Nasty Women and Bad Hombres

Nasty Women and Bad Hombres

Gender and Race in the 2016 US Presidential Election

Edited by Christine A. Kray,
Tamar W. Carroll, and Hinda Mandell

UNIVERSITY OF ROCHESTER PRESS

The University of Rochester Press gratefully acknowledges generous support from the College of Liberal Arts of Rochester Institute of Technology.

First published 2018

University of Rochester Press
668 Mt. Hope Avenue, Rochester, NY 14620, USA
www.urpress.com
and Boydell & Brewer Limited
PO Box 9, Woodbridge, Suffolk IP12 3DF, UK
www.boydellandbrewer.com

ISBN-13: 978-1-58046-936-4
ISSN: 2152-6400

Cataloging-in-Publication Data available from the Library of Congress.

This publication is printed on acid-free paper.
Printed in the United States of America

To our daughters—
Annalea, Sabina, and Mirabelle
—and also, Eddie

CONTENTS

Part 3. Baking Cookies and Grabbing Pussies:
Misogyny and Sexual Politics

Part 4. Election Day: Rewriting Past and Future

ILLUSTRATIONS

FOREWORD

It was the best of times, it was the worst of times, it was the age of wisdom, it was the age of foolishness.

—Charles Dickens, *A Tale of Two Cities*

The energy in the air as thousands made their way to Mt. Hope Cemetery in Rochester on Election Day 2016 to place "I Voted Today" stickers on Susan B. Anthony's headstone was unique, and powerful. The spectacle captured an international audience, as millions of viewers watched John Hucko's live feed of the day on Facebook.[1] Barbara Streisand and the BBC tuned in. CNN was there.

The mood at the cemetery was like nothing I had ever experienced. It was a brisk fall morning. The brilliant blue sky was a vivid backdrop for the gray cemetery markers set in thick, deep-green grass below the branches of ancient trees dressed in vibrant gold and crimson leaves. There was a palpable sense of expectation and a pervasive joy, but there was also a hint of caution, of uncertainty.

The crowd was gentle with one another. People with walkers, toddlers on hips, men alone, women in multigenerational groups, and smiling faces and bodies of all shapes and shades waited patiently for their turn to place their sticker and take a selfie at the modest limestone marker. Some waited as long as three hours, but no one tried to rush others along. People said they were participating in a historic moment. And indeed, they were.

By 8:00 a.m. the next morning, the sky and the cemetery were gray and damp with cold fog and drizzle, and the election results were in. History had been made, but the results angered some, confused others, and left many brokenhearted. What were we to make of the 2016 election?

In this book, the editors have brought together twenty-four chapters by scholars and writers who disassemble what happened from their location and expertise so that we can assemble a response from ours.

For those who were appalled or impressed by the ways in which social media affected public mood and opinion, here is an evidence-based analysis.

For those who are perplexed about why religious fundamentalists voted in droves for a twice-divorced man who confessed to assaulting women, here's an analysis that makes sense.

For those who don't understand why educated white women turned out for Trump or why fellow Democrats campaigned passionately against Clinton, here are some insights.

For those who have been keenly aware of the racism and bias in our systems of government, education, and corrections, here are tools to help others understand the systems that oppress and abuse.

For those who are distressed by the press and media, here are tools to sort through the propaganda, step outside your own echo chambers, and expose the forces that benefit from telling less than the whole story.

Musicians, artists, playwrights, and preachers: read here. These writers will open your imaginations to consider the motivations and concerns of characters who are different from those in your world.

For those feminists who seek to lift up equality for all, but don't understand why their strategies may perpetuate racism, classism, xenophobia, and transphobia: read here to see how that happened in Susan B. Anthony's day and in 2016.

During the Civil War, Susan B. Anthony said, "We want a Union which is a Union in fact, a Union in spirit, not a sham."[2] After the 2016 election, will the United States head toward a union that truly is of the people, by the people, and for *all* the people? Or will we be a sham?

Will the 2016 election prove to be the best of times, or the worst of times? It will be what we make of it. Here's a start to making history for humanity's sake.

—Deborah L. Hughes
President and CEO of the
National Susan B. Anthony Museum and House

Notes

1. "Live Broadcast: Susan B. Anthony Being Honored," News 8 WROC Rochester, November 8, 2016, http://www.facebook.com/News8WROC/videos/10155359367104386/?hc_ref=PAGES_TIMELINE.

2. Ida Husted Harper, *The Life and Work of Susan B. Anthony: Including Public Addresses, Her Own Letters, and Many from Her Contemporaries during Fifty Years*, vol. 1 (Indianapolis: Bowen-Merrill, 1899), 228.

ACKNOWLEDGMENTS

The editors wish to express their deep gratitude to many people who provided support, material and intellectual, to this book project. We are grateful to the College of Liberal Arts at Rochester Institute of Technology and Dean James Winebrake for providing a faculty development grant that financed various elements of the book. We appreciate the unfailing and cheerful encouragement of the press editor, Sonia Kane, and the series editors, Alison Parker and Carol Faulkner, who saw that the history of last week is history, after all, and considered a volume about a twenty-first-century election for a series otherwise about the nineteenth and twentieth centuries. They expertly guided and gently massaged the volume throughout the process.

We are grateful to our many colleagues in the College of Liberal Arts for intellectual and creative input as we turned our attention to Mount Hope Cemetery in the fall of 2016 and imagined what an interdisciplinary conversation about politics, performance, commemoration, critical history, gender, and women's rights might entail. In addition to those represented in these pages, we also acknowledge Kijana Crawford, Elisabetta D'Amanda, Juilee Decker, Christine Keiner, and Uli Linke.

Deborah Hughes, the president and CEO of the National Susan B. Anthony Museum and House, has set for us an example of how to walk the tightrope of principled scholarly investigation over the raging waters of national debate. We are very grateful to scholars and community members who asked probing questions and offered feedback on earlier versions of parts of this manuscript, including participants in the Rochester United States History Workshop, in the annual meeting of the New York chapter of the National Organization for Women (NOW-NY), and in the VoteTilla celebration of the centennial of women's suffrage in New York State. We appreciate the critical insights offered by Jacqueline Fewkes, Carol Mukhopadhyay, and Peggy Sanday.

Throughout this endeavor, we have relied on our families. We thank our parents and families, deeply, for their keen observations and for the many long, excited conversations about the day's breaking news. Throughout it all, our children's giggles lifted our spirits and reminded us of what matters, and why we do the work we do.

On April 4, 2018, as we write these final lines for the book, the nation is marking the fiftieth anniversary of Martin Luther King Jr.'s assassination. May we all strive to live up to his dream.

INTRODUCTION

The Historical Imagination and Fault Lines in the Electorate

Christine A. Kray,
Tamar W. Carroll, and Hinda Mandell

Such a nasty woman," Republican candidate Donald J. Trump muttered under his breath about Democratic candidate Hillary Clinton during the third presidential debate on October 19, 2016. Earlier in the evening, when speaking about his proposal for a wall along the US-Mexico border, he said, "we have some bad hombres here and we are going to get them out."[1] Within minutes, a #BadHombre Twitter hashtag had been created, and the next day, T-shirts and mugs with "Nasty Woman" and "Bad Hombre" were for sale online. Those two phrases were recognized immediately not only as derogatory terms, but as phrases whose rhetorical force rests upon deep-seated cultural conventions and stereotypes that have aimed to relegate women and Latinos to subordinate positions within the US social body.

Hillary Clinton was a "nasty woman" because she transgressed cultural expectations of submissive femininity. And when Trump spoke of "bad hombres" he invoked stereotypes of Mexican criminality enshrined in Hollywood Westerns from as early as *Broncho Billy and the Greaser* in 1914. That's why these two phrases form the title of this book: together they illustrate how gender and racial politics were at the center of the 2016 United States presidential contest between Donald Trump and Hillary Clinton.[2] Multiple factors contributed to the outcome of the election, which will be addressed in other scholarship, yet because gender and race electrified campaign rhetoric and behavior from the outset, this book examines how they were invoked and performed throughout the campaign season.

This book is concerned both with history and the historical imagination. Historical chapters trace how certain gendered and racialized policies, behaviors, and ways of speaking relevant to the election developed over time. Yet we are also interested in the "historical imagination," which refers to how people engage with the past, including the stories they tell about it and intentional actions coordinated around its symbols and artifacts. The election was often called "historic" because it was the first time a woman received the nomination from a major political party for the office of the presidency. Yet the election was also historical in the sense that it stimulated profound national introspection and reflection on the nation's past, as well as its composition and values.

The candidates strategically positioned themselves in relationship to United States history and powerful historical icons. Echoing the "Let's Make America Great Again" slogan from Ronald Reagan's 1980 presidential bid, Donald Trump promised to "Make America Great Again," conjuring up nostalgia for the 1950s, a time of relative prosperity and privilege for white men.[3] Hillary Clinton aligned herself with the suffragists at key moments, including by wearing a white suit when she accepted the Democratic Party's nomination. For many, the election of the first woman president just short of a century after women gained the right to vote in 1920 took on the aura of destiny. In the middle of this tumultuous culture war and competing historical imaginations, citizens themselves turned to history to make the case for their candidate of choice, situating themselves within larger historical narratives and demarcating their communities of obligation.

Indeed, Rochester, New York, where we—the book's editors—live, demonstrated renewed interest in one of our city's most illustrious citizens, suffragist Susan B. Anthony (1820–1906). In recent years, a small number of voters started the practice of affixing their "I Voted" stickers to her gravestone on election days. Attention to this practice grew throughout 2016, spread by social media and national news coverage. This renewed interest in Anthony in the midst of a presidential race that seemed likely to produce the first woman president served as the immediate inspiration for this book. On Election Day itself, many women across the United States planned to wear white in honor of the suffragists, and an estimated 8,000–12,000 people visited Anthony's gravesite.[4]

As the election results came in, though, it became clear that women were not united in support of a woman candidate. Voter exit polls revealed that 52 percent of white women voted for Donald Trump, while 94 percent of Black women and 69 percent of Latinas voted for Hillary Clinton.[5] This particular rift necessitates an *intersectional* analysis in this book. Intersectionality, a term first introduced by legal scholar Kimberlé Crenshaw, emerges out of the recognition that gender and race are not separate realms of experience.[6] Rather, in the United States in the twenty-first century, all bodies are gendered and

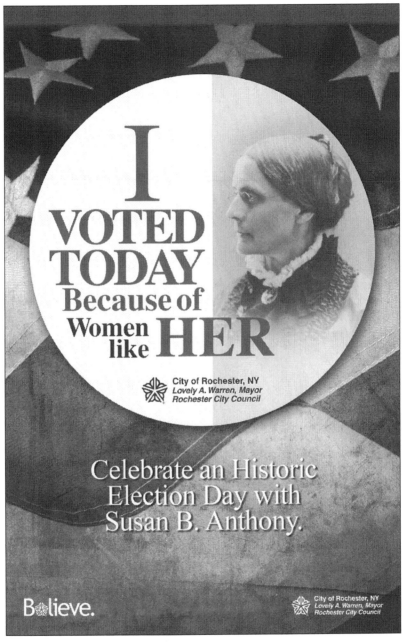

I.1. Digital poster prepared by the City of Rochester for Election Day, 2016. City of Rochester Communications Bureau. Used with permission.

racialized all of the time. Consequently, a specific gender (such as male or female) is not a homogeneous category; rather, the persons occupying it are divided among themselves by racial distinctions. There is no homogeneous experience of "womanhood," because the experiences of Black women, white women, Jewish women, and so on are different. As Crenshaw put it, race *intersects* with gender. Black feminists have noted that the issues that have often taken priority in the women's movement are those of white middle-class women. Such politicking can actually further oppress women of color and working-class women by rendering their priorities invisible.[7]

In fact, Rochester's history and its present illustrate the agonistic consequences of the misrecognition of the intersections of race and gender and the way in which our political culture often pits one interest group against another. In the city's commemorative events, the social reformers Susan B. Anthony and Frederick Douglass (ca. 1818–95) are often paired. They both lived, worked, and collaborated in Rochester, and both are buried in Mount Hope Cemetery. Both were abolitionists (Douglass having escaped from slavery himself), and both worked to advance the rights of women. In 1869 they had a falling out over the proposed Fifteenth Amendment to the Constitution, which was to grant the vote to African American men. Susan B. Anthony felt that preserving suffrage exclusively for men was unjust and insisted that social reformers should press for women's suffrage simultaneously, whereas Douglass did not want to wait for American legislators to come around to that notion as well. Anthony and Douglass's friendship was repaired soon after the Fifteenth Amendment was ratified (in 1870), but that rift demonstrates how committed activists can share strong views on social justice issues, yet when it comes to setting priorities linked to race or gender, they may part ways.

Another key reason this volume pursues an intersectional analysis is because gender and race are *co-constitutive*. In other words, as categories, gender and race create one another as they are performed. Since bodies are always gendered and racialized, what any one person does is "read" by others as related to the race and gender of that person. Similarly, statements made about a person carry, simultaneously, implications for understandings of gender and race. The co-constitution of gender and race are considered here because Trump's campaign strategy rested on it. His performance of leadership entailed an aggressive, combative masculinity seeking to subdue dark-skinned Others, protecting some women in the manner of a benevolent patriarch.[8] Yet against female opponents, he leveraged cultural, visceral feelings of misogyny—with misogyny defined as hatred or loathing of women, especially those who violate traditional expectations of femininity.

Much of the commentary about Trump's ascendance during the campaign and in the immediate postelection period focused on the economic plight of the white working class and their disaffection from the Democratic Party.[9] In contrast, this volume aims for a more holistic analysis that examines the ways in which race and gender were often co-implicated, as Trump mobilized racist and gendered tropes from US history, including the myth of men of color as predatory rapists of white women, to unite white voters in support of his candidacy. This book explores how Donald Trump, Hillary Clinton, and their supporters invoked gender and race, and it explores the co-constitutive effects of their rhetoric and actions.

Squaring Off

The chapters in this book examine various developments and themes in the electoral contest, but here we briefly sketch the ways in which Trump and Clinton positioned themselves with respect to race, gender, and history to lay the groundwork for common understanding. On the face of it, Donald Trump seemed to champion all Americans, as his slogans were nationalistic: "America First" and "Make America Great Again." Yet over time, it became clear that his nationalism slanted toward white nationalism—defined as a desire to secure the privileges of whites in the nation-state—insofar as his rhetoric and policy proposals favored white, native-born, and Christian Americans over ethnic minorities, immigrants, and people of other faiths.[10] Prior to his campaign run, he had earned a reputation for harboring racist views, in part through using his national celebrity status to push the Birther conspiracy theory that Barack Obama was not born in the United States and was ineligible for the office of president.[11] His campaign employed populist strategies, promising to raise the living standards of the lower economic classes, as he vowed to raise up the "silent majority." Trump's proposals to deregulate business and combat "globalist" economic forces through instating protectionist measures were pillars of his populist plan.[12] His rhetoric was tinged with white supremacy—a belief in the racial superiority of whites—as he decried "inner-city" (read: Black) crime and depicted African American neighborhoods as decaying.[13] He employed nativist (privileging native-born citizens) strategies as he pledged to "take our country back" and protect Americans from criminal immigrants and Muslim terrorists through strict immigration policies.[14] His campaign was also masculinist, as his signature interests—manufacturing, mining, the military, construction, and policing—sit comfortably within the traditional preserve of men.

Consequently, the kinds of jobs he promised to restore—factory work, mining, and construction—are those in which men can feel masculine just by going to work. In combination, Trump's masculinist, nativist, and protectionist stances established him as the strong, authoritative patriarch of the nation.

In contrast, Hillary Clinton's campaign began in April 2015 with a confidently feminist slogan ("I'm with Her"). While Bernie Sanders in the primary race and Donald Trump in the general election contest aimed to depict her as corrupt, indifferent to working-class concerns, and beholden to corporate interests, her campaign message envisioned acceptance and cooperation among people of all genders, sexualities, ethnicities, religions, and class backgrounds.[15] This inclusive vision became articulated even more strongly as Donald Trump emerged as her likely Republican opponent. By the time of the Democratic National Convention in July 2016, Clinton's slogan had become "Stronger Together." Her convention speech promise that "love trumps hate" indicted Trump for promoting hatred and also creatively wielded traditional notions of womanly love as a feminist foil against him.[16]

Hillary Clinton symbolically aligned herself with the suffragists by wearing, on the night she clinched the nomination for the Democratic Party (June 7, 2016), a cream-colored jacket—white having symbolized purity of person and cause for the suffragists—and called the night "historic." She credited the organizers of the 1848 Seneca Falls, New York, Convention on women's rights, and noted that her mother had been born on June 4, 1919, the very day on which Congress passed the Nineteenth Amendment to the Constitution, which recognized women's right to vote.[17] She wore a white pantsuit when she accepted the nomination at the Democratic National Convention in July, and again at the third presidential debate on October 19.[18] In her campaign memoir, she writes how she had even planned to wear a white suit to the election night victory party.[19]

The contest in 2016 was especially fraught because voters were being asked to vote on gender—and not just because Hillary Clinton was running, but also because Trump represented a new kind of presidential masculinity. What was at stake was the very conception of "presidential" behavior. Liberal political theory, the inspiration for the American Revolution and the basis for the US government, posits a division between the public sphere of politics and commerce, which it gave to men as their province, and the private sphere of home and family, which it assigned to women.[20] Although American women have successfully fought for the right to be included in the public sphere, the concept of separate spheres has had a lasting cultural influence,

I.2. Hillary Clinton accepts the Democratic nomination for the presidency, Philadelphia, PA, July 28, 2016. Voice of America. Photo: Ali Shaker.

so that women who either fail to meet the obligations of domesticity or who insert themselves into the public sphere prominently are penalized for doing so.[21] Hillary Clinton started at a disadvantage because she was transgressing expectations about separate spheres. However, recent scholarship urges us to attend, not just to the gender identity of candidates, but also to how they are assigned gendered characteristics in media discourses. Gender conflict framing theory has explored how US voters tend to prefer candidates that they identify as having more "masculine" than "feminine" traits, and therefore how media discourses frame the candidates in gendered terms is of critical importance.[22]

This book goes beyond gender identity, separate spheres, and gender conflict framing to consider gender performance.[23] Beyond her identity and how the media depicted her, Hillary Clinton as the first female major-party nominee for the presidency had to perform, or to fashion—through her behavior, voice, and clothing—a way of being presidential that was also feminine.[24] She was tasked with creating a *presidential femininity*. As she transgressed traditions of female submission, voters wondered: Would men accept a woman's leadership? If she became authoritative, would women accept her as a woman? In her memoir, Clinton reflects on the "tightrope" that she and other women "have had to walk in order to participate in American politics."[25]

I.3. Donald Trump accepts the Republication nomination for the presidency, Cleveland, OH, July 21, 2016. Voice of America.

For his part, Donald Trump represented a new type of *presidential masculinity*. We had seen approximations of his style of masculinity on the national stage before, although usually as the villains in films such as *Revenge of the Nerds*: brash, braggadocious, rude, dismissive, brutish, brutal, comfortable in the privileges afforded to him by race, class, and gender—taking what he wanted, aggressively, if need be. We were used to our presidents being male, but their public comportment aimed at combining emotional fortitude, diplomacy, sternness toward foes, and gentility toward women. Trump came in like a gender wrecking ball, decrying political correctness, encouraging violence against protestors, and asserting that the weakness of other men is what had landed our country in trouble, and that only his strength (even if sometimes rude— maybe *especially* if he was sometimes rude) could guard the fatherland.[26] The presidential masculinity he performed was that of the strongman, the alpha male.[27] Consequently, whether the result would be the first female president or the first brutish president, the 2016 election was a contest between different visions of proper gender behavior.

The Election Results: Sisterhood, Sundered

Hillary Clinton was the projected winner in all of the major national media polls throughout the fall of 2016.[28] Particularly after the *Access*

Hollywood tape in which Trump bragged about "grab[ing] 'em by the pussy" was made public on October 7, leading pundits predicted that women in large numbers would cast protest ballots against Trump.[29] Hillary Clinton won the popular vote by over 2.8 million people, but Donald Trump eked out a win by securing the votes of less than 80,000 people in three key swing states (the Rust Belt states of Michigan, Wisconsin, and Pennsylvania), thereby clinching the electoral vote and the presidency.[30]

Fifty-two, ninety-four, and seventy-one—these are the numbers that resound, as they revealed deep fault lines in the electorate by race, gender, and class. Again, according to the CNN exit polls, 52 percent of white women voted for Trump, whereas 94 percent of African American women backed Clinton. Of white men without a college degree, 71 percent chose Trump.

Overall, women preferred Clinton (54 percent versus 41 percent for Trump), and men preferred Trump (52 percent versus 41 percent for Clinton).[31] The existence of a female candidate on the ballot did not make a significant difference, as women's voting patterns were essentially unchanged from 2012 to 2016. In every presidential election from 1996 to 2016, between 51 and 56 percent of women have voted for the Democratic candidate; in 2012, 55 percent backed Obama, and Hillary Clinton's support among women in 2016 was only slightly below that (54 percent).[32]

Racial disparities in voting were more marked than gender disparities: 57 percent of whites voted for Trump, while 74 percent of nonwhites voted for Clinton.[33] Over the previous decade, whites in the United States had drifted solidly toward the Republican Party; whereas in 2008, similar numbers of whites identified as Republican and Democrat (46 percent and 44 percent, respectively), by 2016, they were divided by 15 percentage points (with 54 percent of whites identifying as Republican and 39 percent as Democrat).[34]

The aforementioned division among women by racial identity shattered any notion of sisterhood. As is discussed in the final section of this book, this striking disparity in voting patterns among women by racial identity precipitated a great deal of postelection anger directed by feminist commentators at white women, who were seen as resting in the comforts of race privilege while betraying women of color. While intersectionality has been a key analytical concept in women's and gender studies since 1989, Trump's victory was the moment that the concept entered the mainstream popular discourse, and it became a major theme of organizing in the Women's March of January 2017.[35]

Differences in voting patterns by socioeconomic class also were striking. Exit poll analyses often take level of education as a gross indicator of economic class. Of white voters without a college degree, 66 percent voted for Trump, as compared with 29 percent for Clinton—a stark 37-percentage-point difference.[36]

A more fine-grained analysis that considers race, class, and gender simultaneously shows that the demographic group that showed the strongest support for Trump was white men without a college education: 71 percent (as compared with 23 percent for Clinton). Similarly, 61 percent of white women without a college degree backed Trump (34 percent chose Clinton).[37] This latter trend is not altogether surprising, as political scientist Kelly Dittmar noted that "among white women without a college degree, Republican party identification has grown over the past 24 years."[38]

Even though pundits expected that Trump's sexist behavior would lead women to hand a victory to Hillary Clinton, the fact that race and class turned out to be stronger predictors of voting patterns than gender perhaps should not have been surprising, given longer-standing political trends. Social science scholarship published in the run-up to the election had shown that white antagonism against ethnic Others had become a powerful political force.[39] Three notable books published in 2016 documented the growing alienation and resentment among members of the white working-class population, especially rural residents.[40] Anthropologist Jeff Maskovsky has discussed how Donald Trump mastered a "white nationalist postracialism," in which he eschewed "political correctness," blaming liberal economic, educational, criminal justice, and immigration policies for the nation's ills, including racial inequalities, consequently allowing voters to engage in white nationalist politics without having to feel themselves to be "racist."[41]

Widening our focus to include gender as well, sociologist Michael Kimmel recently showed how ideas about gender further complicate feelings about race and class—specifically how cultural notions of masculinity have fueled white working-class resentment. He noted how the decline of the old industrial economy led to underemployment and stagnant wages for white working-class males and deprived them of work that shored up masculine pride.[42] Shortly after the election, Kimmel remarked about Trump, "Essentially, I wrote a book about his followers—for whom the leader hadn't showed up yet."[43] Our book builds on these insights about the interworking of race, class, and gender by also bringing into focus women and how ideas about femininity intersected with race and class in the candidates' campaigns and in voter reactions.

In fact, in one political science survey conducted in October 2016, participants' responses to attitudinal questions reveal that even though Trump had strong support among the white working class, that support was determined less by economic dissatisfaction than it was by racist and sexist attitudes.[44] CNN election exit polls further illustrate that concerns about threats posed by outsiders were crucial in Trump's victory. When asked, "What is the most important issue facing the country?," exit poll interviewees who answered that it was immigration or terrorism strongly preferred Trump (by 31 percent and 17 percent margins, respectively).[45]

This pattern of ethnonationalist fears generating support for Trump is also seen in a postelection study by political scientist John Sides, who analyzed the responses of 8,000 survey respondents in December 2016, most of whom had also been interviewed in 2011–12. Sides concluded that even prior to the 2016 election, race had become a polarizing element in the United States, with more whites without a college degree siding Republican. However, between 2012 and 2016, heightened concerns about immigrants, Blacks, and Muslims represented the single greatest shift in attitudes captured by the survey, leading Sides to conclude that the fact that Trump's campaign rhetoric spoke to their fears was the deciding factor in Trump's victory.[46]

Although the ultimate impact of Russian electoral interference remains unknown, we can see that Trump designed a persuasive campaign strategy of "America First" and "Make America Great Again." His implicit promise to raise up white working-class men through protectionist economic, immigration, and criminal justice policies gained him large and enthusiastic rallies throughout his campaign. Apparently, for many, Trump's overt sexism was not viewed as a deficit, but as a plus. Indeed, as Smith put it, "this alleged toxicity [toxic masculinity] did not poison Trump's candidacy; instead, it served to fortify it, giving voice to an underclass that attributed its failures to the rise of others."[47] Hillary Clinton's inclusive vision of "Stronger Together" was decidedly optimistic and persuaded the majority of voters overall, yet failed to clinch the support of the majority of voters in crucial swing states.

By slight margins, Trump peeled away white working-class voters in those key swing states. Concerns about the rights and status of women in a Trump presidency were not enough to dissuade voters who perceived that the greatest threats facing them were racial/ethnic and religious Others. This book aims to show how the final stage of the electoral contest entailed a prolonged battle over gender issues, and yet, despite the furor, nativism and white nationalism held greater sway over the electorate, in part because of entrenched misogyny (including internalized misogyny) and in part because of the way in which Donald Trump fused gender and racial discourses, configuring himself as the brash fighter who would protect (white) America First.

Ultimately, more swing-state voters may have been inspired by a nostalgic vision of strong, blue-collar men working in hard hats to build walls than the vision of a white-pantsuit-wearing woman breaking the highest glass ceiling. In fact, a wealthy woman wearing a tailored, designer pantsuit might have been a painful reminder to some men that they might never own a tailored suit. Her achievement, as she was inches from the presidency, might have forced recognition that their lives had fallen short of their aspirations.

Interdisciplinarity, Multivocality, and Feminist Scholarship

This book employs an interdisciplinary feminist methodology. Our contributors include scholars of African American studies, anthropology, communication and media studies, Hispanic studies, history, legal studies, philosophy, sociology, and women's and gender studies, as well as journalists and creative writers. Together, we examine a rich range of sources, from data on crime and immigration to campaign memorabilia, social media conversations, speeches and debates, television appearances, and the political creativity expressed in clothing and ritual performance. We also gather the voices of diverse groups including parents of transgender children, African American women political activists, and pro-Trump white female voters. Collectively, we seek to understand both the experiences of individual women and men as such *and* the social construction of gender roles and race as relationships of power. In order to understand how those dynamics worked in the 2016 election—the first to feature a female candidate nominated by a major political party and following on the heels of the eight-year presidency of Barack Obama, the first African American president—we emphasize the necessity of historical context.

Interdisciplinarity is a critical strategy in feminist scholarship additionally because of the way in which gender is a diffuse cultural system. This book utilizes historian Estelle Freedman's definition of feminism, which is that it is "a belief that women and men are inherently of equal worth."[48] The legal system in and of itself is insufficient to ensure gender equality because of the embeddedness of gender within culture. Social contract theory's gendered separate spheres incorporated an older cultural gender system of patriarchy, which situates the husband and father at the head of the family. The corollary to patriarchy is misogyny, or loathing of women who step out of their subordinate role, which functions to maintain men's authority over women as a group. Americans do not often voice these notions explicitly, and yet patriarchy and misogyny persist because they are woven throughout the cultural fabric. Virtually everything in the cultural world—from clothing to postures, gestures, vocal intonation, joking styles, foods, jobs, domestic tasks, leadership, parenting, sports, emotions, and sexual acts—is assigned a gendered value and consequently affects how we interpret and evaluate the masculinity and femininity of others. These gendered meanings often escape conscious awareness and yet reinforce one another through their logic. And because items coded as masculine are evaluated more positively, when women disrupt the gendered order, code-word jabs—such as "nasty woman" or references to menstruation—can be used to stir up gut-level misogynistic feelings. Scholarship that aims to promote gender equality, therefore, must identify and interrogate patriarchal and misogynistic attitudes and behaviors across all domains in social life—underscoring the importance of diverse methods of research, listening to multiple voices, and comparing findings across disciplines. This book explores the ways in which a cultural system of patriarchy was both challenged and reproduced in 2016, as a woman seemed likely to win the office of the presidency and become the commander in chief, challenged by a man with a history of objectification of women and who was tainted by accusations of misogyny, sexual harassment, and sexual assault.

A unique aspect of this book is the inclusion of personal essays from academics and journalists. Since the election touched Americans in visceral and personal ways—and repudiated, vindicated, refuted, and enraged so many voters depending on which candidate they backed—we felt strongly that a "marriage" of academic scholarship with incisive essays and reporting would bring diverse voices and experiences into the conversation. Perhaps we can grasp intuitively sociologist Margaret Somers's insight that

> people construct identities (however multiple and changing) by locating themselves or being located within a repertoire of emplotted stories; that "experience" is constituted through narratives; that people make sense of what has happened and is happening to them by attempting to assemble or in some way to integrate these happenings within one or more narratives; and that people are guided to act in certain ways, and not others, on the basis of the projections, expectations, and memories derived from a multiplicity but ultimately limited repertoire of available social, public, and cultural narratives.[49]

By opening up space in the book to explore life during the election and its outcomes as complicated and confusing, we view the transformative act of telling stories—and the process by which we construct these narratives—as offering a highly readable mechanism for unpeeling "what is true and what is meaningful in life."[50] With storytelling and story construction so intricately and intimately tied to personal identity, we hope you too will find new meaning in these personal essays, as these writers lift the curtain on their personal lives through the lens of the 2016 election.

Overview of the Book

This book is divided into five parts, which, collectively, examine how gender was performed and invoked throughout the presidential race and how gender and feminist consciousness experienced a resurgence in late 2016, even while notions of race crosscut and divided voters of the same gender. The chapters in part 1 explore how, in American political culture, dominant white masculinity is associated with leadership. Trump displayed this hegemonic masculinity through his emphasis on virility, power, willingness to use physical force, and the denigration of opponents. Those opponents who should have remained subordinate—particularly women, and men who represent marginalized masculinities such as those who are nonwhite or physically disabled—were frequent targets for Trump and his supporters. In chapter 1, women's and gender studies scholar Jane Caputi surveys commercial campaign paraphernalia such as T-shirts, bumper stickers, and buttons, showing how they used misogynistic notions frequently focused on the candidates' genitals in order to marshal support for Trump and mobilize disgust in opposition to Clinton. Communication scholars Roy Schwartzman and Jenni Simon examine in chapter 2 how Trump's performance on the daytime television program *The Dr. Oz Show* established his healthy, potent masculinity, drawing on the Western medical tradition contrasting male strength and female weakness and also entrenched ideas about white genetic fitness. In chapter 3, Hispanic studies scholar Joshua D. Martin places Trump's rhetoric of the "bad hombre" within a long history of American nationalism and border tropes, finding that Trump's use of anti-Mexican stereotypes, particularly depicting Mexican men as sexual predators, positioned him as the strong father protector (patriarch) of the nation. Sociologist Nicholas Robertson demonstrates in chapter 4 that Trump's claims of immigrant criminality are not borne out by official crime statistics, even though such exaggeration fits into a long-standing tradition in the United States of xenophobic racialization of immigrants by casting them as dangerous Others. In chapter 5, communication scholars Beth Boser and Brandon Anderson take up a cultural conundrum: If the president is a woman, does that emasculate the men closest to her? They show how in key July 2016 speeches, Clinton's vice presidential running mate Tim Kaine tried to perform a "subordinate masculinity" to demonstrate male deference to female leadership.

Part 2 examines varying ways in which the history of women's leadership and political participation was invoked in the 2016 election, sometimes as examples of opposition faced by women seeking political office and sometimes as examples of successful strategic feminist activism. In chapter 6, historian Barbara Winslow chronicles the pioneering 1972 presidential campaign of civil rights and feminist leader Shirley Chisholm, the first African American woman elected to Congress. Too often overlooked today, Chisholm's campaign is instructive both because she called for an intersectional analysis of social problems and because she was met with intense racist and misogynistic opposition. Historian Michael Brown turns in chapter 7 to the rift between abolitionist Frederick Douglass and women's rights leader Susan B. Anthony over the Fifteenth Amendment to the Constitution, which granted Black men but not women the right to vote, and its rekindling by the Obama-Clinton rivalry in 2008. The rift between Anthony and Douglass, while often glossed over in popular memory, is crucial to understanding the ways in which American political culture treats minority group advancement as a zero-sum game. Historian Einav Rabinovitch-Fox examines Clinton's sartorial messaging in chapter 8, arguing that her adoption of pantsuits allowed Clinton to position herself as both feminine and fashionable, like the suffragists whose white garb she adopted, and also to use fashion as a means of asserting women's abilities to lead. In chapter 9, historian Ana Stevenson compares pro– and anti–women's suffrage postcards to 2016 election-related Internet memes, finding that antisuffrage and anti-Clinton imagery were popular because they relied on misogynistic humor, in contrast to innocuous but less memorable images deployed by advocates of women's suffrage and by Clinton supporters. Political commentator Joanna Weiss concludes in chapter 10 that Americans' belief in the gendered "self-made man" myth made Hillary Clinton's personal history—particularly her status as a former First Lady—a liability with voters, who viewed her as both too ambitious for a political wife and not independent enough as a candidate.

The chapters in part 3 analyze how misogyny and the sexual double standard influenced voters' perceptions of the candidates and contributed to Trump's victory. In chapter 11, communication scholar Mark Ward Sr. shows how Hillary Clinton's embrace of feminism was anathema to evangelical leaders and voters, for whom she represents "out of control" women threatening godly order. Communications scholars Jiyoung Lee, Carol Liebler, and Neal Powless report on their interviews with white Republican female voters in chapter 12, finding that these voters disliked Clinton because of her transgression of traditional gender roles, while they gave Trump a pass for his attacks on women because his behavior matched their expectations for men. Sociologist Pamela Aronson confirms this finding, arguing in chapter 13 that internalized misogyny and the inability of the Clinton campaign to overcome it by fully activating gender consciousness contributed to Trump's victory. In chapter 14, feminist writer Leora Tanenbaum applies her concept of "slut-shaming" to show that during the 2016 presidential debates, Hillary Clinton missed an opportunity to correct the manner in which she had handled sexual misconduct accusations made against her husband in the 1990s, thereby lessening her ability to hold Trump accountable for his own sexual misconduct. Essayist Steve Almond reflects in chapter 15 on how misogyny led his friend and other "Bernie Bros" to circulate anti-Clinton propaganda stories and memes that originated in Russian electoral interference.

The contributors to part 4 examine the ebullience of Clinton supporters participating in new feminist rituals leading up to and on Election Day, followed swiftly by scrambling for new narratives to ground and reorient the self within a Trump-ascendant world. In chapter 16, communication scholars Gina Masullo Chen and Kelsey Whipple document the creation of an intimate, online public through women's use of Twitter to oppose Trump, contending that the 2016 election fomented a digital movement for female empowerment in the United States that continued after Trump's election. In chapter 17, anthropologist Christine Kray investigates the Election Day phenomenon when, coinciding with a resurgence in feminist sentiment, thousands of people visited Susan B. Anthony's grave, ceremoniously taking a stand in celebration and defense of women's (and others') rights. In the days following the election, cemetery goers experienced an existential crisis, struggling to believe that American voters elected Donald Trump—someone who, in their view, violated the sacred principles of the nation. Among the visitors to Susan B. Anthony's grave was communication scholar and essayist Hinda Mandell. In chapter 18, Mandell discusses the rewriting of self that she had to do when her son was born on Election Day, the start of the Trump era.

Like many families, that of essayist Rachel Parsons was divided by the campaign. In chapter 19, Parsons explores how disability and downward mobility made Trump's siren call of restoring manufacturing jobs so appealing to her mother and many other middle- and working-class whites in the Rust Belt, despite her mother's support for Parsons as an out lesbian and Parson's expressed concern over the future of LGBTQ rights under a Trump presidency. Anthropologist Sally Campbell Galman, in her ethnography of the parents of transgender children in chapter 20, found them employing "negative memory" in the aftermath of the election, looking to historical referents, particularly

1930s Vienna, to reframe their family narratives from hopeful to traumatic. Concern over the rollback of transgender rights and persistence in advocacy for their children, Galman shows, led some parents to reframe activism as they "constructed the everyday as a form of protest." American Muslims similarly confronted a more hostile political context as the Trump administration pushed for a travel ban on visitors from many Muslim-majority nations; in chapter 21, legal scholar and attorney Asma Uddin finds grounds for optimism in the US Constitution's safeguards of religious liberty and their application by the courts in past cases involving Roman Catholics and Mormons.

Part 5 asks: How can we learn from our history to craft a truly inclusive social justice movement? In chapter 22, historians De Anna Reese and Delia Gillis highlight the key role played by Black women within the Democratic Party in shaping the 2016 Clinton campaign and its inclusive message, "Stronger Together." Through their leadership, especially in helping to orchestrate the Democratic National Convention, these women provide a strategy for future campaigns to see (and display) the diversity of the American public as an asset. In chapter 23, philosopher Katie Terezakis applies Nietzsche's three modes of history to analyze racial inequalities in Rochester, past and present. A renewed critical history is necessary, she argues, to inform contemporary social justice movements, which must embrace racially relevant intersectional politics. In chapter 24, activist Jamia Wilson calls for renewed consciousness-raising, arguing that until white women repudiate the false security of benevolent patriarchy and its inherent racism, progress toward gender equality will stall.

In the epilogue, we look to the January 2017 Women's March and the renaissance in women's activism, while noting that the names of Susan B. Anthony and Elizabeth Cady Stanton have been adopted by antiabortion activists, stirring up, once again, discussion about bodily autonomy and the meanings of feminism. As a nation divided and restive, we are still writing our stories, looking to the past for critical insights and inspiration as we stumble forward, unsure and unsteady. While much seems uncertain, it is clear that people from the right and the left of the political spectrum are fighting over the legacies of these historic giants within their own social movements today, as history is revisited, retold, and reclaimed.

Notes

1. Politico staff, "Full Transcript: Third 2016 Presidential Debate," Politico.com, October 20, 2016, http://www.politico.com/story/2016/10/full-transcript-third-2016-presidential-debate-230063.

2. This book starts with the premise that "race" and "gender" are social constructions. That is, although commonly believed to be rooted in biology, they are cultural concepts that demonstrate extraordinary variability between and within cultures and over time, often shaped by and put in service to larger political and economic forces. See, for example, Margaret L. Andersen and Patricia Hill Collins, eds., *Race, Class, and Gender: An Anthology*, 9th ed. (Boston: Cengage Learning, 2015); R. W. Connell, *Masculinities*, 2nd ed. (Berkeley: University of California Press, 2005); Alan H. Goodman, Yolanda T. Moses, and Joseph L. Jones, *Race: Are We So Different?* (Malden, MA: Wiley-Blackwell, 2012); and Ellen Lewin and Leni M. Silverstein, *Mapping Feminist Anthropology in the Twenty-first Century* (New Brunswick, NJ: Rutgers University Press, 2016).

3. Gregory Krieg, "Donald Trump Reveals When He Thinks America Was Great," CNN.com, March 28, 2016, http://www.cnn.com/2016/03/26/politics/donald-trump-when-america-was-great/index.html.

4. Erica Gonzales, "The Case for Wearing White on Election Day," *Harper's Bazaar*, November 7, 2016, http://www.harpersbazaar.com/fashion/trends/news/a18710/wearing-white-on-election-day/; Steve Orr, "Susan B. Anthony's Grave a Sad Place Two Days after Election," *USA Today*, November 10, 2016, https://www.usatoday.com/story/news/politics/elections/2016/11/10/susan-b-anthonys-grave-after-election/93615030/.

5. "Election 2016, Exit Polls," CNN.com, November 23, 2016, http://www.cnn.com/election/results/exit-polls.

6. Kimberlé Crenshaw, "Demarginalizing the Intersection of Race and Sex: A Black Feminist Critique of Antidiscrimination Doctrine, Feminist Theory and Antiracist Politics," *University of Chicago Legal Forum 1* (1989): 139–68. Several other elements of identity intersect, including class, sexuality, (dis)ability, religion, immigration status, and education, of course. In this volume, we prioritize gender and race because of their prominence in popular discussions of the electoral contest.

7. Patricia Hill Collins, *Black Feminist Thought: Knowledge, Consciousness, and the Politics of Empowerment*, 2nd ed. (New York: Routledge, 2000); Angela Y. Davis, *Women, Race and Class* (New York: Random House, 1981); Evelyn Brooks Higginbotham, "African American Women's History and the Metalanguage of Race," *Signs* 17, no. 2 (1992): 251–74; bell hooks, *Ain't I a Woman: Black Women and Feminism* (Boston: South End Press, 1981); *Audre Lorde, Sister Outsider: Essays and Speeches* (Freedom, CA: Crossing Press, 1984); Cherríe Moraga and Gloria Anzaldúa, eds., *This Bridge Called My Back: Writings by Radical Women of Color* (Watertown, MA: Persephone Press, 1981).

8. The co-constitution of race and gender through the trope of the white, male benevolent protector of the helpless white woman against the dark-skinned predatory male has a long history in the United States. See, for example, Philip Dray, *At the Hands of Persons Unknown: The Lynching of Black America* (New York: Modern Library 2003); Susan Faludi, *The Terror*

Dream: Myth and Misogyny in an Insecure America (New York: Picador, 2007); and Crystal N. Feimster, *Southern Horrors: Women and the Politics of Race and Lynching* (Cambridge, MA: Harvard University Press, 2011).

9. Karen Kamp, "Class in America and Donald Trump," BillMoyers. com, August 1, 2016, http://billmoyers.com/story/class-america-donald-trump/; Robert Reich, "What Donald Trump's Election Really Means," Alternet.org, November 10, 2016, http://www.alternet.org/election-2016/robert-reich-what-donald-trumps-election-really-means; J. D. Vance, "How Donald Trump Seduced the White Working Class," *Guardian*, September 10, 2016, http://www.theguardian.com/commentisfree/2016/sep/10/jd-vance-hillbilly-elegy-donald-trump-us-white-poor-working-class; Joan C. Williams, "What So Many People Don't Get about the U.S. Working Class," *Harvard Business Review*, November 10, 2016, http://hbr.org/2016/11/what-so-many-people-dont-get-about-the-u-s-working-class.

10. Jeff Maskovsky, "Toward the Anthropology of White Nationalist Postracialism: Comments Inspired by Hall, Goldstein, and Ingram's 'The Hands of Donald Trump,'" *Journal of Ethnographic Theory* 7, no. 1 (2017): 433–40.

11. Nicholas Kristof, "Is Donald Trump a Racist?," *New York Times*, July 23, 2016, http://www.nytimes.com/2016/07/24/opinion/sunday/is-donald-trump-a-racist.html; see also German Lopez, "Donald Trump's Long History of Racism, from the 1970s to 2016," *Vox*, accessed February 16, 2017, http://www.vox.com/2016/7/25/12270880/donald-trump-racism-history.

12. "Protectionist" economic policies are (ideally) designed to shield nationally owned companies against foreign competition, although Trump's ideas about economic nationalism were widely criticized by economists. See, for example, Stuart Anderson, "Economists Say 'Economic Nationalism' Is Economic Nonsense," *Forbes*, February 25, 2017, https://www.forbes.com/sites/stuartanderson/2017/02/25/economists-say-economic-nationalism-is-economic-nonsense/#434fc5ff306f. On the "silent majority," see Nicholas Fanidos, "Donald Trump Defiantly Rallies a New 'Silent Majority' in a Visit to Arizona," *New York Times*, July 11, 2015, http://www.nytimes.com/2015/07/12/us/politics/donald-trump-defiantly-rallies-a-new-silent-majority-in-a-visit-to-arizona.html?_r=0. Other of Trump's key speeches that reveal these themes are found in "Here's Donald Trump's Presidential Announcement Speech," *Time*, June 16, 2015, http://time.com/3923128/donald-trump-announcement-speech/; Politico staff, "Full Text: Donald Trump 2016 Draft Speech Transcript," Politico.com, July 21, 2016, http://www.politico.com/story/2016/07/full-transcript-donald-trump-nomination-acceptance-speech-at-rnc-225974; and Paul Blake and Brionna Jimerson, "Inside Trump's View of African-Americans and Inner Cities," ABCNews.com, October 12, 2016, http://abcnews.go.com/Politics/inside-trumps-view-african-americans-cities/story?id=42724385.

13. Blake and Jimerson, "Inside Trump's View."

14. Fanidos, "Donald Trump Defiantly Rallies"; "Trump's Presidential Announcement Speech."

15. Hillary Clinton, "Getting Started," YouTube.com, video, April 12, 2015, https://www.youtube.com/watch?v=0uY7gLZDmn4&feature=you tube; Hillary Clinton, "Learn More about Hillary's Vision for America," accessed March 13, 2017, http://www.hillaryclinton.com/issues/.

16. Politico staff, "Full Text: Hillary Clinton's DNC Speech," Politico. com, July 28, 2016, http://www.politico.com/story/2016/07/full-text-hillary-clintons-dnc-speech-226410.

17. Katie Reilly, "Read Hillary Clinton's Historic Victory Speech as Presumptive Democratic Nominee," *Time*, June 8, 2016, http://time. com/4361099/hillary-clinton-nominee-speech-transcript/.

18. Erica Gonzales, "Hillary Clinton Wore Red, White, and Blue for Her Debate Pantsuits," *Harper's Bazaar*, October 20, 2016, http:// www.harpersbazaar.com/fashion/trends/news/a18336/hillary-clinton-presidential-debate-pantsuits/.

19. Hillary Rodham Clinton, *What Happened* (New York: Simon & Schuster, 2017), 18.

20. Feminist theorist Carole Pateman argues that it is through this social contract theory that "modern patriarchy is constituted." Pateman, *The Sexual Contract* (Stanford, CA: Stanford University Press, 1988), 2.

21. On the ways in which women challenged exclusion from the public sphere, see Mary P. Ryan, *Women in Public: Between Banners and Ballots, 1825–1880* (Baltimore: Johns Hopkins University Press, 1990). For an overview of the development of the idea of separate spheres and its consequences for women's citizenship in the US, see Mary P. Ryan, *Mysteries of Sex: Tracing Women and Men through American History* (Chapel Hill: University of North Carolina Press, 2006).

22. Meredith Conroy, *Masculinity, Media, and the American Presidency* (New York: Palgrave Macmillan, 2015); Justin S. Vaughn and Lilly J. Goren, eds., *Women and the White House: Gender, Popular Culture, and Presidential Politics* (Lexington: University Press of Kentucky, 2013).

23. For gender performance theory, see Judith Butler, *Gender Trouble: Feminism and the Subversion of Identity* (New York: Routledge, 1999); and Aidan Smith, *Gender, Heteronormativity, and the American Presidency* (New York: Routledge, 2018).

24. On Clinton's voice, see Olga Khazan, "Would You Really Like Hillary More If She Sounded Different?," *Atlantic*, August 1, 2016, https:// www.theatlantic.com/science/archive/2016/08/hillarys-voice/493565/.

25. Clinton, *What Happened*, 111.

26. On violence against protestors, see Alan Rappeport and Maggie Haberman, "For Donald Trump, 'Get 'Em Out' Is the New 'You're Fired,'" *New York Times*, March 13, 2016, http://www.nytimes.com/2016/03/14/us/politics/donald-trump-security.html.

27. Ishaan Tharoor, "Trump Is the U.S.'s First Latin American President," *Washington Post,* January 26, 2017, http://www.washingtonpost.com/news/worldviews/wp/2017/01/26/trump-is-the-u-s-s-first-latin-american-president/?utm_term=.61ca87ced3c5.

28. "Who Will Win the Presidency?," FiveThirtyEight.com, November 8, 2016, http://projects.fivethirtyeight.com/2016-election-forecast.

29. Aaron Blake, "Three Dozen Republicans Have Called for Donald Trump to Drop Out," *Washington Post,* October 9, 2016, https://www.washingtonpost.com/news/the-fix/wp/2016/10/07/the-gops-brutal-responses-to-the-new-trump-video-broken-down/?utm_term=.6fecb cdd24cd.

30. "2016 Election Results," CNN.com, November 23, 2016, http://www.cnn.com/election/results; Philip Bump, "Donald Trump Will Be President Thanks to 80,000 People in Three States," *Washington Post,* December 1, 2016, https://www.washingtonpost.com/news/the-fix/wp/2016/12/01/donald-trump-will-be-president-thanks-to-80000-people-in-three-states/?utm_term=.d91589077e48.

31. "Election 2016, Exit Polls," CNN.com.

32. Richa Chaturvedi, "A Closer Look at the Gender Gap in Presidential Voting," Pew Research Center, July 28, 2016, http://www.pewresearch.org/fact-tank/2016/07/28/a-closer-look-at-the-gender-gap-in-presidential-voting/. The same CNN exit polls show that Donald Trump's treatment of women played into voters' preferences, as those who were bothered "a lot" strongly preferred Clinton (83 percent), while those who were bothered "not at all" strongly preferred Trump (86 percent). In fact, overall, 70 percent of those interviewed indicated that Trump's treatment of women bothered them "a lot" or "some." Nonetheless, being bothered did not discourage many voters from supporting Trump, as 11 percent of the people who said it bothered them "a lot" and 73 percent of the people who said it bothered them "some" voted for him. Thus, while concerns about Trump's sexism were widespread, they were not decisive. "Election 2016, Exit Polls," CNN.com.

33. Ibid.

34. "The Parties on the Eve of the 2016 Election: Two Coalitions, Moving Further Apart," Pew Research Center, September 13, 2016, http://www.people-press.org/2016/09/13/the-parties-on-the-eve-of-the-2016-election-two-coalitions-moving-further-apart/.

35. The Women's March Organizers and Condé Nast, *Together We Rise: Behind the Scenes at the Protest Heard around the World* (New York: HarperCollins, 2018), 13, 57.

36. "Election 2016, Exit Polls," CNN.com.

37. Ibid.

38. Clare Foran, "Women Aren't Responsible for Hillary Clinton's Defeat," *Atlantic,* November 13, 2016, http://www.theatlantic.com/politics/archive/2016/11/hillary-clinton-white-women-vote/507422/.

39. Marisa Abrajano and Zoltan Hajnal, *White Backlash: Immigration, Race, and American Politics* (Princeton, NJ: Princeton University Press, 2015); Carol Anderson, *White Rage: The Unspoken Truth about Our Racial Divide* (New York: Bloomsbury, 2016); Christopher S. Parker and Matt A. Barreto, *Change They Can't Believe In: The Tea Party and Reactionary Politics in America* (Princeton, NJ: Princeton University Press, 2013).

40. Arlie Russell Hochschild, *Strangers in Their Own Land: Anger and Mourning on the American Right* (New York: New Press, 2016); Nancy Isenberg, *White Trash: The 400-Year Untold History of Class in America* (New York: Viking, 2016); J. D. Vance, *Hillbilly Elegy: A Memoir of a Family and Culture in Crisis* (New York: HarperCollins, 2016).

41. Maskovsky, "Anthropology of White Nationalist Postracialism."

42. Michael S. Kimmel, *Angry White Men: American Masculinity at the End of an Era* (New York: Nation Books, 2013). See also Susan Faludi, *Stiffed: The Betrayal of the American Man* (New York: William Morrow, 1999).

43. J. Oliver Conroy, "'Angry White Men': The Sociologist Who Studied Trump's Base before Trump," *Guardian*, February 27, 2017, http://www.theguardian.com/world/2017/feb/27/michael-kimmel-masculinity-far-right-angry-white-men.

44. Brian F. Schaffner, Matthew MacWilliams, and Tatishe Nteta, "Explaining White Polarization in the 2016 Vote for President: The Sobering Role of Racism and Sexism" (paper presented at The U.S. Elections of 2016: Domestic and International Aspects Conference, Interdisciplinary Center–Herzliya, Herzliya, Israel, January 8–9, 2017), http://people.umass.edu/schaffne/schaffner_et_al_IDC_conference.pdf.

45. "Election 2016, Exit Polls," CNN.com.

46. John Sides, "Race, Religion, and Immigration in 2016: How the Debate over American Identity Shaped the Election and What It Means for a Trump Presidency" (report, Democracy Fund Voter Study Group, June 2017), accessed August 3, 2017, https://www.voterstudygroup.org/reports/2016-elections.

47. Smith, *Gender, Heteronormativity, and the Presidency*, 204–5.

48. Estelle Freedman, *No Turning Back: The History of Feminism and the Future of Women* (New York: Ballantine Books, 2002), 7.

49. Margaret R. Somers, "The Narrative Constitution of Identity: A Relational and Network Approach," *Theory and Society* 23, no. 5 (1994): 614.

50. Dan P. McAdams, *The Stories We Live By: Personal Myths and the Making of the Self* (New York: Guilford Press, 1993), 11.

Part One

Aggressive and Subordinate Masculinities

Chapter One

FROM (CASTRATING) *BITCH* TO (BIG) *NUTS*

Genital Politics in 2016 Election Campaign Paraphernalia

Jane Caputi

"Life Is a Bitch—Don't Vote for One"

—anti-Clinton sticker[1]

"Trump 2016: I Have Serious Balls"

—pro-Trump sticker[2]

Reflecting long-standing social hierarchies of race, gender, class, and sexuality, every president of the United States—until the 2008 election and the victory of Barack Obama—had been a white (as far as anyone knew), Christian (more or less), well-off, and (to all appearances) cisgender and heterosexual man. The uniformity of this public face of "the most powerful man in the world" had long served as a potent symbol of the "rightness" and seeming inevitability of the status quo. The 2016 campaign featured two especially dramatic candidates. The Republican nominee, Donald Trump, a celebrity real-estate tycoon and reality-TV star, seemed to be a hyperbolic expression of that presidential tradition and, to his ardent supporters, the essence of America itself. As one pro-Trump poster read, "I'm Voting Trump to Get My America Back."[3] On the Democrat side was Hillary Clinton, the former US secretary of state and First Lady, now making a historic run as the first female presidential candidate nominated by a major party. A pro-Clinton T-shirt read, "A Woman's Place Is in the White House."[4]

The challenges to tradition in both the 2008 and 2016 elections brought out long-standing fears, resentments, hatreds, and bigotries around race, gender, national origin, age, sexuality, religion, and

class, vividly represented in (unofficial) commercial paraphernalia—
bumper stickers, buttons, caps, T-shirts—many of which were then
exchanged in images sent via email and posted on websites and social-
media platforms.[5]

The National Museum of American History at the Smithsonian, in
Washington, DC, collects such paraphernalia. It deems campaign artifacts to be "material culture that represents political engagement . . .
reflecting the infinite richness and complexity of American history."[6]
This chapter samples and interprets a specific subset of the artifacts
produced in response to the 2016 election—the vivid, vulgar, funny,
angry, and often offensive and bigoted merchandise and related Internet images focused on sex and gender.

Genital Politics

"Word Association: You Say Hillary, I think C.U.N.T."

—anti-Clinton T-shirt[7]

"Trump—Finally Someone with Balls! 2016"

—pro-Trump T-shirt[8]

One of the most consistent themes in pro-Trump paraphernalia is the
claim that Trump is the candidate with the biggest "nuts" or "balls,"
which means that he is the most macho and alpha of males, dominant
over all others. Many feminists link this sort of patriarchal masculinity
to an ongoing epidemic of violence in the United States, the devalu-
ation of women and LGBTQ people, sexual assault, domestic violence, bullying, racism, degradation of the environment ("rape of the
Earth"), and militarism.[9]

A typical pro-Trump poster showed the candidate grimacing and
looking tough. The copy read, "Trump 2016: I Have Serious Balls."[10]
This assertion of genital power was by no means confined to the paraphernalia, nor did it stand unchallenged. Decades earlier, one critic
had described Trump as a "short fingered vulgarian," and the insult
stuck.[11] In 2016, after Trump demeaned the short-statured Cuban
American Marco Rubio as "Little Marco," Rubio pushed back by making jokes about Trump's "small hands." Trump responded directly in
a subsequent debate, holding up his hands and declaring: "Look at
those hands. Are they small hands? If they are small, something else
must be small. I guarantee you there is no problem, I guarantee you."[12]

While this vulgarism aroused some negative commentary, it didn't undo Trump's candidacy as it might have for a man differently situated socially. Race, class, sexuality, and gender politics are powerfully at play here. A common racist stereotype is that black men, by virtue of their race, have bigger penises.[13] This is dehumanization, conveying the racist belief that blacks are inferior to whites, more "animal," carnal, sexual, and sexually dangerous. If supporters of a heterosexual African American candidate issued posters proclaiming his genital magnitude—let alone the candidate himself, no matter how well off and well educated, say Barack Obama or Ben Carson—that candidate's political career might be over. The billionaire Trump famously adopts the bold, tell-it-like-it-is style associated with the "common man." But if another candidate without Trump's wealth swaggered and spoke in this way, or if the candidate's supporters proclaimed his penile largeness in popular paraphernalia, classist stereotypes might ensure that the majority would dismiss him for having "no class." Homophobic stereotypes also come into play. If fans of a gay candidate effused in bumper stickers over the seriousness of his "balls," or that candidate averred the same, he might well be seen as hypersexual, even predatory. A rich, white, celebrity billionaire like Trump can boast about and be associated with huge testicles and penis, because, for him, they signify straight, white, and male dominance—over women as well as over other men.

Paraphernalia reflected this outsized attention to "size" in less blatant ways, as well. One bizarre pro-Trump T-shirt depicted Trump as a grown man wearing a sling that holds a child-sized Marco Rubio wearing a beanie with a propeller on it. The copy reads, "Don't Cry Little Marco."[14] A yard sign hailed Trump as an enormous Uncle Sam–type figure, dangling a tiny Obama by the back of his pants and declaring, "You're Fired" (echoing Trump's signature line from his NBC reality-TV show *The Apprentice*).[15]

Several anti-Trump artifacts turned the size issue back against Trump, including a miniscule bar of soap, "Trump's Small Hand Soap . . . For Dirty Politics."[16] Another is a tiny naked bobblehead, "Baby Penis Trump."[17] The Internet artist Fernando Sosa featured it on Etsy, with an accompanying statement expressing outrage at racist statements by Trump. More publicly, the activist artist group Indecline put up naked life-size statues of Trump labeled "The Emperor Has No Balls" in several urban locations.[18] Whatever one thinks of Trump, critiques based in this phallic framework are problematic from a feminist perspective. Associating proper (white) masculinity with superior size promotes not only body-shaming, but also aggressive and dominant masculinity as the norm. Males must be perceived as dominant over others, or they are perceived as not *men*. Women too are diminished by this framework, for in patriarchal philosophies from Aristotle to Freud, women are the lesser sex because they have no penis at all.[19]

Negative stereotypes of female carnality and genital inferiority if not monstrosity abound.[20] Patriarchal medicine, religion, philosophy, and folk culture continue to associate the vulva and womb, along with menstruation and menopause, with irrationality if not evil.[21] Anti-Clinton items that originated in 2008 when she was sixty years old warned that with a woman as president, the nation would be on the verge of war every "28 days" and that disasters were sure to follow if "hot flashes" were allowed to occur in the White House.[22]

The preponderance of "big balls" pro-Trump items indicates that men can be applauded for being self-assuredly "cocky," but there is no acceptable language or valorized tradition of genital pride for girls and women.[23] During both the 2008 and the 2016 election season, paraphernalia regularly sought to apply genital politics of shame against Hillary Clinton. She was commonly labeled a *cunt*, one of the most taboo words in the English language.[24] Former television actor Scott Baio, a speaker at the 2016 Republican National Convention, retweeted a popular meme casting this aspersion, a slur replicated in an anti-Clinton rebus puzzle T-shirt for country music fans.[25] Similarly themed items focus negatively on female genitals, disparaging female Clinton supporters as favoring her only because of genital identification: "Hillary Clinton 2016: Because I Have a Va-Jay-Jay."[26] Another postcard shows a haggard Clinton admonishing female voters to "Vote with Your Genitals, Not with Your Brains."[27]

In October 2016, a 2005 tape was released showing Trump boasting about how his star power gave him license to "grab 'em [women] by the pussy." It was met with outrage, but, again, not enough to undo his candidacy.[28] Among multiple feminist responses, Amanda May issued a T-shirt reading "Vaginas Against Trump," worn proudly for a photo shoot by some members of the cast and crew of *Orange Is the New Black*.[29] Some might well question the wisdom of this phrase that appears to identify women with their vaginas. Certainly, though, there is reason for women, including transwomen, to vote against a candidate who identifies himself with sexual abuse.

My title "Genital Politics" is flippant, but simultaneously serious. The reality remains that since the country's inception genital politics have ensured that Americans have been voting for male presidential candidates because these politicians were men in a "man's world." Hillary Clinton's candidacy challenged this. It also raised the question of whether women *as women* should vote for female candidates. Few feminists would argue that women should vote for a female candidate regardless of the candidate's politics. But shouldn't women affirmatively and proudly vote for women they determine to be progressive as part of a strategy to terminate the male grip on the White House and disrupt at the same time this tradition's potent symbolic support for (white) male supremacy?

Misogyny: The Bitch, Gorgon, Witch, and Hag

"This Bitch is Bat Shit Crazy"

—anti-Clinton sticker[30]

"And You Thought Medusa Was a Bitch: Beware Hillary"

—anti-Clinton sticker[31]

"Cackle Cackle: Hillary Rotten Clinton"

—anti-Clinton (as witch) sticker[32]

"Hillary Is a Socialist Hag!"

—anti-Clinton postcard[33]

Multiple misogynist slurs, based in hatred, dread, and disgust for women, appeared regularly throughout anti-Clinton paraphernalia. One of the most common was the aspersion that she was a *bitch* and, implicitly and explicitly, a *castrating bitch.* Indeed, if you look up the phrase *castrating bitch* online, you will quickly be directed to the vernacular *Urban Dictionary.* There, the "top definition" begins with the name "Hillary Rodham Clinton."[34]

Countless artifacts reiterate the message: "This Bitch Again";[35] "Queen Bitch";[36] "Life's a Bitch: Don't Vote for One."[37] Andi Zeisler, a founder of the feminist magazine *Bitch,* explains that *bitch* is used as an epithet to describe any "woman who is strong, angry, uncompromising and often uninterested in pleasing men . . . the woman who has a better job than a man and doesn't apologize for it . . . the woman who doesn't back down from a confrontation."[38] This anti-Clinton paraphernalia reflected the sexist frame that holds that when a woman is empowered, a man is necessarily disempowered, that strength in women translates inevitably into weakness and emasculation for men. Hence the words *castrating* and *bitch* so often appear together. The underlying fear is not so much about men actually losing their genitals. It's about men losing their "patriarchal dividend,"[39] their status and privileges (like higher pay and an exclusive lock on the presidency) that are cut off—they maintain—when women attain equality. Significantly, feminists since the 1970s have reclaimed the word *bitch* and some pro-Clinton artifacts incorporate this—for example, a T-shirt with a photo of an unsmiling Clinton wearing sunglasses and peering at her phone, with the emblazoned phrase: "Bitches Get Stuff Done."[40]

"The Hillary Clinton Nutcracker" openly plays on the *castrating bitch* theme. It casts her pantsuited form as fully able to crack a walnut between her thighs. The 2008 version dubbed her a "ball-breaker,"[41] but the campy 2016 one hailed her as hopefully able to "keep the nuts out of the White House."[42]

Patriarchal fears of castration provide the basis for the myth of the *vagina dentata*, the castrating toothed vagina,[43] which informs multiple depictions of Clinton. Many represent her as the fanged and snake-haired Gorgon Medusa, understood by Sigmund Freud and others as a symbol of castration.[44] Medusa was originally an archaic Greek goddess, but patriarchal myth turned the goddess into a monster, righteously beheaded by a "hero" Perseus.[45] One sticker, showing a sour-faced and snake-haired Clinton, names her an even worse "bitch" than "Medusa." And an Internet pro-Trump image actually shows Trump as Perseus, brandishing the severed head of Hillary/Medusa over the words "Make America Great Again."[46]

Vagina dentata imagery also informs buttons and bumper stickers depicting Clinton as a generic fanged and hideous monster about to "eat our babies,"[47] perhaps alluding to abortion. A related flamboyant road sign displayed by a gun shop in Maine lambasted Clinton as inhuman, a dread "Hildabeast" set to commit genocide of males: "THE HILDABEAST CLINTON AND ITS VAGENDA OF MANOCIDE."[48] The incendiary and fantastic language immediately made its way into related T-shirts and buttons, including some that ironically flip the meaning to give it a feminist flair.[49]

Along with *bitch*, Clinton is commonly branded a *witch*. She is depicted with a green face and pointed black hat, cackling crazily and riding a broom, when not being crushed under a falling house or burned at the stake.[50] One pro-Trump item called openly for Hillary's execution: "Burn the Witch 2016."[51] A pro-Sanders sticker followed suit with "Hillary's a Witch! Bern Her."[52] These lines, so easily tossed off, grossly trivialize if not celebrate the misogynist atrocity of the European witch hunts. For about three centuries in Europe (1450–1750), powerful men of both church and state labeled women who were troublesome to them—those who were single, community leaders, skilled at herbs and healing, wise elders—as *witches*. They legally tortured and executed (including by burning) about 300,000 people, most of them women, in an outbreak of mass femicide.[53]

Finally, a misogynist double standard is evident in the ageism directed at Clinton far more than her male opponents. Top candidates in 2016 all were older than previous front-runners. Bernie Sanders was seventy-four during his campaign, and Donald Trump seventy. But age-based insults were almost all directed at the youngest of the three, Clinton, sixty-eight. She was regularly caricatured by her detractors as a politically unviable "grandma" and as repellently "old" and grotesquely wrinkled, a hideous "hag."[54] Age-related disability-bashing infused an Internet image mocking Clinton. The cranky-looking, wrinkled, and bespectacled face of Hillary Clinton was placed atop the blue wheelchair insignia indicating a handicapped parking spot; the red arrow of her campaign logo pointed the way.[55]

I found no paraphernalia explicitly targeting Trump's age. Ageism was directed a bit against Bernie Sanders,[56] but many more pro-Sanders items depicted him favorably by identifying him with youthful pursuits, such as skateboarding and playing a guitar in a punk rock band.[57] Several associated him with revered male elders, like the estimable artist/illustrator Emek's homage, "Bernie Wan Kenobi."[58]

Homophobia and Transphobia

"Hillary Stinks, Just Ask Her Girlfriend"

—anti-Clinton bumper sticker[59]

"Hillary for Lezident"

—anti-Clinton T-shirt[60]

Ultimately, any ambitious, smart, and powerful woman, no matter if she conforms to feminine presentation, is viewed as a sexual and gender deviant. Haters vilify both Hillary Clinton and former First Lady Michelle Obama as secret men and/or closeted lesbians. A typical image depicts Clinton sneaking into the men's room and using a urinal;[61] a related Internet meme shows a photo of Michelle Obama supposedly with a penis visible under her dress.[62]

Homophobic and transphobic jabs aimed at men issued from both left and right. Some of these mock straight and gender-conforming men by depicting them in feminine attire. Anti–Hillary Clinton items depict Bill Clinton in makeup, pearls, and a skirt, dubbing him the

"First Lady."[63] Internet visuals disparage Donald Trump also by representing him as a woman. Sometimes the intent is pure mockery. Other times, the purported aim is to critique the double standard that allows Trump to get away with behaviors that would likely sink female candidates: refusing to release tax returns; interrupting opponents during debates; grimacing instead of smiling; declaring bankruptcy multiple times; and cheating, divorcing, and marrying younger partners.[64] But this gender-mocking strategy is problematic because it dehumanizes nonconforming, transgender, or sex- and gender-ambiguous people by casting them to be inherently ridiculous, as "freaks."

Homophobic characterizations mark a popular anti-Trump theme that mocks him with the suggestion that he and hypermacho, homophobic, and antifeminist Russian president Vladimir Putin are lovers. A critical outdoor mural of the two kissing appeared first in Lithuania in May 2016, recalling the conventional kiss between Soviet-era dictators.[65] The image went viral and soon was replicated in a poster sold in the United States—"Trump Putin '16. Make Tyranny Great Again"[66]— and expanded into many overtly homophobic, mostly Internet-based variations. One of these photoshopped images was posted by Queensryche singer Todd La Torre on Facebook and shared on the Facebook page for "Occupy Democrats."[67] It shows Putin and Trump as a pair of leather-garbed, dominant (Putin)/submissive (Trump) lovers, as Putin stands over the sitting Trump, holding him on a chain. Scholars Randy Conner and David Sparks identify such anti-Trump jokes as virulently antigay, pointing out that Putin and Trump "are heterosexist misogynists who have allied themselves with white supremacy."[68] But images like this bypass this crucial recognition and instead critique Trump and Putin by associating them with a gay subculture, eliciting and reinforcing disgust—not for tyrants, but for gay men.

Underlying all of the misogynist, homophobic, and transphobic aspersions expressed in the paraphernalia discussed here is the discriminatory dogma that assertive, powerful women and anyone who doesn't conform to sexual and gender norms is inferior, deviant, and unsuitable for political office.

Electoral Violence

"Beat Hillary!"

—anti-Clinton sticker[69]

"Wanna See Hillary Run? Throw Rocks"

—anti-Clinton calendar print[70]

"Trump That Bitch"

—anti-Clinton bumper sticker[71]

"Hang the Bitch"

—Cries from the audience at a Trump rally[72]

The candidacy of Hillary Clinton (in both 2008 and 2016) was met by a scourge of misogynist abuse and threats. Many items not only insulted and sought to shame and discredit her, but openly called for her to be raped ("Hillary: Bump Her, Stick Her")[73] and murdered in an act of domestic violence ("I Wish Hillary Had Married OJ").[74] A popular biker T-shirt bears this slogan on its back: "If You Can Read This, the Bitch Fell Off." The visual of one 2016 pro-Trump shirt, set in front of the White House, showed a grinning motorcycle-riding Trump wearing that shirt and with Hillary Clinton, "the bitch," pitching off the back of the bike.[75] There were Internet images and sites suggesting that Trump be beaten up or "punched"[76] (the same site also offered the chance to "punch Hillary"), but virtually no commercial paraphernalia endorsing violence against Trump.

In 2008 the demand was to get Clinton "back to the kitchen."[77] In 2016 that shifted to sending her to jail. Trump branded her "Crooked Hillary," and surrogates led rally chants of "Lock Her Up," sentiments echoed in bumper stickers combining the two phrases.[78] Many items depict Clinton behind bars in an orange jumpsuit, demanding "Hillary for Prison 2016."[79] Trump promised that she would be incarcerated following his election, something dictators are wont to do to their opponents. But he dropped this immediately upon winning the presidency. It is true that Clinton was being investigated by the FBI in relation to her emails (twice), though the FBI also cleared her (twice).[80] Arguably much of this animosity was due to Hillary Clinton's "crime" of being an ambitious, feminist-identified woman, daring to make a bid for the highest office in the land.

These kinds of aspersions and threats against a candidate are what international democracy rights groups call *electoral violence*: "any harm or threat of harm to any person or property involved in the election process, or the process itself, during the election period."[81] The misogynist character of the venom directed at Hillary Clinton comprises intimidation not only against her, but implicitly against all women who might think of making a presidential run. And it is crucial to remember that violence is not only physical, but takes verbal, emotional, and psychological forms including threats, name-calling, cultivation of anxiety and despair, humiliation, blaming, shaming, accusing, isolating, and reality control, all of which can be noted in many of the items described here.[82]

Cultural studies scholar John Cawelti observes that American violence has long been "associated with the protection of white male supremacy."[83] The psychological electoral violence aimed at Hillary Clinton is part of that tradition. The rhetoric of hate previously confined to the fringe, but now issuing from Trump supporters as well as Trump himself; the fervent support of Trump by members of the KKK, the alt-right, and neo-Nazi groups; and the significant upswing in hate crimes since the election suggest that what is really going on is what is emblazoned on one anti-Trump baseball cap: "Make America Hate Again."[84]

Historian Nell Irwin Painter notes that Trump's winning promise to "Make America Great Again" was heard by many as "Make America White Again." She wryly observes that "without Barack Obama, there is no Donald Trump."[85] Still, if Obama's presidency inspired a nativist backlash, perhaps Trump's presidency will bring its own unintended consequences. A 2016 poll of Americans of all ages and backgrounds indicated that four women, in this order, have emerged as the current face of feminism: Michelle Obama, Oprah Winfrey, Hillary Clinton, and Beyoncé.[86] Black voters, especially black women voters who gave Trump only 4 percent of their vote, as well as LGBTQ voters led the way in opposition to Trump.[87] Intersectional feminism, which recognizes that feminism is necessarily enmeshed with all other social justice concerns,[88] informs a newly reenergized movement. One of these four feminists, Hillary Clinton, won the popular vote by almost 3 million votes. Another of these four leading feminists, Oprah Winfrey, said in February 2017 that she would not rule out a presidential run in 2020. Whether Oprah runs or not, some of the values she represents—racial inclusion and equality, women's and girls' empowerment, LGBTQ rights, nurturance, community and relationship building, listening, and healing—are necessary in our deeply divided country facing what seems to many on all sides to be an especially uncertain future.

One mug depicting Hillary Clinton as a witch read, "I'm Coming for Your Children to Destroy Their Future."[89] The scapegoating of Hillary Clinton as the one who will destroy our future is a denial and displacement of far more realistic concerns. It's not the "witch"— female empowerment—that is threatening to consume our younger generations. The threats facing all of us derive more from those practices and values associated with "balls" and sexist notions of masculinity. These include domination; violence; hierarchy; war; hate crimes; contamination of land, air, and water; the consequences of global warming, including food shortages and displacement of people; and the potential use of weapons of mass destruction.

I collected these artifacts (along with others marked with biases based in race, ethnicity, religion, and nationality) because these aspects of material culture are an essential part of the historical record. But, along with the Museum of American History, I also hope that our reflection on them will help us to recognize and reject bias and thus increase our ability and our propensity to shape what the museum calls a "more humane future," one ever more consonant with national ideals of justice and equality for all.

Notes

1. Barefoot Graphix, "Life's a Bitch DON'T VOTE FOR ONE!" window vinyl decal for sale [purchased 2016], accessed August 7, 2017, https://www.amazon.com/Lifes-Bitch-DONT-VOTE-ONE/dp/B00VZ5O442.

2. WildThreadz, "Trump 2016: I Have Serious Balls," vinyl sticker posted for sale July 23, 2015, CafePress.com, item webpage discontinued.

3. Ibid.

4. HilTee, "A Woman's Place Is in the White House," T-shirt posted for sale September 1, 2015, https://www.amazon.com/Kids-Womans-Place-White-House/dp/B01M71A2RQ/ref=sr_1_1?s=apparel&ie=UTF8&qid=1502130939&sr=1-1&nodeID=7141123011&psd=1.

5. I collected these for two visual culture exhibits: 3-Ring Political Circus (2008) and Political Sideshow (2016), cocurated with Adrienne Gionta, both sponsored by Florida Atlantic University Galleries. The artifacts from both the 2008 and 2016 exhibits are collected in the Visual Archives of the Florida Atlantic University Wimberly Library.

6. "Smithsonian Curators to Collect 2016 Presidential Convention Memorabilia from RNC, DNC," National Museum of American History, July 15, 2016, http://americanhistory.si.edu/press/releases/presidential-conventions.

7. "Word Association: You Say Hillary, I Think C.U.N.T.," T-shirt for sale [purchased 2008], CafePress.com, item webpage discontinued.

8. "Trump—Finally Someone with Balls! 2016," T-shirt for sale [purchased 2016], FunnyShirts.net, item discontinued.

9. See, for example, James Gilligan, *Violence: Reflections on a National Epidemic* (New York: Vintage, 1997); bell hooks, *The Will to Change: Men, Masculinity and Love* (New York: Washington Square Press, 2004).

10. WildThreadz, "Trump 2016: I Have Serious Balls."

11. Emily Shapiro, "The History behind the Donald Trump 'Small Hands' Insult," ABC News, March 4, 2016, http://abcnews.go.com/Politics/history-donald-trump-small-hands-insult/story?id=37395515.

12. Ibid.

13. Scott Poulson-Bryant, *Hung: A Meditation on the Measure of Black Men in America* (New York: Doubleday, 2005).

14. goatlady_Get-Yer-Goat, "Donald Trump—Don't Cry Little Marco," T-shirt posted for sale March 6, 2016, http://www.cafepress.com/mf/103730133/donald-trump-dont-cry-little-marco_tshirt?productId=1737021303.

15. RightWingStuff, "Trump Uncle Sam—You're Fired! Yard Sign," yard sign posted for sale November 2, 2015, http://www.cafepress.com/+trump_uncle_sam_youre_fired_yard_sign,1671044205.

16. The Unemployed Philosophers Guild, "Trump's Small Hand Soap," soap [purchased 2016], accessed August 7, 2017, http://www.philosophersguild.com/Trumps-Small-Hand-Soap.html.

17. Fernando Sosa, "Baby Penis Trump Bobblehead," doll for sale [purchased 2016], accessed August 7, 2017, http://politicalsculptor.com/babypenistrump.html.

18. Elisabeth Garber-Paul, "Naked Trump Statues," *Rolling Stone*, August 19, 2016, http://www.rollingstone.com/culture/features/trump-statues-meet-anarchists-behind-emperor-has-no-balls-w435341.

19. Rosemary Agonito, *History of Ideas on Woman: A Source Book* (New York: Berkeley Publishing Group, 1977).

20. Barbara Creed, *The Monstrous Feminine: Film, Feminism, Psychoanalysis* (New York: Routledge, 2002).

21. Nancy Tuana, *The Less Noble Sex: Scientific, Religious, and Philosophical Conceptions of Woman's Nature* (Bloomington: Indiana University Press, 2002).

22. Katkramer, anti–Hillary Clinton paraphernalia [purchased 2008], Zazzle.com, item webpage discontinued; "Why Not Hillary? Because No One Needs to Go to War Every 28 Days," anti–Hillary Clinton paraphernalia [purchased 2008], CafePress.com, item webpage discontinued.

23. For feminist rebuttal and commentary, see Eve Ensler, *The Vagina Monologues* (New York: Villard, 1998); Emma L. E. Rees, *The Vagina: A Literary and Cultural History* (New York: Bloomsbury, 2013); and Inga Muscio, *Cunt: A Declaration of Independence* (Seattle: Seal Press, 2002).

24. Benjamin K. Bergen, *What the F: What Swearing Reveals about Our Language, Our Brains, and Ourselves* (New York: Basic Books, 2016), 15.

25. Allegra Kirkland, "RNC Speaker Scott Baio Tweeted Meme Referring to Hillary Clinton as a C**T," *Talking Points Memo*, July 18, 2016, http://talkingpointsmemo.com/livewire/scott-baio-speaker-republican-convention; This T-shirt uses visual symbols that sound out "I Love Country Music," putting Clinton's face next to a tree to signify country: "I Love Country Music Anti Hillary Clinton T-shirt," T-shirt for sale [purchased 2016], accessed August 7, 2017, http://www.betterthanpants.com/i-love-country-music-anti-hillary-clinton-t-shirt#.

26. "Because I Have a Va-Jay-Jay—Anti-Hillary Political Bumper Sticker," bumper sticker for sale, September 19, 2016, http://www.ebay.com/itm/

BECAUSE-I-HAVE-A-VA-JAY-JAY-ANTI-HILLARY-POLITICAL-BUMPER-STICKER-4169-/121723009680.

27. Politiclothes.com, "Vote with Your Genitals, Not with Your Brains—Hil Bumper Sticker," bumper sticker for sale [purchased 2016], accessed August 7, 2017, http://www.zazzle.com/vote_with_your_genitals_not_with_your_brains_hil_bumper_sticker-128976920242409406.

28. Jill Filipovic, "Donald Trump's 'P—y' Comment Is the Root of Sexual Violence," *Time*, October 8, 2016, http://time.com/4523972/donald-trumps-comment-root-sexual-violence/.

29. Tara McCoy, "Vaginas Against Trump," *Huffington Post*, October 19, 2016, http://www.huffingtonpost.com/entry/vaginas-against-trump_us_5807829de4b00483d3b5cdf5.

30. goatlady_GetYerGoat, "Hillary Bitch Bat Shit Crazy Sticker," bumper sticker posted for sale December 26, 2015, http://www.cafepress.com/mf/102853036/hillary-bitch-bat-shit-crazy_sticker?productId=1705323601.

31. "And You Thought Medusa Was a Bitch: Beware Hillary," sticker for sale [purchased 2008], CafePress.com/HillaryScaresMe, item webpage discontinued.

32. "Cackle Cackle: Hillary Rotten Clinton," sticker for sale [purchased 2008], CafePress.com, item webpage discontinued.

33. First Principles, "Hillary Is a Socialist Hag!" sticker for sale [purchased 2016], Zazzle.com, item webpage discontinued.

34. DBaltimore, "Castrating Bitch," UrbanDictionary.com, February 15, 2007, http://www.urbandictionary.com/define.php?term=castrating%20bitch.

35. Charles C. Johnson, "Anti-Hillary Street Art Hits LA Ghetto," GotNews.com, October 20, 2014, http://gotnews.com/streetart-welcomes-hillary-clinton-hood/.

36. Shirtuosity, "Anti-Hillary: Queen Bitch Trucker Hat," hat posted for sale December 1, 2007, http://www.cafepress.com/+antihillary_queen_bitch_trucker_hat,195245774.

37. "Life's a Bitch, Don't Vote for One—Political Bumper Sticker," bumper sticker for sale [purchased 2016], accessed August 7, 2017, https://www.amazon.com/lifes-bitch-dont-vote-for/dp/b0144r4utq.

38. Andi Zeisler, "The B-Word: You Betcha," *Washington Post*, November 18, 2007, http://www.washingtonpost.com/wp-dyn/content/article/2007/11/16/AR2007111601202.html.

39. Raewyn Connell, "The Social Organization of Masculinity," in *Exploring Masculinities: Identity, Inequality, Continuity, and Change*, ed. C. J. Pascoe and Tristan Bridges (New York: Oxford University Press, 2016), 136–44.

40. "Bitches Get Stuff Done—Hillary Clinton for President 2016," T-shirt for sale [purchased 2016], nstapparel.com, item discontinued (available at http://www.hillaryclintonmerchandise.com/hillary-clinton-merchandise/bitches-get-stuff-done-hillary-clinton-for-president-2016/). The phrase is originally from Tina Fey. See Alex Abad-Santos, "SNL's

2008 'Bitches Get Stuff Done' Sketch Foreshadowed Trump Calling Clinton a 'Nasty Woman,'" *Vox*, October 20, 2016, https://www.vox.com/2016/10/20/13346106/hillary-clinton-nasty-woman.

41. "The Hillary Nutcracker," stainless steel nutcracker for sale [purchased 2008], https://www.ebay.com/p/Hillary-Clinton-Nutcracker-Stainless-Steel-Thighs-2007-Gag-Joke-Gift-Hilary/1200159750.

42. Damn Handy Products, "The Hillary Nutcracker," stainless steel nutcracker for sale [purchased 2016], accessed August 7, 2017, http://www.hillarynutcracker.com/.

43. Penelope Dane, "Vagina Dentata," in *The International Encyclopedia of Human Sexuality* (John Wiley and Sons, 2015), 1409–30, https://doi.org/10.1002/9781118896877.wbiehs525.

44. Elizabeth Johnston, "The Original 'Nasty Woman,'" *Atlantic*, November 6, 2016, https://www.theatlantic.com/entertainment/archive/2016/11/the-original-nasty-woman-of-classical-myth/506591/; Sigmund Freud, "Medusa's Head (1940, 1922)," in *Standard Edition of Complete Psychological Works of Sigmund Freud*, ed. and trans. James Strachey (London: Hogarth Press, 1955), 18:273–77.

45. Jane Ellen Harrison, *Prolegomena to the Study of Greek Religion* (New York: Meridian Books, 1955), 199.

46. "Trump—Make America Great Again," Internet image, accessed August 7, 2017, https://pbs.twimg.com/media/Cvctmb3VIAAI8Ql.jpg.

47. "Hillary Will Eat Our Babies," anti–Hillary Clinton unofficial campaign paraphernalia for sale, [purchased 2008], www.bewareHillary.com, item webpage discontinued.

48. April Siese, "'Vagenda of Manocide' Marquee Is but One of This Gunsmith's Hilariously Offensive Election Signs," *Daily Dot*, August 24, 2016, https://www.dailydot.com/unclick/vagenda-manocide-election-sign/.

49. See, for example, Awkward Design Co., "The Vagenda of Manocide Pro–Hillary Clinton Feminist T-shirt," T-shirt for sale, posted September 1, 2015, https://www.amazon.com/Vagenda-Manocide-Pro-Hillary-Clinton-Feminist/dp/B01L8DU16A.

50. For examples and commentary, see Jason Markey, "Hillary Clinton as Witch," *Patheos*, November 1, 2016, http://www.patheos.com/blogs/panmankey/2016/11/hillary-clinton-as-a-witch/.

51. Brad Camis, "Burn the Witch Decal," vinyl sticker, posted for sale August 3, 2016, cafepress.com, item discontinued.

52. bumpa001, "In Hillary We Don't Trust! Bumper sticker," bumper sticker for sale [purchased 2016], https://www.zazzle.com/in_hillary_we_dont_trust_bumper_sticker-128490559347323514.

53. Anne Barstow, *Witchcraze: A New History of the European Witch Hunts* (San Francisco: HarperCollins, 1994).

54. Anti–Hillary Clinton T-shirts and Apparel, "Sorry Grandma—Anti Hillary-png.png Baby Blanket," baby blanket for sale [purchased 2008], accessed August 7, 2017, https://www.zazzle.com/sorry_grandma_

anti_hillary_png_png_baby_blanket-256298506977781315; *First Principles*, "Hillary is a Socialist Hag." See also analysis and imagery at JR Thorpe, "Hillary Clinton and the Psychology of Disliking Older Women," *Bustle*, September 26, 2016, http://www.bustle.com/articles/184675-hillary-clinton-the-psychology-of-disliking-older-women.

55. See design by John Ekdahl in Kemberlee Kaye, "The Internet Reacts to Hillary's Campaign Logo," LegalInsurrection.com, April 14, 2015, http://legalinsurrection.com/2015/04/the-internet-reacts-to-hillarys-campaign-logo/.

56. Sabo, "Bernie Diaper Poster," archival giclée print for sale, February 8, 2016, accessed August 7, 2017, http://unsavoryagents.com/?projects=bernie-diaper-poster.

57. Tara-draws, "Skater Bernie," vinyl sticker for sale [purchased 2016], accessed August 7, 2017, https://www.redbubble.com/people/tara-draws/works/21635089-skater-bernie?p=sticker&size=small&utm_source=google&utm_medium=cpc&utm_campaign=g.pla+notset&co; ABCnt, "Bernie So Punk," image created September 2015, T-shirt for sale, item discontinued.

58. Emek, "Bernie Wan Kenobe," screen print on foil, posted for sale December 18, 2015, artist4bernie.com, item discontinued. Emek generously donated this print to the Political Sideshow exhibit.

59. "Hillary Stinks, Just Ask Her Girlfriend," bumper sticker for sale [purchased 2008], CafePress.com, item webpage discontinued.

60. shirtsandgiggles, "Hillary for Lezident T-shirt," T-shirt for sale [purchased 2008], CafePress.com, item webpage discontinued.

61. RightWingStuff, "She's Not What She Seems!" T-shirt posted for sale October 26, 2006, http://www.cafepress.com/mf/15340677/shes-not-what-she-seems_tshirt?productId=1812195644.

62. eden30jasp, "Shocking Video: Michelle Obama(first Lady) [*sic*] Is a Man," *Nairaland Forum*, June 22, 2016, http://www.nairaland.com/3180880/shocking-video-michelle-obama-first.

63. ArtMuvz, "Bill Clinton First Lady Square Pin," square pin for sale [purchased 2016], https://www.zazzle.co.uk/bill_clinton_first_lady_square_pin-145754387656321544.

64. One such image that pointed to gender double standards in the election is discussed in Joe Vesey-Byrne, "This Viral Meme is Completely Changing the Way People Think about the US Election," Indy100.com, September 30, 2016, https://www.indy100.com/article/if-donald-trump-was-a-woman-7340491. One such image was forwarded to me in an email in 2016. I applaud the astute political critique of the image, but disagree with the visual strategy.

65. Katie Reilly, "Street Mural of Donald Trump Kissing Vladimir Putin Goes Viral," *Time*, May 14, 2016, http://time.com/4336396/lithuania-mural-donald-trump-vladimir-putin-kiss/.

66. Titikaryati, "Trump Putin 2016," poster print for sale [purchased 2016], https://us.dizinga.com/en/artists/titikaryati/artworks/35546/poster-print-portrait/12800256/.

67. "Queensryche Singer Slammed as 'Disrespectful' after Posting Trump-and-Putin Friendship Meme," *Blabbermouth.net,* January 5, 2017, http://www.blabbermouth.net/news/queensryche-singer-slammed-as-disrespectful-after-posting-trump-and-putin-friendship-meme/. I was alerted to this image by Randy Conner.

68. Randy Conner, personal communication, March 19, 2017.

69. "Beat Hillary!" sticker for sale [purchased 2008], RightWingStuff.com, item webpage discontinued.

70. Shirtuosity, "Wanna See Hillary Run? Calendar Print," calendar for sale created June 11, 2007, cafepress.com, item discontinued.

71. "Trump That Bitch Anti Hillary—Bumper Sticker," bumper sticker for sale [purchased 2016], accessed August 7, 2017, http://www.stickershoppe.com/mm5/merchant.mvc?Screen=PROD&Product_Code=SSBS489&Category_Code=anti-hillary-clinton&Store_Code=SS&gclid=CJyNxKv-4tMCFdcUgQod3WIAfg.

72. This sentence can be overheard in a video posted in Ashley Parker, Nick Corasaniti, and Erica Berenstein, "Voices from Trump Rallies, Uncensored," *New York Times,* August 3, 2016, https://www.nytimes.com/2016/08/04/us/politics/donald-trump-supporters.html?_r=0.

73. "Hillary Bumpher Stickher Classic Thong," thong underwear for sale [purchased 2008], accessed August 7, 2017, http://www.cafepress.com/bumpstickhillar.248303773.

74. John Aravosis, "Amazon Selling 'I Wish Hillary Had Married OJ' T-shirts," AmericaBlog, July 29, 2016, http://americablog.com/2016/07/amazon-selling-wish-hillary-married-oj-t-shirts.html.

75. Biker Life Clothing, "Trump/Clinton Fell Off T-shirt," T-shirt for sale [purchased 2016], accessed August 7, 2017, https://www.amazon.com/Trump-Clinton-Fell-Off-T-Shirt/dp/B01DJDB0U8/ref=sr_1_1?ie=UTF8&qid=1494339179&sr=8-1&keywords=biker+life+trump.

76. "Punch the Trump," online game, accessed August 7, 2017, http://www.crazygames.com/game/punch-the-trump.

77. Anti–Hillary Clinton campaign paraphernalia [purchased 2008], CafePress.com, item webpage discontinued.

78. BrattyTees, "Crooked Hillary Lock Her Up Bumper Sticker," bumper sticker for sale [purchased 2016], accessed August 7, 2017, https://www.zazzle.com/crooked_hillary_lock_her_up_bumper_sticker-128630556017491192.

79. StickerDog, "Hillary Prison 2016—Anti-Hillary Bumper Sticker," bumper sticker for sale [purchased 2016], accessed August 7, 2017, https://www.amazon.com/HILLARY-PRISON-2016-Anti-Hillary-Sticker/dp/B00D8U0A86/. See also "Lock Her Up Posters," accessed August 7, 2017, https://www.zazzle.com/lock+her+up+posters.

80. Eric Bradner, Pamela Brown, and Evan Pere, "FBI Clears Clinton—Again," CNN.com, November 7, 2016, http://www.cnn.com/2016/11/06/politics/comey-tells-congress-fbi-has-not-changed-conclusions/index.html.

81. "Preventing Violence through Enhancing Security, Trust, and Electoral Security," International Foundation for Electoral Systems, http://www.ifes.org/news/preventing-electoral-violence-through-enhancing-security-trust-and-electoral-integrity.

82. Patricia Evans, *The Verbally Abusive Relationship* (Holbrook, MA: Adams Publishing, 1996).

83. John G. Cawelti, *Mystery, Violence, and Popular Culture* (Madison: University of Wisconsin Popular Press, 2004), 211.

84. Sarah Harvard, "Hate Crimes since the Election," *AOL News*, February 13, 2017, https://www.aol.com/article/news/2017/02/13/hate-crimes-since-the-election-heres-whos-been-targeted-since/21712876/; M_Ga, "Make America Hate Again—Anti–Donald Trump 2016 Trucker Hat," hat for sale [purchased 2016], accessed August 7, 2017, https://www.zazzle.com/make_america_hate_again_anti_donald_trump_2016_trucker_hat-148151975218671021.

85. Nell Irwin Painter, "Without Obama There Would Be No Trump," *New York Times*, August 9, 2016, https://www.nytimes.com/roomfordebate/2016/08/09/what-is-with-those-crowds-at-trump-rallies/without-obama-there-would-be-no-trump.

86. Kyle Munzenrieder, "These Four Women Are the Face of Feminism according to New Poll," *W Magazine*, March 8, 2017, https://www.wmagazine.com/story/faces-of-feminism-poll-oprah-michelle-obama-hillary-clinton-beyonce.

87. Laura Morgan Roberts and Robin J. Ely, "Why Did So Many White Women Vote for Donald Trump," *Fortune*, November 17, 2016, http://fortune.com/2016/11/17/donald-trump-women-voters-election/; Matthew Tharrett, "How Many LGBT People Voted for Trump?," *Logo*, November 9, 2016, http://www.newnownext.com/lgbt-vote-donald-trump/11/2016/.

88. Kimberlé Crenshaw, "Mapping the Margins: Intersectionality, Identity Politics, and Violence against Women of Color," *Stanford Law Review* 43, no. 6 (1991): 1241–99.

89. Anti–Hillary Clinton paraphernalia, mug for sale [purchased 2016], Zazzle.com, item webpage discontinued.

Chapter Two

TRUMP IN THE LAND OF OZ

Pathologizing Hillary Clinton and the Feminine Body

Roy Schwartzman and Jenni M. Simon

Disclosure of a candidate's medical history has become de rigueur in presidential campaigns, a mundane ritual since Thomas Eagleton's history of psychiatric treatment sank his vice presidential bid in 1972. The 2016 presidential election redramatized the issue of health. Hillary Clinton's physician had provided a written health assessment on July 28, 2015. That two-page letter discussed her well-publicized concussion incurred while secretary of state, seasonal allergies, a list of medications, and the lab results from a March 2015 checkup. The letter attested that she was "a healthy female" with "a healthy lifestyle," and that a "full medical evaluation" shows her "in excellent physical condition and fit to serve as President of the United States."[1] Her sudden illness in September 2016 raised questions about the health of both major parties' candidates, as Donald Trump remained evasive about his own health status.

Prior to that, the sole official assessment of Donald Trump's health had consisted of a fourteen-line letter dated December 4, 2015, referencing "a recent [undated] complete medical examination that showed only positive results."[2] The "laboratory test results [quantifying only blood pressure] were astonishingly excellent." Trump was taking a low-dose aspirin and an unspecified dosage of an unspecified statin daily. The letter concluded: "If selected, Mr. Trump, I can state unequivocally, will be the healthiest individual ever selected to the presidency." This onslaught of vague superlatives raised suspicions, which increased when the physician admitted to writing the letter in a few minutes without proofreading it.[3]

On September 11, 2016, Hillary Clinton attended a ceremony in New York commemorating the fifteenth anniversary of the 9/11 terrorist attacks. She abruptly departed during the ceremony, staggering and needing physical assistance to return to her vehicle. The extensively aired video footage ignited speculations about the candidate's health. After initially claiming she was simply faint from hyperthermia, her campaign eventually disclosed that she had been diagnosed with pneumonia two days before the event—a fact unknown by many of her own staff.[4] Her physician prescribed complete rest (a veritable "rest cure"), and Clinton vanished entirely from the campaign trail for three days. Trump reacted to Clinton's confinement by booking a September 15 appearance on *The Dr. Oz Show*, a popular daytime television program that offers medical advice.

Our essay homes in on this pivotal moment in the 2016 campaign, wherein several long-standing cultural narratives about women in the political realm converged to disadvantage Hillary Clinton and strengthen the perceived stature of Donald Trump as a desirable leader. We explore how Clinton's illness, followed by Trump's appearance on *The Dr. Oz Show* while she recuperated, crystallized the contrast between healthy manhood and degenerate femininity. This episode provides an opportune moment to interrogate how gender and racial norms intersect in the political realm, illustrating how patriarchal parameters of white femininity are constructed, reinforced, and challenged. The subsequent analysis of how health intersects with race and gender illuminates the complicated, pitfall-riddled path toward enacting both femininity and political leadership.

We approach this project through an unconventional hybrid format that blends a creative component, original poetry, with traditional research and analysis. Poetry brings to bear a wide range of tools unavailable or discouraged in canonically practiced scholarly research.[5] Unlike traditional academic prose, poetry privileges play. Verbal and visual experimentation push the limits of language by exploiting all of its available resources. Poetry's intensely figurative language can interrogate taken-for-granted systems of thought and constructively offer new ways of approaching and acting in the world.[6] In this spirit, the poems enter our essay as figurations: invitations to expand interpretive possibilities, contrasting with the figures and tables that lend numerical precision. Poems also beckon the body, serving "in the writer or the reader as a new sense organ, opening a new field or a new dimension to our experience."[7]

Poetry's embodiment of discourse, expressed in the preceding quote from French philosopher Maurice Merleau-Ponty, blends well with the central theoretical concept underlying the health narratives we discuss. Merleau-Ponty embraced the notion of the body-subject.[8] All knowledge, experience, and perception flows through the body. Rather than view communication as simply transmitting some sort of message that exists apart from performance and utterance, acknowledging the body-subject recognizes that meaning necessarily includes the physical enactment of communication. Instead of merely conveying a message, the human body that delivers a message is implicated in its meaning. Thus, the content of communication lies not in disembodied words constituting a text. The inseparability of communication from the body-subject renders all meaning corporeal, intertwining interpretation with the enacted layers of the communicator's identities—which include performance of gender.

The following sections focus on the roles four primary body-subjects—Hillary Clinton, Donald Trump, his wife Melania Trump, and his daughter (by previous marriage) Ivanka Trump—played in the cultural narratives about women that informed public discussions regarding health and fitness for leadership in the 2016 presidential campaign. We examine how Hillary Clinton's publicly witnessed collapse and Donald Trump's movement of medical discussions to the popular daytime talk show arena energized narrative trajectories that stigmatize women who vie with men for leadership as "sick."

The Wizard of (Dr.) Oz

The Dr. Oz Show airs in thirty-minute segments every weekday. The host, Dr. Mehmet Oz, established his professional reputation as a notable medical researcher and cardiothoracic surgeon affiliated with Columbia University. He catapulted to prominence due to his appearances on *The Oprah Winfrey Show,* and he has hosted *The Dr. Oz Show* since 2009. His program offers wide-ranging health and medical advice. Oz, a registered Republican active in the GOP in New Jersey (his home state), donated to the campaigns of several prominent candidates, including Bill Frist and John McCain.[9] Oz even dallied with the idea of running for office himself. Prior to the Trump episode, *The Dr. Oz Show* had been sinking in the ratings, with its average daily audience declining from 3.8 million in 2011–12 to 1.8 million in 2015.[10] The one-hour episode (double the usual length) on September 15 featuring Donald Trump spiked ratings to a 64 percent increase compared to the previous year.[11] *The Dr. Oz Show* has since been renewed through the 2018–19 season.[12]

Hillary Clinton's campaign eventually released more of her medical information (not complete records, but a more extensive snapshot than

Trump provided to Dr. Oz) on the same day that Trump appeared on *The Dr. Oz Show.* In a two-page, single-spaced letter, Hillary's physician listed her medications, vital signs and a summary of lab results from a recent physical, details of a past sinus infection, and the genesis of her recent pneumonia diagnosis.[13] CNN's chief medical correspondent, Dr. Sanjay Gupta, noted, "This is certainly not a release of medical records by any means."[14] The Clinton campaign faced an uphill battle to convince voters its candidate was healthy while she remained mute and incapacitated.

Hillary Clinton's Body in Absentia

Hillary's bodily absence from the program enabled Dr. Oz and Donald Trump to position her vis-à-vis the male bodies that hosted the show and occupied the stage. She was invoked twice during the program. Introducing the episode that featured Donald Trump, Dr. Oz stated that his staff had "also invited" Hillary Clinton and that "she is considering our invitation."[15] Hillary occupied the grammatical position of the add-on, with Donald the headliner. Immediately after seating his guest, Dr. Oz asked Donald to agree "not to talk about" Hillary. Donald replied, "I think it's fine. We want her to get well." Both momentary references to Hillary rhetorically positioned her as physically absent, a negation. She had no presence on stage. She was the taboo topic. She had not responded to Oz's invitation. Hillary's illness confined her to the sickbed, a site of convalescence and—most important—of silence while Donald's Trump's narrative spun through audiovisual space.

The comparative health of the candidates also served as a measure of their merit. Donald asserted that "when you're running for President, I think you have an obligation to be healthy." He added, "I don't think you can represent the country properly if you're not a healthy person." Ascribing health to the person—you *are* healthy rather than have good health—essentializes the physical condition. Suffering from illness reflects deeper pathologies of character.

Over the next three weeks, the Trump campaign unleashed a fusillade of attacks that equated Hillary's physical debilitation with ineptitude and moral decrepitude. Donald complained that Hillary took too many days off, adding: "All those day offs and then she can't even make it to her car. Isn't it tough?"[16] Presumably she was so feeble that even a rest cure could not rehabilitate her. Donald continued to equate Hillary's fragility with dis-ability, in the sense of both immobility and incompetence: "Here's a woman, she's supposed to fight all these different things, and she can't make it fifteen feet to her car. Give me a break."[17] Donald proceeded to wobble and stagger, mocking Hillary's stumble and brief collapse on September 11. On October 11, the Trump campaign released a television ad that included still photos of Clinton coughing, stumbling on stairs, and being helped into a van after collapsing at the 9/11 commemoration. A voice-over asserted, "Hillary Clinton doesn't have the fortitude, strength, or stamina to lead in our world."[18] Hillary literally could not stand up to the demands of the presidency. "Stamina" had evolved into an evocation not only of Donald's physical prowess, but also of broader and more durable cultural narratives that position masculine physical superiority and feminine physical fragility as indexes of gender quality. The poem "Bodies of Evidence," constituting Figuration 1, represents some of the quandaries Hillary confronted.

The gendered body-subject is a product of enforced performances of gender and the policing of gender boundaries.[19] Gendered performances, being static, normative practices, become "visible markers 'on' the body, markers that reveal the sexual essence 'in' the body."[20] Gender signifiers (dress, mannerisms, language) are conflated to the signified (biological) sex, creating a gendered body-subject inseparable from its performance. Political and gender identities involve performances, and Hillary's political and gender positioning vis-à-vis her husband complicated her situation. Physical appearance and vocal delivery are sites where the "gender policing of political women's voices" occurs, and it becomes "particularly acute when running for the most masculine office in American politics."[21]

Other candidates—including Bernie Sanders as well as Donald Trump—accused Hillary of "shouting," reinforcing coverage of her along with other female candidates as "shrill, whiny, or unnecessarily angry or nagging."[22] Such discourse attempts to restore the "natural order" of gender, discursively retrofitting Hillary into the "proper" and deeply ingrained gender stereotypes of the emotionally volatile woman too irresponsible for the presidency. Donald's insistence on stamina invoked long-standing connections between political leadership and masculine strength.[23] Hillary cultivated an "iron lady" persona to "appropriate these imagined qualities of national manhood into a woman who biologically cannot possess them."[24]

As Hillary's political prominence and fortitude rose, her husband's declined. Her firm, carefully modulated oratorical voice contrasted sharply with her husband: the formerly defiant, hypersexual seducer of women now gaunt and frail, speaking in a raspy whisper. Hillary's signs of virility, however, also became a liability from a patriarchal political perspective. The more Hillary solidified her "iron lady" persona, the more she embodied a reversal—patriarchally encoded as a perversion— of gender norms in politics. She literally wore the pants(suits) in her marriage, a fashion choice that drew consistent, widespread scorn.[25] As sociolinguist Robin Lakoff observed, narratives about Hillary "are provoked less by her actual behavior and more by the symbolic function she plays and the narratives we wrest from her."[26]

The three poems ("figurations") in this chapter are original pieces by the chapter's coauthor Roy Schwartzman.

Figuration 1
Bodies of Evidence

Bill's most famous proclamation
a false negation:
"I did not have sex with that woman."
And now his main action:
subtraction.
Voracious seducer
now vegan humanitarian.
His gaunt, frail frame
squeezes out
hoarse, creaky words powdered with sawdust.
We strain to hear him
just as I strained to be heard.
If I pump up my volume, that makes me Shrillary.

To be heard
I must lose my voice.
Giggles and whispers catch my ear,
muffled talk of "Billary" again.
I must wear the pants
suits in this family.
I am suitable
as a display rack for my wardrobe.
Everybody else seems to know
just what suits me.
Trouble is, everything seems to fit.
So I clothe my shapeless body
in a giant consignment shop,
consigned to serve
as receptacle for everything noxious in womanhood.
Hosts of contradictions
lay embedded in my womb
where they gestate and fester.
My battered body harbors whatever
others cast out.

I am the permanent presence
of absence.

Donald Trump and the Body Politic

Dr. Oz initially addressed candidate Trump: "As a doctor, I am always concerned with the person in front of me, and we should agree that we're not going to discuss Secretary Clinton. Is that OK?" Avoiding discussion of Hillary arose not out of concern for her, but from the host's concern that Donald, "the person in front of" Oz, remain at the forefront of attention. Hillary's ill-timed illness defined her as a deficit—not only absent, but unmentionable.

Immediately Donald agreed, reminding the audience of her sickness: "We want her to get well." Dr. Oz then introduced a sharp contrast to Hillary's incapacitation. He asked, "How do you stay healthy on the campaign trail?" This first question neatly revealed Clinton's frailty and, in contrast, naturally assumed Trump's health. Before even discussing any medical history, Oz treated Donald as presumptively well, so he merely had to "stay healthy" while Hillary had to "get well." Dr. Oz proceeded to conduct a verbal "review of systems" to assess Donald's health. His health status was confirmed by unchallenged self-affirmations of health rather than from long-term, fully documented medical history. When Oz asked why, if Donald is as healthy as he claims, he does not share his medical records, Donald replied, "I have them right here." He then asked the audience, "Should I do it?" Amid cheers and applause, Donald handed Dr. Oz two sheets of paper: one with lab results and one certifying the reappointment of his physician to the hospital staff.[27] Despite the paucity of actual data, Donald appeared to give the studio audience exactly what they wanted.

Donald ensconced himself squarely as the picture of healthy living, as affirmed by Dr. Oz—both a medical and celebrity endorsement—and demonstrating his own eugenic lineage. On *The Dr. Oz Show*, Donald touted his genetic destiny: "But genetically—I think you're probably a believer in—that's sort of the most important thing. My parents lived very long lives." When releasing his initial, brief medical summary in 2015, Trump attributed his health to "great genes."[28] For Donald, health resided in the bloodline, just as essentialist concepts of race view racial identity as inherent and inherited rather than constructed and performed.

Ivanka's inclusion on *The Dr. Oz Show* propelled the narrative logic of Donald's health. Ivanka's youth, vigor, and beauty articulate a genetic enthymeme: health (and wealth) begets health (and wealth). When his daughter Ivanka joined him on the show, she demonstrated Donald's healthy genetic legacy. During a 2003 appearance on Howard Stern's radio show, Trump touted his own genetic superiority: "You know who's one of the great beauties of the world, according to everybody. And I helped create her. Ivanka. My daughter, Ivanka. She's six feet tall, she's got the best body."[29] Ivanka's salubrious and seductive presence offered physical proof that only healthy specimens sprout from Donald Trump's loins.

Donald displayed an orderly array of body-subjects, with everyone enacting their properly designated role. When Donald welcomed Ivanka onto the stage, she assumed her role by performing care through her dutiful service to her father and instilling hope for future mothers and children. By implication, her performance cast women who defy sociobiological narratives of womanhood as femmes fatales—dangerous women who pose a threat to themselves and society. When women refuse to heed nature's call and venture into traditionally masculine domains, their choice is portrayed as the cause of illness.[30]

Donald presented himself as his own body of evidence. As embodied masculinity, Donald's persona exhibited virility and strength, and in particular, the healthy male body's inherent endeavor to pass on its genetic lineage. When Dr. Oz quantified Donald's testosterone level and praised it as "good," the audience laughed while Donald smugly grinned. "Material Witness," the poem included as Figuration 2, portrays Donald's embodied argument and attitude.

Figuration 2
Material Witness

My body, my world: first person singular

Pay no attention to that man behind the curtain
All you need to know lies
skin deep
Don't unbutton my shirt or loosen my tie
Don't eavesdrop on my locker room talk—
besides, you don't belong and boys will be boys
so don't worry your pretty little head
calm down
don't sweat
don't get your panties in a bunch
after I grab you by the pussy
Just kidding—where's your healthy sense of humor?
Good. Clean. Fun.

I get my exercise by
raising my voice
raising your hopes
You do the heavy lifting
Carry the bricks to "Build the wall!"

Slam the iron door shut and "Lock her up!"
Command and Control
obey and submit
Progressive resistance
just makes me stronger.

Systems check:
Any history of history?
        None that I am aware of. Believe me.
Is biology destiny?
        I bet my wife on it. Believe me.

I am my body. I am every body.
Take my sputtered utterances
since they spring from your silent mouth,
the half-formed words you yearned to hurl.
I cure laryngitis. Hallelujah!

Ah, the wizardry of Oz

Melania Trump as Malleable Model

Donald's wife Melania remained a cipher throughout the campaign, enabling her husband to define her role as a glamourous but muted accoutrement. The media treated the Republican National Convention in July as her oratorical debut, "a rare public-speaking appearance."[31] Unlike Hillary's compulsory absence due to illness, Melania's invisibility allowed her to be appropriated seamlessly as a supporting character in Donald's hypermasculine narrative. Unlike Hillary, Melania presumably knew her place: as an ornamental augmentation of Donald's heterosexual prowess. Following the debacle of her partially plagiarized speech at the convention,[32] Melania still carried some residual baggage. She might not have fared well in a more spontaneous interview format, plus any inquiries about her own health could risk spoiling her pristinely mysterious and presumably spotless medical history. Melania's invisibility rendered her a vessel, a blank slate for the inscribing of a male-molded essence. Unlike Hillary, Melania had not trespassed into the masculine domain of politics. Quite the contrary, Melania's professional history resided at the epicenter of femininity: as the sexually idealized and fantasized female body, a position both of Donald's previous wives also occupied.

  Melania's relative obscurity provided narrative flexibility and rhetorical opportunities. Simone de Beauvoir suggests that relegating woman to a mystery does not simply silence her, but renders her inscrutable and hidden.[33] As a cipher, apart from the masculine order, she can serve as a free-floating signifier available to take on whatever roles and meanings patriarchy assigns. As Lisa Disch explains, "we [women] are interpellated (or called) into existence by socially sanctioned forms of address that put us in our place even as they make us feel at home."[34] Paradoxically, Melania could play both the seductive object of heterosexual male desire and the obedient wife/nurturing mother. Figuration 3 expresses the complexities of Melania's stature within this narrative framework.

Figuration 3
M-Bodied Artifice

This poem has no subject.

Pygmalion/Pig-male-lion,
Your male gaze sculpts me
into a self-portrait of Your desire
airbrushed to perfection,
rendered more alluring by its statuesque
hollowness.
You mold me,
malleable, sex-soaked modeling clay in your masculine grasp
caressing while crushing, squeezing
the breath from Your voluptuous vessel.
You fill me
with wonder,
with other people's words
that give me voice.
Tabula rasa that you tattoo as Yours.

You parade me down the runway;
You march me across the tarmac.
Me, object? Me: object.
No object-
ions [to]
Your Honor[ifics].

Ivanka Trump as Physical Specimen

The "discordant feminine body" originates in eighteenth- and nineteenth-century medical discourse that linked social behavior with the biological realities of motherhood and reproduction. Our current "truth" of gender was shaped by a male-dominated medical profession that viewed feminine bodies in terms of their (in)capabilities in relation to male bodies.[35] Narratives of women as physically and mentally weak established cultural beliefs that women who sought power were dysfunctional and deviant. Power, in these terms, was unnatural to the feminine body. Women who violated gender norms required treatment to discipline their bodies into behaving in accordance with the medically authorized "truth" of gender.[36] Conflation of physical illness with other types of incapacity reinforces larger cultural narratives that equate women's ailments with their inherent deviance and shortcomings. At least since the nineteenth century, Western medical, literary, and artistic representations of female pathology emphasized not only her own dysfunction and degeneracy, but also raised threats of contaminating women and men who conformed with authorized gender roles.[37]

A racial component also infuses narratives of the discordant feminine body. Women of color, specifically black women, have been depicted as hypersexual and corrupt. Their seductive power lures white men and tempts white women to embrace perversely deviant sexual desires and behaviors (such as lesbianism, masturbation, and promiscuity).[38] The body-subject offers a compelling conceptual framework for approaching the status of women as by nature physically, socially, and morally deviant. Samantha Murray, a researcher on gendered violence, observes that "the issue is the embodying, and bodying forth, of gendered modes of bodily comportment, of historically and culturally specific 'knowledges' about femininity: the perception of the world against the 'backdrop' of these knowledges about gender haunts the comportment of women."[39] Ivanka's presence on stage restored order by reuniting desirable female identity with whiteness. Ivanka looked and comported herself in ways congruent with cultural attitudes that privilege the beautiful, innocent, youthful, white female.

Semiotically, Ivanka served as a standard-bearer of whiteness. Prior to entering the conversation between her father and Dr. Oz, the audience was already aware of her genetic gifts, in part from her father's effusive (self-)promotion: "My daughter, Ivanka. She's six feet tall, she's got the best body. She made a lot of money as a model—a tremendous amount";[40] "What a beauty, that one. If I weren't happily married and, ya know, her father. . . ."[41] In her own right, Ivanka is known for her various fashion and cosmetic lines that cater to the rich, white women Ivanka represents with her "flawless" and "perfect" skin.[42] The website for Ivanka's product line (www.ivankatrump.com) has a pure white background with a pale pink banner. The lithe models on the site uniformly have straight hair and complexion no darker than slightly tan.

Ivanka's outfit—typical of her public attire—accentuated her conformity to a white standard of beauty. Her burgundy dress, while not overly revealing, sharply contrasted with her pale skin. The slit of the dress teased viewers with a long expanse of white, toned—but slim—leg, peeking out with every high-heeled step. The sheath cut of the dress hugged her body, which is the ideal ratio of curves to slenderness. Her only visible jewelry was a delicate gold bracelet that adorned her equally delicate wrist. The image embodied a perfect paradoxical portrait of the patriarchally authorized bodily ideal for the working white woman: revealing, but innocent; curvaceous, but thin; sexually pleasing, but modestly understated. Even her naturally blonde hair, flowing and left untied to reveal its sensual plushness, had been dyed and highlighted to a shade of white-blonde, and straightened into shiny perfection.[43] Her lips and nails, painted a shade of pale pink, complemented her dress and skin tone. She was the image of European perfection and feminine beauty—an Aryan princess taking her place in the Trump dynasty. In the course of their conversation, Dr. Oz referred to Ivanka as the "secret weapon" behind her father's campaign, a reference that supports unconscious cultural attitudes of women's power as secretive, sneaky, and submissive.

Ivanka assumed a multipurpose role as the nurturing mother that Hillary could not be and as the female crusader for traditional womanhood that ill suited the exotic Melania. In contrast to Melania, Ivanka was homegrown, unencumbered by status as an immigrant or by a heavy "non-American" accent. Ivanka continues to serve as a surrogate First Lady, occupying an office in the White House (where Melania did not reside until June 2017), being escorted by her father to official events, and even standing in for the president during part of the G20 summit in July 2017.

The Dr. Oz Show framed Ivanka as a political crusader who never shed her wifely domesticity. During the conversation with Ivanka, full-screen still images of Ivanka with her three young children portrayed a blissful family life. These images followed similar photos of the entire Trump family that aired while Dr. Oz asked Donald how he felt about being a grandfather. When asked about her potential role in the White House, a question usually reserved for a First Lady, Ivanka navigated her answer toward the domestic sphere. Ivanka returned woman's focus to the home and family through her "revolutionary" plan to augment child care options, a move that would save American families and finally give stay-at-home mothers the "recognition they deserve."[44]

Ivanka embodied the culturally accepted feminine narrative. Her presence bespoke beauty, health, and elegance, and her demeanor captured the empathetic nature of femininity. As she sat next to her father, her body constituted a rhetorical site, a body-subject both enmeshed in and extending the skeins of narratives that sustain perceptions of womanhood.

Every Body's Business

A woman's body always embodies her narrative being, especially in war and politics. The degree to which her body correctly performs her gender (i.e., comports itself to behavioral and visual expectations/desires) affects how the public perceives her political abilities. She disciplines her body; thereby she avoids being disciplined for violating her patriarchally defined "place." Her gender performance is strictly governed through references to the feminine artifice (what she wore, how she looked) and how she performs traditional gender roles (wife and mother).[45] The female candidate is constrained by a double-bind: Is she man enough? And if she is, do we want her (can we trust her) as an inauthentic woman? This dilemma confronted Hillary Clinton throughout her political career. Hillary had supposedly betrayed her womanhood by being too assertive, politically hawkish, and ambitious.[46]

The four main body-subjects embody somatic narratives that solidified as they intersected during *The Dr. Oz Show.* Hillary's status as thoroughly debilitated thwarted her attempt to establish an aura of competence and vigor that did not rely on androcentric notions of health. Donald reinforced female fragility as ongoing proof of his virility. Melania's body-subject augmented the narrative of the female body as (sexually) desirable because desired, yet unproductive (as a vessel for delivering plagiarized words). Ivanka embodied the beautiful fruits that sprang from Donald's loins.

Collectively, the original poems included as the figurations in this essay, combined with the critical analysis of the imagery and discourse surrounding Donald Trump's appearance on *The Dr. Oz Show,* track the evolution of larger cultural narratives that link women's malfunctioning bodies with professional malfeasance and moral misbehavior. The rhetorical force of this narrative thread helps explain why Donald's physical attributes augmented his stature as a locker-room legend, relegating Hillary to the sickbed.

The poems demonstrate not only how these narratives played out at the time, but how they engage and enrage long past the presidential election. The poetic component of this essay may qualify as a body-subject itself. Each poem invites the reader to inhabit and interrogate possible worlds wrought by lived practices of gender. Dwelling within this discourse enables us to experience the dynamic dialogues between narratives and counternarratives of gender. In this poetry-infused essay, the poems directly reflect and give voice to the constant tensions between predominant and promiscuous narratives that constitute the ambivalent status of women enveloped in patriarchal politics. Our more traditional critical analysis points to how gender narratives propel political behaviors, in this case protecting long-standing investments in perpetuating masculine leadership. Alongside this investigation, the poetry embraces indeterminacy, the unfinalizability of narratives that cast (out) others as the Other.[47] While chapters march toward conclusions, poems revel in dis-closure.

Notes

1. Caitlin Cruise, "Clinton Releases Medical Records Showing She's 'Fit to Serve as President,'" *Talking Points Memo*, July 31, 2015, http://talking pointsmemo.com/livewire/hillary-clinton-medical-records. The quotes come from the physician's letter, reproduced in full within the article.

2. Chris Cillizza, "Donald Trump's Shell Game with His Health Records," *Washington Post*, September 14, 2016, https://www.washington-post.com/news/the-fix/wp/2016/09/14/donald-trump-is-playing-a-shell-game-on-his-medical-records/?utm_term=.4cbf555e1141. All quotes are from the physician's letter, reproduced in full within the article.

3. Anna R. Schecter, Chris Francescani, and Tracy Connor, "Trump Doctor Wrote Health Letter in Just 5 Minutes as Limo Waited," NBC News, August 26, 2016, http://www.nbcnews.com/news/us-news/trump-doctor-wrote-health-letter-just-5-minutes-limo-waited-n638526.

4. Jonathan Martin and Amy Chozick, "Hillary Clinton's Doctor Says Pneumonia Led to Abrupt Exit from 9/11 Event," *New York Times*, September 11, 2016, http://www.nytimes.com/2016/09/12/us/politics/hillary-clinton-campaign-pneumonia.html?_r=0.

5. Roy Schwartzman, "Poeticizing Scholarship," *American Communication Journal* 6, no. 1 (2002), http://ac-journal.org/journal/vol6/iss1/special/schwartzman.pdf; Roy Schwartzman, "Unma(s)king Education in the Image of Business: A Vivisection of Educational Consumerism," *Cultural Studies ↔ Critical Methodologies* 17, no. 4 (2017): 333–46.

6. Paul de Man, "The Epistemology of Metaphor," *Critical Inquiry* 5, no. 1 (1978): 13–30.

7. Maurice Merleau-Ponty, *The Essential Writings of Merleau-Ponty*, ed. Alden L. Fisher (New York: Harcourt, 1969), 195.

8. Ibid., 185–213.

9. Tom Kershaw, "The Religious and Political Views of Mehmet Oz," *Hollowverse*, September 21, 2012, http://live.hollowverse.com/mehmet-oz/;

Lizzy Ratner, "The Great and Powerful Dr. Oz," *New York Observer*, August 14, 2007, https://observer.com/2007/08/the-great-and-powerful-dr-oz/.

10. Ana-Marija Dolaskie, "Dr. Oz Audience Down 50 Percent—So We're Halfway There," American Council on Science and Health, September 15, 2015, https://acsh.org/news/2015/09/15/dr-oz-viewers-are-off-50-percent-so-were-halfway-there.

11. Paige Albiniak, "'Dr. Oz' Scores Ratings Bump with Trump," *Broadcasting & Cable*, September 16, 2016, https://www.broadcastingcable.com/news/distribution/dr-oz-scores-ratings-bump-trump/159680.

12. Daniel Holloway, "'Dr. Oz' Renewed through 2018–19 Season," *Variety*, June 9, 2016, https://variety.com/2016/tv/news/dr-oz-renewed-1201791854/. The article notes that the program airs on Fox network affiliates in its largest markets.

13. Evan Halper, "Hillary Clinton's Doctor Releases Note, Disclosing Some Additional Medical Information," *Los Angeles Times*, September 14, 2016, https://www.latimes.com/nation/politics/trailguide/la-na-trailguide-updates-clinton-releases-doctor-s-1473886160-htmlstory.html.

14. Dan Merica, "Clinton Campaign Releases New Health Information," CNN.com, September 15, 2016, https://www.cnn.com/2016/09/14/politics/clinton-campaign-releases-new-health-information/.

15. "Dr. Oz Exclusive: One-on-One with Donald Trump," *The Dr. Oz Show*, produced by Mehmet Oz, Harpo Productions, aired September 15, 2016, http://www.doctoroz.com/episode/dr-oz-exclusive-one-one-donald-trump. All quotations from the program are taken from this source. To avoid ambiguity in referring to the Trump and Clinton families, each individual will be mentioned by first name only unless the context makes identification obvious.

16. C-SPAN, "Presidential Candidate Donald Trump Rally in Council Bluffs, Iowa," video, September 28, 2016, http://www.c-span.org/video/?415991-1/donald-trump-campaigns-ottumwa-iowa.

17. C-SPAN, "Donald Trump Rally in Mannheim, Pennsylvania," video, October 1, 2016, http://www.c-span.org/video/?416260-1/donald-trump-campaigns-manheim-pennsylvania.

18. David Weigel, "New Trump Ad Revives—and Mainstreams—'Sick Hillary' Attack," *Washington Post*, October 11, 2016, https://www.washingtonpost.com/video/politics/donald-trump-dangerous--campaign-2016/2016/10/11/46c09464-8fc9-11e6-bc00-1a9756d4111b_video.html?utm_term=.92b4bb6d6645.

19. Shannon Holland, "The Dangers of Playing Dress Up: Popular Representations of Jessica Lynch and the Controversy Regarding Women in Combat," *Quarterly Journal of Speech* 92, no. 1 (2006): 27–50.

20. Ibid., 29.

21. Kelly Dittmar, "Watching Election 2016 with a Gender Lens," *PS: Political Science & Politics* 49, no. 4 (2016): 808.

22. Ibid.

23. Rebecca S. Richards, "Cyborgs on the World Stage: Hillary Clinton and the Rhetorical Performances of Iron Ladies," *Feminist Formations* 23, no. 1 (2011): 15.

24. Ibid.

25. See, for example, Amanda Prestigiacomo, "Hillary Breaks Out the Ugliest Outfit in Human History," *Daily Wire*, August 25, 2016, http://www.dailywire.com/news/8658/hillary-breaks-out-ugliest-outfit-human-history-amanda-prestigiacomo#. For a discussion of Clinton's pantsuits as artifacts of feminist resistance, see Deirdre Clemente, "Presidential Pantsuits: Why Clinton's Outfits Are So Controversial," *LiveScience*, November 7, 2016, https://www.livescience.com/56779-why-hillary-clinton-pantsuits-bother-americans.html.

26. Robin Tolmach Lakoff, *The Language War* (Berkeley: University of California Press, 2000), 193.

27. For the complete documents, see Jessica Taylor and Joe Neel, "Trump Releases Weight, Cholesterol, Blood Sugar and Other Medical Information," NPR, September 15, 2016, http://www.npr.org/2016/09/15/494081537/trump-releases-weight-cholesterol-blood-sugar-and-other-medical-information.

28. Jessica Taylor, "Doctor: Trump Would Be 'Healthiest Individual Ever Elected' President," NPR, December 14, 2015, http://www.npr.org/2015/12/14/459700154/doctor-trump-would-be-healthiest-individual-ever-elected-president.

29. Hannah Al-Othman, "Thanks Dad," *Daily Mail*, October 26, 2016, http://www.dailymail.co.uk/news/article-3870754/The-thing-common-sex-Bizarre-interview-Donald-Ivanka-Trump-resurfaces-three-years-later.html.

30. Marilyn Boyer, "The Disabled Female Body as Metaphor for Language in Sylvia Plath's *The Bell Jar*," *Women's Studies in Communication* 33, no. 2 (2004): 199–223.

31. Ali Vitali, "In Rare Appearance, Melania Trump Adds Softer Tone to RNC," NBC News, July 18, 2016, http://www.nbcnews.com/politics/2016-election/donald-trump-introduce-wife-melania-s-speech-rnc-n612061; Mythili Sampathkumar, "Melania Trump Makes Rare Public Appearance with Speech on Female Empowerment," *Independent*, March 29, 2017, http://www.independent.co.uk/news/world/americas/us-politics/melania-trump-speech-female-empowerment-women-donald-wife-rare-appearance-a7656776.html.

32. Gregory Krieg, Eric Bradner, and Eugene Scott, "No One to Be Fired after Melania Trump Speech Plagiarism Episode," CNN Politics, July 19, 2016, http://www.cnn.com/2016/07/19/politics/melania-trump-michelle-obama-speech/index.html.

33. Simone de Beauvoir, *The Second Sex*, ed. and trans. H. M. Parshley (New York: Vintage, 1974), 290.

34. Lisa Disch, "Judith Butler and the Politics of the Performative," *Political Theory* 27, no. 4 (1999): 546.

35. Cathy Lubelska, "Chasing Shadows: Issues in Researching Feminist Social Histories of Women's Health," in *Representing the Past: Women and History*, ed. Ann-Marie Gallagher, Cathy Lubelska, and Louis Ryan (London: Routledge, 2001), 180.

36. Judith Butler, *Gender Trouble* (New York: Routledge, 2006), 198–200.

37. Sander Gilman, *Difference and Pathology: Stereotypes of Sexuality, Race, and Madness* (Ithaca, NY: Cornell University Press, 1985), 15–58.

38. Ibid., 76–129.

39. Samantha Murray, *The 'Fat' Female Body* (Hampshire, UK: Palgrave Macmillan, 2008), 161.

40. Regina F. Graham, "Trump Called His Daughter Ivanka 'a Voluptuous Piece of Ass': How Donald Talked about Threesomes and His Distaste for Women Over 35 during 17 Years of Misogynistic 'Banter' with Shock Jock Howard Stern," *Daily Mail*, October 8, 2016, http://www.dailymail.co.uk/news/article-3829021/Trump-called-daughter-Ivanka-piece-17-years-crude-misogynistic-banter-Howard-Stern.html#ixzz4o29cvCpZ.

41. Adam Winthal, "Donald Trump's Unsettling Record of Comments about His Daughter Ivanka," *Independent*, October 10, 2016, http://www.independent.co.uk/news/world/americas/us-elections/donald-trump-ivanka-trump-creepiest-most-unsettling-comments-a-roundup-a7353876.html.

42. "Ivanka Trump's Makeup Artist Alexa Rodulfo Reveals the First Daughter's Beauty Secrets," *Hello Magazine*, February 15, 2017, http://us.hellomagazine.com/health-and-beauty/12017021421193/ivanka-trump-beauty-secrets-makeup-artist-alexa-rodulfo/.

43. Ivanka's hair has changed dramatically since she began modeling. In 1996–97 she was a noticeably darker shade of blonde. See Samantha Faragalli, "26 of Ivanka Trump's Most Memorable Beauty Moments," *Instyle*, April 27, 2017, http://www.instyle.com/beauty/makeup/ivanka-trump-beauty-looks#1001246. Kyle White, one of her hairdressers, reveals how to "get" Ivanka's hair in Liz Ritter, "Ivanka Trump's Colorist Reveals Exactly How to Get Her Gorgeous Blond Hair," New Beauty, January 26, 2017, http://www.newbeauty.com/blog/dailybeauty/10462-ivanka-trump-hair-color/.

44. "Dr. Oz Exclusive."

45. Caroline Heldman, Susan J. Carroll, and Stephanie Olson, "'She Brought Only a Skirt': Print Media Coverage of Elizabeth Dole's Bid for the Republican Presidential Nomination," *Political Communication* 22, no. 3 (2005): 315–35; Lindsey Meeks, "Is She 'Man Enough'? Women Candidates, Executive Political Offices, and News Coverage," *Journal of Communication* 62, no. 1 (2012): 175–93.

46. Sarah-Jane Leslie, "'Hillary Clinton Is the Only Man in the Obama Administration': Dual Character Concepts, Generics, and Gender," *Analytic Philosophy* 56, no. 2 (2015): 111–41.

47. Frances Rapport and Graham Hartill, "Poetics of Memory: In Defence of Literary Experimentation with Holocaust Survivor Testimony," *Anthropology and Humanism* 35, no. 1 (2010): 28.

Chapter Three

THE BORDER, BAD HOMBRES, AND THE BILLIONAIRE

Hypermasculinity and Anti-Mexican Stereotypes in Trump's 2016 Presidential Campaign

Joshua D. Martin

In the United States, border tropes have long held a close relationship with nationalism, particularly in regard to the country's southern border with Mexico. In recent years, however, both nationalism and talk of the US-Mexico border have become increasingly salient in discussions regarding culture, belonging, and identity. Oftentimes, too, discourses centering on border tropes and nationalism draw on hyper (Anglo) masculinity as a resource to combat perceived social ills.[1] In the 2016 Donald J. Trump presidential campaign, these tactics proved especially effective. In fact, Trump's use of border imagery and anti-Mexican stereotypes played a critical role throughout his campaign, delineating a call to defensive action that found its footing in his own brand of aggressive masculinity. Trump configured overdue brawn, exceptional resilience, and unfettered strength as solutions to rectify real or imagined social problems emanating from Mexico or beyond, and the aggressors were often assumed to be Mexican men— or "bad hombres," to use his terminology.

Invoking the US-Mexico border as a rallying point for political ends is a strategy as old as it is effective. This chapter examines anti-Mexican stereotypes used by Trump throughout his presidential campaign and explores how the discursive construction of Mexican men as criminal and sexually predatory reifies US nationalism through a binary gendered logic. Trump's disparaging comments pit an imagined Anglo body politic against a criminally invasive brown specter, contrasting the civic duty and law-and-order respectability of the former against the alleged malice, criminality, and sexual predation of the latter.[2] Of equal importance is the gendered imagery that permeates Trump's comments. The alleged porosity of the United States' southern border with Mexico renders the United States a vulnerable and feminine entity, a revelation that proves even more alarming when Latino/a (im)migration is then represented as an invasive and penetrative force. The closed-masculine/open-feminine dichotomy would play a critical role in shaping national politics and anti-Latino/a discourse, doing so with an impressive ideological force that embroiled fear, anxiety, gender, and questions of American identity at the heart of the 2016 US presidential race. Border imagery and border metaphors play a critical role, too: on the one hand, they foreground two different communities ("us" versus "them"), and on the other, they establish a moral calculus of defensive action that beseeches hyper Anglo masculinity to solve a series of real or imagined problems—a sentiment that found its logical conclusion in Trump.

Defining Masculinities

Gender can be understood in part as the effects of what we do and how we perform as social actors in a given time and space,[3] and thus, as "a way in which social practice is ordered."[4] Accordingly, masculinity is "an essence or commodity" inasmuch as it "draws and impinges on a number of different elements, domains, identities, behaviours and even objects."[5] A given masculinity is also a place in gender relationships that informs hierarchies, questions of power, and how those social positions affect both men and women.[6] This study of Trump's own masculine brand remains conscious of how nationalism and the concept of the autonomous "self-made man" shape masculine ideals, since Anglo men are largely remembered as the principal architects of the nation-state and its cultural heritage, and since the ways in which Anglo men have understood themselves as "men" have oftentimes intersected with national interests.[7] If, as sociologist James Messerschmidt has argued, we must study masculinities in order to understand structures of power and inequality,[8] it is also true that "the control of space is an integral part of power relations."[9] This chapter recognizes how the policing of, and reference to, geopolitical borders reflects and reinforces claims to national identity,[10] and it argues that in the phenomenon studied here, hyper Anglo masculinity is invoked as a resource to preserve the stability of the United States' cultural heritage and combat a perceived feminization or weakening of the country by securing its porous borders.

Drugs, Crime, and Rapists: Creating Antagonisms through Border Metaphors and Anti-Mexican Stereotypes

On June 16, 2015, real-estate mogul and reality-TV star Donald Trump descended the grand escalator in Trump Tower and took the stage to announce his candidacy for the Republican nomination for president of the United States. In that speech, Trump emphasized his leadership, entrepreneurial ingenuity, and status as a Washington outsider, contrasting the opulence of his estate and affluence of the Trump name with the alleged incompetence of the political status quo. In many ways, Trump's speech was fittingly hyperbolic for his larger-than-life personality. Arguably the most cited segment of Trump's speech lacked specific policy proposals, but it did provide a clear picture of the antagonists that he promised to combat: "When Mexico sends its people, they're not sending their best. . . . They're sending people that have lots of problems, and they're bringing those problems with [them]. They're bringing drugs. They're bringing crime. They're rapists. And some, I assume, are good people."[11] Trump's comments reflect an antiquated disdain toward Mexicans that ties sexual politics to a racialized nationalism. Many Anglo men in the nineteenth century, for example, portrayed Mexican men, and Latin America as a whole, in decidedly feminine terms, often as a way to justify continental expansion.[12] During the Mexican Revolution, the "macho, tequila-drinking image" of Pancho Villa "established a racialized metaphor" regarding Mexican masculinity in the United States, and convinced many Anglos of the need to increasingly police the United States' southern border.[13] During the World War II era, anti-Mexican stereotypes acquired an even more sinister tenor. In Los Angeles, for example, men of Mexican descent were typecast as potential rapists, criminals, gang members, and arsonists, and therefore "a morally bankrupt drain on the war effort."[14] Accordingly, conflict between Anglo men and Mexican American men, as in the case of the Zoot Suit Riots, emerged in part along gendered lines, where upholding white masculinity demanded the protection of white women from their allegedly menacing and sexually promiscuous colored male counterparts.[15] Following a long tradition of anti-Mexican stereotypes, Trump hypersexualizes Mexican men but then configures them as doubly invasive actors: in sexual terms they are rapists, and in geopolitical terms they are illegal border-crossers.

The hierarchy that emerges from Trump's xenophobic ploys locates the United States in a position of weakness and vulnerability, a maneuver that beseeches immediate action in response to the alleged incompetence of status quo political actors. Trump regularly reminded audiences of his billionaire status, and his business ventures quickly emerged as a rallying point for the success of hardheaded (masculine) pragmatism and business acumen. Trump's nativist sympathies would acquire a higher tenor and garner widespread support with registered voters by repeatedly drawing attention to the United States' southern border with Mexico and recycling stereotypes that homogenized Mexican immigrants (usually men) as criminally invasive, located somewhere outside of the United States' cultural collective.

While Trump criticized the United States' long-standing trade policies in broad terms, specifically targeting China and Mexico, he did not mention the political machinations and neoliberal trade deals that maintain asymmetrical economic and political relationships between the United States and Mexico, in ways that simultaneously favor US economic interests and promote US-bound undocumented immigration.[16] These asymmetries have led social anthropologist Jorge Durand and sociologists Douglas S. Massey and Nolan J. Malone to affirm that "U.S. policy toward Mexico is inherently self-contradictory, simultaneously promoting integration while insisting on separation."[17] In conjunction with neoliberal economic globalization as a whole, the North American Free Trade Agreement (NAFTA) privileges a "transnational economic structure that serves the interests of large multinational firms such as agribusinesses."[18] This creates a cyclical demand for cheap, undocumented labor that militarized border enforcement both complicates and contradicts: the demand for undocumented labor persists following neoliberal reforms, but undocumented immigrants have been forced to cross more dangerous and isolated parts of the border, and they have often encountered more burdens upon trying to leave the United States.[19] NAFTA also disadvantaged Mexico's poor farmers. While the treaty reduced tariffs, it allowed government subsidies (which usually help wealthier countries) to flourish.[20] Since the 1994 implementation of NAFTA, the United States has increased farm subsidies by 300 percent, which has worked to promote "genetically engineered, corporately grown corn from the U.S. Midwest" over the locally grown corn of Mexico's small-scale farmers.[21] As historian Timothy J. Henderson explains, "Mexico was cast in the role of perennial junior partner to its richer cosignatories, its chief contribution being cheap labor."[22] Decrying US policies in Latin America, however, does little to rally Americans' feelings of national belonging. Border tropes continue to function as convenient props that bypass complex phenomena, such as transnational trade deals or the United States' interventionist policies throughout Latin America. Communication scholar Cari Lee Skogberg Eastman is therefore correct in her observation that in political discourse "borders become a distraction, focusing attention on the *result* of policy— unauthorized crossings—rather than the *nature* of the policy itself."[23]

Trump's racist and nativist tactics were nothing new in the court of national identity politics. The tried-and-true stereotypes of Mexicans as figures in need of corrective American action have existed since at least the nineteenth century, and immigration has always operated as a contentious topic on the national stage, receiving increased vitriol during periods of economic upheaval or widespread anxiety. Historian David Lorey reminds us that "depressed economic conditions in the 1930s along with an increase in anti-Mexican sentiment motivated U.S. officials to impose severe restrictions on the entry of immigrants," with the end result being that "one-half million Mexicans were forcibly repatriated between 1929 and 1935."[24] In 1983, amidst "economic insecurity and cold war hysteria," President Reagan bemoaned what he foresaw as the imminent "'tidal wave of refugees'" that, in his view, would surely follow Communist insurgencies south of the border.[25] The story is an old one, resurrected at different times for political expediency and almost always with alarming efficacy. As sociologist and migration scholar Stephen Castles argues, "It is much easier to turn these groups into the scapegoats for the social crisis, by blaming them not only for their own marginality, but also for the decline in general standards."[26]

Trump's anti-immigrant tactics weren't particularly surprising given the history of anti-Mexican sentiment in the United States, but the widespread support he garnered along the way has forced scholars to consider how and why these strategies continue to prove so effective. What has not been sufficiently analyzed are the masculinist dimensions of this appeal. Consider briefly the following comments from the same speech:

> I would build a great wall, and nobody builds walls better than me, believe me, and I'll build them very inexpensively, I will build a great, great wall on our southern border. And I will have Mexico pay for that wall. . . . Nobody would be tougher on ISIS than Donald Trump. Nobody. I will find, within our military, . . . the General Patton or I will find General MacArthur. . . . I will find the guy that's going to take that military and make it really work. Nobody, nobody will be pushing us around. I will stop Iran from getting nuclear weapons. And we won't be using a man like Secretary Kerry that has absolutely no concept of negotiation, who's making a horrible and laughable deal, who's just being tapped along as they make weapons right now, and then goes into a bicycle race at 72 years old, and falls and breaks his leg. I won't be doing that. And I promise I will never be in a bicycle race.

Masculine brawn is never far removed from Anglo nationalism and Mexican scapegoating. A number of erroneous claims underpin Trump's diatribe, but the clever symbolic ordering of antagonists (immigrants-terrorists-liberals) nonetheless proves effective, and it does so through a masculine facade of brazen resiliency, no-nonsense unilateralism, and rugged "self-made man" individualism. Why is this effective? The allure has as much to do with gender as it does with grandeur. In the above passage, Trump provides a sequential narrative of threats and weaknesses, giving his audience a cognitive blueprint that culminates in the moral imperative to respond to international threats (ISIS) and national weakness (porous borders, a fragile military, and a feeble secretary of state) with overdue brawn. The comments of political scientist Kathleen Staudt concerning border security are particularly relevant in this regard: "U.S. politicians," Staudt argues, "cannot afford to 'look weak' on border security" because "politicians [are compelled to] exploit fears with spatial metaphors, focusing on, even demonizing borders, especially the two thousand–mile border separating Mexico and the United States, and its migrants and immigrants."[27] If Trump's speech relied on masculine excess (the call to build a wall, the promise to increase military strength, the portrayal of Secretary Kerry as weak and incompetent), his language also worked to entrench a binary that inevitably acquired gendered dimensions given the fact that former secretary of state Hillary Clinton was expected to emerge out of the primaries as his Democratic opponent.

Trump's nativism, racialized discourse, and frequent use of border tropes configure him as a hypermasculine presence, whose dogged fortitude and perceived strength attempt to mitigate the anxieties of his base.[28] Part of why this strategy is so effective is because the shared hostility toward nonwhites advances a false consciousness that displaces one's anxiety onto a voiceless brown monolith—Latino/as, Muslims, immigrants, or indeed any demographic whose racial background, religious affiliation, or language capacities disturb the image of the nation-state as bounded, predominantly white, and English-speaking. Accordingly, the perceived dissolution of white patriarchy in light of this cultural, linguistic, and racial heterogeneity authorized abrasive rhetoric and questionable actions that might otherwise have been considered unacceptable or appalling.

Make America Masculine (Again): A Capitalist Cowboy in the Pursuit of Greatness

The masculinist dimensions of candidate Trump's appeal have not entirely been overlooked, nor, at times, have they even been avoidable, as when the reality-TV star boasted about the size of his penis during a nationally televised Republican debate.[29] Cognitive linguist George

Lakoff postulates that much of Trump's support is likely derived from the symbolic aura that he projects through the ploys of "strict father morality," whereby "a well-ordered world" emerges from "a moral hierarchy in which those who have traditionally dominated should dominate."[30] *New York Times* columnist Charles M. Blow contends that Trump "appeals to a regressive, patriarchal American whiteness in which white men prospered," and that for the candidate's white male supporters, American history is conflated and embellished with ambiguous exceptionalism, lauding "white men [who] reigned supreme in the idealized history [when] all was good with the world."[31] This revelation should not surprise us.

Trump pointed to the beginning and middle of the twentieth century as times when America was "great," lauding the United States' respective entrepreneurialism and military strength at those times.[32] Still, his nativist rhetoric and border proposals allude to an amorphous ideal of greatness, and that is part of the allure. The scapegoating of Latino/as (and of Mexicans in particular) only advanced this process. By constructing metaphorical borders (citizen/alien, us/them, American/Mexican), Trump consolidated a vision of the nation-state in exclusionary terms, and his tactics resonated with many who feared a depreciation, or total dissolution, of their own culture.[33] The strategy, again, is an old one, but it should remind us of how the disparagement of those who stand outside an imagined cultural collective can fortify local and national identities. All identity categories arise from different forms of exclusion, and their legitimacy depends on the types of language that we use to authorize these constructions. The hypermasculinity that permeated Trump's campaign should not be overlooked.[34] Trump's stereotyping of Mexicans does not account for real data, but it does allow his voting bloc to identify themselves within a horizontal camaraderie with the nation's white male forebearers, and it establishes a vertical moral hierarchy that privileges no-nonsense initiative and manly autonomy.

The array of borders that Trump invokes complements a cultural script of entrepreneurial ingenuity and Anglo male superiority. Geographers Alexander C. Diener and Joshua Hagen observe that "while borders continue to serve to order our daily lives, they also perpetuate difference and 'othering' along with belonging and identity."[35] This framework, in turn, reifies the nation-state as an imagined community of Anglo nationals, while configuring Anglo men as architects and guardians of the country and its cultural heritage. The binaries are simple, but the cognitive blueprint that they encode legitimizes a type of cultural exceptionalism that requires a hypermasculine Anglo presence to combat real or imagined social ills. Because of its estimated cost of nearly \$40 billion,[36] Trump's border wall between the United States and Mexico would be economically attainable only after Congress's approval of serious budget adjustments, such as billions of dollars in cuts to infrastructure, medical research, and community grants.[37] In terms of geographical feasibility, its prospects are far more nebulous.[38] What's more, the deportation of 11 million undocumented immigrants would require both a projected twenty years to undertake and an estimated \$400–600 billion in funding.[39] Part of the rhetorical success behind Trump's geopolitical and metaphorical borders is that they function as a springboard for national identity and exclusion, creating (b)orders of cultural intelligibility by marginalizing brown bodies from the cultural script, and by promoting the erasure of their linguistic, cultural, and religious heterogeneity. Trump's hypermasculine aura and exclusionary vision of the nation reach for a disappearing horizon of an idealized past, one where the social and economic capital of the nation's Anglo male architects remained unburdened by the complexities of neoliberal trade deals and what essayist Richard Rodriguez has termed "the browning of America."[40]

The Border as Political Theater: Economic Asymmetries, Increased Militarization, and Direction for Future Research

The US-Mexico border has received numerous monikers since it was "carved in the midst of U.S. imperialism."[41] Borderland feminist writer Gloria Anzaldúa, for one, famously termed it "*una herida abierta* [an open wound] where the Third World grates against the first and bleeds."[42] The reasons behind this disparity are many and complex. To cite just a few examples: the increase in *maquiladoras* along the border, especially after NAFTA, has created a northward flow for low-wage labor, which in turn has disadvantaged Mexico's interior manufacturing.[43] Furthermore, the disregard for environmental regulations by US firms, the few or nonexistent taxes paid by "*maquila* capitalists," and "runaway urbanization" have also contributed to the long-standing structural inequalities between the two countries and along the border.[44] In political discourse, though, the border often functions as a useful partisan football, with the ability to consolidate loyalties by cementing superficial binaries. Trump's representation of Mexicans as criminally invasive and hypersexual occludes the macroprocesses by which these same individuals experience what gender theorist Judith Butler, in her coauthored study with social anthropologist Athena Athanasiou, would call "dispossession"—the increasing disposability of brown bodies and their labor through the "exploitative excess" of "neoliberal forms of capital."[45] While nationalism holds significant appeal in the shaping of cultural imaginaries (who "we" are) and political initiatives (what "we" must do), the relationship between Mexico and the United States reflects a transnational reality of interdependent economies, cultural exchange, and labor networks.[46]

Trump's wall proposal is dubious in terms of its economic and geographical feasibility, but the message, one emerging from nativist anxiety and a binary logic of "us" versus "them," of billionaire versus bad hombres, has found solid footing in the imaginations of millions of voters. In many ways, Trump's comments correspond to the insights of Kathleen Staudt regarding border rhetoric and hypermasculinity:

> At the U.S.-Mexico border . . . two hypermasculinity variants collide and collude: one related to national security and the consequent militarization of everyday life . . . and the other related to a backlash against real and perceived threats (men's backlash against women, and xenophobes' backlash against immigrants). Rather than producing security, the results of these forces aggravate human insecurity in terms of everyday violence, sporadic violence, and policy-induced deaths at and near borders, as well as lingering poverty from policy-generated, market-based inequalities that fester from free-trade regimes.[47]

Rather than prioritize one or the other, Trump built much of his campaign by embodying both of these proposed "hypermasculinity variants." Borders and their exclusionary logic are old staples in the American mythos, recycled at different times and given legitimacy through appeals to social, cultural, or economic imperatives.

In his final debate with Democratic presidential candidate Hillary Clinton, Trump again reached for border imagery and, again, reduced Latino men to criminals, all while representing the United States as weak and porous:

> They're coming in illegally. Drugs are pouring in through the border. We have no country if we have no border. . . . We need the wall. . . . We're going to get them out. We're going to secure the border. And once the border is secured, at a later date, we'll make a determination as to the rest. But we have some bad hombres here and we're going to get them out.[48]

The reduction of complex phenomena to simple binaries (law-and-order Americans versus bad hombres) plays into the hierarchies and dichotomies that permeated Trump's past speeches. What's more, the representation of the United States as a violated figure at the hands of nonwhite foreigners gave urgent primacy to a hypermasculine candidate whose proposals, however vague or seemingly unfeasible, nonetheless responded to this gendered logic with palpable brawn. The fact that Secretary Clinton, the first woman nominee of a major US political party, promised a pathway to citizenship for potentially millions of qualifying undocumented immigrants, further established a binary that reflected a closed-masculine (build a wall) / open-feminine (welcome immigrants) dichotomy.

Throughout his campaign, Trump's disparagement of Latino/as, and in particular of Mexican men, entrenched a gender binary that configured the United States as porous and feminine, with the effect of framing his perceived strength and entrepreneurial success as resources that could remedy this same vulnerability. Border metaphors, I have argued, are particularly effective in consolidating nationalist loyalties by promoting the idea that cultures are homogeneous and atemporal—unchanging across space and time, and beginning and ending at nation-state boundaries. Scholars should continue to take note of the gendered dimensions that inform the representations of Latino/as here in, and en route to, the United States, as well as how these same representations affect both Latino/a and Anglo cultural scripts. Though the United States and Mexico have grown increasingly interconnected in terms of economic exchange and immigration networks, cross-cultural dialogue has not always triumphed, and border imagery and hyper Anglo masculinity continue to hold significant appeal in national discourse and politics.

Notes

1. The term "Anglo" is commonly used in the borderlands, instead of "Caucasian" or "white," as a contrast to "Hispanic."

2. Research does not support Trump's characterization of immigrants as more prone to criminality. See O. Nicholas Robertson's chapter in this volume.

3. Judith Butler, *Gender Trouble: Feminism and the Subversion of Identity* (New York: Routledge, 1999), 43–44.

4. R. W. Connell, *The Men and the Boys* (Berkeley: University of California Press, 2000), 58–59.

5. Andrea Cornwall and Nancy Lindisfarne, "Dislocating Masculinity: Gender, Power and Anthropology," in *Dislocating Masculinity: Comparative Ethnographies*, ed. Andrea Cornwall and Nancy Lindisfarne (New York: Routledge, 1994), 12.

6. R. W. Connell, *Masculinities*, 2nd ed. (Berkeley: University of California Press, 2005), 71.

7. Joane Nagel, "Masculinity and Nationalism: Gender and Sexuality in the Making of Nations," *Ethnic and Racial Studies* 21 (1998): 242–45. For a summary of the rise and evolution of the "self-made man" in the United States, see Michael Kimmel, *Manhood in America: A Cultural History* (New York: Free Press, 1996), 13–42.

8. James Messerschmidt, *Nine Lives: Adolescent Masculinities, the Body, and Violence* (Boulder, CO: Westview Press, 1999), 2.

9. Joseph Nevins, *Operation Gatekeeper: The Rise of the 'Illegal Alien' and the Making of the U.S.-Mexico Boundary* (New York: Routledge, 2002), 162.

10. Yosef Lapid, "Identities, Borders, Orders: Nudging International Relations Theory in a New Direction," in *Identities, Borders, Orders: Rethinking International Relations Theory*, ed. Mathias Albert, David Jacobson, and Yosef Lapid (Minneapolis: University of Minnesota Press, 2001), 7.

11. "Here's Donald Trump's Presidential Announcement Speech," *Time*, June 16, 2015, http://time.com/3923128/donald-trump-announcement-speech/.

12. Amy S. Greenberg, *Manifest Manhood and the Antebellum American Empire* (New York: Cambridge University Press, 2005), 95–106.

13. Marie Sarita Gaytán, *¡Tequila! Distilling the Spirit of Mexico* (Stanford, CA: Stanford University Press, 2014), 62.

14. Luis Alvarez, *The Power of the Zoot: Youth Culture and Resistance during World War II* (Berkeley: University of California Press), 53.

15. Ibid., 216.

16. Jason Ackleson, "Constructing Security on the U.S.-Mexico Border," *Political Geography* 24 (2005): 167.

17. Douglas S. Massey, Jorge Durand, and Nolan J. Malone, *Beyond Smoke and Mirrors: Mexican Immigration in an Era of Economic Integration* (New York: Russell Sage Foundation, 2002), 83.

18. Ackleson, "Constructing Security," 167.

19. Ibid., 167–68.

20. Seth Holmes, *Fresh Fruit, Broken Bodies: Migrant Farmworkers in the United States* (Berkeley: University of California Press, 2013), 25.

21. Ibid., 41.

22. Timothy J. Henderson, "Mexican Immigration to the United States," in *A Companion to Mexican History and Culture*, ed. William H. Beezley (Malden, MA: Wiley-Blackwell, 2011), 612.

23. Cari Lee Skogberg Eastman, *Shaping the Immigration Debate: Contending Civil Societies on the U.S.-Mexico Border* (Boulder, CO: First Forum Press, 2012), 79.

24. David E. Lorey, *The U.S.-Mexican Border in the Twentieth Century* (Lanham, MD: SR Books, 2005), 71–72.

25. Massey, Durand, and Malone, *Beyond Smoke and Mirrors*, 86.

26. Stephen Castles, "Citizenship and the Other in the Age of Migration," in *Nations and Nationalism: A Reader*, ed. Philip Spencer and Howard Wollman (New Brunswick, NJ: Rutgers University Press, 2005), 305.

27. Kathleen Staudt, "Violence at the Border," in *Human Rights along the U.S.-Mexico Border: Gendered Violence and Insecurity*, ed. Kathleen Staudt, Tony Payan, and Z. Anthony Kruszewski (Tucson: University of Arizona Press, 2009), 13.

28. Alec Tyson and Shiva Maniam write that "Trump won white voters by a margin almost identical to that of [Republican presidential candidate] Mitt Romney, who lost the popular vote to Barack Obama in 2012." Additionally, the authors report that "women supported Clinton over Trump by 54% to 42%" and that "by 53% to 41%, more men supported Trump than Clinton." See Alec Tyson and Shiva Maniam, "Behind Trump's Victory: Divisions by Race, Gender, Education," Pew Research Center, November 9, 2016, http://www.pewresearch.org/fact-tank/2016/11/09/behind-trumps-victory-divisions-by-race-gender-education/.

29. The Fix, "The Fox News GOP Transcript, Annotated," *Washington Post*, March 3, 2016, https://www.washingtonpost.com/news/the-fix/wp/2016/03/03/the-fox-news-gop-debate-transcript-annotated/?utm_term=.ea6ef6d9c85e.

30. George Lakoff, "Understanding Trump," *Huffington Post*, July 23, 2016, http://www.huffingtonpost.com/george-lakoff/understanding-trump_b_11144938.html.

31. Charles M. Blow, "Trump Reflects White Male Fragility," *New York Times*, August 4, 2016, https://www.nytimes.com/2016/08/04/opinion/trump-reflects-white-male-fragility.html.

32. Gregory Krieg, "Donald Trump Reveals When America Was Great," CNN.com, March 28, 2016, http://www.cnn.com/2016/03/26/politics/donald-trump-when-america-was-great/index.html.

33. According to 2014 data, there were 55.3 million Hispanics in the United States, which accounted for 17.3 percent of the total US population. By contrast, in 1980, Hispanics in the United States numbered 14.8 million and represented only 6.5 percent of the total US population. See Renee Stepler and Anna Brown, "2014, Hispanics in the United States Statistical Portrait," Pew Research Center, April 19, 2016, http://www.pewhispanic.org/2016/04/19/statistical-portrait-of-hispanics-in-the-united-states/.

34. The violence that Trump endorsed at his campaign rallies and his promise to "bomb the hell" out of suspected terrorists and to execute their families are but two examples of hypermasculinist discursive strategies. See Jenna Johnson, "Donald Trump Promises to 'Bomb the Hell Out of ISIS' in New Radio Ad," *Washington Post*, November 18, 2015, https://www.washingtonpost.com/news/post-politics/wp/2015/11/18/donald-trump-promises-to-bomb-the-hell-out-of-isis-in-new-radio-ad/?utm_term=.79385f294569; and Nick Gass, "Trump: We Have to Take Out ISIL

Members' Families," Politico.com, December 2, 2015, http://www.politico.com/story/2015/12/trump-kill-isil-families-216343.

35. Alexander C. Diener and Joshua Hagen, "Conclusion: Borders in a Changing Global Context," in *Borderlines and Borderlands: Political Oddities at the Edge of the Nation-State*, ed. Alexander C. Diener and Joshua Hagen (New York: Rowman & Littlefield, 2010), 193.

36. Danielle Ivory and Julie Creswell, "One Certainty of Trump's Wall: Big Money," *New York Times*, January 28, 2017, https://www.nytimes.com/2017/01/28/business/mexico-border-wall-trump.html.

37. Associated Press, "White House Calls for Domestic Cuts to Finance Border Wall," *ABC News*, March 28, 2017, http://abcnews.go.com/amp/Politics/wireStory/white-house-eyeing-18-billion-list-social-program-46415161. In addition, the Justice Department would lose $1 billion, Federal Emergency Management Agency (FEMA) $667 million, and the TSA $80 million. See Nicholas Fandos, "Trump's Border Wall Gets Billions in Budget Proposal," *New York Times*, March 16, 2017, https://www.nytimes.com/2017/03/16/us/politics/donald-trump-border-wall-budget.html.

38. The border wall would have to withstand the Rio Grande. The Trump administration would also face legal obstacles given that about two-thirds of the land that the nearly 2,000-mile border crosses is privately owned (while the remaining third is either federal or tribal). Additionally, the wall would disturb the natural habitats of threatened wildlife. See Matthew Daly and Alicia A. Caldwell, "Zinke: Border Wall 'Complex,' Faces Geographic Challenges," Associated Press, March 30, 2017, https://apnews.com/fec7a51f830442ee977a9c1b5df44ef9.

39. Russell Berman, "The Conservative Case against Enforcing Immigration Law," *Atlantic*, March 6, 2015, https://www.theatlantic.com/politics/archive/2015/03/the-conservative-case-against-enforcing-immigration-laws/387004/.

40. Richard Rodriguez, *Brown: The Last Discovery of America* (New York: Penguin Books, 2002), xiii.

41. José David Saldívar, *Border Matters: Remapping American Cultural Studies* (Berkeley: University of California Press, 1997), 8.

42. Gloria Anzaldúa, *Borderlands/La frontera: The New Mestiza* (San Francisco: Aunt Lute Books, 2007), 25.

43. Mike Davis, *Magical Urbanism: Latinos Reinvent the US City* (New York: Verso, 2000), 29–30.

44. Ibid., 32.

45. Judith Butler and Athena Athanasiou, *Dispossession: The Performative in the Political* (Malden, MA: Polity, 2013), 29.

46. Lorey, *U.S.-Mexican Border*, 117–52.

47. Staudt, "Violence at the Border," 4.

48. Politico staff, "Full Transcript: Third 2016 Presidential Debate," Politico.com, October 20, 2016, http://www.politico.com/story/2016/10/

full-transcript-third-2016-presidential-debate-230063. The historical record does not affirm Trump's correlation of border buildup with increased national security. For example, increased border security and militarization during the 1990s and early 2000s did not curb cross-border sales of illegal drugs. See Robert Lee Maril, *National Security, Public Safety, and Illegal Immigration along the U.S.-Mexico Border* (Lubbock: Texas Tech University Press, 2011), 96–97.

Chapter Four

THE MYTH OF IMMIGRANT CRIMINALITY

Early Twentieth-Century Sociological Theory and Trump's Campaign

O. Nicholas Robertson

Despite the myth of the United States as a nation that welcomes immigrants, historically most migrant groups have been greeted by racialized nativism in a process that constructs immigrants as fearsome racial others.[1] Imputing dubious moral character to immigrants and tying it to "race" permits white, native-born Americans to maintain an advantageous position within the social and economic order, and historically occurs more frequently during times when they experience insecurity about that position. The process by which whites use an ideology of nonwhite criminality to maintain their advantage can take various forms, such as terroristic violence via lynching, or the systemic criminalization and imprisonment of African Americans following the gains of the civil rights movement.[2]

During Donald Trump's 2016 presidential campaign, he mobilized fallacious racist/nativist claims that immigrants—and in particular Mexican immigrants—have a propensity toward criminality beyond that of native-born Americans, and are a threat to Americans' personal safety and to national security, and he vowed to stem the tide of criminal immigrants. These claims were effective among many voters, especially white voters, because they promised the reestablishment of white supremacy at a time when whites will soon no longer constitute the majority and when many confront severe inequality and economic precariousness in a neoliberal economic order. This chapter examines Trump's statements regarding immigrant criminality, his proposals regarding border security and deportation, and how the statistical data in fact belie a link between immigration and crime, and takes up the question of why falsehoods about immigrant crime were appealing in 2016.

Immigrant Crime: Discourse and Policy in the Trump Campaign

Throughout his campaign, Trump engaged in racialized nativism to garner votes, seeking to link immigrants, especially undocumented immigrants, to crime in his speeches, interviews, and policy proposals. In the June 16, 2015, speech in which he announced his candidacy for the Republican nomination, he offered a glimpse of what would become a major theme of his campaign, stating, "When Mexico sends its people, they're not sending their best. . . . They're sending people that have lots of problems, and they're bringing those problems with us. They're bringing drugs. They're bringing crime. They're rapists. And some, I assume, are good people."[3] Notably, he does not distinguish between documented and undocumented Mexicans, implying that the danger emanates from both their status as immigrants and their national origin. Additionally, singling out rape as a particular problem echoes historical discourses about the need for white men to "protect their women" against defilement by non-white men.[4]

Responding to criticism that his comments about Mexicans were racist, on July 5, 2016, he stated, "I can't apologize for the truth. I said tremendous crime is coming across. Everybody knows that's true. And it's happening all the time. So, why, when I mention, all of a sudden I'm a racist. I'm not a racist. I don't have a racist bone in my body."[5] He deflected charges of racism by deploying post–civil rights movement color-blind rhetoric about not having "a racist bone" in his body. Trump referenced relationships he had with members of racial minority groups, stating that over the years he had employed thousands of Mexicans, that he "loves" the "Mexican people," and that "they are fantastic."[6] The next day, he added, "What can be simpler or more accurately stated? The Mexican Government is forcing their most unwanted people into the United States. They are, in many cases, criminals, drug dealers, rapists, etc." Despite his insistence, when, in a presidential debate on October 19, 2016, he referred to the "bad hombres" coming across the border, he revealed that his concern was racial and nationalist as much as concerned with crime.[7]

One of the mechanisms in the process of racialized nativism is to advocate that certain racial or nationality groups be prevented from entering the country and those that are present be removed.[8] Trump sought to inform voters that he would ensure their safety by preventing Mexican and other immigrants inclined to criminality from entering the United States and would deport the undocumented. He promised a "big, beautiful wall" on the US-Mexico border, that Mexico would pay for it, and that he would begin working on the "impenetrable physical wall . . . on day one."[9] He also aimed to challenge the constitutionality of a right guaranteed by the Fourteenth Amendment known as "birthright citizenship," in which all those born in the United States are automatically conferred citizenship, arguing that those children born to undocumented parents should not qualify. He conceded that US-born children would be allowed to migrate back if they were found to be "good people."[10]

Trump promised an end to Obama's "catch-and-release" policy in which some undocumented border-crossers who were not considered a criminal threat were released on their own recognizance prior to their scheduled immigration hearing, and he promised that "anyone who illegally crosses the border will be detained until they are removed out of the country." This would be accomplished via the tripling of the number of ICE (Immigration and Customs Enforcement) agents, and "joint operations with local, state, and federal law enforcement." He proposed "an end to sanctuary cities" and rescinding of the Deferred Action for Childhood Arrivals (DACA) program, which defers removal for two years for qualifying undocumented migrants who were brought to the United States as children. Additionally, he advocated the establishment of a "biometric entry-exit visa tracking system . . . at all land, air, and sea ports," and to ensure that "other countries take their people back" when they have been ordered deported.[11]

And yet, in his claims about immigrant criminality, Trump often misused or outright fabricated statistical data. For example, at a campaign rally in Austin, Texas, Trump stated: "According to the Texas government, nearly 200,000 illegal immigrants were booked into Texas jails between 2011 and 2016. Collectively, those arrested were responsible for more than half a million criminal offenses, including 1,055 homicides, 5,516 sexual assault charges and more than 50,000 charges of either burglary or theft. Not going to happen folks. We're not going to let it happen to our country. It's enough."[12] However, the data referenced concern all "criminal aliens" charged with a crime, both documented and undocumented. Moreover, the half million criminal offenses to which he refers are charges made over the entire lifespan of the immigrants and not the five-year period from 2011 to 2016. Most importantly, the criminal offenses represented charges and not convictions. Hence, his statement contained three significant falsehoods that exaggerate the threat posed by immigrants.[13]

Theories on the Immigration-Crime Relationship

To unpack why Trump's claims about immigrant criminality resonated with many voters in 2016, it is instructive to consider both how academic researchers have conceptualized any possible link between immigration and crime, as well as what actual crime statistics reveal. Several sociological/criminological theories offer predictive models about the relationship between immigration and crime. Three main theories (social disorganization, cultural approaches, and opportunity structure) all predict that increased immigration will correspond to increases in criminal activity either at the individual or aggregate level, such as across different types of neighborhoods, whereas one (immigrant revitalization) predicts a decrease in crime. As we shall see, it is important to note that social disorganization, cultural, and opportunity structure theories of crime were formed in the early twentieth century to explain crime in ghettos of the urban North and Midwest. These ghettos were peopled mostly by European immigrants and Blacks who had moved north seeking economic opportunities and fleeing white terrorism in the South. In contrast, immigration revitalization theory emerged in the early twenty-first century.

First, based largely on research conducted in early twentieth-century immigrant destination cities such as Chicago, social disorganization theory suggested that immigration increases the concentration of poverty and neighborhood disadvantage, population turnover, and the racial and ethnic composition of a neighborhood, contributing to higher rates of neighborhood crime.[14] Many immigrants (who were overwhelmingly poor) often settled together with Blacks in urban ghettos, compounding the concentration of poverty. Social disorganization theorists argued that as earlier groups of immigrants became socially and economically mobile, population turnover ensued as one racial/ethnic group begins to move out and is replaced by another (invasion followed by succession). Efforts by neighborhood residents to engage in social control were undermined by assumed racial conflict among the groups. While it is important to note the explicitly sociological explanation of crime offered by social disorganization theory at a time when individualistic and racist biological explanations were dominant in the larger society, hypotheses derived from this perspective predicted a positive correlation between immigration and crime.

Writing in the same historical context of urbanization and heightened immigration to the United States in the early twentieth century, sociologist Thorsten Sellin argued that the cultural traditions of the sending country impacted the types of criminal involvement of particular immigrant groups.[15] In *Culture Conflict and Crime*, Sellin argued that conduct norms define what behaviors are acceptable or unacceptable. As immigrants adjust to a new cultural setting, they go through a process of "adjustment to heterogeneous conduct norms" and may violate cultural norms, or worse, criminal statutes.[16] Consequently, this cultural theory predicts a positive correlation between immigration and crime.

Also emerging in the early twentieth century, opportunity structure theories predicted a correlation between immigration and crime. Merton's anomie/strain theory was one of the first and most influential statements, as he drew attention to the stratification of American society, and how some individuals and groups are blocked from opportunities. The inability to realize the cultural goal of monetary success leads to frustration/strain among some individuals, who may in turn innovate a path to success by resorting to illegitimate/criminal means.[17]

Following Merton's strain theory, one can hypothesize that immigrants, especially immigrants on the lower end of the class structure, and their children might be particularly vulnerable to the temptation to forge a path to financial success through criminal innovation. Many immigrants settle in disadvantaged neighborhoods characterized by concentrated poverty, residential instability, underperforming schools, limited access to employment, and racial residential segregation. Immigrants may also face language barriers if they are not fluent in English, and in the case of Latinos, the disproportionate number of male migrants could lead to higher rates of crime than might otherwise be expected, as young men are consistently found to be more likely than young women to be involved in crime, especially violent crime.[18]

In contrast to the other three theories, the immigrant revitalization perspective posits that immigrants may be less likely to be involved in crime and that crime rates will be lower in areas where they are residentially concentrated, for several reasons. Immigrants to the United States generally do not come from the bottom rung of the economic ladder of their sending countries, and they tend to have more human capital than the people they left behind, which they can then use to help realize their dreams of upward mobility in the United States.[19] Furthermore, most immigrants do not migrate to the United States intending to engage in criminal acts. In communities where immigrants are concentrated, the social ties, networks, and informal social control that occur among migrants may help to prevent crime.[20] Additionally, immigrant entrepreneurs who establish businesses in their communities tend to hire coethnics, thus reducing the number of jobless individuals in the community.[21] Immigrants are often a source of low-wage labor for businesses in and outside the communities in which they reside, and they replenish institutions such as schools and churches especially when they settle in communities that have lost much of their native-born population.[22] Attempts at cultural preservation by immigrant parents may also be important in preventing immigrant adolescent involvement in crime and delinquency. In short, the immigrant revitalization perspective suggests that immigration reduces crime.

Analysis

The twentieth-century theories of the immigration-crime relationship (social disorganization, cultural approaches, and opportunity structure) and the Trump campaign all argue that increasing immigration leads to an increase in crime. The earlier theories were conceptualized during a period of virulent nativism directed at immigrants, and it may be tempting to argue that they simply reflect the racialized nativism of the early twentieth century. That would be, however, a simplistic argument, as they are sociological understandings that stand in stark contrast to the individualistic and overtly racist biological explanations that dominated US discourses about immigrants during the late nineteenth and early twentieth centuries. These theories are potentially limited, however, in explaining the contemporary immigration-crime relationship for several reasons. While European immigrants at the turn of the twentieth century settled primarily in the urban core of northern and midwestern cities close to low-wage jobs, immigrants in more recent decades tend to settle in regions, cities, and towns that have historically not been destinations for immigrant groups. As such, the process of population turnover (invasion and succession) that social disorganization theory suggested undermined the ability of neighborhood residents to maintain social control may not be occurring to the same degree among contemporary immigrants. Due to global cultural flows, contemporary immigrants are likely more familiar with American culture, thus decreasing the potential for cultural conflicts that the cultural theory predicted would be criminogenic. Finally, as a counter to opportunity structure theories, while most of the immigrants in the period 1880–1920 were poor, rural Europeans, contemporary immigrants are generally not from the poorest classes of people from the sending countries. With comparatively more social and human capital, they may be less inclined to innovate via crime.

Empirical Evidence on the
Immigration-Crime Relationship

We have seen that three major theories predict an increase in crime associated with increasing immigration, whereas immigrant revitalization theorists posit the opposite. What do the data tell us?

We can examine the relationship between immigration and crime through a variety of quantitative analyses. First, we can examine how national crime rates varied over time in relationship to the size of the immigrant population. In 1990 the foreign-born population was 7.9 percent of the total population, and by 2013 it had increased to 13.1 percent. During the same period, estimates of the unauthorized population increased from 3.5 million to 11.2 million. And during this same period of historic increase in both documented and undocumented migration to the United States, crime was on the decline. From 1990 to 2013, data from the FBI indicate that violent crime declined by 48 percent. This decline was not limited to a specific type of violent crime, as the numbers of people arrested for aggravated assault, robbery, rape, and murder all declined. Additionally, the overall property crime rate declined by 41 percent. While the crime drop was not evident in all localities, significant decreases in motor vehicle theft, larceny/robbery, and burglary were reported to the FBI by police departments from around the country including traditional and newly emerging immigrant destinations.[23]

Data on those incarcerated also reveal that immigrants represent a relatively small number of prisoners. An analysis of 2010 American Community Survey census data by Walter Ewing, Daniel Martinez, and Rubén Rumbaut reveals that of immigrant males age eighteen to thirty-nine, 1.6 percent are incarcerated while among native-born males the number increases to 3.3 percent. This disparity in incarceration is not new and reflects similar findings from analyses of 1980, 1990, and 2000 census data. These data also reveal that the native-born imprisonment rate was two to five times that of immigrants. While 2010 census data do not provide specific information on whether immigrants are documented or undocumented, the authors attempted to estimate rates of incarceration of undocumented immigrants by examining those rates among "less-educated Mexican, Salvadoran, and Guatemalan men who make up the bulk of the unauthorized population."[24] They found that among native-born young men eighteen to thirty-nine, the incarceration rate was 10.7 percent compared to 2.8 percent among Mexican men, and 1.7 percent for Salvadoran and Guatemalan men, which would suggest that undocumented immigrants have been less prone to criminal activity than native-born Americans.[25]

Similar to the census data findings, an analysis of two waves of the National Epidemiologic Survey on Alcohol and Related Conditions (NESARC) finds that compared to the native-born population, immigrants are less likely to be involved in violent and nonviolent antisocial behavior. NESARC is a nationally representative sample of the noninstitutionalized US population from eighteen to thirty-four years old. Violent and nonviolent antisocial behavior is measured by thirty-one items from the antisocial personality disorder module of the AUDADIS-IV (Alcohol Use Disorder and Associated Disabilities Interview Schedule–DSM-IV). Item measures include questions regarding involvement in intimate partner violence, truancy, weapon use in a fight, and general involvement in illegal activities. This age cohort also corresponds to the period when men are most likely to engage in crime and especially the violent crime that is most often feared. Of the respondents in this survey sample, 14.6 percent ($n = 7,320$) are immigrants, while 85.4 percent are native-born ($n = 35,622$). The authors compare African, Latin American, Asian, and European immigrants to native-born Americans and find that regardless of their region of origin, immigrants are less likely to be involved in antisocial behavior. More specifically, migrants from Asia and Africa are four times less likely to engage in antisocial behavior compared to the native-born, and immigrants from Latin America three times less likely. Of the regions of migrant origin, Europeans are closest to native-born Americans regarding their involvement in antisocial behavior. Research among natives finds that those who are male, poor, have less than a high school education, and reside in urban areas have higher rates of involvement in antisocial and specifically violent behavior, but this is not the finding among immigrants of whom the majority fit this description.[26]

While the studies discussed thus far dispel the myth of immigrant criminality echoed by Donald Trump, they are limited in their ability to determine any causal impact of immigration on crime. In contrast, analyses that control for theoretically informed variables that are thought to influence the immigration-crime relationship on average indicate that immigration decreases levels of crime.

First, contrary to popular and theoretical expectations, with a few exceptions, research indicates that, controlling for a host of variables, acculturation (or Americanization) actually increases adolescent involvement in crime and delinquency.[27] For example, Min Zhou and Carl Bankston's study of self-reported crime and delinquency among two cohorts of Vietnamese youth in New Orleans finds that compared to a 1994 cohort of Vietnamese adolescents, a 2003 cohort was more likely to engage in drug use and alcohol use, and were more likely to be stopped by the police. This was the case even though the parents in the later cohort were on average better educated and the families were more likely to have consisted of two-parent homes. The 2003 cohort of youth was more likely to be US-born, indicating that acculturation is associated with increased involvement in crime. Research also indicates that most types of violent behavior increase across immigrant generations; that is, immigrant youth who came to the United States at younger ages are more likely to be involved in violent behavior, and youth whose families are more acculturated are more involved in violence compared to youth whose families are partially acculturated or nonacculturated.[28] Using a nationally representative sample to examine delinquency across immigrant generations, Hoan Bui finds that self-reported substance use is more common among later generations.[29]

Research on the immigration-crime relationship also seeks to identify the impact of immigration on crime in the communities where immigrants settle. In other words, do national trends regarding the link between immigration and crime hold true at the metropolitan or city level? A recent study by Robert Adelman and colleagues on the impact of immigration on urban crime rates across four decades indicates that there is a negative relationship between immigration and violent and property crime.[30] They analyze 1970, 1980, 1990, 2000, and 2010 census data on 200 metropolitan statistical areas across the country in addition to data from the FBI's Uniform Crime Report. Specifically, they find that over this four-decade period, there was a negative effect of immigration on property crime, robbery, and murder (but no effect on assault). Previous research by Graham Ousey and Charis Kubrin sought to understand the causal impact of immigration on crime by analyzing its impact on violent crime rates in American cities from 1980 to 2000.[31] They use data from 159 cities to "examine whether within-city, over-time change in immigration was associated with within-city change in a violent crime index," and the extent to which various theories adequately explain the immigration-crime relationship in light of factors such as "demographic structure, economic deprivation, labor markets, illegal drug markets, police force capacity, and family structure."[32] Among these cities of at least 100,000 people, they find that increases in immigration are negatively associated with change in violent crime. Furthermore, they suggest that one of the factors that significantly produces this negative relationship is that immigration is negatively associated with divorce and single parenthood.[33] Research with data at the track (neighborhood) level also reveals similar findings to analyses at the metropolitan and city level. Using data from the National Neighborhood Crime Study (NNCS), María Velez and Christopher Lyons sought to examine the relationship between "neighborhood disadvantage," immigration, and crime. Similarly, using data collected in 2000, they find a negative relationship between recent immigration and neighborhood violent crime.[34]

Discussion and Conclusion

Throughout Trump's 2016 presidential run, he routinely mobilized racist and nativist discourse regarding immigrant criminality. He constructed immigrants, especially undocumented immigrants, as a threat to individual safety and national security. Much of this rhetoric was directed at Mexicans, and at campaign events, he led supporters in chants of "Build that wall!"[35] Deflecting criticism by using color-blind ideology, and misusing government data to exaggerate the threat posed by immigrants, he advocated the use of security forces at the local, state, and federal levels to coordinate a wholesale removal of the undocumented.

The existing research on the immigration-crime relationship finds, however, that increasing immigration does not lead to increasing crime. Since 1965, the number of immigrants to the United States has increased significantly at the same time that we have witnessed a significant drop in property and violent crime. Research also confirms that immigrant males have lower levels of incarceration than their native-born counterparts, immigrants are less likely to be involved in violent and nonviolent antisocial behavior, Americanization increases adolescent involvement in crime and delinquency, and on average crime decreases in the areas in which immigrants settle.

Research findings also cast doubt on the explanatory power of traditional sociological/criminological theorizing on the immigration-crime relationship. Contrary to the claims of social disorganization theory, urban neighborhoods characterized by greater influxes of immigrant residents are not experiencing detectable increases in violence. The finding that acculturation leads to heightened involvement in crime and delinquency contradicts the cultural theory predictions, suggesting that American culture is criminogenic (crime-producing), more so than the culture of immigrants. Additionally, immigrants of similar social class backgrounds to their native-born counterparts experience lower levels of violence and are less likely to engage in antisocial behavior. Much of the research findings are consistent with the new immigrant revitalization perspective, and there is an emerging scholarly consensus that increased immigration decreases crime.

In light of the empirical evidence to the contrary, why is it that Trump's racist and nativist rhetoric resonated with many Americans, especially native-born whites? One possible clue lies in the changing demographic composition of the United States. Prior to 1965, country-specific immigration quotas ensured that that the vast majority of immigrants hailed from Europe and that the United States remained an overwhelmingly white and Christian nation. The Hart-Cellar Act of 1965 dismantled the country-specific quota system, opening the door to immigrants from world regions previously underrepresented in the country. Most immigrants in the post-1965 era hail from Latin America, Asia, and the Caribbean. In 2014 the foreign-born comprised roughly 42 million individuals, representing about 13 percent of the total US population. Mexicans make up around 28 percent of the foreign-born population; the next three largest nationality groups among the foreign-born are from Asia: India, China, and the Philippines.[36] The racialized nativism of Trump's campaign appealed to white Americans who may be fearful of losing their position atop the United States' racial, social, and economic hierarchies. For many of these individuals, the "real America" (or the America that matters most) is, according to Christopher Parker and Matt Barreto, "white, middle class, middle-aged, Christian, heterosexual, mostly male."[37] They fear the demographic changes brought about by post-1965 immigration, and are unsure if they will continue to be the winners in the contemporary neoliberal economic order.[38]

Notes

1. John Higham, *Strangers in the Land: Patterns of American Nativism, 1860–1925* (New Brunswick, NJ: Rutgers University Press, 2002); Matthew T. Lee and Ramiro Martinez, "Immigration Reduces Crime: An Emerging Scholarly Consensus," in *Immigration, Crime and Justice*, ed. William F. McDonald (Bingley, UK: Emerald Group, 2009), 3–16; Juan F. Perea, ed., *Immigrants Out! The New Nativism and the Anti-Immigrant Impulse in the United States* (New York: New York University Press, 1997); George J. Sanchez, "Face the Nation: Race, Immigration, and the Rise of Nativism in Late Twentieth Century America," *International Migration Review* 31, no. 4 (1997): 1009–30.

2. Stewart E. Tolnay and E. M. Beck, *A Festival of Violence: An Analysis of Southern Lynchings, 1882–1930* (Urbana: University of Illinois Press, 1995); Loïc Wacquant, "Deadly Symbiosis: When Ghetto and Prison Meet and Mesh," *Punishment & Society* 3, no. 1 (2001): 95–133.

3. "Here's Donald Trump's Presidential Announcement Speech, *Time*, June 16, 2015, http://time.com/3923128/donald-trump-announcement-speech/.

4. Philip Dray, *At the Hands of Persons Unknown: The Lynching of Black America* (New York: Modern Library, 2003); Andrea Smith, *Conquest: Sexual*

Violence and American Indian Genocide (Durham, NC: Duke University Press, 2015).

5. Michelle Ye Hee Lee, "Donald Trump's False Comments Connecting Mexican Immigrants and Crime," *Washington Post*, July 8, 2015, https://www.washingtonpost.com/news/fact-checker/wp/2015/07/08/donald-trumps-false-comments-connecting-mexican-immigrants-and-crime/?utm_term=.d2c251a17a15.

6. Gerhard Peters and John T. Woolley, "Press Release—Trump on Mexico Comments: 'I Can't Apologize for the Truth,'" American Presidency Project, July 6, 2015, http://www.presidency.ucsb.edu/ws/?pid=116584.

7. Erin McCann and Jonah Engel Bromwich, "'Nasty Woman' and 'Bad Hombres': The Real Debate Winners?," *New York Times*, October 20, 2106, https://www.nytimes.com/2016/10/21/us/politics/nasty-woman-and-bad-hombres-the-real-debate-winners.html?mcubz=1&_r=0.

8. Julia G. Young, "Making America 1920 Again? Nativism and US Immigration, Past and Present," *Journal on Migration and Human Security* 5, no. 1 (2017): 217–35.

9. "Immigration," DonaldJTrump.com, accessed September 7, 2017, https://web.archive.org/web/20161114081213/https:/www.donaldjtrump.com/policies/immigration/; Matthew Boyle, "Donald Trump Throws Down in Phoenix: Champions 10-Step Immigration Reform Plan," Breitbart.com, August 31, 2016, http://www.breitbart.com/2016-presidential-race/2016/08/31/donald-trump-throws-down-in-phoenix-champions-10-step-immigration-reform-plan/.

10. Associated Press, "Trump Would Deport Children of Illegal Immigrants," *Boston Globe*, August 17, 2015, https://www.bostonglobe.com/news/politics/2015/08/16/trump-would-deport-children-illegal-immigrants/0k8tnLoq6mlOygt3oGV67M/story.html.

11. "Immigration," DonaldJTrump.com.

12. D'Angelo Gore, Lori Robertson, and Eugene Kiely, "FactChecking Trump on Immigration," FactCheck.org, August 30, 2016, http://www.factcheck.org/2016/08/factchecking-trump-on-immigration/.

13. Ibid.

14. Clifford R. Shaw and Henry Donald McKay, *Juvenile Delinquency in Urban Areas: A Study of Rates of Delinquents in Relation to Differential Characteristics of Local Communities in American Cities* (Chicago: University of Chicago Press, 1942).

15. Thorsten Sellin, *Culture Conflict and Crime* (New York: Social Science Research Council, 1938).

16. Ibid., 85.

17. Robert K. Merton, "Social Structure and Anomie," *American Sociological Review* 3, no. 5 (1938): 672–82.

18. Alejandro Portes and Rubén G. Rumbaut, *Immigrant America: A Portrait*, 4th ed. (Berkeley: University of California Press, 2014).

19. Ibid.

20. Ramiro Martinez Jr., Matthew T. Lee, and Amie L. Nielsen, "Segmented Assimilation, Local Context and Determinants of Drug Violence in Miami and San Diego: Does Ethnicity and Immigration Matter?," *International Migration Review* 38, no. 1 (2004): 131–57.

21. Karin Aguilar–San Juan, "Staying Vietnamese: Community and Place in Orange County and Boston," *City and Community* 4, no. 1 (2005): 37–65.

22. David M. Ramey, "Immigrant Revitalization and Neighborhood Violent Crime in Established and New Destination Cities," *Social Forces* 92, no. 2 (2013): 597–629.

23. Walter Ewing, Daniel E. Martínez, and Rubén G. Rumbaut, "Special Report: The Criminalization of Immigration in the United States," American Immigration Council, July 13, 2015, https://www.americanimmigrationcouncil.org/research/criminalization-immigration-united-states.

24. Ibid., 7.

25. Ibid.

26. Michael G. Vaughn, Christopher P. Salas-Wright, Matt DeLisi, and Brandy R. Maynard, "The Immigrant Paradox: Immigrants Are Less Antisocial Than Native-born Americans," *Social Psychiatry and Psychiatric Epidemiology* 49, no. 7 (2014): 1129–37.

27. Hoan N. Bui, "Parent-Child Conflicts, School Troubles, and Differences in Delinquency across Immigration Generations," *Crime & Delinquency* 55, no. 3 (2001): 412–41; Jeffrey D. Morenoff and Avraham Astor, "Immigrant Assimilation and Crime: Generational Differences in Youth Violence in Chicago," in *Immigration and Crime: Race, Ethnicity, and Violence*, ed. Ramiro Martinez Jr. and Abel Valenzuela Jr. (New York: New York University Press, 2006), 36–63; Rubén G. Rumbaut, Roberto G. Gonzales, Golnaz Komaie, Charlie V. Morgan, and Rosaura Tafoya-Estrada, "Immigration and Incarceration: Patterns and Predictors of Imprisonment among First- and Second-Generation Young Adults," in *Immigration and Crime*, ed. Martinez and Valenzuela, 64–89; Min Zhou and Carl L. Bankston III, "Delinquency and Acculturation in the Twenty-first Century: A Decade's Change in a Vietnamese American Community," in *Immigration and Crime*, ed. Martinez and Valenzuela, 117–39.

28. Zhou and Bankston, "Delinquency and Acculturation."

29. Bui, "Parent-Child Conflicts."

30. Robert M. Adelman, Lesley Williams Reid, Gail Markle, Saskia Weiss, and Charles Jaret, "Urban Crime Rates and the Changing Face of Immigration," *Journal of Ethnicity in Criminal Justice* 15, no. 1 (2017): 52–77.

31. Graham C. Ousey and Charis E. Kubrin, "Exploring the Connection between Immigration and Violent Crime Rates in U.S. Cities, 1980–2000," *Social Problems* 56, no. 3 (2009): 447–73.

32. Ibid., 466.

33. Ibid.

34. María B. Vélez and Christopher J. Lyons, "Situating the Immigration and Neighborhood Crime Relationship across Multiple Cities," in *Punishing Immigrants: Policy, Politics, and Injustice*, ed. Charis E. Kubrin, Marjorie S. Zatz, and Ramiro Martínez Jr. (New York: New York University Press. 2012), 159–77.

35. Jenna Johnson, "'Build That Wall' Has Taken on a Life of Its Own at Donald Trump's Rallies—but He's Still Serious," *Washington Post*, February 12, 2016, https://www.washingtonpost.com/news/post-politics/wp/2016/02/12/build-that-wall-has-taken-on-a-life-of-its-own-at-donald-trumps-rallies-but-hes-still-serious/?utm_term=.c9f7877e322b.

36. Portes and Rumbaut, *Immigrant America*; Jie Zong and Jeanne Batalova, "Frequently Requested Statistics on Immigrants and Immigration in the United States," Migration Policy Institute, March 8, 2107, http://www.migrationpolicy.org/article/frequently-requested-statistics-immigrants-and-immigration-united-states.

37. Christopher S. Parker and Matt A. Barreto, *Change They Can't Believe In: The Tea Party and Reactionary Politics in America* (Princeton, NJ: Princeton University Press, 2013), 35.

38. Jessica Autumn Brown, "Running on Fear: Immigration, Race and Crime Framings in Contemporary GOP Presidential Debate Discourse," *Critical Criminology* 24, no. 3 (2016): 315–31; Parker and Barreto, *Change They Can't Believe In*, 35.

Chapter Five

AMERICA, MEET YOUR NEW DAD

Tim Kaine and Subordinate Masculinity

Beth L. Boser and R. Brandon Anderson

In a drama- and conflict-filled election season, Hillary Clinton's choice of Tim Kaine as running mate seemed, perhaps, underwhelming. Kaine was portrayed as a centrist, a pragmatist who "dedicated himself to incremental progress in a red-turned-purple state."[1] Falling just short of selection by Obama in 2007, Kaine offered the Clinton campaign a seemingly safe choice. As a longtime Democratic insider, Kaine was a reliable and, in his own words, "boring" vice presidential selection.[2] In contrast, we contend that Kaine is anything but boring; rather, he provides a fascinating case study of masculine ambivalence in the contemporary political sphere.

Political campaigns are heavily gendered contexts. Prior work in the field of rhetoric demonstrates that presidential campaigns, in particular, offer highly visible gendered spectacles that place cultural tensions relating to gender roles and ideologies on display. However, gender seems only to come to the forefront of national campaigns when something disrupts the normative gendered conventions of the executive office. The US presidency is traditionally a masculine space; contenders for the office have always been required to perform a specific and narrow masculinity to appear presidential. When women appear on the scene, the stability of patriarchal constructions is called into question and debated in a range of public contexts. Prior scholars have illustrated the ways in which Geraldine Ferraro, Sarah Palin, and of course, Hillary Clinton spurred such debate.[3] In 2016 dynamics of gender disruption were evident as the public, media, and the candidates themselves seemed intent on centering gender discourses.[4] The most prominent of these stemmed from conflict between Clinton and Bernie Sanders during the primary contest, and Clinton and Donald

Trump during the general. The importance of such conflicts should not be understated; yet, these are not the only gendered disruptions to emerge from this election cycle.

Indeed, such obvious gender rhetorics may obscure other significant discourses. The gendered rhetoric of Tim Kaine, for example, may seem insignificant when compared to the aggressive masculinity displayed by Trump and the persistent gendered double-binds publicly navigated by Clinton. However, we contend that relatively mundane constructions of masculinity reflected in Kaine provide subtle yet powerful insight into the complexity of contemporary political gender roles. In particular, the ways in which Kaine constructed and negotiated masculinity was significant, at least in part, because of the supportive and subordinate role he played with respect to Clinton. Not only did Kaine's subordinate masculine role reflect historical constructions of profeminist men, it also illustrated a supportive masculinity that simultaneously subverted some aspects of hegemonic masculinity while reinforcing others. In this chapter, we illustrate this claim by (1) providing a review of prior work centering on masculinity and politics and (2) offering an analysis of rhetorical constructions of Kaine's masculinity. Specifically, we examine Kaine's July 23 introduction speech in Miami and his July 27 vice presidential nomination acceptance speech, in combination with popular responses to both. This analysis illuminates a less obvious, but nonetheless important, gendered disruption from the 2016 campaign.

Masculinity and (Vice) Presidential Politics

US politics comprises a collection of patriarchal institutions. The office of the presidency is noted, in particular, for its connection to hegemonic masculinity.[5] According to sociologist R. W. Connell, hegemonic masculinity is the style of masculinity "culturally exalted" in a given time.[6] The notion that a style of masculinity is hegemonic presumes the following: masculinity is (along with femininity) socially constructed, as opposed to natural or given; constructions of gender are discursive, composed by a range of public and mediated rhetorics; and such constructions are reaffirmed, perpetuated, and/or transgressed in and through individual performances of gender in dialogic relation to cultural norms and systems.[7] Furthermore, hegemonic masculinity is not the only type of masculine construction; some performances of masculinity are "expelled from the circle of legitimacy."[8] These "subordinated" performances of masculinity are commonly associated with gay identities and symbolically feminized.[9]

Thus, notions of masculinity are not static; yet, in a given epoch a collection of characteristics and roles may be identified as "exalted." More specifically, more than twenty-five years ago, communication scholar Nick Trujillo claimed that features of hegemonic masculinity in US culture included (1) physical force and control, as the male body represents power; (2) occupational achievement, as "men's work" is valued in capitalist society; (3) familial patriarchy, as men hold dominant roles over women in families; (4) frontiersmanship, as the white working-class cowboy is archetypical in US culture; and (5) heterosexuality, as sexual relationships with women are normative.[10] Although such characteristics may be performed in a range of ways, and may manifest more or less prominently over time, recent analyses indicate that notions of these traditionally dominant features of masculinity continue to structure or otherwise have bearing on a range of political and mediated cultural texts.[11]

Additional characteristics of hegemonic masculinity relate to the presidency. For example, qualities of heroism, courage, military prowess, battle readiness, athleticism, power, control, and determination have been connected to the role of "commander-in-chief."[12] Simultaneously, the president must embody a national father-figure and protective breadwinner.[13] Such a narrowly masculine image of the US presidency combined with systemic patriarchy has, to date, severely limited the ability of women to contend for the office. Even Barack Obama, whose historic election represented a major disruption in the presumed whiteness of the presidency, was able to fulfill the other normative requirements of presidential masculinity in ways that a woman could not.[14]

The vice presidential role has a complex relationship to that of the president. The vice president must be seen as a person who could step into the presidency at a moment's notice. At the same time, the vice president is subordinate to the president and must enact a submissive posture. Historically, the vice president was seen as relatively unimportant; John Adams stated that he was a "placeholder," lamenting, "My country has in its wisdom contrived for me the most insignificant office that has ever the invention of man contrived or his imagination conceived."[15] Recent vice presidents Al Gore, Dick Cheney, and Joe Biden have expanded the role. Still, according to communication scholar Denise Bostdorff, the largely ceremonial nature of the office and the fact that vice presidents must "submerge their independence and individualism" within that of the president feminizes the vice presidency and makes it a "traditional female role."[16]

Media constructions complicate this gendering of the vice president, and not all are created equal. Dick Cheney, a former secretary of defense, five-time heart attack survivor, advocate of "enhanced interrogation," and notorious hunter from Wyoming, embodied many characteristics of hegemonic masculinity. Candidate Paul Ryan was an athletic "gym rat"; his fitness regimen led one journalist to quip, "In case you haven't heard, Paul Ryan works out. A lot."[17] And although such masculine roles were not available to candidate Sarah Palin in conventional ways, communication scholars Katie Gibson and Amy Heyse observe that the "faux maternal" persona constructed in Palin's 2008 Republican National Convention speech—wherein she emphasized her role as a "hockey mom" and virtuous protector of her children—enacted traditional gender scripts and reinforced the hegemonic masculinity of (conservative) politics.[18] More recently, driven primarily by the satirical publication *The Onion*, "Uncle Joe" Biden was constructed as a cheap six-pack-toting, Trans Am–driving party-boy, who enjoyed a deep and meaningful, albeit one-sided, bromance with President Obama.[19] Such comedic representations paved the way for Kaine. As journalist Alexandra Petri quipped, "Onion Joe Biden's iconic Trans Am is about to pull out from the driveway of the vice president's residence. But don't worry. Tim Kaine's minivan is here to take its place. And it's full of healthy snacks!"[20] Communication scholars Kherstin Khan and Diane M. Blair remind us that gendered images are ultimately cocreated by candidates' "rhetorical actions and the rhetorical framing of those actions by the media."[21]

An additional complicating factor in 2016 was the role reversal necessitated by Clinton's unprecedented candidacy. A woman at the top of the ticket presented a major disruption to established gendered patterns of the presidency and vice presidency. The incongruity of Clinton in this role laid gendered constructions bare and spurred reworkings of taken-for-granted norms. When a woman, always in a position subordinate to men in hegemonic gender hierarchies, ran for the top political office in the nation surrounded by men occupying support positions, gendered tensions emerged. Others previously examined such tensions in the relationship between Hillary and Bill Clinton, both in her 2007–8 primary run and in the most recent election.[22]

Of course, the mere fact that Clinton is a woman did not, in itself, disrupt the hierarchical gendered constructions of the offices. Prior scholarship demonstrates that the insertion of the "feminine" into the political sphere does not necessarily amount to the sphere's "feminization." For example, man candidates frequently utilize a "feminine style" of rhetoric, marked by inductive form and personal tone.[23] However, this style of communication is often used to forward a patriarchal agenda and "mask the patriarchy of contemporary politics."[24] That which may seem to put forth empowering gendered possibilities in politics may actually solidify the supremacy of the existing hierarchy. Similarly, men who occupy roles subordinate to prominent woman candidates may, through their discourse, reinforce hegemonic masculinity and subvert the goals of the very women they seek to support.

For example, Kherstin Khan and Diane M. Blair illustrated ways in which Bill Clinton's campaigning for Hillary Clinton in the 2008 election actually marginalized her candidacy. With media framing Bill as the "popular, patriarchal head" of the Democratic Party, "hegemonic discourses about masculinity and the presidency" were reinforced.[25] Bill was celebrated for his ability to "seduce" voters, as a "securer" of votes, and as a "defender/rescuer of Senator Clinton's campaign."[26] References to his sexual virility and indiscretions also reinforced perceptions that Clinton was unable to "'control' her husband," and his "popularity was often presented in contrast to [her] perceived coldness and lack of likeability."[27] Of course, Bill's goal was to support Clinton's candidacy for president, and he "did promote a liberal feminist agenda"; however, Bill's discourse "resulted in the (re)affirmation of the presidency as the hegemonic masculine role."[28] Similar conclusions have been drawn regarding Bill's role in the 2016 election. In particular, musings on Bill's role as the presidential spouse once again demonstrated and reinforced the hegemonic masculinity of the presidential office.[29] Jokes about whether or not he would be in charge of selecting the White House flowers and china pattern (as First Ladies have traditionally done) as well as questions about how much influence he would hold over Hillary (would her presidency be just another term for Bill?) enacted cultural gender scripts that constrained Hillary.[30] Of course, these scripts did not similarly constrain Bill, nor have man presidential candidates been constrained in such ways by their spouses. The subordinate, helpmate role of presidential spouse remains a "natural" fit for a woman.

Historical studies of men who were supporters of women's rights offer additional layers of meaning to the current context. Throughout the 2016 campaign, histories of nineteenth-century woman suffrage activism echoed in symbolic and material ways. Discourses centered on prominent men who were Hillary Clinton's allies may be compared to those centered on men who advocated for woman suffrage. Sociologist Michael Kimmel and Thomas Mosmiller noted that "male participants in suffrage demonstrations were labeled 'Aunt Nancy men,' or 'miss-Nancys,' or 'man-milliners,' turn-of-the-century versions of 'Momma's boys.'"[31] Indeed, they claimed that "the most common theme in public reaction to men's support of women's rights has been a questioning of their masculinity."[32] Historian Stacey Robertson's work on suffrage activist Parker Pillsbury illustrated how activists responded to such labels.[33] Pillsbury, she claimed, subverted traditional notions of manhood because he viewed male dominance as unmanly. Pillsbury constructed an alternative version of masculinity that was composed of bodily strength (to use in defense of the exploited), self-control, and civic morality (comprised of self-sacrifice, virtue, and independence).[34] Although Pillsbury's new masculinity opposed more aggressive and domineering forms, it was certainly not a critique of paternalism, nor did it constitute women as equals. In fact, conceptions of women as defenseless and in need of protection and instruction undergirded Pillsbury's construction of a more virtuous masculinity.[35]

Evidently, masculinity is comprised of a complex constellation of discourses and symbols that shift and bend to meet the contextual constraints of the moment. Even subversions or disruptions to previously stable systems of gender oftentimes yield ambivalent results vis-à-vis gender-based oppression, as subordinate men enact masculinist scripts to constrain a woman superior, or one system of masculinity is replaced by another, different, but nonetheless domineering, masculinity. These tensions manifested in Kaine's campaign rhetoric. Although Kaine may seem an unlikely person through which to analyze hegemonic masculinity when compared with the more blatant example of Trump, we contend that within his seemingly harmless and unremarkable enactment of paternalistic scripts persisted everyday, mundane, and pervasive gender-based domination. Of course, the relevance of such scripts extends beyond gender; thus, ways in which Kaine's paternalistic performances pertained to race and other identity-based axes of oppression are also evident in our analysis.

Constructing Tim Kaine's Masculinity

To articulate the ways in which masculinity was constructed by and through Kaine, we examined two speeches very similar in content—his July 23 introduction and his July 27 acceptance of the nomination—as well as mediated responses to both. Despite having served as governor of and senator from Virginia, prior to his selection as Clinton's running mate, Kaine was relatively unknown at the national level. These two speeches represented his introduction to a wide audience; thus, they provided good texts through which to analyze the construction of Kaine's image. Additionally, a range of mediated responses to these two "first impression" speeches provided insight into co-constructions of his public identity. The following section draws examples from the speeches to illustrate how Kaine constructed a subordinate *and* paternalist masculine image. Then, we briefly examine ways in which mediated responses picked up on these themes to more overtly construct images of Kaine as a particular sort of "dad." Importantly, many of the symbolic messages that constructed such masculine images did not overtly pertain to gender. Instead, we found that a range of ideas and meanings came together to both implicitly and explicitly construct gender.

The Subordinate Paternalist Role

To begin, Kaine engaged in discursive practices that echoed Bostdorff's claim about the "feminized" vice presidential role.[36] He defined himself, first, not as an individual but in relation to others. He expressed gratitude to his wife and three adult children, and said, "I am the luckiest dad and the luckiest husband in the world."[37] Women have more readily been cast in such ways, as someone's wife, mother, daughter, or sister. At the same time, he claimed that he and Clinton would be "compañeros de alma."[38] Meaning "companions of the soul" or soul mates, this constituted he and Clinton as intimate collaborators. Platonic, to be sure. However, this choice of phrasing could also be read to imply a gendered marriage of sorts; a significant reversal given the vice presidential subordinate "helpmate" role.[39] The phrase also foreshadowed Kaine's frequent practice of weaving Spanish into his public campaign speeches. Previously, he garnered some attention when he delivered the first ever full speech in Spanish on the Senate floor, in support of an immigration bill.[40] Kaine's fluency in the language and perceived cultural competency positioned him somewhat differently with regard to Latinx communities than typical white male politicians.[41] Perceptions of his Spanish-speaking were mixed;[42] however, Kaine constructed himself as a candidate who could transcend cultural and racial divides and work as a partner rather than a dominator.

Kaine's tone was humble, conversational, and at times, passive. He stated, "This might be the first time you're hearing me speak, and hey . . . for many of you this is the first time you've even heard my name. But that's okay, because I'm excited for us to get to know one another."[43] He assumed a submissive posture, and framed his candidacy as two new acquaintances beginning a conversation and learning about one another. Such submission was also evident in the way Kaine described his career. He remarked that he "became" the mayor of Richmond, the lieutenant governor of Virginia, and then the governor of Virginia.[44] Significantly, this phrasing connoted that these things "happened to" Kaine—they came to be. He did not make them happen; he was not the agent. Furthermore, the reason such things happened to him related to his talent for "listening to people, learning about their lives, and trying to find consensus."[45] He painted himself as someone who did not assume command and dole out expertise and instructions; rather, he was a collaborator who allowed others to speak first and set the agenda.

Kaine's subordination shifted to supportiveness, as an emphasis on collaboration was reflected in collectivist themes throughout the speeches. He noted that the motto of his Jesuit boys' high school was "Men for others" and that the school influenced his decision to "devote [him]self to social justice."[46] He said his experience volunteering in Honduras "convinced [him] that we've got to advance opportunity and equality for everybody, no matter where they come from, how much money they have, what they look like, what accent they have, or who they love."[47] Furthermore, Kaine stated of his seventeen years as a civil rights lawyer: "I brought dozens of lawsuits when I was in private practice battling banks, landlords, real estate firms, insurance companies, and even local governments that treated people unfairly. . . . I won a historic verdict against a national insurance company because they had been redlining minority neighborhoods, treating them unfairly."[48] The focus on collectivism in these examples constructed Kaine as concerned with communities of varying socioeconomic status, culture, sexuality, and race, and echoed the masculine construction of men who were advocates for woman suffrage. This masculinity rejected "masculine virtues of self-interest and individualism" and instead emphasized "selflessness and concern with the social good."[49] Strong men could use both their physical and intellectual strength to advocate for the marginalized. Such constructions indicate an attitude that is at once supportive *and* paternalistic.

Kaine's version of paternalism was further reflected in messages about family. He spoke of the "union-organized ironworking shop in the stockyards of Kansas City" run by his dad. He said, "That ironworking business was tough" and illustrated how the rest of the family supported dad. Kaine recalled:

> My mom, in addition to all the challenges of my two brothers and me . . . was my dad's best saleswoman. . . . My two brothers and I, we all pitched in. Sometimes we were scheduled to pitch in and sometimes dad would just shake us in the morning and say, "I got an order to get out and I really need you guys today." . . . But that's what families do. . . . That's what families do. That's what families do.[50]

Kaine's father, in a tough blue-collar profession, represented rugged white masculinity and the closely linked value of an honest day's work. His mom was an empowered professional, a "saleswoman," in addition to her motherly duties. Dad exercised control over his sons, but they consented to help, to serve the collective. The repetition of "That's what families do" emphasized that such a familial relationship was not one of top-down domination, but rather of concordance; each member "consented" to the role they had no choice but to play.

Additionally, the theme of paternalism extended beyond family to Kaine's experiences as a missionary in Honduras, which he undertook as part of his commitment to social justice. He stated: "When I got to Honduras . . . my recently acquired knowledge of constitutional law was pretty useless. But the experience of working in my dad's ironworking shop was actually kind of helpful. So I taught teenagers the basics of carpentry and welding, and they helped me learn Spanish. And I tell you. My time in Honduras changed my life in so many ways."[51] Many have critiqued the practice of white Western missionary work and "voluntourism" in developing countries. Writer Teju Cole conceptualized such work as contributing to a paternalistic white savior complex, and wrote that the complex "is not about justice. It is about having a big emotional experience that validates privilege."[52] Beyond being supportive and paternalistic at once, couching missionary work within an overarching concern for justice and collective well-being masked the paternalism and subtle domination that accompany such activities.

Kaine's fatherly enactments starkly contrasted with Donald Trump. Once again in the context of Honduras, Kaine described getting a "firsthand look at a system . . . a dictatorship where a few folks at the top had all the power, and everybody else got left behind."[53] This not-so-subtle dig at perceptions of Trump's rhetorical and leadership style as dictator-like created an image of a dominant, overbearing, controlling, even violent father. Kaine compounded his critique of Trump as he returned to his second language. He stated, "Aprendí los valores del pueblo—fe, familia, y trabajo. Los mismos valores de la communidad Latina aquí en nuestro país,"[54] meaning "I learned the values of the people—faith, family, and work. The same values of the Latin community here in our country." Here, Kaine foregrounded the significant influence of Latinx culture on his moral upbringing and worldview, all the while calling for a presidential morality lacking in Trump. By returning to the Spanish language, Kaine obscured his whiteness and suggested that he would govern from a position of cultural compassion, as a "good" patriarch should. The image was extended when Kaine said, of Trump, "From Atlantic City to his so-called university, he leaves a trail of broken promises and wrecked lives wherever he goes.

We can't afford to let him do the same thing to our country."[55] Donald Trump, to put it simply, is a deadbeat dad.

A final notable characteristic of Kaine's speeches, which indicated his ambivalent relationship to cultural norms of masculinity, was the pairing of hegemonically masculine and more subordinate or feminized masculine ideas. For example, Kaine discussed the military and the importance of upholding commitments to the nation's military allies; yet, he did so in the context of his son, who is a marine, and the need to keep individual troops out of harm's way. He also spoke of "fighting for children and families" and "fighting for equal rights" for a range of marginalized groups.[56] Over and over again, he paired the aggressive "fight" with helping kids and others who are in need of such help. He illustrated, in a range of ways throughout the speeches, that his masculinity is strong, but also benevolent.

Safe Dad, Creepy Dad

Our focus on fatherly paternalism may seem strange, given that Kaine did not talk much about his own experiences as a father in the speeches examined here. Yet, Kaine's perceived identity as a "dad," gleaned from his messages and style overall, animated a barrage of mediated responses that gave further substance to the sort of masculinity he promoted. "#TimKaineDadJokes" began trending on Twitter during his July 27 acceptance speech. The humorous barbs came primarily from supporters, and were good-natured and celebratory. For example, one user wrote, "I bet if Tim Kaine has leaked voicemails at the DNC they were all reminders to stay hydrated."[57] Another wrote, "Tim Kaine is that soccer dad who can sing along to any rap song, but hums the curse words."[58] Riffing on Kaine's reputation as a skilled harmonica player, one tweet stated, "$50 says Tim Kaine plays 'Wagon Wheel' on harmonica at his daughter's wedding. 'Join in if you know the words,' he'll say enthusiastically."[59] The same user later quipped, "Tim Kaine respectfully declined to have the Secret Service drive for him. Didn't like how the agent handled the wheel. '10 and 2,' he said."[60] Still others remarked, "Tim Kaine is your friend's dad who brought extra corsages just in case your Homecoming dates forgot"[61] and "Tim Kaine wanted to make sure your sleepover was all right—oh, and he made nachos, he'll just leave 'em on the ping pong table."[62] Taken together, such tweets did significant work to construct Kaine as a safe, nerdy, benevolent, white heterosexual patriarch. To many of his supporters on the left, Kaine's masculinity was not in line with hegemonic masculinity inasmuch as it did not connote, for example, power, aggression, or military prowess. Though responses were designed to poke fun at

Kaine, they also signaled admiration; thus, to those on the left inclined to care about political gender roles, Kaine would have been perceived as a progressive and even feminist alternative to the Republican ticket.

In opposition to such tongue-in-cheek celebratory constructions were responses from the right. A range of conservative commentators and bloggers referred to Kaine as "Creepy Kaine."[63] On Twitter and various other social media sites, visual juxtapositions of Kaine to images including Rip Taylor, Jack Nicholson's portrayal of "The Joker," a dummy from *The Twilight Zone*, or "creepy" clowns often accompanied the label.[64] Some portrayed Kaine driving a van with no windows and "free candy" written on the side, while others questioned why he seemed to enjoy spending so much time with young boys in Honduras.[65] Others called him a "cuckold" or "cuck."[66] These examples jumbled together a range of meanings to suggest that the image perceived by supporters as "safe" actually masked a nefarious character and aberrant masculinity. For instance, some implied a deviant sexuality connected with pedophilia. Such comparisons functioned, at least in part, to question Kaine's integrity and his manhood, presenting complex iterations of the "feminized" narrative some conservatives have long built up around the Democratic Party.[67] Gender scholar Jackson Katz argued that the right has constructed Democrats as "weak and politically spineless"[68] and that "millions of white male voters . . . equate liberal policies with emasculation and weakness."[69] To his detractors on the right—at least those who participated in the "Creepy Kaine" discourse—Kaine's version of masculinity was not in line with hegemonic masculinity inasmuch as it came across as emasculated, and demonstrated a lack of virile heterosexuality, manly aggression, power, and dominance.

Complicity and Constraints

Conclusions to be drawn from this analysis are more complex than a simple either/or, as in, *either* Kaine reinforces the hegemonic masculinity of the political sphere *or* he does not. His role as subordinate to Clinton in concert with a constellation of symbolic acts detailed above make this plain. R. W. Connell argued that one need not conform to all the tenets of a given period's hegemonic masculinity in order to enact "complicity" with them, stating:

> If a large number of men have some connection with the hegemonic project but do not embody hegemonic masculinity, we need a way of theorizing their specific situation. This can be done by recognizing another relationship among groups of men, the relationship of

complicity with the hegemonic project. Masculinities constructed in ways that realize the patriarchal dividend without . . . being the front-line troops of patriarchy, are complicit in this sense.

. . . Marriage, fatherhood and community life often involve extensive compromises with women rather than naked domination or an uncontested display of authority. A great many men who draw the patriarchal dividend also respect their wives and mothers, are never violent towards women, do their accustomed share of the housework . . . [70]

Kaine may not overtly embody hegemonic masculinity, but he still "draws the dividend." In doing so, he provided an appealing alternative (for some) to the far more aggressive masculinity presented by Trump and others on the right. However, he also "draws the dividend" by enacting elements of hegemonic masculinity that advance his particular political goals, making him an appropriately masculine figure to embody political leadership in the United States. The ways in which Kaine presented himself as subordinate bolstered his image as a supportive figure who champions justice for those who are oppressed because of their gender, race, class, or sexual orientation. Simultaneously, his paternalistic image as a safe, white, middle-class, heterosexual father-figure was solidified and celebrated. He reaped the benefits of being a white man in politics, all the while positioning himself as a person who could subvert such characterizations at will.

Ultimately, this chapter is less about Kaine himself than it is about the gendered discourses he draws on and enacts. Kaine's performance of masculinity was grounded in cultural scripts bigger than he or any one individual. In other words, just as Clinton has been constrained by scripts that prescribe appropriate and limited roles for women in politics, so too was Kaine constrained by the rhetorical options at his disposal pertaining to masculinity in the political sphere and the vice presidential role. Given the conventions of the vice presidency and a need to not dominate Clinton's candidacy, Kaine's enactment of a persona that was simultaneously supportive and paternal makes a great deal of sense. Still, considering the implications of such constraints is necessary. Even if Kaine is a *nice* dad, his positioning as *any* sort of dad calls forth images of the executive branch as the rightful place for the "father" of the country. Furthermore, given deeply embedded gender role conventions both within and outside of the political sphere, if Kaine is dad then Clinton is mom and placed right back into a subordinate position. As the political sphere hopefully becomes more diverse in terms of gender and other facets of identity, new sorts of power dynamics will inevitably continue to bump up against the limitations of persistent historical frameworks. Thus, we would be remiss to allow subtle examples of masculine domination to go uncritiqued. Much like the virtuous masculinity of nineteenth-century prosuffrage men,[71] Kaine's particular version of masculinity continued to position women and people of color as subordinate, in need of saving. Years from now, Donald Trump's infamous "grab 'em by the pussy" remark may have faded from memory.[72] For now, it is illustrative of a particular sort of aggressive and misogynist masculinity, to which Tim Kaine stands in stark contrast. Put another way, masculinity does not always "grab [one] by the pussy," and relatively more hidden and seemingly innocuous enactments allow systems of gender domination to persist unchecked.

Notes

Chapter title adapted from Alexandra Petri, "America, Meet Tim Kaine, Your New Stepdad," *Washington Post,* July 28, 2016, https://www.washingtonpost.com/blogs/compost/wp/2016/07/28/america-meet-tim-kaine-your-new-stepdad/?utm_term=.22ce2171eadd.

1. Ibid.

2. Andrew Buncombe, "Hillary Clinton Picks 'Boring' Tim Kaine to Be Her Running Mate," *Independent,* July 23, 2016, http://www.independent.co.uk/news/people/hillary-clinton-picks-boring-tim-kaine-to-be-her-running-mate-a7151926.html.

3. Denise M. Bostdorff, "Vice-Presidential Comedy and the Traditional Female Role: An Examination of the Rhetorical Characteristics of the Vice Presidency," *Western Journal of Speech Communication* 55 (1991): 1–27; Katie L. Gibson and Amy L. Heyse, "'The Difference between a Hockey Mom and a Pit Bull': Sarah Palin's Faux Maternal Persona and Performance of Hegemonic Masculinity at the 2008 Republican National Convention," *Communication Quarterly* 58, no. 3 (2010): 235–56; Karlyn Kohrs Campbell, "The Discursive Performance of Femininity: Hating Hillary," *Rhetoric & Public Affairs* 1, no. 1 (1998): 1–19.

4. Kelly Wilz, "Bernie Bros and Woman Cards: Rhetorics of Sexism, Misogyny, and Constructed Masculinity in the 2016 Election," *Women's Studies in Communication* 39, no. 4 (2016): 357–60.

5. Jackson Katz, *Man Enough? Donald Trump, Hillary Clinton, and the Politics of Presidential Masculinity* (Northampton, MA: Interlink Books, 2016); Shawn J. Parry-Giles and Trevor Parry-Giles, "Gendered Politics and Presidential Image Construction: A Reassessment of the 'Feminine Style,'" *Communication Monographs* 63 (1996): 337–53; Kristina Horn Sheeler and Karrin Vasby Anderson, *Woman President: Confronting Postfeminist Political Culture* (College Station: Texas A&M University Press, 2013).

6. R. W. Connell, *Masculinities,* 2nd ed. (Berkeley: University of California Press, 2005), 77.

7. Ibid.; Judith Butler, *Gender Trouble: Feminism and the Subversion of Identity* (New York: Routledge, 1999).

8. Connell, *Masculinities*, 79.

9. Ibid.

10. Nick Trujillo, "Hegemonic Masculinity on the Mound: Media Representations of Nolan Ryan and American Sports Culture," *Critical Studies in Mass Communication* 8 (1991): 291–92.

11. See, for example, Anna Cornelia Fahey, "French and Feminine: Hegemonic Masculinity and the Emasculation of John Kerry in the 2004 Presidential Race," *Critical Studies in Media Communication* 24, no. 2 (2007): 132–50; Gibson and Heyse, "Difference," 235–56; Elizabeth Fish Hatfield, "'What It Means to Be a Man: Examining Hegemonic Masculinity in Two and a Half Men," *Communication, Culture & Critique* 3 (2010): 526–48; Simon Lindgren and Maxime Lelievre, "In the Laboratory of Masculinity: Renegotiating Gender Subjectivities in MTV's Jackass," *Critical Studies in Media Communication* 26, no. 5 (2009): 393–410; Mark A. Rademacher and Casey Kelly, "'I'm Here to Do Business. I'm Not Here to Play Games': Work, Consumption, and Masculinity in Storage Wars," *Journal of Communication Inquiry* 40, no. 1 (2016): 7–24.

12. Parry-Giles and Parry-Giles, "Gendered Politics," 343–46.

13. Ibid., 345.

14. Sheeler and Anderson, *Woman President*, 171.

15. Jaime Fuller, "Here Are a Bunch of Awful Things the Vice President Has Said about Being No. 2," *Washington Post*, October 14, 2014, https://www.washingtonpost.com/news/the-fix/wp/2014/10/03/a-brief-history-of-vice-presidents-bemoaning-the-vice-presidency/?utm_term=.11e9c708e2d8.

16. Bostdorff, "Vice-Presidential Comedy," 2.

17. Bill Gifford, "Paul Ryan, Ubermensch," *Slate*, September 17, 2012, http://www.slate.com/articles/news_and_politics/politics/2012/09/paul_ryan_claims_he_has_6_to_8_percent_body_fat_.html.

18. Gibson and Heyse, "Difference," 236.

19. "The President of Vice," *Onion*, http://www.theonion.com/interactive/biden.

20. Petri, "America, Meet Tim Kaine."

21. Kherstin Khan and Diane M. Blair, "Writing Bill Clinton: Mediated Discourses on Hegemonic Masculinity and the 2008 Presidential Primary," *Women's Studies in Communication* 36 (2013): 57.

22. Ibid., 56–71; Roseann M. Mandziuk, "Whither the Good Wife? 2016 Presidential Candidate Spouses in the Gendered Spaces of Contemporary Politics," *Quarterly Journal of Speech* 103, nos. 1–2 (2017): 136–59.

23. Karlyn Kohrs Campbell, *Man Cannot Speak for Her: A Critical Study of Early Feminist Rhetoric* (New York: Greenwood Press, 1989), 13.

24. Parry-Giles and Parry-Giles, "Gendered Politics," 348.

25. Khan and Blair, "Writing Bill Clinton," 57.

26. Ibid., 60–61.

27. Ibid., 61.

28. Ibid., 67.

29. Mandzuik, "Whither the Good Wife?"

30. Ibid., 151–53.

31. Michael S. Kimmel and Thomas E. Mosmiller, eds., *Against the Tide: Pro-Feminist Men in the United States, 1776–1990* (Boston: Beacon Press, 1992), 6.

32. Ibid.

33. Stacey M. Robertson, "'Aunt Nancy Men': Parker Pillsbury, Masculinity, and Women's Rights Activism in the Nineteenth-Century United States," *American Studies* 37, no. 2 (1996): 33–60.

34. Ibid.

35. Ibid.

36. Bostdorff, "Vice Presidential Comedy."

37. The full transcript of Tim Kaine's introductory speech is drawn from "In Miami, Tim Kaine Joins the Democratic Ticket," Hillary for America, July 23, 2016, https://www.hillaryclinton.com/briefing/updates/2016/07/23/in-miami-tim-kaine-joins-the-democratic-ticket/.

38. Ibid.

39. Bostdorff, "Vice Presidential Comedy."

40. Erin Banco, "A Speech in Spanish Is a First for the Senate," *New York Times*, June 11, 2013, http://www.nytimes.com/2013/06/12/us/politics/tim-kaines-immigration-speech-in-spanish-is-a-first-for-the-senate.html?smid=fb-share.

41. Russel Contreras and Amy Taxin, "Sen. Tim Kaine Speaks Spanish: Does That Matter to Latino Voters?," *Christian Science Monitor*, July 27, 2016, https://www.csmonitor.com/USA/Politics/2016/0727/Sen.-Tim-Kaine-speaks-Spanish-Does-that-matter-to-Latino-voters.

42. Ed O'Keefe, "Tim Kaine Can Speak Spanish, but Most Hispanics Don't Care," *New York Times*, July 24, 2016, https://www.washingtonpost.com/politics/tim-kaine-can-speak-spanish-but-most-hispanics-dont-care/2016/07/24/9925fd74-510e-11e6-a7d8-13d06b37f256_story.html?utm_term=.d2f7477d50bb.

43. "Kaine Joins the Democratic Ticket."

44. The full transcript of Tim Kaine's nomination acceptance speech is drawn from "Transcript and Video: Tim Kaine Accepts the Vice Presidential Nomination," *Los Angeles Times*, July 27, 2016, http://www.latimes.com/politics/la-na-pol-tim-kaine-convention-speech-transcript-20160727-snap-story.html; "Kaine Joins the Democratic Ticket."

45. "Kaine Joins the Democratic Ticket."

46. Ibid.

47. Ibid.

48. Ibid.

49. Robertson, "Aunt Nancy Men," 41–42.

50. "Kaine Joins the Democratic Ticket."

51. Ibid.

52. Teju Cole, "The White-Savior Industrial Complex," *Atlantic*, March 21, 2012, https://www.theatlantic.com/international/archive/2012/03/the-white-savior-industrial-complex/254843/.

53. "Kaine Joins the Democratic Ticket."

54. "Tim Kaine Accepts Nomination."

55. Ibid.

56. "Kaine Joins the Democratic Ticket."

57. Alexandra Petri, quoted in Matt Fuller, "A Definitive Guide to the Best Tim Kaine Jokes Twitter Has to Offer," *Huffington Post*, October 4, 2016, http://www.huffingtonpost.com/entry/tim-kaine-dad-jokes-twitter_us_57f3de7fe4b0d0e1a9a9f609.

58. Kelly Cohn, quoted in Fuller, "Best Tim Kaine Jokes."

59. Fuller, "Best Tim Kaine Jokes."

60. Ibid.

61. Jenny Han, quoted in L. V. Anderson, "Here Are the Best Dad Jokes from Twitter during Tim Kaine's DNC Speech," *Slate*, July 27, 2016, http://www.slate.com/blogs/xx_factor/2016/07/27/here_are_the_best_dad_jokes_from_twitter_during_tim_kaine_s_dnc_speech.html.

62. Jason O. Gilbert, quoted in Anderson, "Best Dad Jokes from Twitter."

63. See, for example, #creepykaine, Twitter hashtag, https://twitter.com/hashtag/creepykaine?lang=en; David Limbaugh, "'Creepy Kaine' Exposes Emptiness of Dems' Policies," *World Net Daily*, October 6, 2016, http://www.wnd.com/2016/10/creepy-kaine-exposes-emptiness-of-dems-policies/.

64. #creepykaine, Twitter hashtag, https://twitter.com/hashtag/creepykaine?lang=en&lang=en.

65. Ibid.

66. Ibid.

67. Katz, *Man Enough?*, 263.

68. Ibid.

69. Ibid., 256.

70. Connell, *Masculinities*, 79–80.

71. Robertson, "Aunt Nancy Men."

72. "Transcript: Donald Trump's Taped Comments about Women," *New York Times*, October 8, 2016, https://www.nytimes.com/2016/10/08/us/donald-trump-tape-transcript.html.

Part Two

Feminist Predecessors

Chapter Six

PLEASE PUT STICKERS ON SHIRLEY CHISHOLM'S GRAVE

Assessing the Legacy of a Black Feminist Pioneer

Barbara Winslow

The 2016 election was notable for being the first time a woman ran for the US presidency nominated by a major political party. The campaign and election of Donald Trump—an unending spectacle of misogyny, racism, Islamophobia, xenophobia, bullying, and the most venal nationalistic chest-thumping—upended this "first." To show support for Hillary Clinton and to pay homage to earlier suffragists, women went to Rochester, New York, to put "I Voted" stickers on the grave of Susan B. Anthony, one of the most prominent nineteenth-century suffragists. Women of color, especially African American women, were furious at their constant erasure from the narrative of women's rights activism. Feminist writer Roxane Gay tweeted, "I'd put my voting sticker on Ida B. Wells's grave" (@rgay, November 8, 2016). Mikki Kendall, a self-described "occasional feminist" and writer, tweeted, "I owe my right to vote to Sojourner Truth, Ida Wells, Mary Church Terrell, Mary Cary, Nannie Burroughs, Frances Harper and Daisy Langphen" (@Karynthia, November 8, 2016). And Everette Dionne pleaded with a tweet to "please put stickers on Shirley Chisholm's grave" (@freeblackgirl, November 8, 2016), which is in Buffalo, New York.

As the Democratic Party candidate trying to break "that highest glass ceiling," Hillary Clinton was subjected to endless, horrific, and often baseless attacks on her character, honesty, and commitment to the democratic process—expectedly from the right, and surprisingly from the left. Whatever one makes of her campaign, there should be little doubt that race and misogyny—along with the Democratic Party leadership's failure to recognize the devastation resulting from thirty years of neoliberalism, Clinton's own mistakes, voter suppression, FBI director James Comey's letter to Congress regarding the reopening of the investigation of her emails shortly before the election, Russian hacking, combined with twenty-five years of systematic character assassination—played major roles in her electoral defeat.[1]

Clinton, however, was not the first woman to have endured vicious racial, class, and gender attacks while trying to make a presidential run. In 1972 Shirley Chisholm, who claimed a number of firsts including being the first African American woman elected to Congress, in 1968, was the first African American and the first woman to mount a campaign for the Democratic Party nomination for the US presidency. In her career as an elected official, first in Albany, in the New York Assembly and then in Congress, she was ignored, mocked, and slandered, not only by whites, but also by some African Americans, mainly men, who unfortunately internalized racist misogyny. Even with the outright sexism of the 2016 presidential election evident in slogans such as "Trump That Bitch" and "Hillary for Prison," probably no other candidate has been subjected to the type of vicious gendered smear attacks as was Chisholm.[2]

This is part of the price that confident, ambitious political women must pay, especially if and when they are to be firsts. And, too often, these pioneering women are not supported by their expected allies— Chisholm, not having support from male African American civil rights leaders; Clinton, losing support from white, suburban, college-educated women.[3] Aside from the obvious, there were other significant differences between the 1972 Chisholm campaign and the 2008 and 2016 Clinton campaigns. One, Chisholm was not even close to winning a presidential election (she only won one primary, New Jersey's, which was not a delegate-electing primary) let alone the Democratic Party nomination. Therefore, the party leadership and the press did not have to take her as seriously as they did Clinton. Chisholm was ignored, or as Florynce (Flo) Kennedy, African American, feminist, militant, founder of the Feminist Party, and supporter of the Chisholm presidential candidacy pointed out, Chisholm was "white-ed" out of history.[4] Shirley Chisholm's life and political activism is living proof of the centrality of the intersection of class, race, sexuality, and gender. Her story reveals how different our political culture would be if women of color suffragists and feminists were put front and center of the historical narrative.

Shirley Chisholm rose to prominence in 1968 when she ran for Congress, and for the most part, given the overall political climate— liberalism, support for civil rights, the social welfare programs of the

New Deal and Great Society, growing opposition to US militarism, and grudging support for women's rights—her politics and persona were not subject to constant attack until 1972. Clinton, on the other hand, became a public political figure during the conservative ascendancy of Reagan and George H. W. Bush, which included a growing attack on the gains made by the women's movement, in particular a woman's right to abortion, sexuality, and equality on the job, in marriage and in politics.

In 1992 the growing conservative movement and media made Clinton their poster child for all their fears about strong women and feminism. The right portrayed Clinton as a dishonest, ambitious, man-hating (even castrating) harpy who wanted a nanny state. As a First Lady who wished to be an active participant in the Bill Clinton White House, she was constantly reviled. Elected as US senator from New York in 2000, she was reelected in 2006. She then ran for the Democratic Party's presidential nomination *twice*—losing in 2008 in a bitter, racially charged, and gendered primary struggle against an African American male, Barack Obama, and then in 2016 defeating Bernie Sanders, a white Jewish male, in an equally bitter and gendered struggle. In those two races, much of the media adored Obama, for the most part ignored Sanders, and attacked Clinton.

Shirley Chisholm's persona, life experiences, and public activism were the embodiment of intersectionality. Like Hillary Clinton, she was a fiercely ambitious woman, a strategic politician and activist, and committed to public service. But there were obvious racial and class differences. Chisholm's life, first as a student, then a teacher, manager, elected official, and political activist, was a constant struggle against the barriers of race, class, and gender oppression. Born in Brooklyn in 1924 of working-class, Afro-Caribbean immigrants, she lived in Barbados from 1929 to 1938 during the early years of that nation's struggle for independence. No doubt, this experience gave young Chisholm an understanding of the need to stand up and fight for one's principles, self-respect, and independence from oppressive and racially unjust relationships—whether personal or imbedded in economic or social relationships. Her later feminist consciousness was due in part to having been raised by two strong, hardworking Barbadian women.

Chisholm moved back to the Bedford-Stuyvesant neighborhood of Brooklyn, New York, in 1933, to an urban world dominated by highly structured hierarchies of class, ethnicity, gender, and race. Her early life in Brooklyn, navigating and excelling in the racialized and gendered public school system, gave her the context for her future political philosophy and electoral ambitions. She attended Brooklyn College of the City University of New York, majoring in sociology with a minor in Spanish, and plunged into the world of student politics, including the all-black organization the Harriet Tubman Society, the Debating Society, the National Association for the Advancement of Colored People (NAACP), and the Brooklyn chapter of the Urban League. She also campaigned for women running for college government positions, whether white or black. Aware that women of color were excluded from the college's sorority system, Chisholm founded IPOTHIA (In Pursuit of the Highest in All). Her growing race and gender consciousness was a central legacy of her experience at Brooklyn College and would continue to be a motivating force throughout her political career.[5]

After graduation Chisholm earned a master's degree in childhood education from Columbia Teachers' College. In the late 1940s she entered local politics; she enjoyed the tumult but chafed at its racism and sexism. The 17th Assembly District Democratic Club (or 17AD) was located in Bedford-Stuyvesant, populated overwhelmingly with African Americans and Afro-Caribbeans, and highly influential in electing state senators, assemblymen, and local city council members. Yet the 17AD's leaders were all white; they did everything they could to prevent African Americans from running for office; they held segregated meetings with blacks on one side, whites on the other; women were not present.

Disgusted but determined to change this political scene, Chisholm plunged into the fray, first bringing black women to the meetings and then challenging the white, male leadership. She was a tireless political activist. She demanded that the women's community work be funded and appreciated. She worked with other black political activists canvassing neighborhoods, ringing doorbells, registering voters, preparing voters to fight against voter suppression, organizing and speaking at rallies, working phone banks, and fund-raising. Through this grassroots organizing, political activists successfully challenged the apportionment of political districts in Brooklyn. By 1962, after a decade of hard political organizing, the grassroots activists formed the Unity District Club and succeeded in ousting the entrenched white, male leadership. Chisholm had been in the leadership of that campaign.[6]

Once the 12th District was organized, Chisholm notified the Unity Democrats that she wanted the nomination for state representative in Albany. She believed she had earned the nomination. She had spent ten years doing almost every job in Brooklyn party politics, except run for elective office. In addition, she was confident she was the most qualified person to represent this new district in the statehouse, and furthermore, she said, "I was not going to be denied because of my sex." Once Chisholm stepped forward to claim what she saw as her destiny, she ran into both entrenched gendered and racial chauvinism from her former political comrades. According to Chisholm, she had to face down men in her own political club who "had a taste of how I operated." To them she was "a little woman who didn't know how to play the game or when to shut up."[7] She stood her ground in face of white and male opposition. By the standards of the 2016 presidential election, she was a "nasty woman."

Chisholm was acutely aware of how black women had been reviled, made invisible, or cast as the historical stereotypes of mammies, Jezebels, or Sapphires. Daniel Patrick Moynihan, a Harvard sociologist and adviser to then president Lyndon Johnson, gave these racially gendered stereotypes academic social science credentials. His inflammatory 1965 report, "The Negro Family: The Case for National Action," argued that the primary cause of the "tangle of pathology" in the black community was the matriarchal nature of the black family. Moynihan asserted that the dominant black mother emasculated the black man. Feminists and many African Americans criticized the report; nonetheless, it was accepted as a serious analysis of the problems of racism and a blueprint for policy proposals, which particularly sought to penalize black mothers and demonize strong black women. Chisholm herself referenced the damage done by the Moynihan report to African American women in their families, in their communities, in their activism, and in their personal relationships.[8]

She was elected to the state legislature in 1965 and proved to be a hardworking and effective legislator. She was also determined to be her own person, often defying the leadership of the UDC as well as the New York State Democratic Party. Chisholm was very aware of the challenges facing someone who was a woman, African American, and a novice legislator. But much of the initial hostility she faced was a reaction to her being an outspoken black woman, who chose not to go along with "the rules of the political game" for she believed they were "designed to make it possible for men in power to control the actions of their supporters."[9] She also paid a price for being an African American woman in the white, male world of Albany politics. While her days were busy with committee hearings, legislative sessions, and meeting with constituents, her evenings were lonely. She was separated from her husband and far away from the community, church, and women's social and political organizations that sustained her in Brooklyn. In the 1960s, Albany was not very hospitable to African Americans, and "respectable" women did not go to bars or restaurants on their own. These gendered social relationships meant Chisholm was even further excluded and distanced from centers of power—male power. Often male legislators would hold informal caucusing in their hotel rooms, meetings where legislative details and personnel issues were hashed out. Chisholm was never invited. When not politicking, officials would go out to dinner, bars, movies, and clubs, where again, political deals were worked out and social relationships were strengthened. Chisholm was never invited. She confided to an interviewer, "I don't blame the fellows for not asking me out to dinner. I think there was a little fear of 'how do we handle her socially,'" adding that "men don't like independent women."[10]

Chisholm hid her disappointment and loneliness by being an engaged legislator. She was not afraid of partisan combat, willing to aggressively jump into debates, speaking up with confidence—something few female legislators did. Working with three other African American legislators—Percy Sutton, Charles Rangel, and David Dinkins—Chisholm helped enact legislation creating the first unemployment insurance for agricultural and domestic workers, as well as job protection for pregnant teachers. She was most proud of the passage of the 1966 Search for Education, Elevation and Knowledge (SEEK) legislation, which reflected her lifelong commitment to greater access to higher education. SEEK, an educational assistance program, enabled high school students from underfunded public schools to be enrolled in the City University of New York (CUNY) and the State University of New York (SUNY) with financial assistance for tutoring and counseling.[11]

Chisholm's four-year tenure in the state legislature convinced her that she had the talent, the ability, and the passion to represent her constituents at the national level. Her major obstacle was the male chauvinism of her colleagues in Albany as well as in the Democratic Party leadership. "This whole question of women, it gets to you," she remarked in an interview. "You can use a woman to do all sorts of tasks, but to put a woman in power, well that's another thing."[12]

As a result of a successful Supreme Court decision creating the 12th Congressional District, which gave Bedford-Stuyvesant voters the chance to elect one of their own, Chisholm announced she was going to run for Congress in 1968. And, once again, she faced the opposition from the all-male state and county leadership, who didn't like her independence from party strictures. "If we can't control her in Albany, how are we to control her in Washington?" was a common complaint. The men offered at least twelve other candidates, all men, to oppose Chisholm. But Chisholm had the support of Brooklyn's women, many of whom had been demanding greater women's representation. In an unusual twist, the Republican nomination went to James Farmer, an African American who had a national reputation and following because of his leadership in the militant civil rights organization the

Congress of Racial Equality (CORE). In this election, it seemed that everything went against Chisholm. Farmer had national name recognition, a huge war chest, a well-oiled political machine, and he did not have to support or campaign for the Republican presidential nominee, Richard Nixon.[13]

But Chisholm remained confident. First, she knew that 60 percent of the registered voters in her district were women. Having been a grassroots community and political activist, she knew the women in her neighborhood, and she made a point of involving women in her campaign. "Make no mistake about it," she would say over and over again at women's meetings. "You will send me to Congress." She contacted every neighborhood woman leader and asked for help. They held raffles, teas, bake sales, and barbecues. Chisholm knew that these women were transforming the traditional meaning of "woman's work": working for a man. This time the women were doing the same work, but for a woman. "If they were successful," she said, "they would have helped elect the first black woman ever to serve in the House of Representatives." Chisholm was also confident of Farmer's negatives. He did not live in the neighborhood, he was running as a Republican, and he had a white wife. Chisholm also took up the slogan "Unbought and Unbossed." These words were more than a campaign slogan. "Unbought" meant more than just that her vote was not for sale. It referenced liberation from slavery and colonialism. In the same vein, "unbossed" signified not only that she was not going to be dominated by any one political organization, but also that she was a strong woman, not to be bossed around at work, in the home, or in the House.[14]

Farmer ran an aggressive, masculinist campaign emphasizing gender differences. His campaign cannot really be compared to the aggressive racist, xenophobic, masculinist Trump campaign, because Farmer, like Chisholm, was a strong supporter of the black freedom struggle, supported unions, and opposed the war in Vietnam. Instead, Farmer's campaign literature argued for a "strong man's image." Chisholm might be a nice woman, he would say, but the 12th District needs "a man's voice" in Washington. Chisholm understood that Farmer was using this rhetoric, as well as the analysis of the Moynihan report, against her: "To the black men—even some of those supporting me—sensitive about female domination, they were running me down as a bossy female, a would-be matriarch."[15] At the time when the assumption was that black women's activism and Black Nationalism were irreconcilable, Chisholm's campaign demonstrated that it was possible to wage a campaign that brought ordinary women front and center, and at the same time organize inclusively for greater social justice. She mobilized the women in the district and turned Farmer's male chauvinist campaign strategy against him. "Men always under-estimate women," Chisholm wrote. "They underestimated me and they underestimated the women like me." She went into the projects, attended community meetings, and organized her car caravans, which stopped on busy streets, using her gender as her campaign weapon. "I am a woman and you are a woman, and let's show Farmer that woman-power can beat him."[16]

Television and print media ignored her altogether, another gall-ing aspect of the sexism she endured. An NBC weekend special, "The Campaign and the Candidates," reported only on Farmer without even mentioning Chisholm. The manager of one station sneered, "Who are you? A little school teacher who happened to go to the Assem-bly."[17] The *New York Times* erased her altogether with the headline "Farmer and Woman in Lively Bedford-Stuyvesant Race."[18] In the end, Chisholm defeated Farmer by 34,885 votes. Farmer, who later became friends with Chisholm and believed that she had "performed well" in Congress, was somewhat chagrined and perhaps a bit bitter about his loss. In his autobiography, he ruefully commented that he now "had a most unique distinction: I was the first black man in U.S. history to be defeated by a woman in a congressional race."[19]

The racial and misogynist treatment Chisholm experienced in Brooklyn politics barely prepared her for Washington, DC. While she became an instant celebrity upon her election, she continued to be insulted and demeaned. One southern congressman would take a cloth and wipe off any chair Chisholm sat in; another southerner constantly confronted Chisholm about her salary. She wasn't quiet and she wasn't conventional. She hired an all-female staff—the first person in Congress to do so. She upended commonly accepted congressio-nal rules of conduct when she refused to accept her first committee assignment, the Agricultural Committee, after pointing out that put-ting an African American from an urban district on a forestry commit-tee was a waste of her time. "If you do not assist me," she warned, "I will have to do my own thing."[20] Chisholm persisted and won a seat on the Veterans Committee. She continued to speak up and speak out. Her first speech in Congress was in opposition to the US war in Vietnam and a promise to vote against every bill brought to the House that pro-vided money to the Department of Defense. She continued to speak her mind on issues such as child poverty, police brutality, the Black Panther Party, labor unions, support for abortion rights, and for the Equal Rights Amendment. After giving a riveting speech after being inducted into the Delta Sigma Theta sorority, an African organization founded in 1913, she thrilled the audience as she concluded, "One thing people in New York and Washington are afraid of in Shirley Chisholm is *her mouth.*"[21]

It was the overall disgust with what she saw as Richard Nixon's corrupt, militaristic, and racist administration, combined with confidence growing out of the social justice movements, that convinced Chisholm she should be a double first—the first woman and the first African American to run for the presidency on the Democratic Party ticket. That Chisholm had the nerve, the chutzpah, the brazen guts to challenge the all-white male presidents' club thrilled her supporters and enraged her detractors. Flo Kennedy was one of her earliest supporters, urged her to run, and produced Chisholm's first campaign button: "Miz Chiz for Pres." Kennedy exulted that the campaign was "the most exciting, the most dangerous, the most likely . . . to blow the minds of [the] various parts of the establishmentarians," because Chisholm was a "fighting black woman who doesn't accept the sexist, racist, prop-war bull."[22] As her campaign progressed, she won support from a wide range of political activists and organizations.[23]

However, while she won the support of many grassroots organizations, a number of leading feminist individuals and organizations did not back her. Sister New Yorker Bella Abzug, for example, refused to endorse her candidacy, arguing that Chisholm had no chance of winning the nomination. In addition, the leadership of the civil rights movement and African American elected officials were hostile, patronizing, and unsupportive. According to Carolyn Smith, one of Chisholm's staffers, members of the Congressional Black Caucus (which Chisholm helped found) were most upset by Chisholm's candidacy. William Clay from Missouri asked sarcastically, "Who does she think she is, running for President of the United States? She needs to know where her place is." Smith said that Clay thought it was fine for Chisholm to be a legislator and represent her district. "In other words, tend to your business. It was okay for Jesse Jackson to run, and it's okay for the men to run—but a lady's place was either in the home, the schools, as a teacher." In language not that dissimilar to some of Bernie Sanders's supporters, one unnamed CBC member stated, "I would love to see a woman running for president, just not this one." Florida's Alcee Hastings (who was impeached as a judge in 1989) argued, "Chisholm would embarrass a lot of her own people." Jessie Jackson was so opposed to her candidacy that during the Illinois primary campaign he refused to let Chisholm speak at the Operation Push offices in Chicago. Julian Bond, a civil rights icon, used traditional sexist language to explain his lack of support: "I don't think her gender had anything to do with it as her style." Or as an unnamed CBC member told the *New York Times*, "she's a militant feminist and she rubs us the wrong way."[24]

Flo Kennedy provocatively summed up the misogyny and racism Chisholm faced throughout her entire political career. Some white feminists and African American men claimed they wanted to disrupt and overthrow the racist patriarchy, but when a chance to do so really appeared, they could not bring themselves to support Shirley Chisholm, the first African American and the first woman to run for the Democratic Party presidential nomination—the only candidate who was arguably their best representative. "The Chisholm candidacy not only freaked out the Establishment and the niggerizers," Kennedy acidly commented. "It also confused and unsettled the niggers—and by niggers, I don't mean just the black niggers, but also the student niggers, and the women niggers and the poor niggers—plus a whole lot of other people who thought they were revolutionaries but discovered they couldn't dig her wig."[25]

Chisholm ran in seventeen state primary elections; she won only the nonbinding New Jersey primary. She campaigned with little money, a disorganized but loyal staff, and enthusiastic supporters. She had to fight tooth and nail to get on television or in the newspapers. The tepid interest by the press, and lack of support from traditional Democratic Party and civil rights leaders, however, were nothing compared to the racial and gendered assault she faced—this time from the Republican Party. On the eve of the final primary campaign, in California, the FBI alerted Chisholm that she had been a victim of a smear campaign. This was doubtless part of Richard Nixon's "dirty tricks" campaign strategy. But what happened to Chisholm was more than a trick. It was an execrable attack that demonstrated the depths of Nixon's amoral corruption.

In early June, someone broke into one of Hubert Humphrey's campaign headquarters, stole letterhead stationery, and wrote an ungrammatical, poorly spelled press release claiming that Chisholm had been committed to a private home for the mentally ill, that she was a "transvestite," and that she was hostile and aggressive to the people she met. It said her physician had written that Chisholm "makes facial grimaces, talks and gesters [*sic*] to herself, exhibits inexplicable laughter and weeping, and at times has an abnormal interest in urine and feces which she smears on walls and herself." The letter concluded, "the voters of the nation should be aware of candidates [*sic*] full record and background so an intelligent and meaningful choice can be made. Black voters should be made aware of these facts as her strongest appeal is to them." According to later FBI investigations, this bogus press release was sent to a number of African American publications.[26]

Given the atrocious spelling and grammar, one can only assume that serious organizations and news outlets knew immediately that the charges were false and immediately alerted the FBI. An appalled Humphrey denied having anything to do with the press release, and the FBI subsequently absolved him of any involvement. Chisholm never mentioned this smear in Shola Lynch's documentary about Chisholm's presidential run, or in her own account of her presidential bid, *The Good Fight*, nor did filmmakers and writers who chronicled the 1972 Democratic primary.[27] Perhaps it was too hateful an incident for even Chisholm to acknowledge. Perhaps if she had acknowledged it, it would only have encouraged even more racial and gendered attacks on her. Nonetheless, this Nixonian smear presaged the venal and violent attacks and smears on Hillary Clinton forty-four years later. Trump made a series of wild accusations against Clinton, promised to jail her if he were elected president, and encouraged his supporters' wild conspiracy theories. One such fantasy, which connected Clinton to a child sex ring being run out of a pizzeria in Washington, DC, ended with a deluded conspiracy follower shooting up the pizza parlor.[28]

Chisholm went to the Democratic National Convention with 151 delegates. Once again, it was black men who disappointed her. Walter Fauntroy, the nonvoting representative from the District of Columbia, who had promised his votes to Chisholm, gave them to the white candidate, George McGovern. And in a heartbreaking betrayal, Representative Ron Dellums from California, who had promised to place her name in nomination, refused at the last minute. During the campaign, she had experienced endless disappointments, political and personal attacks, snubs, and racist and sexist behavior. But this rejection came from a colleague and friend. Percy Sutton, black activist and New York City businessperson, and Charles Evers, brother of Medgar Evers, put her nomination forward, and Chisholm became the first African American and the first woman to have her name placed in nomination for the Democratic Party presidential ticket. In retrospect, looking at how African American men had treated her, it becomes clear why Chisholm said repeatedly that she experienced more discrimination "as a woman than as a black."[29] She never fully recovered from her bitter disappointment; however, she remained in Congress, serving as a more conventional, albeit very liberal, legislator until 1982.

Chisholm was always aware of her historic first and the doors to racial and gender equality she wished to open. As an elected official and an activist, Chisholm constantly referred to the role of black women in the struggle for social justice. However, in subsequent elections, the press and pundits chose to ignore relevant stories about black women. In the 2008 primary, for example, the press chose to focus on the conflict between white women (Clinton/Elizabeth Cady Stanton) and black men (Obama/Douglass), ignoring black suffragists and Chisholm altogether.[30]

In the midst of her '72 campaign, Chisholm honored the legacy of African women's activism by taking time to lay a wreath on the grave of the abolitionist, feminist, and suffragist Sojourner Truth. While putting stickers on ancestors' graves shows respect for past struggles, it would be better if we followed in the footsteps of Chisholm and her supporters by working together to change the political system. In fact, if we knew more about Chisholm's campaign and also more about the histories of African American women as well as other marginalized people, we would learn about the importance of coalition building as the most positive way forward in the struggle for social justice. Chisholm always believed that black women (and I would argue that if she were alive today, she would amend her belief to women of color) must be front and center in order to address issues of class and gender. As long as historians and popular media ignore the history and activism of those most marginalized and as long as activists pit one group against another, we miss the opportunity to examine how ability, age, class, gender, race, nationality, and sexuality intersect. So that we never again experience an election like that of 2016, we need to build a multiracial, intergenerational, inclusive coalition of nasty people (women included) and bad hombres as a powerful tool for social change.

Notes

1. As Sean McElwee and Jason McDaniel reported, "Donald Trump successfully leveraged existing resentment towards African Americans in combination with emerging fears of increased racial diversity in America to reshape the presidential electorate, strongly attracting nativists towards Trump and pushing some more affluent and highly educated people with more cosmopolitan views to support Hillary Clinton. Racial identity and attitudes have further displaced class as the central battleground of American politics." McElwee and McDaniel, "Fear of Diversity Made People More Likely to Vote for Trump," *Nation*, March 14, 2017, https://www.thenation.com/article/fear-of-diversity-made-people-more-likely-to-vote-trump/.

2. For more on misogynistic and racist slogans and election paraphernalia such as bumper stickers and T-shirts, see Jane Caputi's chapter in this volume.

3. Of white women with college degrees, 51 percent voted for Clinton, less than anticipated, while 62 percent of white women without college degrees voted for Trump. Katie Rogers, "White Women Helped Elect

Donald Trump," *New York Times*, November 9, 2016, https://www.nytimes.com/2016/12/01/us/politics/white-women-helped-elect-donald-trump.html.

4. Barbara Winslow, *Shirley Chisholm: Catalyst for Change* (New York: Westview Press, 2013), 116.

5. See, for example, the Brooklyn College yearbook, *The Breuklundiar*, and Shirley Chisholm, *Unbought and Unbossed* (Washington, DC: Take Root Media, 2010), chap. 4.

6. Chisholm, *Unbought and Unbossed*, chaps. 5–6; Winslow, Shirley Chisholm, chap. 4.

7. Chisholm, *Unbought and Unbossed*, 69.

8. Sam Klug, "The Moynihan Report Resurrected," *Dissent*, Winter 2016, https://www.dissentmagazine.org/article/moynihan-report-resurrected-daniel-geary-black-power.

9. Chisholm, *Unbought and Unbossed*, 77.

10. Ibid.

11. Winslow, *Shirley Chisholm*, 52.

12. Susan Brownmiller, "This Is Fighting Shirley Chisholm," *New York Times Magazine*, April 13, 1972, 34.

13. See Winslow, *Shirley Chisholm*, chap. 6.

14. Ibid., 64.

15. Chisholm, *Unbought and Unbossed*, 68.

16. Ibid., 83.

17. Ibid., 88.

18. John Kifner, "Farmer and Woman in Lively Bedford-Stuyvestant Race," *New York Times*, October 26, 1968, 22.

19. James Farmer, *Lay Bare the Heart: An Autobiography of the Civil Rights Movement* (New York: Arbor House, 1985), 314. For a full discussion of the 1968 primary and congressional elections, see Winslow, *Shirley Chisholm*, 56–70.

20. Chisholm, *Unbought and Unbossed*, 106.

21. Susan Brownmiller, *Shirley Chisholm: A Biography* (New York: Doubleday, 1970), 153; emphasis in original.

22. Sherie M. Randolph, *Florynce 'Flo' Kennedy: The Life of a Feminist Radical* (Chapel Hill: University of North Carolina Press, 2016), 209.

23. Shirley Chisholm, *The Good Fight* (New York: Harper and Row, 1973); Winslow, *Shirley Chisholm*, chaps. 7–8; Rev. Al Sharpton, "Shirley Chisholm's Influence," YouTube.com, video, December 3, 2014, https://www.youtube.com/watch?v=2zlUA6r8Xo&list=UUZnCXaCEHJWdj_ADxF8rmUw&index=1.

24. Frank Kynn, "What Makes Shirley Run?," *New York Times*, January 30, 1972, 174; see also Winslow, *Shirley Chisholm*, 71–105.

25. Randolph, *Florynce 'Flo' Kennedy*, 202.

26. FBI File, Shirley Chisholm, no.453411-000, Shirley Chisholm Project, Brooklyn College Archives and Special Collections, Brooklyn College Library.

27. *Chisholm '72: Unbought and Unbossed,* directed by Shola Lynch (2004; New York, REALside Production), DVD.

28. Cecelia Kang and Adam Goldman, "In Washington Pizzeria Attack, Fake News Brought Real Guns," *New York Times,* December 5, 2016, https://www.nytimes.com/2016/12/05/business/media/comet-ping-pong-pizza-shooting-fake-news-consequences.html?_r=0.

29. Carol Moseley Braun, the first African American woman elected to the US Senate, in 1992, who also ran for president in the Democratic primaries in 2004, echoed Chisholm's reflections. See Carol Moseley Braun, "Epilogue: Gender and Race as Cultural Barriers to Black Women in Politics," in *Interconnections: Gender and Race in American History,* ed. Carol Faulkner and Alison Parker (Rochester, NY: University of Rochester Press, 2012), 260–66.

30. Mark Leibovich, "Rights vs. Rights: An Improbable Collision Course," *New York Times,* January 13, 2008, http://www.nytimes.com/2008/01/13/weekinreview/13leibovich.html. See also Michael J. Brown's chapter in this volume.

Chapter Seven

COMMEMORATION AND CONTESTATION

Susan B. Anthony, Frederick Douglass, Hillary Clinton, and Barack Obama

Michael J. Brown

Antislavery and women's rights icons Frederick Douglass and Susan B. Anthony are often paired in ways that blend representations of the past with inspirational approaches to the future. The two are linked in a progressive narrative that celebrates their tenacity, their courage, and, ultimately, how these fierce advocates for equality and justice "saw many of their dreams come true." These "friends for freedom," as the title of Suzanne Slade's 2014 children's book suggests, "helped America grow up." Similarly, Dean Robbins's 2016 *Two Friends: Susan B. Anthony and Frederick Douglass* presents the life experiences of the reformers as parallel, emphasizing their shared struggle for comparable goals. "The two of them bravely spoke out for each other's causes, making appearances together throughout their lives," Robbins writes. "They never stopped fighting, and they never doubted that victory would come." In the end, "Anthony and Douglass won their battles."[1]

The commemorative pairing of Anthony and Douglass as "friends for freedom" is highly visible in Rochester, New York—the city they shared in the mid-nineteenth century. The Frederick Douglass–Susan B. Anthony Memorial Bridge spans the Genesee River in the city's center. The University of Rochester's campus has buildings named for the two, as well as the Susan B. Anthony Institute for Gender, Sexuality, and Women's Studies and the Frederick Douglass Institute for African and African-American Studies. In the city's west, the National Susan B. Anthony Museum and House sits across Susan B. Anthony Square Park from the Frederick Douglass Resource Center. A sculpture depicting Douglass and Anthony conversing over tea occupies the center of the square. "It's a social statement," said Laotian American sculptor Pepsy M. Kettavong of his work. "A black man and a white woman are drinking tea together. A Laotian makes their sculpture. It could be a metaphor for American democracy."[2] And in Rochester's Mount Hope Cemetery, where the grave of Susan B. Anthony drew crowds on Election Day 2016, Frederick Douglass is also interred.

The commemorative pairing of Anthony and Douglass obscures the rupture within their relationship and their broader reform coalition over the Fifteenth Amendment to the US Constitution, which in 1870 granted African American men the right to vote in the wake of the Civil War. While Douglass supported the amendment, Anthony and other advocates for women's rights opposed it on the grounds that it enshrined a specifically male definition of suffrage. The "friends for freedom" were divided by a political culture that denied their fundamental civil rights and afforded precious few opportunities for progressive reform. In this culture of competitive liberal individualism, black men's and white women's political advancement appeared to be possible only sequentially but not concurrently—a view that pushed the intersectionality of race and gender for black women to the periphery.

Anthony, Douglass, and a contested rather than commemorative approach to the political achievements of American women and African Americans were rekindled by the 2008 Democratic primary, in which Hillary Clinton and Barack Obama vied for their party's presidential nomination. Commentators invoked the rupture between Anthony and Douglass to frame the contest between Clinton and Obama. The progressive narrative that either of them winning the nomination would mark a historic breakthrough sat uneasily alongside the fact that victory for one meant that breaking through for the other would have to wait—but how long?

What Wendell Phillips called "the Negro's hour"—in particular, ratification of the Fifteenth Amendment (1870)—came fifty years before the Nineteenth Amendment wrote national suffrage for American women into the Constitution (1920).[3] The wait for a woman president, however, seemed like it might follow quickly on the heels of the first African American president. With the support of Barack Obama, Hillary Clinton mounted what appeared on track to be a winning campaign for the presidency in 2016. On Election Day, thousands gathered at Anthony's grave to celebrate the shattering of "the highest, hardest glass ceiling." Celebration turned to something else as it became clear that the arrival of women's hour for the presidency, like the arrival of women's hour for national suffrage rights a century and a half earlier, would have to wait.

The story of Douglass and Anthony, like the 2016 election itself, challenges the notion that progress toward racial and gender equality in the United States is linear, steady, or inevitable. How might public memory in a place like Rochester—at the center of the commemorative Douglass-Anthony pairing—pivot to address an ambiguous, unresolved story about race, gender, and American politics?

The tensions between the commemorative, progressive pairing of Anthony and Douglass and the uneven political realities of their own lifetimes reflect the process by which history becomes memory. Historians have long observed that memory, both individual and cultural, is mediated and constructed. Memory, in turn, serves as a basis for identity—national, as well as personal. So imbricated are the two that historian John Gillis has suggested "that the notion of identity depends upon the idea of memory, and vice versa."[4]

In American memory, exceptionalist understandings of national identity are manifest in an emphasis on exceptional historical figures. While these heroes loom large in the historical imagination, the role of social movements and collective action is obscured. Such hero-centered memory is often at odds with historiographical understanding. Recent scholarship on the nineteenth-century women's movement, for example, has criticized the traditional focus on Anthony and Elizabeth Cady Stanton at the expense of a wider world of activists, including women of color.[5]

In addition to its focus on heroes, American memory emphasizes narratives that, when not entirely uplifting, at least offer an upward trajectory. "Americans see themselves as progressive people and therefore enshrine the artifacts of technological advancement," historian Diane F. Britton writes, "while they tear down vestiges of conflict and strife."[6] Such progressive modes of memory extend to social and political, as well as technological, history. In their critique of potent memory-maker Ken Burns's film *Not for Ourselves Alone: The Story of Elizabeth Cady Stanton and Susan B. Anthony* (1999), Vivien Ellen Rose and Julie Corley point to the ways in which Burns downplays the complex, uncomfortable features of the suffrage movement, which are crucial for understanding the division between advocates of woman and black suffrage. Instead, Burns "simply retrac[es] the well-trodden triumphal march to the passage of the Nineteenth Amendment after their deaths."[7] Such stories of triumphal marches include struggle and sacrifice, but they do not make room for contingency—the real possibility that the march could have (or may have) concluded in something other than a complete triumph.

7.1. Timihya Flowers sets the table with crocheted treats for Susan B. Anthony and Frederick Douglass in Rochester, NY, before the Suffragist City Parade, July 22, 2017. Photo: Max Schulte. From Rochester *Democrat and Chronicle*, October 15, 2017. © 2017 Gannett-Community Publishing. All rights reserved. Used by permission and protected by the copyright laws of the United States. The printing, copying, redistribution, or retransmission of this content without express written permission is prohibited.

Burns is far from the only maker of memory concerning Anthony, Stanton, and the reform coalition to which they belonged. Indeed, Anthony and Douglass were powerful makers of memory themselves. Douglass produced four versions of his autobiography between 1845 and 1892.[8] Anthony was the only person to edit all of the first four volumes of the *History of Woman Suffrage*. Anthony's attic became, by the later years of her life, an "unrivaled" archive of US women's rights history—major parts of which she ultimately consigned to the flames.[9] Through authorship, editorship, and the control of archives, Anthony and Douglass sought to fashion their own narratives. In doing so, they engaged in "the politics of memory."[10]

In post–Civil War political culture, memory was both a contested field and a strategically valuable one. Anthony, Stanton, and other suffragists knew that "to enter politics in this era was to enter a conversation about memory." Thus, historian Lisa Tetrault writes, "women entered the memory wars by telling their own version of history." The result, she argues, was "the myth of Seneca Falls"—an origin story that emphasized the 1848 women's rights meeting in Seneca Falls as the birth of the women's movement in the United States.[11] The Seneca Falls story subordinated the broad social and economic agenda of the famous Declaration of Sentiments to one overriding sentiment: that women should have the ballot, a "right . . . by which all others could be secured."[12] This mode of remembering Seneca Falls highlighted the role of Stanton, though "Anthony also entered the story, even though she had not been present at the creation associated with 1848."[13]

Unlike Anthony, Douglass had been "present at the creation" in 1848. He would play a vital role in the central drama of the convention narrative, speaking decisively on behalf of Stanton's most controversial resolution, the one calling for woman suffrage.[14] As the events of Seneca Falls gave way to the memory of Seneca Falls, with Anthony looming larger and larger in that memory, Douglass's intervention on behalf of women's suffrage linked these "friends for freedom" at the very heart of the movement's story.

As new generations of women joined the women's rights movement after the Civil War, the account of that movement's history generated by Anthony and Stanton placed their own efforts at the center of the struggle, drawing a line from Seneca Falls in 1848 through the establishment of the National Woman Suffrage Association in 1869 to Anthony's arrest for voting in Rochester in 1872. That line would continue on, ultimately, to the passage of the "Anthony Amendment"—as the Nineteenth Amendment was sometimes called. This account thus traced the arc of an "independent women's movement" from 1848 to 1920.[15] As an "origin myth," this story of Seneca Falls served "to legitimate and unify the messy contingencies of political struggle." It "promotes the forgetting of struggles within the struggle, the debates and rivalries within the movement itself."[16] Of the struggles, debates, and rivalries that the myth obscured, none was more difficult to reckon with than the division over the Fifteenth Amendment, which split the women's movement in two.

In 1869 the coalition of reformers seeking equality and justice for both African Americans and American women became badly fractured. Though this broad alliance antedated the Civil War, it took on a new organizational form with the establishment of the American Equal Rights Association (AERA) in 1866. The immediate postwar years were a malleable moment, a time during which the United States might be reshaped. "Reconstruction" is an apt label for the period. The emancipation of enslaved people raised the question of political rights: would freedpeople be merely nonslaves, or would they become citizens? The uncertain status of freedpeople, not to mention that of the former Confederate states, brought the boundaries of the national political community to the forefront of debate. Citizenship was linked to the right of suffrage, and as Americans adjudicated the character of the former, they understood its implications for exercising the latter. The Fourteenth Amendment thus came as a disappointment to members of the reform coalition for a variety of reasons. It established the citizenship of the freedmen without guaranteeing their right to vote, and it brought the word "male" into the Constitution as a descriptor of enfranchised citizens, establishing penalties "when the right to vote . . . is denied to any of the male inhabitants of [a] State, being twenty-one years of age, and citizens of the United States, or in any way abridged, except for participation in rebellion, or other crime."[17] The drafting of the amendment in early 1866 and its passage by Congress later that year (it would not be ratified by the states until 1868) were overseen by Republicans, who wielded most of the political power in Washington. Though reformers found much to criticize in the amendment, they continued to see the Republican Party as the best vehicle—if not the ideal one—for their aims.[18]

Republicans recognized that, in addition to principled arguments on its behalf, an additional amendment explicitly guaranteeing African American male suffrage would bring a substantial population of new voters onto their party's rolls. Abolitionist leaders had already signaled their support for such a measure, in spite of its marginalization of women, both white and black. At the head of the American Anti-Slavery Society, Wendell Phillips had proclaimed: "One question at a time. This hour belongs to the negro."[19] In the interval between the ratification of the Fourteenth Amendment and the shaping of the Fifteenth, however, it looked possible to press for "universal suffrage" under the banner of the AERA at the state level.[20]

Anthony, Stanton, and other activists traveled to Kansas in 1867, where separate referenda on black and women's suffrage were on the November ballot. After an acrimonious campaign, both propositions failed. Anthony and other women working in Kansas noted the lukewarm support they had received from some Republicans and the outright hostility directed at them by others. They saw, too, that eastern abolitionist leadership had failed to support them until it was too late—offering meager financial support for campaigners and only providing newspaper editorials on behalf of the referenda at the end of the campaign.[21] When Anthony and Stanton returned east, they came with George Francis Train, a wealthy Democrat who offered to underwrite their publication of a newspaper, the *Revolution* (1868–72). A "flamboyant racist" whose "attacks on the intelligence and integrity of black people were basic to his political arsenal," Train raised the ire of AERA members who questioned how Anthony and Stanton could ally with him.[22]

The advent of the Fifteenth Amendment exacerbated these tensions. In opposing the amendment, Anthony and Stanton's *Revolution* employed racist rhetoric.[23] Stanton claimed that those in Congress who supported the amendment would "degrade their own mothers, wives, and daughters, in their political status, below unwashed and unlettered ditch-diggers, bootblacks, hostlers, butchers, and barbers." That "Patrick and Sambo and Hans and Yung Tung" would elect lawmakers to govern cultivated women outraged her. At the Illinois Woman Suffrage Association in 1869, Anthony introduced a resolution that "the Republican cry of 'manhood suffrage' creates an antagonism between the black man and all women, and will culminate in fearful outrages on womanhood, especially in the Southern States."[24]

The stage was set for the May 1869 AERA meeting, at which Anthony and Douglass clashed on the platform. Douglass said that when a woman "is shot down by the Kuklux, or hung to a lamp-post at every turn, simply for being a woman, then he was willing to admit that there would be something like an equality of urgency between her and the negro in the matter of having extended to them the right of suffrage." Anthony replied, "When Mr. Douglass tells us that the case of the black man is so perilous, I tell him that wronged and outraged as they are by this hateful and mean prejudice against color, he would not today exchange his sex and color, wronged as he is, with Elizabeth Cady Stanton." She had earlier argued that if "the whole loaf of justice" was not to be provided at once but rather given "piece by piece, then give it first to women, to the most intelligent and capable portion of the women at least, because in the present state of government it is intelligence, it is morality which is needed." The conversation had turned, Anthony lamented at the outset, from the advocacy of equal rights for all to the question of whose situation—that of women or black men—was more dire and deserving.[25]

Three days after her exchange with Douglass, Anthony led the founding of the National Woman Suffrage Association (NWSA), which was dedicated to pursuing woman suffrage through a federal constitutional amendment, opposed to the Fifteenth Amendment, and interested in an array of women's rights issues. While the Fifteenth Amendment prohibited the restriction of voting "on account of race, color, or previous condition of servitude," NWSA appealed for an amendment that would "prohibit the several States from disfranchising any of their citizens on account of Sex."[26] Six months after NWSA's formation, AERA members who supported the Fifteenth Amendment created the American Woman Suffrage Association (AWSA). The reform movement was sundered.

Subsequent events, however, would allow this painful moment to be remembered as "a severe bump in the road" rather than a fork in it.[27] NWSA and AWSA joined to form the National American Woman Suffrage Association (NAWSA) in 1890, and this new organization would—though not without significant splintering of its own—see passage of the Nineteenth Amendment. Neither Anthony nor Douglass would live to see that achievement. On the day of his death in 1895, Douglass had been accompanied to the platform at the National Council of Women's meeting in Washington, DC, by Anthony.[28] These "friends for freedom" had, it seemed, been united in the end, their now-past dispute an aberrant moment in their relationship and a bump on the long road of reform that was, ultimately, the path of progress.

And yet, the same year Anthony escorted Douglass at the National Council of Women in Washington, she had told him not to attend the NAWSA meeting in Atlanta for fear that his presence would alienate potential white southern allies.[29] By that time, African American men were no longer able to exercise their Fifteenth Amendment rights in the South. The great achievement of the ballot had been rolled back by physical intimidation, poll taxes, grandfather clauses, and a host of other disfranchisement measures. The path of progress was not assured.

The history of Anthony and Douglass points to a contested past, one that may disrupt commemorations of these two figures and their struggles for justice. The 2008 Democratic primary contest between Barack Obama and Hillary Clinton was a moment when that disruptive potential surfaced. Writing in January of that year, journalist Mark Leibovich observed that either candidate's win would mark a "breakthrough," but that such "politics can be a zero-sum game, with distinct groups striving for a finite piece of the change pie. It brings to mind that the civil rights movement and the women's movement have a long, complicated history dating back to abolitionism and the origins of modern feminism." By May, historian Debby Applegate, writing in the *New York Times*, noted that with Obama on the verge of securing the nomination, the "historical analogy" between the primary contest and the rupture over the Fifteenth Amendment "is being used to support a variety of points: that in the 'oppression sweepstakes' women always 'lose' to blacks, that when thwarted in their ambitions, white women will resort to angry racism, that liberal coalitions are mere screens for self-interested identity politics that fracture whenever real power is at stake." Early scholarship on the campaign affirmed the journalistic impressions formed while it was under way. "Though Senator Clinton has had a long history of working on behalf of women and all racial groups," sociologists Adia Harvey Wingfield and Joe Feagin wrote, "when it came down to gaining access to power, she chose to emphasize her whiteness as an ascendant feature and a characteristic that supposedly made her more deserving of the political rewards she sought—just like the white women abolitionists of the 19th century."[30] After losses in the North Carolina and Indiana primaries, Clinton attempted to diminish the results by citing polls indicating that "Obama's support among working, hard-working Americans, white Americans, is weakening again, and how whites in both states who had not completed college were supporting me."[31] Clinton touted her electability in relation to the "hard-working" vote, which she conflated with white voters.

When President-Elect Obama chose Hillary Clinton as secretary of state, commentators reached for another analogy from the 1860s: Abraham Lincoln's cabinet as—in the words of Doris Kearns Goodwin's popular 2005 book—a "team of rivals."[32] Like Douglass and Anthony, Obama and Clinton had, with the season of rivalry ended, reunited on behalf of shared aims. When Clinton announced her candidacy to succeed Obama as president, she quickly became the front-runner for the Democratic nomination, which she ultimately secured—the first woman to become the nominee of a major party. With predictive models giving Clinton better than a 70 percent chance to win as late as the day of the general election, she looked poised to succeed the first African American president as the first woman president.[33]

When the electoral votes were tabulated, Americans across the political spectrum were shocked, and many Clinton supporters appalled, that Donald Trump—whose campaign featured misogynist attacks on Clinton and Republican candidate Carly Fiorina, among others, and who had boasted about grabbing women by their genitals—had been elected president. Instead of consummating the journey toward justice that Anthony, Douglass, and others walked, Election Day 2016 told another story about American history—one of long and uncertain struggles continued, rather than progressive ends achieved.

Public memory and historical narratives that elide such complexities may leave people not only uninformed about the past but also unprepared for the contingencies of the present. Just as the schism over the Fifteenth Amendment disrupts memory of Anthony and Douglass as "friends for freedom," so the outcome of the 2016 presidential election disrupts the narrative of an American project organized around the progressive, inexorable achievement—spurred on by leaders of courage and conscience—of racial and gender equality, modes of justice that make good on the essential American story rather than marking radical departures from it.

Historian David Roediger has observed "how remembering the past reflects a sometimes enervating desire for solidarity to be easy." He points to the Kettavong sculpture in Rochester, which "implies an ease in solidarity that the lives of Douglass and Anthony both exemplify and contradict." American historians and political actors alike have sought to construct "usable" pasts—sometimes entering the politics of memory to mobilize, salvage, or control social movements. Anthony and Douglass worked to fashion such usable pasts themselves, versions of history that both smoothed rough edges and served to inspire. And yet, Roediger writes, understanding "the power of those pressures working against solidarity is also a usable part of remembering the past." Such accounts of the past may be more uncomfortable than they are reassuring, but "the desire for reassurances that social motion is proceeding in our favor can lead in practice to immobilization, especially when defeats accumulate and hollow victories are extolled."[34] Despite their importance, complex, uncomfortable histories are rare in places of public memory, like Rochester's Mount Hope Cemetery, where Anthony, Douglass, and, after dark on November 8, 2016, Hillary Clinton's candidacy for the presidency of the United States, were laid to rest.

Notes

1. Suzanne Slade, *Friends for Freedom: The Story of Susan B. Anthony and Frederick Douglass*, illustrated by Nicole Tadgell (Watertown, MA: Charlesbridge, 2014), front matter, 33; Dean Robbins, *Two Friends: Susan B. Anthony and Frederick Douglass*, illustrated by Sean Qualls and Selina Alko (New York: Orchard Books, 2016), authors' note, back matter. Leigh Fought has recently challenged the notion that Douglass and Anthony were friends at all: "Theirs was hardly the 'lifelong friendship' that Anthony described after Douglass had died. While he supported her cause and they found one another useful political allies, they had little fondness for one another." Fought writes that the Anthony-Douglass friendship is largely the construction of "popular history, aided by *The History of Woman Suffrage*," which was compiled by Anthony, Elizabeth Cady Stanton, and Matilda Joslyn Gage. Fought, *Women in the World of Frederick Douglass* (New York: Oxford University Press, 2017), 201, 168, fig. 6.2.

2. Rochester Institute of Technology, "Tea Time for Two," Success Stories (from *University Magazine*, Spring 2002), https://www.rit.edu/success.php?s=24.

3. Phillips's phrase comes from his keynote address to the American Anti-Slavery Society. "Thirty-Second Anniversary of the American Anti-Slavery Society," *National Anti-Slavery Standard,* May 20, 1865.

4. John R. Gillis, "Introduction: Memory and Identity: The History of a Relationship," in *Commemorations: The Politics of National Identity,* ed. John R. Gillis (Princeton, NJ: Princeton University Press, 1994), 3. See also David Thelen, "Introduction: Memory and American History," in *Memory and American History,* ed. David Thelen (Bloomington: Indiana University Press, 1990).

5. Diane F. Britton, "Public History and Public Memory," *Public Historian* 19 (Summer 1997). Faye Dudden has argued that Anthony and Stanton "cannot be replaced by a broader cast of grassroots feminists . . . because they *were* so widely influential" (emphasis in original). Dudden, *Fighting Chance: The Struggle over Woman Suffrage and Black Suffrage in Reconstruction America* (New York: Oxford University Press, 2011), 12. Other scholars, however, have offered accounts of the women's movement that decenter Anthony and Stanton. They point to a movement that spanned activists in the Midwest and West, that included African American women, that comprised an array of activist intellectuals, and that operated largely independent of central coordination. Alison M. Parker, *Articulating Rights: Nineteenth-Century American Women on Race, Reform, and the State* (De Kalb: Northern Illinois University Press, 2010); Stacey M. Robertson, *Hearts Beating for Liberty: Women Abolitionists in the Old Northwest* (Chapel Hill: University of North Carolina Press, 2010); Martha Jones, *All Bound Up Together: The Woman Question in African American Public Culture, 1830–1900* (Chapel Hill: University of North Carolina Press, 2007); Julie Roy Jeffrey, *The Great Silent Army of Abolitionism: Ordinary Women in the Antislavery Movement* (Chapel Hill: University of North Carolina Press, 1998).

6. Britton, "Public History and Public Memory," 16.

7. Vivien Ellen Rose and Julie Corley, "A Trademark Approach to the Past: Ken Burns, the Historical Profession, and Assessing Popular Presentations of the Past," *Public Historian* 25, no. 3 (Summer 2003): 55.

8. *Narrative of the Life of Frederick Douglass, an American Slave* (1845), *My Bondage and My Freedom* (1855); *Life and Times of Frederick Douglass* (1881, revised 1892).

9. Lisa Tetrault, *The Myth of Seneca Falls: Memory and the Women's Suffrage Movement, 1848–1898* (Chapel Hill: University of North Carolina Press, 2014), 141–44, 178, 181.

10. The literature on "the politics of memory" is extensive—interdisciplinary and international. For a recent appraisal of the field, see Nicole Maurantonio, "The Politics of Memory," in *The Oxford Handbook of Political Communication,* ed. Kate Kenski and Kathleen Hall Jamieson (Oxford University Press, published online July 2014), https://doi.org/10.1093/oxfordhb/9780199793471.013.026.

11. Tetrault points to a variety of other possible "origin" points for an American women's rights—if not specifically a suffrage—movement, going back to the Grimké sisters' work in the 1830s. Lori D. Ginzberg has shown that women in northern New York State submitted a suffrage petition to the New York state constitutional convention in the summer of 1846. Ginzburg argues that such petitions make clear that women undertook "both private conversations and public appeals for women's political rights years earlier" than the traditional emphasis on Seneca Falls suggests. Lori D. Ginzberg, *Untidy Origins: A Story of Women's Rights in Antebellum New York* (Chapel Hill: University of North Carolina Press, 2005), 7. Other works that reexamine the origins of the antebellum women's movement include Nancy Isenberg, *Sex and Citizenship in Antebellum America* (Chapel Hill: University of North Carolina Press, 1998); Bonnie S. Anderson, *Joyous Greetings: The First International Women's Movement, 1830–1860* (New York: Oxford University Press, 2000); Katherine Kish Sklar, "Women's Rights Emerges within the Anti-slavery Movement: Angelina and Sarah Grimké in 1837," in vol. 1 of *Women and Power in American History: A Reader*, 2nd ed., ed. Thomas Dublin and Katherine Kish Sklar (Englewood Cliffs, NJ: Prentice Hall, 2002); Susan Zaeske, *Signatures of Citizenship: Petitioning, Antislavery, and Women's Political Identity* (Chapel Hill: University of North Carolina Press, 2003); and Rosalyn Terborg-Penn, "African American Women and the Vote: An Overview"; Willi Colman, "Architects of a Vision: Black Women and Their Antebellum Quest for Political and Social Equality"; and Bettye Collier-Thomas, "Frances Ellen Watkins Harper, Abolitionist and Feminist Reformer, 1825–1911"; in *African-American Women and the Vote, 1837–1865*, ed. Ann D. Gordon and Bettye Collier-Thomas (Amherst: University of Massachusetts Press, 1997).

12. Susan B. Anthony, "Woman's Rights," *Johnson's New Universal Cyclopaedia*, quoted in Tetrault, Myth of Seneca Falls, 110.

13. Tetrault, *Myth of Seneca Falls*, 8, 2, 174, 184–86.

14. Lori D. Ginzberg, *Elizabeth Cady Stanton: An American Life* (New York: Hill and Wang, 2009), 59.

15. Historians, as well as Anthony and Stanton themselves, have subscribed to portions of this narrative. Ellen Carol Du Bois's seminal *Feminism and Suffrage: The Emergence of an Independent Women's Movement in America, 1848–1869* (Ithaca, NY: Cornell University Press, 1978) emphasized the radicalism of the women's movement—its breadth of concerns beyond suffrage—and the importance of the rise of a movement led by women and dedicated specifically to women's rights, with Seneca Falls and the formation of the National Woman Suffrage Association as the crucial moments in its story.

16. Tetrault, *Myth of Seneca Falls*, 4.

17. United States Constitution, Amendment XIV, section 2.

18. Du Bois, *Feminism and Suffrage*, 53–78; Dudden, *Fighting Chance*, 61–107; Laura E. Free, *Suffrage Reconstructed: Gender, Race, and Voting Rights in the Civil War Era* (Ithaca, NY: Cornell University Press, 2015), 104–39.

19. Phillips, "Thirty-Second Anniversary."

20. Du Bois, *Feminism and Suffrage*, 64–66; Free, *Suffrage Reconstructed*, 133–39.

21. Both Du Bois and Dudden characterize the Kansas campaign as a moment when, frustrated by their erstwhile allies in the Republican Party and the antislavery cause, Anthony and Stanton began looking for new potential alliances (e.g., with Democrats) and a means of organizing, as Du Bois puts it, "a politically autonomous woman suffrage movement." Dudden emphasizes the extent to which Wendell Phillips's control over the Jackson and Hovey funds—two bequests on behalf of reform—deprived Anthony and Stanton of the resources necessary to conduct their work in Kansas, where, they believed, unlike Phillips, "that they actually had a 'fighting chance' to win woman suffrage." Anthony and Stanton's alliance with Train took shape under these circumstances and, Dudden argues, "historians have not realized how a hidden conflict about money exacerbated their slide into overt racism." Du Bois, *Feminism and Suffrage*, 81; Dudden, *Fighting Chance*, 10. On the lack of financial and editorial support for the Kansas campaign, see Dudden, 120, 126.

22. Du Bois, *Feminism and Suffrage*, 93.

23. Scholars have critically assessed both the whiteness and the racism of feminism in this period. Rosalyn Terborg-Penn, "Discrimination against Afro-American Women in the Woman's Movement, 1830–1920," in *The Afro-American Woman*, ed. Sharon Harley and Rosalyn Terborg-Penn (Port Washington, NY: Kennikat, 1978), 17–27; Angela Davis, *Women, Race, and Class* (New York: Random House, 1981), 70–86; bell hooks, *Ain't I a Woman: Black Women and Feminism* (Boston: South End Press, 1981); Paula J. Giddings, *When and Where I Enter: The Impact of Black Women on Race and Sex in America* (New York: Morrow, 1984); Bettina Aptheker, "Abolitionism, Women's Rights, and the Battle over the Fifteenth Amendment," in *Women's Legacy: Essays on Race, Sex, and Class in American History* (Amherst: University of Massachusetts Press, 1982); Louise Michele Newman, *White Women's Rights: The Racial Origins of Feminism in the United States* (New York: Oxford University Press, 1999).

24. Elizabeth Cady Stanton, "Manhood Suffrage," *Revolution*, December 24, 1868; and "Meeting of the Illinois Woman Suffrage Association in Chicago," February 12, 1869; both in *Against an Aristocracy of Sex*, vol. 2 of *The Selected Papers of Elizabeth Cady Stanton and Susan B. Anthony*, ed. Ann D. Gordon (New Brunswick, NJ: Rutgers University Press, 2000), 196, 215. Dudden has recently argued with respect to Anthony and Stanton's racist rhetoric that "political opportunism . . . drove them onward: had they not believed they had a fighting chance, they would not have reached so far or stooped so low." Dudden, *Fighting Chance*, 10. Laura Free argues that

"partisan politics, and the linguistic culture it created, constrained both the political choices and the political rhetoric of the postwar moment, making partisan racist speech seem like a viable strategic choice to these two activists." Free, *Suffrage Reconstructed*, 7.

25. "Equal Rights," *New York Times* (1857–1922), May 13, 1869, accessed April 9, 2017, http://search.proquest.com.ezproxy.rit.edu/docview/92514780?accountid=108; "Remarks by SBA to the American Equal Rights Association in New York," May 12, 1869, in *Against an Aristocracy of Sex*, 238–40.

26. United States Constitution, Amendment XV, section 1; Elizabeth Cady Stanton, Matilda Joslyn Gage, and Susan B. Anthony, "Appeal for a Sixteenth Amendment," from the National Woman Suffrage Association, November 10, 1876, National Archives Record Group 233: Records of the US House of Representatives, 1789–2015, https://catalog.archives.gov/id/306647.

27. Ruth Rosenberg-Naparsteck, speaking in the film *Let's Have Tea: A Sculpture of Conversation*, produced by Novat Corp. and Silver and Ink Media, directed by Matt Cottom, 2006.

28. Jay S. Walker, "Frederick Douglass and Woman Suffrage," *Black Scholar* 14 (1983): 18.

29. Tetrault, *Myth of Seneca Falls*, 179.

30. Mark Leibovich, "Rights vs. Rights: An Improbable Collision Course," *New York Times*, January 13, 2008, http://www.nytimes.com/2008/01/13/weekinreview; Debby Applegate, "Two Can Make History," *New York Times*, May 25, 2008, http://www.nytimes.com/2008/05/25/opinion/25applegate.html; Adia Harvey Wingfield and Joe R. Feagin, *Yes We Can? White Racial Framing and the Obama Presidency*, 2nd ed. (New York: Routledge, 2013), 67–68.

31. Kathy Kiely and Jill Lawrence, "Clinton Makes Case for Wide Appeal," *USA Today*, May 27, 2008, http://usatoday30.usatoday.com/news/politics/election2008/2008-05-07-clintoninterview_N.htm.

32. "Assessing Obama's Team of Rivals," *All Things Considered*, NPR, June 10, 2012, http://www.npr.org/2012/06/10/154710832/assessing-obamas-team-of-rivals; Doris Kearns Goodwin, *Team of Rivals: The Political Genius of Abraham Lincoln* (New York: Simon & Schuster, 2005).

33. "Who Will Win the Presidency?," FiveThirtyEight.com, November 8, 2016, https://projects.fivethirtyeight.com/2016-election-forecast/.

34. David Roediger, "Making Solidarity Uneasy: Cautions on a Keyword from Black Lives Matter to the Past," *American Quarterly* 68, no. 2 (June 2016): 240, 244–45.

Chapter Eight

DRESSING UP FOR A CAMPAIGN

Hillary Clinton, Suffragists, and the Politics of Fashion

Einav Rabinovitch-Fox

Among the topics that drew the most attention at the Democratic National Convention in Philadelphia in July 2016 was the outfit Hillary Clinton wore to her acceptance speech. Dressed in an all-white pantsuit and a crewneck white shirt underneath, nude kitten heels, adorned with a golden pendant necklace and earrings, Clinton's appearance did not only convey a presidential demure but was also—as many in the media were quick to acknowledge—filled with symbolism regarding women's long struggle for equal rights and a fair share in politics. Designed by Ralph Lauren, one of Clinton's favorite designers, the white suit served both as a reference to the outfit Geraldine Ferraro (the first female major-party vice presidential candidate) wore to her acceptance speech in 1984, and perhaps more importantly, to the outfits worn by suffragists in the early twentieth century.[1]

Capitalizing on what has become her signature silhouette, Clinton used the white pantsuit as an effective means to promote her political message, situating herself as the successor of the suffrage cause and as the new model of the female politician. Her appearance, which conveyed both strength and femininity, unity and pride, served to amplify the agenda she set in her speech. Commenting that "standing here as my mother's daughter, and my daughter's mother, I'm so happy this day has come," Clinton framed her nomination not only as a personal achievement, but as a feminist one, situating herself as part of a matriarchal lineage of strong women. "Let's keep going, until every one of the 161 million women and girls across America has the opportunity she deserves," Clinton called from the convention stage, "because even more important than the history we make tonight, is the history we will write together in the years ahead."[2]

And history indeed played an important role for Clinton in her effort to rally supporters. While Clinton's convention speech was very much geared toward the future, her appearance was an important acknowledgment of the past, and of the crucial role women played in enabling her to reach this achievement. Yet, Clinton's use of fashion at the DNC and throughout the 2016 presidential campaign was more than a simple honorary nod toward suffragists who fought for their right to vote. Like the suffragists, Clinton understood the power of clothing in conveying political messages and the usefulness of fashion to political campaigns. And like the suffragists, she also proved her willingness to leverage her femininity and appearance, harnessing them to advance her political goals.

The association of fashion and politics, especially when it comes to female politicians, is fraught with tensions and complexities. Many have argued that the scrutiny and criticism female politicians receive on their fashion choices is a testament to the prevailing sexism that still defines much of our political system. Women are being judged on their appearance much more than men, who can basically get away with almost anything regarding their looks: age, sloppiness, weight, even bad hair. Moreover, critics claim, focusing on women's clothing instead of their actions and record belittles them and perpetuates the misogynic notion that women cannot play significant roles in politics. Relegated to an impossible position of "damned if you do, damned if you don't," women need to negotiate a fine line with their appearance to be taken seriously as politicians.[3] However, as the examples of Clinton and the suffragists show, fashion can also be used as a powerful means to convey ideas and to construct images. Both suffragists in the early twentieth century and Clinton in her 2016 presidential campaign used attire in creative ways to promote their agendas, infusing fashion with political meaning and turning it into a useful element in their campaigns. They used fashion to garner public support for their claims, as well as a feminist tool of pleasure and self-assertion. Suffragists emphasized their femininity through the adoption of fashionable attire as a way of refuting derogatory images that portrayed them as masculine and unattractive. Through careful attention to appearance, they presented their respectability as women and their worthiness as voters.[4] Clinton, although sticking to her famous pantsuits, also used appearance to emphasize her feminine traits, by softening her look through hairstyle and makeup and creating a gentler image to draw voters.[5]

Instead of treating fashion as a frivolous matter, seeing it only as an oppressive tool to curb women's influence in the public sphere, this essay reconsiders the political meaning of fashion statements and their role in political campaigns. By examining both the symbolic meaning of clothes, seeing them as a form of communication, and clothes as material objects, it argues that fashion offers women new ways to experience the public sphere and to use it in their favor. Recently scholars have examined the feminist uses and applications of fashion, understanding it as a critical site of political expression.[6] Expanding on these studies, this essay examines the politics of fashion as they manifested in both the women's suffrage and the 2016 election campaigns, pointing to the long trajectory of women's use of clothing to convey their political message and to advance their agendas, thus reclaiming fashion as a feminist means of resistance.

From its early stages in the 1850s, the political use of clothing was part of the feminist struggle for women's rights and equality.[7] Yet, by the 1910s, with the rise of mass consumption and the growing dissemination of visual images through opulent department stores displays, periodicals, and advertising, a new understanding of the connection between clothing and women's rights emerged.[8] As a New York suffragist informed a *New-York Tribune* reporter in 1911, "the latest move [in the women's suffrage campaign] concerns the clothes question. It is a personal affair with most of us, but it is frequently hinted by the big leaders that the dress question is perhaps the most vital of all." Since the most pressing issue of the campaign was to gain public support by drawing positive attention to the suffrage cause, it was decided that "the Suffragette . . . hereafter is to be the leading exponent of fashion. . . . [E]ach and every one will dress as she never has before. It's all been planned and agreed to, signed and sealed."[9] This new attention to women's appearance and the insistence that suffragists can be and are fashionable women marked a change in the campaigning strategy. After a decade of facing serious impediments to the broadening of the franchise, suffragists in the 1910s began utilizing all kinds of theatrical and spectacular tactics—from outdoor gatherings, to colorful parades, to theatrical pageantry and picketing—that pushed the issue of women's rights to the forefront of popular imagination and debate.[10] Clothing choices in particular were central to these efforts, offering suffragists new ways to shape their public image.

As they marched and gave speeches, suffragists emphasized the importance of cultivating a feminine, appealing, and less threatening public appearance through fashion.[11] According to Anna Shaw, a leader of the National American Woman Suffrage Association (NAWSA), this meant avoiding every attribute that did not conform to

traditional notions of how a woman should look and behave.[12] Only in
this way, Shaw believed, suffragists could avoid being identified as masculine, dowdy, and unattractive, an accusation women faced as they
began to demand equality with men, and which proved to be a serious obstacle for gaining suffrage.[13] In emphasizing their femininity by
appearing dignified, attractive, and stylish, suffragists implied that they
were likable and virtuous women, thus undermining the association of
political participation with a threat to gender hierarchies.[14] As suffragist Lydia Commander declared, women were "determined to take an
active part in the community and look pretty too."[15]

The cultivation of an appealing image was done through the
adoption of fashionable silhouettes and styles. By 1908, the year in
which suffrage parades began, new trends in women's fashions that
reduced the number and weight of undergarments created a narrower
silhouette that accentuated a woman's curves on the one hand, yet
provided more comfort and physical mobility on the other (see fig.
8.1).[16] Suffragists readily embraced these new fashions. In addition
to the benefits of greater comfort and health that the styles provided,
the circumference of the dress—which was not too wide and not too
narrow—together with the ankle-length hemline, made marching in
city streets more convenient and more feasible, thus turning parades
and other theatrical spectacles into a popular publicity tactic. As mainstream fashions became more and more suitable to women's active
lifestyles, suffragists could easily use them in their assertion of their
political presence in the public sphere. "Marching costumes," consisting of tight trousers underneath a mid-calf-length skirt with a deep slit,
enabled suffragists to march comfortably, even a few miles, without
being worried of the dress getting dirty, wet, or becoming a health haz-
ard (see fig. 8.2).[17]

Clothing silhouettes and designs were not the only elements that
made marching an effective tactic. Color, and particularly the suffrage
colors—white, purple, and yellow/gold[18]—proved to be a central
technique through which suffragists conveyed their ideas visually.[19] As
Glenna Tinnin, one of the organizers of the 1913 Washington, DC,
suffrage parade, explained, "An idea that is driven home to the mind
through the eye produces a more striking and lasting impression
than any that goes through the ear."[20] The 1913 parade plan speci-
fied the order of the marchers, divided by professions, countries, and
states, and the color of their dresses, hats, and banners. Social workers were supposed to wear dark blue, writers wore white and purple,
and artists wore pale rose. The overall picture created a compelling
and organized sight of color and harmony.[21] But the use of colors had
an additional effect. Marching in their costumes and with handmade

8.1. B. Altman Catalog, 1908. The new fashions that became popular in 1908 were narrower and lighter than previous trends and enabled greater mobility and freedom to the women who wore them. The Winterthur Library, Printed Book and Periodical Collection. Used with permission.

8.2. Marching costume for Chicago's Suffrage Parade, 1916. This marching costume, with its skirt with a deep slit and trousers underneath, enabled suffragists to march comfortably while maintaining their modesty. Library of Congress Prints and Photographs Division.

8.3. New York Suffrage Parade, 1915. Suffragists' emphasis on color, form, and spectacle asserted a new female presence in the public sphere that helped to gain support for suffrage. Library of Congress Prints and Photographs Division.

banners, emphasizing color and arrangement, as well as the portrayal of their womanly talents of embroidery and fashion, suffragists asserted their political presence in what was considered to be a male territory, thus transforming the urban landscape as a site of visual politics. A photograph of a 1915 parade exemplifies this idea, showing suffragists marching in formation, their bright clothing contrasting sharply with the sidewalk crowds of men in dark-colored suits (see fig. 8.3). This visual contrast, between women and men, bright and dark, order and disorder, provided a perceptible manifestation to suffragists' arguments and conveyed to viewers the possible contribution women might add to politics after receiving the vote.

While suffragists adhered to popular fashion trends, it would be difficult, however, to identify a specific "suffrage dress" or "style" that suffragists promoted apart from colors. One explanation could be that as mainstream styles in the 1910s became more convenient, suffragists felt more comfortable to adopt them without needing to create a "special" style of their own. Specialty suffrage stores sold suffrage regalia that included sashes, hats, dresses, and blouses, and the suffrage press advertised specific "suffrage designs," such as the "suffrage blouse," that adhered to the latest trends. While the blouse did not contain any distinct feature, the magazine identified it as a distinct design since it was "ready-to-wear-to-anything-and-not-at-all expensive" and as such suited suffragists' needs.[22] Yet, as this example shows, one could have a "suffrage costume" by buying an "ordinary" white dress or blouse and then adding a decorative accessory in purple or yellow. "Many of us buy our frocks at department stores, and special suffrage regalia is not, alas, a specialty of these stores," explained suffragist Elizabeth Newport Hepburn.[23] Indeed, although stores like Macy's offered "official" suffrage costumes, and suffrage organizations encouraged women to buy specific outfits as a form of financial contribution and support, the fact that a woman could be identified with the suffrage cause by wearing "mainstream styles" in specific colors expanded participation in suffrage parades and activities to women who did not necessarily come from the middle and upper classes.[24]

Indeed, activists who were excluded from the mainstream movement due to their class or race used suffrage fashions to claim their role as partners in the cause. Especially for black suffragists, adopting the fashionable imagery of the suffrage colors and silhouettes allowed them to show their support for suffrage and at the same time to challenge the prevalent racism and class bias of many of the suffrage leaders. By dressing like their white counterparts, black suffragists could demand their right to equal citizenship as women, while also promoting racial equality as African Americans, laying claims to middle-class respectability. Although white suffragists also had to capitalize on their feminine appearance to gain public support and ameliorate fears of "desexualizing" the race, fashion contained a dual political function for black suffragists, who used it as a form of racial uplift, claiming access to the privileges of white womanhood. By adopting the color white that was associated with sexual and moral purity—qualities long deprived from African American women in public discourse—black suffragists like Mary Church Terrell and Ida B. Wells used fashion as a political means to advance racial equality, reclaiming their bodies, their humanity, and their respectability as women and mothers.[25]

The only garment that ever came close to becoming a "suffrage uniform" was a replica of prison garbs that National Woman's Party (NWP) activists wore during their time at the Occoquan Workhouse in Virginia after being arrested for picketing in front of the White House in 1917. While in Occoquan, suffragists viewed their garb as a sign of the denial of their rights as political prisoners; however, once released, they capitalized on the same imagery in order to gain publicity and legitimacy for their claims. In 1919, two years after their jailing first began, the NWP organized a cross-country "Prison Special" speaking tour in which suffragists recounted their experience in jail as a way to promote their cause. Speakers on the tour wore "calico wrappers designed exactly after the pattern of those which they were forced to wear in the work-house, thereby making the accounts of their experiences in the jail more vivid."[26] As fashion scholar Katherine Feo Kelley argues, suffragists used the prison dresses as a tool of visual rhetoric, turning their own bodies into political sites for advocating suffrage. By creating reproductions of the prison garb—a fashionable version of the original garment—suffragists stripped away the connotation of criminality and powerlessness that the prison dress entailed and turned it into a symbol of struggle and power as well as into a political performance.[27]

The creative use of fashion and the increasing visibility of suffragists in the streets, as well as the circulation of suffragists' photographs in national magazines, provided contemporaries with tangible evidence that suffragists were not devilish amazons but "ordinary women" wearing fashionable styles.[28] In their ability to become less conspicuous in the public sphere yet still noticeable for their sense of style and organization, suffragists pushed women's suffrage into the cultural mainstream and, eventually, into a constitutional amendment. As they employed mainstream styles in the creation of their image, suffragists refashioned the ways in which urban politics were played out, contributing to the creation of a modern political landscape based on appearance.[29]

The use of clothing in the service of promoting political agendas went beyond suffragists' successful campaign. As female politicians sought to break new ground and to play new roles in government, clothing became not only another aspect on which their candidacy and suitability for the job was judged, but also an opportunity to define (and redefine) the meaning of women in politics and their images as political leaders.[30] Staying true to the need to present a feminine image, female politicians like Shirley Chisholm turned fashion into a powerful form of self-expression that was integral to the construction of both her individual and political identity. Being the first African American woman elected to Congress in 1968, and running for the Democratic presidential nomination in 1972, Chisholm became famous for her bouffant coiffure, cat-eye glasses, and bright colored and printed ladylike suits. Like black suffragists, Chisholm also embraced a feminine look, emphasizing her gender and racial respectability. Yet, despite sticking to suits and skirts, Chisholm nevertheless shaped a political style that did not shy away from color or creativity and offered an alternative to what a woman in politics should look like. And like Chisholm, Clinton also used fashion to shape an image that encompassed both her individual style and political agenda.

Moving away from dresses and skirt suits that characterized her appearance as First Lady, Clinton the politician—the senator, the secretary of state, and the presidential candidate—opted for pant-suits in solid bold colors, or for colorful printed long jackets over tai-lored pants. Yet Clinton's famous affection for wearing pantsuits on the campaign trail was not an attempt to "dress like a man" but with brighter colors; rather, it was an attempt to create her own signature style that would convey both strength and femininity. Her avoidance of scarves, belts, and hair accessories during the 2016 campaign in favor of a cleaner, streamlined look enabled her to present a serious, con-fident, yet feminine image of the female politician, while at the same time avoiding fashion missteps that characterized her earlier career.[31] Moreover, wearing pantsuits did not mean rejecting the need to look fashionable and trendy. For the 2016 campaign, Clinton upgraded her appearance, using the advice of experts such as the makeup artist Bar-bara Lacy and the stylist Isabelle Goetz, and incorporating items made of leather and more colorful daring jackets.[32] Additionally, with the use of makeup, styled hair, heels, and jewelry, Clinton presented a softer, yet not matronly, look that turned the harsh lines of the masculine suit into a feminine outfit. By choosing bold colors that went beyond the black-navy-gray color scheme of the manly suit, and by adopting more flowing cuts, ruffles, and round collars that broke the severe rectangu-lar silhouette of the jacket, Clinton feminized the pantsuit.

Yet more importantly, Clinton fashioned a personal style that was both completely her own and an epitome for the confident female pol-itician. Describing herself as a "hair icon" and a "pantsuit aficionado," Clinton did not dismiss fashion as a frivolous matter but instead sought to use it in her favor, capitalizing on the association of the pantsuit with the image she wanted to present on the campaign trail.[33] Surprisingly, by turning the pantsuit into her "campaign uniform," Clinton made her appearance less conspicuous, which allowed her to focus on her policies and platform, using fashion to amplify her message instead of being the topic of the discussion. Although some lamented the toning down of her appearance during the Democratic primary debates, argu-ing that by "sapping her clothes of potentially controversial content, Mrs. Clinton had also sapped them of personality," Clinton showed her humor, shrewdness, and her sharp political senses in picking cam-paign outfits once she clinched the nomination.[34] The first Instagram post from her campaign after achieving the needed number of del-egates depicted a rack full of pantsuits in red, white, and blue, with the title "Hard choices." A play on her memoir's title, and conveying patriotic sentiments, the post received 6,600 "likes" in the first four hours, and almost 29,500 in total.[35] Proving that she did not shy away from harnessing clothes to promote her candidacy, the pantsuits' color scheme of red, white, and blue continued throughout her campaign, and more evidentially in the three national presidential debates with Donald J. Trump.

Trying to convey an image that is both serious and confident yet also relatable, Clinton, like the suffragists, used clothing as a way to soften her cold, harsh image, presenting herself as an approachable, "everyday woman" who can form a personal connection with potential voters. However, although her close work with designers and stylists did upgrade her appearance, it also drew criticism of her class privilege. When she wore a $12,000 Armani jacket to her victory speech after the New York primary, in which she spoke on the suffering of families due to the economic recession, the media criticized her imperviousness to working-class concerns.[36] Needing to navigate this thin line, Clinton dodged the criticism by shifting the conversation to her style instead of how much the jacket cost, playing "the woman card" in her emphasis on good appearance that is expected from women.

Unlike her 2008 campaign, when she was more reluctant to use "the woman card" in her favor, Clinton in 2016 was more comfortable in situating herself first and foremost as a woman, emphasizing the historical importance of her candidacy. Like the suffragists, who used theatrical tactics and showcased their skill in embroidery and drama, the Clinton campaign also forged strong relations with the fashion industry and Hollywood to garner voters' support. During 2016 New York fashion week, the campaign hosted a fund-raiser in the form of a runway show, presenting T-shirts designed by notable names such as Marc Jacobs, Diane von Furstenberg, and Tory Burch, which further solidified the connection between fashion and politics. Cohosted by Anna Wintour, *Vogue*'s chief editor, who had also been rumored to advise Clinton on her style, it was a creative method to forge positive coverage of fashion in connection with Clinton. The shirts featured in the event were later sold on the campaign's website for the price of forty-five to sixty dollars, allowing voters not only to show their support for Clinton, but also to present themselves as fashion savvy and proud owners of couture fashion.[37] This association of Clinton with the fashion world helped to make her appealing to a younger and more fashion-forward voter base, turning slogans such as "I'm with Her" and "Stronger Together" into fashion statements. While this move created a more commercialized version of her political message, it also enabled Clinton to present a more mainstream version of feminism with which many could identify.[38]

Clinton's ownership of the pantsuit also enabled her to capitalize on the style as a political means. Artists like Beyoncé showed their endorsements by wearing pantsuits to concerts, yet many other women also embraced the outfit, establishing it as a symbol of feminist pride and empowerment. Under the hashtag of #PantsuitNation, thousands of Clinton's supporters showed up to the polls on election day wearing pantsuits, turning themselves into walking campaign banners.[39] As they sought an empowering symbol around which to be unified, these women merged the fashionable legacies of the suffrage movement with a modern fashionable imagery in the form of the white pantsuit, referencing both the suffragists and Clinton as models.

The political use of clothing as a form of empowerment did not end with Clinton's defeat in November. Nor did the reference to the fashionable legacies of the suffragists and their successful campaign. In her concession speech, Clinton again invoked both in words and fashion her commitment to women's advancement. She wore a black and purple suit—the traditional mourning colors—nodding with the color purple to the suffragists, who used it to signal their loyalty to the cause. "I know we have still not shattered that highest and hardest glass ceiling, but some day someone will and hopefully sooner than we might think right now," Clinton declared.[40]

While Clinton's dream of becoming the first female president did not come true, her fashionable legacy proved inspirational and lasting. Providing a symbol around which women could unify and go to action, Clinton's pantsuit style became an icon for resistance. After the election, what started as a Facebook page calling for going to the polls in pantsuits, evolved into a virtual community and a movement named "Pantsuit Nation." Seeking to "foster connection. Take action. Extend trust," through meetings and social media, the movement reached within its first month 3.7 million members worldwide.[41] However, it soon ignited controversies regarding the movement's desired goals and future direction. Like with the suffragists a century before, people of color and minorities felt excluded, with some arguing that Pantsuit Nation has turned into "a space where white people can claim to fight for the survival of the sisterhood by performing apolitical acts of self-humanizing . . . on the backs of people of color whose lives are directly and disproportionately affected by Trump's policies." Instead of fashion becoming a bridge across racial and class differences, serving as a platform of political resistance, critics charged that Pantsuit Nation stripped the power of the fashionable item, and emphasized its white, excluding nature.[42]

Yet, even if Pantsuit Nation failed on its promise, the inherent connection between fashion and politics continued beyond the campaign, and proved, as in the struggle for suffrage, that it can be a useful tool for feminist protest. As millions of women around the world marched to protest Trump's policies toward women, LGBTQ people, Muslims, and other minorities a day after his inauguration, they donned hand-knitted cat-eared pink "pussyhats," as a symbol of resistance, unity, and power. Employing the association of knitting with femininity and tra-ditional gender roles to create a new image of power and defiance, the hat creatively reclaimed women's dignity in the face of Trump's misogynistic statement of grabbing women "by the pussy."[43] The Pussy-hat Project—an initiative of two women from California who sought to encourage participation in the Women's March—evolved into a move-ment of resistance, and an inspiration to many. Making its way from the streets into the runway, and receiving its official seal as a fashion item after the Victoria and Albert Museum purchased one of the Project's hats for its collection, the pussyhat symbolizes the perfect mergence between fashion and politics in the service of feminist resistance.[44] If suffragists in the early twentieth century had to embrace fashion to gain public support, and Clinton politicized the pantsuit as a fashion-able statement, the pussyhat has the potential of fashioning political protest for years to come.

Demonstrating that a commitment to women's rights can go together with adherence to fashion, and that clothing can be a useful tool to convey political agendas, the white garb of the suffragists, the pantsuit, or the pussyhat are not just accessories to political campaigns, but an integral part of their message. Understanding that not only the content of the message matters, but also how it is being delivered, the use of fashion in political campaigns shows that far from being oppressive, belittling, or just superfluous, clothing plays a crucial role in shaping political images and opinions. Whether they marched in Washington, DC, in their white, yellow, and purple colors in 1913, or in their pink pussyhats in 2017, it was the creative use of fashion that enabled these women activists to shape a new feminist presence in the public sphere.

Notes

1. It is important to note that only a few days after the DNC speech Ralph Lauren did admit to designing the suit, a move that enabled Clinton to keep media attention on her and the meanings of her fashion choices instead of on him. Adam Tschorn, "Provenance of the Pantsuit: Hillary Clinton Wore Ralph Lauren for Her Convention Speech," *Los Angeles Times*, August 1, 2016, http://www.latimes.com/fashion/la-ig-hillary-clinton-ralph-lauren-pantsuit-20160801-snap-story.html.

2. "Transcript: Hillary Clinton's Speech at the Democratic Convention," *New York Times*, July 28, 2016, https://www.nytimes.com/2016/07/29/us/politics/hillary-clinton-dnc-transcript.html.

3. Molly Ball, "No, It's Not Sexist to Describe Women Politicians' Clothes," *Atlantic*, July 2, 2013, https://www.theatlantic.com/politics/archive/2013/07/no-its-not-sexist-to-describe-women-politicians-clothes/277460/; Natalie Geismar, "Why Are We Still Talking about Hillary Clinton's Clothes?," *Ms. Magazine*, June 13, 2016, http://msmagazine.com/blog/2016/06/13/the-one-battle-female-politicians-just-cant-win/.

4. Of course, not all suffragists presented the same attitude. There was never a single suffrage movement, and suffragists differed by class, race, religion, ethnicity, and political affiliation, as well as in their views on why and how to achieve the vote. The National American Woman Suffrage Association (NAWSA), which was the largest organization, supported more conservative tactics of convincing legislators. The National Women's Party (NWP), which was formed by some of the younger NAWSA members who were frustrated by what they saw as a timid approach, was a more radical and militant organization. Black women, who often faced discrimination, and at times were barred from full participation in NAWSA and NWP, formed their own organization: the National Association of Colored Woman (NACW).

5. Liza Darwin, "How Hillary Clinton Softened Her Style to Win Votes," *Observer*, August 19, 2015, http://observer.com/2015/08/how-hillary-clinton-softened-up-her-style-to-win-votes/.

6. See, for example, *Tanisha Ford, Liberated Threads: Black Women, Style, and the Global Politics of Soul* (Chapel Hill: University of North Carolina Press, 2015); Betty Luther Hillman, *Dressing for the Cultural Wars: Style and the Politics of Self-Presentation in the 1960s and 1970s* (Lincoln: University of Nebraska Press, 2015); Einav Rabinovitch-Fox, "This Is What a Feminist Looks Like: The New Woman Image, American Feminism, and the Politics of Women's Fashion 1890–1930" (PhD diss., New York University, 2014).

7. For more on the "bloomer" and its role in the struggle for women's rights, see Elizabeth Cady Stanton, Susan Brownell Anthony, and Matilda Joslyn Gage, *History of Women Suffrage*, vol. 1, 1848–1861 (New York: Fowler & Wells, 1881), 470–71; Gayle Fischer, *Pantaloons and Power: A Nineteenth-Century Dress Reform in the United States* (Kent, OH: Kent State University Press, 2001); Robert Riegel, "Women's Clothes and Women's Rights," *American Quarterly* 15, no. 3 (1963): 390–401.

8. Margaret Finnegan, *Selling Suffrage* (New York: Columbia University Press, 1999), 2, 79–81.

9. Florence Flynn, "'Attract and Allure,' Cries the Suffragette," *New-York Tribune*, April 30, 1911.

10. On the theatrical aspects of the suffrage campaign, see Susan Glenn, *Female Spectacle: The Theatrical Roots of Modern Feminism* (Cambridge, MA: Harvard University Press, 2000); Michael McGerr, "Political Style and

Women's Power 1830–1930," *Journal of American History* 77, no. 3 (December 1990): 864–85; Finnegan, *Selling Suffrage*; Ellen Dubois, "Working Women, Class Relations, and Suffrage Militance: Harriot Stanton Blatch and the New York Woman Suffrage Movement 1894–1909," *Journal of American History* 74, no. 1 (June 1987): 34–58; Mary Chapman, *Making Noise, Making News: Suffrage Print Culture and U.S. Modernism* (New York: Oxford University Press, 2014).

11. "Mrs. Belmont Home for Suffrage War," *New York Times*, September 16, 1910; Marry Holland Kinkaid, "The Feminine Charms of the Woman Militant," *Good Housekeeping*, February 1912, 146–47.

12. Helena Hill Weed, "A Feminist Rises in Defense of Bobbed Hair," *New-York Tribune*, September 18, 1921; Flynn, "Attract and Allure."

13. See, for example, "Woman's Emancipation," *Harper's New Monthly Magazine*, August 1851, 424; "Why Shouldn't We Vote?," http://www.loc.gov/pictures/resource/var.0899/; and "Independence Day of the Future," *Puck*, July 4, 1894.

14. Finnegan, *Selling Suffrage*, 81.

15. Quoted in Dubois, "Working Women," 56.

16. "Paris (from Our Own Correspondent)," *Vogue*, May 21, 1908; "For Outdoor Wear," *Harper's Bazaar*, September 1911, 416; Elizabeth Ewing, *History of Twentieth Century Fashion* (Hollywood, CA: Costume and Fashion Press, 2001), 62, 66.

17. The "bicycle craze" of the late 1890s and early 1900s made these types of skirts popular for riding, and a legitimate attire for women in public.

18. The American suffrage colors took their inspiration from the British suffragettes, whose movement's colors—purple, white, and green—stood for loyalty, purity, and hope, respectively. After campaigning in Kansas, where the state flower (sunflower) was prominently used as a suffrage symbol, American suffragists replaced the British green with yellow/gold for American organizing purposes.

19. Glenn, *Female Spectacle*, 129, 131–32; Finnegan, *Selling Suffrage*; Maria Elena Buszek, *Pin-Up Grrrls: Feminism, Sexuality, Popular Culture* (Durham, NC: Duke University Press, 2006), 129–34; Ann Marie Nicolosi, "'The Most Beautiful Suffragette': Inez Milholland and the Political Currency of Beauty," *Journal of the Gilded Age and Progressive Era* 6, no. 3 (2007): 294–95, 299.

20. Glenda Smith Tinnin, "Why the Pageant?," *Woman's Journal*, February 5, 1913, 50.

21. "March 3, 1913: Parade Plan—List of Floats," Box 16, Folder 239, Alice Paul Papers. MC 399, Schlesinger Library, Radcliffe College, Harvard University. The parade was segregated, however, with black activists only allowed to march together in the back. None of the official photographs or plans included them either. Allison Lange, "We Can Do Better

Than the Suffragists," *Nursing Clio*, January 5, 2017, https://nursingclio. org/2017/01/05/we-can-do-better-than-the-suffragists/#footnoteref4.

22. "The Suffrage Blouse," *Woman Citizen*, June 2, 1917, 10; Finnegan, *Selling Suffrage*, 126.

23. Elizabeth Newport Hepburn, "Suffragists' Clothes," *New York Times*, May 15, 1913.

24. F. F. Purdy, "Notes from New York," *Merchants Record and Show Window* 31 (December 1912): 40; Finnegan, *Selling Suffrage*, 69, 126.

25. Treva Lindsey, *Colored No More: Reinventing Black Womanhood in Washington, D.C.* (Champaign: Illinois University Press, 2017), 97, 100–101, 104–10.

26. "Prison Special," *Suffragist*, February 15, 1919, 5.

27. Katherine Feo Kelly, "Performing Prison: Dress, Modernity, and the Radical Suffrage Body," *Fashion Theory* 15, no. 3 (2011): 316.

28. They also solidify the image of the suffragist as a white woman. Alice Duer Miller, "Who Is Sylvia? An Aspect of Feminism," *Scribner's Magazine*, July 1914, 55; "The Type of Suffragist Has Changed," *New-York Tribune*, February 24, 1911.

29. Race played an important role in suffragists' ability to push the boundaries of female respectability in public. White suffragists, protected by racial privilege, could challenge more fiercely notions of gender propriety without having their femininity, and their access to its privileges, questioned. Black suffragists, on the other hand, were not given that option.

30. Vanessa Friedman, "The New Age in Power Dressing," *New York Times*, July 27, 2016, https://www.nytimes.com/2016/07/28/fashion/hillary-clinton-theresa-may-michelle-obama-power-dressing.html.

31. For examples of the evolution of Clinton's style throughout her career, see "In Photos: Hillary Clinton's Iconic Style through the Years," *Harper's Bazaar*, October 26, 2017, http://www.harpersbazaar.com/celebrity/red-carpet-dresses/news/g6036/hillary-clinton-campaign-fashion/?slide=79; and Darwin, "How Clinton Softened Her Style."

32. Darwin, "How Clinton Softened Her Style."

33. Zeke J. Miller, "Hillary Clinton Joins Twitter," *Time*, June 10, 2013, http://swampland.time.com/2013/06/10/hillary-clinton-joins-twitter/.

34. Vanessa Friedman, "How Hillary Clinton Ended the Clothing Conversation," *New York Times*, January 20, 2016, https://www.nytimes.com/2016/01/21/fashion/hillary-clinton-pantsuit-style-2016-campaign.html.

35. hillaryclinton, "Hard choices," *Instagram*, June 10, 2015, https://www.instagram.com/p/3wNnxBEPpX/.

36. Madelyn Chung, "Hillary Clinton under Fire for Wearing $12,000 Armani Jacket While Giving Speech about Inequality," *Huffington Post*, June 8, 2016, http://www.huffingtonpost.ca/2016/06/07/hillary-clinton-armani-jacket_n_10337460.html.

37. Valeriya Safronova, "Fashion Turns Out, in T-shirts, for Clinton," *New York Times*, September 7, 2017.

38. This image, however, like the suffragists' image, appealed mainly to middle-class white voters.

39. The hashtag #PantsuitNation, as well as #WearWhiteToVote, originated as an invite-only Facebook page before the election, encouraging women to wear white pantsuits to the polls on Election Day. The page became wildly popular, transforming into a feminist forum where Clinton supporters encouraged one another; shared stories of standing up to sexual harassment, racial bullying, and violence; and called for women's empowerment.

40. "Hillary Clinton's Concession Speech," *New York Times*, November 9, 2016, https://www.nytimes.com/video/us/politics/100000004708101/hillary-clinton-concession-full-speech.html.

41. "Pantsuit Nation's Manifesto," November 22, 2016, http://www.pantsuitnation.org/blog/pantsuit-nations-manifesto.

42. Harry Lewis, "Pantsuit Nation Is a Sham," *Huffington Post*, December 20, 2016, http://www.huffingtonpost.com/entry/panstuit-nation-is-a-sham_us_585991dce4b04d7df167cb4d. The controversy broke after the movement's founder, Libby Chamberlain, turned it into a trademarked not-for-profit organization and announced having a book deal based on the Facebook page posts.

43. Unlike the color white, pink carried with it less controversies around race, and instead highlighted the gender aspect of the protest. Although some commentators have pointed out that not every woman's pussy is pink, the hat became a symbol of gender defiance—as pink is a color identified with women—that enabled women of color to claim their equal space in that protest based on their gender.

44. The V&A museum in London has one of the most important costume collections in the world. Janelle Okwodu, "The Women's March Pussyhat Takes Milan Fashion Week," *Vogue*, February 25, 2017, http://www.vogue.com/article/milan-fashion-week-ready-to-wear-fall-2017-missoni-pussyhats; "Pussyhat Goes on Display at V&A," *BBC News*, March 8, 2016, http://www.bbc.com/news/entertainment-arts-39203873.

Chapter Nine

ONE HUNDRED YEARS
OF CAMPAIGN IMAGERY

From Woman Suffrage Postcards
to Hillary Clinton Memes

Ana Stevenson

Around 1910 American postcard publisher J. E. Hale circulated a woman suffrage postcard featuring a photograph of suffragist Susan B. Anthony, alongside what are described as her "talismanic words": "Failure Is Impossible."[1] This was just one of many official suffrage postcards, produced between 1901 and 1915, to celebrate departed nineteenth-century social reformers. Anthony herself featured on postcards by the National American Woman Suffrage Association (NAWSA). The Literature Committee of the Congressional Union for Woman Suffrage depicted sculptor and feminist Adelaide Johnson's marble bust of Anthony. Other publishers printed photographic postcards of her parents, her birthplace, a thirty-six-year-old Anthony, and an elderly Anthony. A Trident Publishing Co. postcard quoted Anthony: "Woman suffrage is coming—no power on earth can prevent it—but the time of its coming will depend upon the loyalty and devotion of the women themselves."[2]

In many ways, the early twentieth-century postcard phenomenon foreshadowed the ephemerality of today's Internet memes. Postcards, scholars suggest, constituted a communications revolution comparable to the digital revolution: nineteenth-century photograph albums have been described as the "Victorian Facebook," while the Edwardian "craze" for postcards is seen as mirroring Twitter's popularity.[3] More than any other turn-of-the-twentieth-century communications technology, postcards "allowed people to see the world around them and to display their contributions to that world."[4] Social media provides similar opportunities in the twenty-first century. Political cartoons, in turn, rely on an understanding of political commonplaces, literary and cultural allusions, character traits, and other contextual factors; they are "enthymemes which invite the reader to respond in accordance with certain values, beliefs, and predispositions."[5] Since political cartoons have appeared continuously in American print culture since the 1860s, political imagery constitutes a rich medium through which to reflect on shifting cultural perspectives toward American women.[6]

The celebration of suffrage pioneers such as Anthony anticipated their memorialization during the 2016 US presidential election a century later. "Women in Congress and a Woman President, Says Susan B. Anthony," a *New York Press* headline proclaimed in 1905, the year before her passing.[7] Echoes of Anthony's determination reverberated in the certainty about a Hillary Clinton victory. Woman suffrage postcards and Hillary Clinton memes offer the opportunity to analyze strategies of campaign imagery in the United States across roughly one hundred years. This chapter examines how these woman-centered political campaigns mobilized mass culture. The earnest moralizing of much prosuffrage and pro-Clinton imagery was arguably less successful than the irreverent misogyny of their antisuffrage and anti-Clinton counterparts. What role, then, do stereotypes and humor play in political debate? And how can these strategies be better harnessed by feminists? This chapter outlines the limitations of invoking the woman suffrage movement for the Clinton campaign and suggests strategies for how future women in politics might promote a feminist message in their political ephemera.

Woman Suffrage Postcards

Picture postcards were a central component of the "Golden Age of Suffrage Memorabilia," which scholar Kenneth Florey situates between 1908 and 1917. American suffragists collected postcards enthusiastically, perhaps with a proportionally greater zeal than the wider public's "craze" for postcards. Most prosuffrage postcards were associated with NAWSA, which inaugurated the National Woman Suffrage Publishing Company in November 1914. After splitting from NAWSA in 1916, the National Woman's Party (NWP) and commercial publishers alike produced comparatively few.[8] Commonly, prosuffrage postcards embraced patriotic themes and responded logically but uninspiringly to antisuffrage arguments. In contrast, antisuffrage postcards were characteristically produced commercially, circulated far more widely, and visually vibrant.

Why the prominence of Susan B. Anthony? A tendency to commemorate deceased social reformers was prevalent in the United States.[9] Other prosuffrage postcards featured the photographs and quotations of women's rights luminary Elizabeth Cady Stanton; the abolitionists and women's rights reformers Lucretia Mott, Julia Ward Howe, Wendell Phillips, and Henry B. Blackwell; antislavery politicians Senator Charles Sumner and President Abraham Lincoln; and temperance reformer Frances Willard. Far fewer postcards featured contemporaries, such as novelist Charlotte Perkins Gillman or suffrage leaders Carrie Chapman Catt, Rev. Anna Howard Shaw, and Alice Paul.

Yet Anthony's prominence in the commemorative landscape was far from coincidental. As historian Lisa Tetrault argues, Stanton and Anthony together used the memory of the 1848 women's rights convention in Seneca Falls, New York, to creatively dominate the leadership of the late nineteenth-century women's movement. While Anthony became an increasingly perceptive and recognizable agitator, Stanton gradually demonstrated a distaste for constant campaigning, annoyance with organizational politics, and frustration with Anthony's mounting acceptance of a suffrage-only platform. Stanton's escalating political and religious radicalism alienated many of her contemporaries by the 1890s, leaving Anthony to emerge at the heart of the movement's historical memory at the century's end.[10] What began with Anthony herself turned into self-perpetuating commemorative efforts. The NWP commissioned a Johnson marble memorial sculpture entitled *Woman Movement* (1920); intended for display in the US Capitol, it featured Anthony rising above Mott and Stanton.[11] During the 1930s and 1940s, Rosa Arnold Powell led a campaign to etch Anthony's face into Mount Rushmore.[12] In 1979 the Susan B. Anthony one-dollar coin was minted.[13] Her prominence in twentieth-century suffrage memorialization explains, in part, why Anthony's gravestone in Rochester's Mount Hope Cemetery has become the site of twenty-first-century "I Voted" ritual activity, particularly on November 8, 2016, as documented in Christine A. Kray's chapter in this volume.

But at the turn of the twentieth century, the prosuffrage postcards that lionized nineteenth-century social reformers had many lackluster, didactic, and propagandistic counterparts. Some suffrage cartoonists, especially Lou Rogers and Nina Allender, managed to mobilize humor for the cause in the *Woman's Journal, Judge,* and *Suffragist,* yet confinement to prosuffrage newspapers limited circulation. Additionally, these illustrations do not appear to have been transferred to postcards.[14] Even moderately humorous prosuffrage postcards tended to be moralizing. Since these postcards were almost exclusively produced and sold directly by suffrage organizations, they often enjoyed less exposure and circulation than their commercial—and usually vividly antisuffrage—counterparts.

Antisuffrage postcards in contrast successfully mobilized an irreverent, misogynistic humor, the strategies of which remain familiar today. The late nineteenth-century humor industry relied on stereotypes, a phenomenon prosuffrage postcards largely failed to exploit. The stereotype was instead "a tool for racism, sexism, and profitable commodification," as Michael H. Epp observes.[15] Antisuffrage postcard manufacturers inadvertently contributed to political discourse. By exploiting existing gender ideologies, they depicted public women in general and suffragists in particular as "topical or humorous types."[16] Commercial publishers produced the "most visually evocative" postcards by appealing to this antisuffrage worldview.[17] The antisuffrage postcards that used misogynistic stereotypes to portray suffragists, such as the shrew or aged harridan, proved commercially profitable. Suffragist women could be infantilized, with their political demands diminished to the trope of little girls wanting to wear pants (fig. 9.1), or presented as transgressive through gender inversions such as the female police officer (fig. 9.2), or the feminized man (fig. 9.3). Since these postcards were largely reactive toward the public controversy about woman suffrage, it is arguable that many individuals wholeheartedly viewed suffragists as "nothing more than scolds and battle-axes."[18]

Constantly limited by financial constraints, suffragists nonetheless sought to mobilize new technologies and embrace consumer culture to promote the cause.[19] According to Amy Shore, suffrage memorabilia and pageantry represented new attempts for suffrage organizations to "capitalize on mass culture as a site of organizing and social movement."[20] In 1913, on the eve of Woodrow Wilson's presidential inauguration, NAWSA's Congressional Committee staged the National Woman Suffrage Parade in Washington, DC. The parade's director, Alice Paul, was a newcomer who understood how dramatic tactics and "visual rhetoric" could have a significant and lasting effect.[21] To soften the spectacle of the public woman, the parade organizers featured suffragist and lawyer Inez Milholland as the "Mounted Herald," adorned with a golden crown. Placed atop a magnificent white horse at the beginning of the pageant for greatest visibility, her dress recalled "an age of heraldry and martyrdom."[22] The *Washington Post* pronounced Milholland "The Most Beautiful Suffragette."[23] The organizers also staged an allegorical tableau featuring classical imagery on the steps of the Treasury Building. As the official event program described, "Columbia, hearing the approach of the Procession, summons to her side, Justice, Charity, Liberty, Peace and Hope, to review with her this 'new crusade' of women."[24] Afterward, merchants published more

9.1. "Will we get em?" (Barton and Spooner, n.d.). Antisuffrage postcard
depicting suffragists as children. Catherine H. Palczewski Postcard Archive,
University of Northern Iowa, Cedar Falls, IA. Used with permission.

9.2. "Suffragette Copette" from "Suffragette Series" (New York: Dunston-Weiler Lithograph Co., 1909). Antisuffrage postcard satirizing the idea of women taking on men's roles, in this case, that of a police officer. Catherine H. Palczewski Postcard Archive, University of Northern Iowa, Cedar Falls, IA. Used with permission.

9.3. "Election Day" from "Suffragette Series" (New York: Dunston-Weiler Lithograph Co., 1909). Antisuffrage postcard depicting gender relations turned upside down as the wife and mother heads out to vote and the husband and father "suffers" at home with two children. Catherine H. Palczewski Postcard Archive, University of Northern Iowa, Cedar Falls, IA. Used with permission.

postcards of the National Woman Suffrage Parade than any other suffrage event, featuring the visually striking formations of row upon row of white women holding political placards and wearing white.[25]

Like woman suffrage postcards, the National Woman Suffrage Parade was also characteristic of the exclusionary, segregationist tendencies of the woman suffrage movement.[26] Although contention arose when southern leaders Laura Clay and Kate Gordon urged the adoption of a specifically whites-only suffrage agenda, the custom of racial segregation in suffrage pageantry failed to provoke widespread controversy. In 1913 NAWSA attempted to have all African American women march together at the parade's end. The Illinois Equal Suffrage Association had intended to present an interracial delegation—including Chicago's Alpha Suffrage Club president, journalist and antilynching advocate Ida B. Wells-Barnett—but its president Grace Wilbur Trout ultimately felt compelled to comply with NAWSA's directive. Yet at the final moment, as a photograph in the *Chicago Tribune* captured, Wells-Barnett positioned herself to march as part of a (forcibly integrated) Illinois delegation.[27] As a corpus, woman suffrage postcards overwhelmingly imagined an electorate comprised of privileged white women and men. Some depicted the working classes, and derogatory ethnic stereotypes were certainly evident (though somewhat rare), yet people of color were largely conspicuous due to their absence. Alice Beach Winter and Mary Ellen Sigsbee's remarkable prosuffrage illustrations of African American women were unlikely to have appeared on postcards.[28]

Postcards represented an important moment in the history of political imagery, a position now dominated by Internet memes. During the 1910s, prosuffrage postcards celebrated admirable though fallible foremothers, made vacillating attempts at humor, aimed to embrace mass culture, and failed to cultivate solidarity. In contrast, antisuffrage postcards succeeded through a reliance on misogynistic stereotypes, from the harridan to the infantilized activist and the gender transgressor, as well as on account of their mobilization of color and humor. As historian Susan Magarey emphasizes, suffrage-era feminists were not without humor; many were adept at "demonstrating irony, performing parody, ridiculing and deflating pompousness and pretension."[29] But the humor of antisuffragists gained far greater cultural currency. The similarities and limitations evident in woman suffrage postcards can be observed in political imagery, especially memes, across the career of Hillary Clinton.

Hillary Clinton Memes

The 2016 presidential campaign of Hillary Clinton perceived failure to be impossible, thus recalling the words of Susan B. Anthony. Her official campaign and many of its unofficial supporters—the individuals, organizations, and media that endorsed her candidacy—went so far as to position a Clinton presidency in anticipation of 2020: the one-hundredth anniversary of the Nineteenth Amendment. Likewise, Clinton's detractors demonstrated an ongoing reliance on the misogynistic stereotypes pioneered in antisuffrage postcards. As the Clinton campaign struggled to convince voters that it prioritized diversity and solidarity, the celebration and memorialization of the woman suffrage movement inadvertently recalled the shortcomings of both.

Many humorists have relied on sexist stereotypes to depict Hillary Rodham Clinton. Her emergence on the national stage coincided with a key moment in the illustration of gender in political imagery. A one-hundred-year analysis of women in July Fourth newspaper cartoons reveals how the theme of women's subordination never truly disappeared, but became somewhat subtler by the 1960s and 1970s.[30] Feminist theorist Angela McRobbie describes how many of the women's liberation movement's goals were institutionally adopted by the 1990s, but popular culture was beginning to self-consciously construct feminism as passé. As postfeminist media discourse developed, it celebrated "female individualism" and presented sexism through the lens of irony.[31] Female politicians such as Clinton reveal how white middle-class women often experience the benefits of feminism most fully, yet remain subject to the vagaries of postfeminist media discourse.[32] To depict Clinton—a First Lady with an agenda—during husband Bill Clinton's presidency, political imagery routinely embraced sexist stereotypes. Since Clinton transgressed many of the gendered expectations associated with the First Lady, cartoonists concocted a usurper of male power; an emasculating radical feminist; a sexualized career woman neglectful of her husband and child; the root of all the Clinton administration's problems; and a wife one would wish to divorce.[33]

The reliance on such stereotypes did not abate during the 2008 presidential primary campaign. Political cartoons depend on stereotypes because the "essence of the cartoon is satire, a distortion of the truth."[34] Humorists found race and sex to be "particularly salient" categories due to the novelty of Barack Obama—a black man—and Hillary Clinton—a white woman—competing as front-runners for the Democratic nomination.[35] But if the question of race versus sex was unprecedented in the Democratic primaries, it actually spoke to a rhetorical rift central to the history of American feminism.[36] The mobilization of racial and sexual stereotypes—together with a particular aversion to Clinton—would continue. Journalists derided Clinton's pantsuits, which supposedly rendered her "not feminine enough"; described her political ambition and age as unattractive; and portrayed her as a scold who exploited her adult daughter. Many also expressed a fear that Clinton, though widely recognized to be competent, would lean politically on her husband.[37]

The digital age offered the possibility of alternate narratives about Clinton in political imagery. As secretary of state in the first Obama administration, her competence was lovingly parodied when Stacy Lambe and Adam Smith's meme-based Tumblr, *Texts from Hillary*, went viral in April 2012.[38] An Internet meme, according to communications scholar Limor Shifman, is a unit of popular culture "circulated, imitated, and transformed" online by individuals, "creating a shared cultural experience in the process." Experienced socially though shared individually, memes are spread "*as is*, by forwarding, linking or copying" as well as through "mimicry and remix."[39] The photograph upon which the memes were based, captured by Kevin Lamarque for Reuters on October 18, 2011, epitomized the digital age. It featured Secretary Clinton as a C-17 military aircraft passenger traveling from Malta to Tripoli; she just happened to be using her Blackberry and wearing snappy sunglasses. Would this photograph enable positive—and perhaps even feminist—digital imagery of a high-powered female politician? While technology baffles many baby boomers, Hillary Clinton appeared cool, calm, and connected. The Tumblr paired Lamarque's photograph with other photographs to create memes depicting imagined digital conversations between Clinton and famous politicians, celebrities, and public figures. *Texts from Hillary* overturned or at least challenged some of the stereotypes mobilized in earlier political imagery.

The humor of *Texts from Hillary* was derived from popular culture and gendered perceptions of a political work ethic. One meme invoked a 2011 Beyoncé song: MSNBC host Rachel Maddow supposedly texted, "Who run the world?" and meme-Clinton replied, "Girls." How ironic, the memes implied, that Obama rather than Clinton became president? Indeed, the "'Texts from Hillary' meme shows Clinton in charge," the *Boston Globe* editorialized.[40] Other memes depicted Clinton as more rational than former vice presidential candidate and governor of Alaska Sarah Palin, as well as more mature and professionally adept than colleagues such as President Obama, Massachusetts governor Mitt Romney, Vice President Joe Biden, President George Bush, and Secretary of State Condoleezza Rice, Secretary of State Colin Powell, and not least Bill Clinton. Fraternization with celebrity "friends"—Oprah, Beyoncé, Anna Wintour, and Meryl Streep—also rendered meme-Clinton "cool," as did her digital trouncing of singer Lady Gaga, actor Ryan Gosling, Facebook cofounder Mark Zuckerberg, and comedian Jon Stewart. Opportunistically capitalizing on the

phenomenon, Clinton made her Twitter debut by inaugurating a fol-
low-on hashtag, #tweetsfromhillary.[41]

But these memes and their offshoots also had their limitations.
As often occurs with female politicians, the emphasis on Clinton's
forename rather than her surname worked to accentuate her womanhood.[42] Ultimately, *Texts from Hillary* and #tweetsfromhillary gained
cultural currency because the humor was based on an "interplay
between elite and quotidian discourses" representative of the rhetorics of postfeminism. A ruse through which antifeminist discourses can
influence public dialogue and popular culture, postfeminism appears
"flexible and playful" whereas feminism is seen to be "intractable and
dour."[43] These very shortcomings—the struggle to effectively mobilize
humor for feminist ends—appeared repeatedly in the digital realm of
the 2016 presidential campaign.

After Clinton officially announced her candidacy for the 2016
presidential election, the need to create a credible digital presence was widely appreciated. Her campaign logo was designed and
donated by Pentagram's Michael Bierut and released in April 12,
2015. It featured the letter "H" in patriotic colors. As design scholar
Juliette Cezzar observed, the logo was somewhat devoid of context—
more "a container than a message"—thus morphing to the expectations of many constituents. "Philosophically, this is very much aligned
with how [Clinton] wants to represent herself and what she wants to
say."[44] Like prosuffrage postcards, the official campaign sometimes
embraced color in the patriotic trio of red, white, and blue. Clinton
perpetually appeared at the center of political rallies with patriotic
banners and large crowds in photographs that later became official
campaign memes. Beyond this, however, many official memes were
visually and rhetorically uninspiring. The official campaign slogan
"I'm with Her" appeared explicitly gendered but also overly earnest, as did an unofficial attempt to reclaim the pantsuits previously
lambasted by journalists: Libby Chamberlain's organization, Pantsuit Nation. Similarly, a black-and-white photograph of Clinton—
in front of a crowd and wearing a white pantsuit often interpreted
as an acknowledgment of the suffragists—was overwritten with the
words: "I'm with her because it's time to make history."[45] The Clinton campaign's official and unofficial digital presence arguably fell
between embracing feminism, but being somewhat bland, or being
thoroughly postfeminist in its meaning or intent.

Conversely, like their antisuffrage predecessors, memes antago-
nistic toward Clinton's candidacy embraced humor. In the twenty-
first century, this humor was defined by its sharp misogyny. The term
"meme magic," developed on the imageboard website 8chan, refers

to the real-life consequences that can be (and arguably have been) effected through political memes.[46] Memes and hashtags such as "Zombie Hillary"—which took advantage of candid photographs where Clinton had wide eyes or prominent teeth, or alternately used photograph-editing software to transform her into a zombie—directly contributed to the sexism and ageism aimed at Clinton.[47] Like anti-suffrage postcards, these memes made Clinton appear untrustworthy by depicting her as a crazed, disdainful usurper or an aged harridan. Despite its extraordinary popularity, *Texts from Hillary* also revealed the real-world consequences of memes. Her use of a Blackberry would ultimately raise questions about her State Department email address.[48] By 2016, *Texts from Hillary* could be positioned to allude to this later scandal and FBI investigation. Other anti-Clinton memes featured widely circulated phrases such as "Life's a bitch, don't vote for one" and "I did not have textual relations with that server," the latter satirizing Hillary Clinton's email scandal through use of Bill Clinton's denial of his sexual improprieties with Monica Lewinsky.

Not only were these anti-Clinton memes humorous; they were far more evocative than phrases such as "I'm with Her." Memes by Clinton detractors may have been amateurish in appearance, yet they collectively embraced many of the overworked stereotypes evident in antisuffrage and political imagery. This rendered them engaging and memorable in ways that the official and unofficial Clinton campaign memes failed to be. The media discourse of postfeminism simultaneously made it difficult to respond to misogynistic imagery without lapsing into ineffective moralizing or earnest sincerity.

Many unofficial Clinton supporters, namely media outlets, framed her candidacy in terms of the memorialization and fulfillment of suffragist history. The Clinton campaign affirmed the contemporary significance of suffragists and even their postcards. In fact, woman suffrage postcards conjured what Adrienne LaFrance described as "The Weird Familiarity of 100-Year-Old Feminism Memes" in a pictorial essay for *The Atlantic*.[49] Once Clinton became the Democratic nominee, even the official campaign could not entertain the possibility of defeat. On Clinton's sixty-ninth birthday, a meme likely developed by staffers appeared on Twitter. It featured a childhood photograph, captioned: "Happy birthday to this future president" (@HillaryClinton, October 26, 2016). Clinton was fulfilling Anthony's vision—"Women in Congress and a Woman President"—from one hundred years earlier. A week prior to the election, LaFrance described the "idea of a woman being elected president of the United States" as no longer a question of "if, but when," alongside a historical photograph of the Treasury Building tableau from the 1913 National Woman Suffrage Parade.[50]

Inez Milholland may have been forgotten in popular memory, but the effect of the rows of white suffragists wearing white was not.

This adulation inadvertently spoke to the limitations of the Clinton campaign. Clinton did not dismiss racial issues like many suffragists: legal and social advocacy for children, women, and racial minorities was an important aspect of her earlier career. But in balancing the interests of many constituents during the 2016 presidential campaign, these efforts were far less palpable. Democratic candidate Bernie Sanders and others positioned Clinton not as a candidate who embraced intersectionality and social revolution, but as a concession to liberal feminism, capitalism, and the political elite.[51] Such a critique resonated with the limitations of "white feminism," colloquially used to describe how much white women's activism overlooks the operation of privilege and the intersectional experiences of people of color. In fabric as in ethnicity, it spoke to the historical and contemporary resonances between the woman suffrage movement and a Clinton presidency. Somewhat like the discourse of postfeminism, a white woman as president—particularly this white woman as president—was anticipated to be a symbolic victory that would merely reproduce the status quo.

Postcards versus Memes: "I'm with Her"?

Despite being produced one hundred years apart, woman suffrage postcards and Hillary Clinton memes share clear consistencies. How, specifically, did the themes and strategies pioneered in these postcards appear in contemporary memes? The corpus of woman suffrage postcards is replete with stark contrasts, from visual coloration to text-based humor. Many prosuffrage postcards were visually lackluster, having the blandest coloration and often tending toward grayscale, whereas antisuffrage postcards were routinely colorful and therefore more eye-catching.[52] Alongside the prosuffrage tendency toward earnest moralizing, the oppositional strategy of embracing irreverent, misogynistic humor rendered antisuffrage postcards visually appealing and entertaining.

Favorable and unfavorable Clinton memes reflected the tendencies of both pro- and antisuffrage postcards. *Texts from Hillary* is based on a photograph that was contextually interesting, yet located in the lackluster and somewhat monochromatic setting of a military aircraft. The humor of these memes, while irreverent, relied on the limiting rhetorics of postfeminism. Following presidential campaign design trends, official Clinton memes mainly featured limited colors—often grayscale or the patriotic trio of red, white, and blue. In contrast, memes hostile toward Clinton embraced both sexist stereotypes and highly misogynistic text-based messages. These memes became far more memorable because they featured widely circulated phrases that were at once more pithy and meaningful than that of the official Clinton campaign or its unofficial supporters. The resonances such political imagery holds across a hundred years speak to the gains of feminism, especially as envisioned by Anthony and the suffragists, but also to the persistence and similitude of specific types of misogyny.

How can political ephemera better resonate to foster national and global solidarity? Too strong an identification with a fraught historical legacy—especially a legacy that reflects a campaign's own limitations—is neither a useful nor an authentic strategy. Specifically identifying how a candidate will address the inequalities of that historical legacy may be more fruitful. Moreover, while prosuffrage visual culture contributed to the movement's ultimate success, the overriding notion that "failure is impossible" is far better suited to a campaign for democratic rights sustained over decades than a two-year presidential campaign.

Official and unofficial campaigns for feminist women politicians should focus on strategies proven to be influential. Political and cultural benefits seemingly emanate from the effective use of color and humor. Online postfeminist gender-difference humor, a backlash against comedy that identifies and critiques gender inequalities, has proven more popular than feminist humor.[53] Stepping away from an abundance of overly moralizing and earnest messages, which tend to appeal more to existing rather than potential supporters, may therefore be a useful strategy. If colorful, eye-catching, well-designed intersectional feminist humor can be developed as digital political ephemera, perhaps more of the electorate will indeed be with her.

Postcards have regained—or retained—significance following the historic Women's March on Washington of January 21, 2017. The organizers of this new movement, aware of feminism's fraught legacies, prioritize intersectional activism. The "Unity Principles"—themselves inspired by Clinton's famous statement about the inseparability of women's rights and human rights, uttered at the 1995 United Nations Fourth World Congress on Women in Beijing, China—emphasize and prioritize the structural inequalities experienced by black, native, poor, immigrant, disabled, Muslim, and LGBTQ women. One of the "actions" associated with the Women's March "10 Actions for the First 100 Days" campaign encouraged individuals to "write postcards" to US senators. Postcards, reimagined, have thus emerged at the center of political action during the twenty-first century.

Notes

1. "Failure is Impossible" (Elmira, NY: J. E. Hale, ca. 1910), National Museum of American History; Ida Husted Harper, *The Life and Work of Susan B. Anthony*, vol. 3 (Indianapolis: Hollenbeck Press, 1908), 1409, 1442. See Kathleen Barry, *Susan B. Anthony: A Biography of a Singular Feminist* (New York: New York University Press, 1988), chap. 13: "'Failure Is Impossible'"; and Lynn Sherr, *Failure Is Impossible: Susan B. Anthony in Her Own Words* (New York: Random House, 2005), esp. 324.

2. "Susan B. Anthony" (Davenport: Trident Publishing Co., ca. 1911). For all postcard examples and further information on provenance, see Kenneth Florey, *American Woman Suffrage Postcards: A Study and Catalog* (Jefferson, NC: McFarland & Company, 2015), esp. chap. 1: "Official Suffrage Postcards"; Kristin Allukian and Ana Stevenson, *The Suffrage Postcard Project*, 2015, http://thesuffragepostcardproject.omeka.net/.

3. Nicole Hudgins, "A Historical Approach to Family Photography: Class and Individuality in Manchester and Lille, 1850–1914," *Journal of Social History* 43, no. 3 (2010): 564–65; Julia Gillen and Nigel Hall, "The Edwardian Postcard: A Revolutionary Moment in Rapid Multimodal Communications" (paper presented at British Educational Research Association Annual Conference, September 5, 2009, University of Manchester).

4. Steven Dotterer and Galen Cranz, "The Picture Postcard: Its Development and Role in American Urbanization," *Journal of American Culture* 5, no. 1 (1982): 45.

5. Martin J. Medhurst and Michael A. Desousa, "Political Cartoons as Rhetorical Form: A Taxonomy of Graphic Discourse," *Communications Monographs* 48, no. 3 (1981): 204.

6. Katherine Meyer, John Seidler, Timothy Curry, and Adrian Aveni, "Women in July Fourth Cartoons: A 100-Year Look," *Journal of Communication* 30, no. 1 (1980): 21.

7. Edwin Tracey, "Women in Congress and a Woman President, Says Susan B. Anthony," *New York Press*, February 26, 1905, in Susan Brownell Anthony Scrapbook, 1905–6, Reel 6, Papers of Susan B. Anthony, Library of Congress Manuscript Division.

8. Florey, *American Woman Suffrage Postcards*, 4, 10–11, 13, 14, 19; Dotterer and Cranz, "Picture Postcard," 45.

9. Florey, *American Woman Suffrage Postcards*, 7–8, 108. In contrast, the British women's suffrage movement, especially the Women's Social and Political Union, produced over 100 postcards celebrating contemporary suffrage leaders. See Lisa Tickner, *The Spectacle of Women: Imagery of the Suffrage Campaign 1907–14* (Chicago: University of Chicago Press, 1988).

10. Lisa Tetrault, *The Myth of Seneca Falls: Memory and the Women's Suffrage Movement, 1848–1898* (Chapel Hill: University of North Carolina Press, 2014).

11. Ibid., 187–88.

12. Simon Schama, *Landscape and Memory* (New York: Vintage Books, 1996), 385.

13. Ana Stevenson, review of *The Myth of Seneca Falls: Memory and the Women's Suffrage Movement, 1848–1898*, by Lisa Tetrault, *Australasian Journal of American Studies* 35, no. 1 (2016): 163–65.

14. Alice Sheppard, "Political and Social Consciousness in the Woman Suffrage Cartoons of Lou Rogers and Nina Allender," *Studies in American Humor* 4, nos. 1–2 (1985): 39–50.

15. Michael H. Epp, "The Traffic in Affect: Marietta Holley, Suffrage, and Late-Nineteenth-Century Popular Humor," *Canadian Review of American Studies* 36, no. 1 (2006): 96–97.

16. Tickner, *Spectacle of Women*, 162.

17. Catherine H. Palczewski, "The Male Madonna and the Feminine Uncle Sam: Visual Argument, Icons, and Ideographs in 1909 Anti-Woman Suffrage Postcards," *Quarterly Journal of Speech* 91, no. 4 (2005): 366.

18. Florey, *American Woman Suffrage Postcards*, 1–2.

19. Margaret Finnegan, *Selling Suffrage: Consumer Culture and Votes for Women* (New York: Columbia University Press, 1999).

20. Amy Shore, "Suffrage Stars," *Camera Obscura: Feminism, Culture, and Media Studies* 21, no. 3 (63) (2006): 3.

21. Katherine H. Adams and Michael L. Keene, *Alice Paul and the American Suffrage Campaign* (Urbana: University of Illinois Press, 2008), 12, 112–16.

22. Ann Marie Nicolosi, "'The Most Beautiful Suffragette': Inez Milholland and the Political Currency of Beauty," *Journal of the Gilded Age and Progressive Era* 6, no. 3 (2007): 288, 298.

23. "The Most Beautiful Suffragette," *Washington Post*, March 2, 1913. See Sarah J. Moore, "Making a Spectacle of Suffrage: The National Woman Suffrage Pageant, 1913," *Journal of American Culture* 20, no. 1 (1997): 89–103.

24. Harriet Connor Brown, ed., "Official Program of the Woman's Suffrage Procession" (Washington: Press of the Sudwarth Company, 1913), Reel 58, *National American Woman Suffrage Association*, Library of Congress Manuscript Division.

25. Florey, *American Woman Suffrage Postcards*, 159.

26. Rosalyn Terborg-Penn, *African American Women in the Struggle for the Vote, 1850–1920* (Bloomington: Indiana University Press, 1998).

27. Mia Bay, *To Tell the Truth Freely: The Life of Ida B. Wells* (New York: Hill and Wang, 2009), 290–91.

28. Alice Sheppard, *Cartooning for Suffrage* (Albuquerque: University of New Mexico Press, 1994), 200–201.

29. Susan Magarey, "'The Color of Your Moustache'; or Have Feminists Always Been Humorless?," *Journal of the Association for the Study of Australian Literature* 2 (2003): 142.

30. Meyer et al., "Women in July Fourth Cartoons," 21–30.

31. Angela McRobbie, "Post-Feminism and Popular Culture," *Feminist Media Studies* 4, no. 3 (2004): 255–64.

32. Mary Douglas Vavrus, *Postfeminist News: Political Women in Media Culture* (Albany: SUNY Press, 2002), 130–31.

33. Charlotte Templin, "Hillary Clinton as Threat to Gender Norms: Cartoon Images of the First Lady," *Journal of Communication Inquiry* 23, no. 1 (1999): 20–36.

34. Ibid., 20.

35. Eileen L. Zurbriggen and Aurora M. Sherman, "Race and Gender in the 2008 U.S. Presidential Election: A Content Analysis of Editorial Cartoons," *Analyses of Social Issues and Public Policy* 10, no. 1 (2010): 223–47.

36. Ana Stevenson, "The Woman-Slave Analogy: Rhetorical Foundations in American Culture, 1830–1900" (PhD diss., University of Queensland, 2015); Tracy A. Thomas, "Sex versus Race, Again," in *Who Should Be First? Feminists Speak Out on the 2008 Presidential Campaign*, ed. Beverly Guy-Sheftall (Albany: SUNY Press, 2010).

37. Diana B. Carlin and Kelly L. Winfrey, "Have You Come a Long Way, Baby? Hillary Clinton, Sarah Palin, and Sexism in 2008 Campaign Coverage," *Communication Studies* 60, no. 4 (2009): 330–32, 334–37.

38. Stacy Lambe and Adam Smith, *Texts from Hillary*, April 4–11, 2012, and June 7, 2016, http://textsfromhillaryclinton.tumblr.com/.

39. Limor Shifman, "Memes in a Digital World: Reconciling with a Conceptual Troublemaker," *Journal of Computer-Mediated Communication* 18, no. 3 (2013): 367, 365.

40. Joanna Weiss, "'Texts from Hillary' Meme Shows Clinton in Charge," *Boston Globe*, April 10, 2012, https://www.bostonglobe.com/opinion/2012/04/09/texts-from-hillary-meme-shows-clinton-charge-meme-her-own/x0Gh1ascWwJbwtWQoyWO7H/story.html.

41. Karrin Vasby Anderson and Kristina Horn Sheeler, "Texts (and Tweets) from Hillary: Meta-Meming and Postfeminist Political Culture," *Presidential Studies Quarterly* 44, no. 2 (2014): 224–43.

42. Zurbriggen and Sherman, "Race and Gender," 231; Ana Stevenson, "Making Gender Divisive: 'Post-Feminism,' Sexism and Media Representations of Julia Gillard," *Burgmann Journal: Research, Debate, Opinion*, no. 2 (2013): 56.

43. Anderson and Sheeler, "Texts (and Tweets) from Hillary," 225, 227.

44. Juliette Cezzar, quoted in Colleen Kane, "What the Critics Say about Jeb Bush's and Hillary Clinton's Campaign Logos," *Fortune*, June 15, 2015, http://fortune.com/2015/06/15/jeb-bush-hillary-clinton-logos/.

45. Hillary Clinton, "I'm with Her Because It's Time to Make History," November 7, 2016, Facebook photo, https://www.facebook.com/hillary clinton/photos/a.889773484412515.1073741828.889307941125736/1 320311824692010/?type=3&theater; Vanessa Friedman, "Why Hillary Wore White," *New York Times*, July 29, 2016, https://www.nytimes.com/

2016/07/30/fashion/hillary-clinton-democratic-national-convention. html.

46. "Meme Magic," *Know Your Meme*, 2017, accessed August 11, 2017, http://knowyourmeme.com/memes/meme-magic.

47. Morgan Brinlee, "The Zombie Hillary Clinton Hashtag Is Yet Another Sexist Attack against Her," *Bustle*, September 18, 2016, https://www.bustle.com/articles/184547-the-zombie-hillary-clinton-hashtag-is-yet-another-sexist-attack-against-her.

48. Angela Chen, "How the 'Texts from Hillary' Photo Sparked an Inquiry into Clinton's Emails," *Gizmodo*, June 11, 2016, https://www.gizmodo.com.au/2016/06/how-the-texts-from-hillary-photo-sparked-an-inquiry-into-clintons-emails/.

49. Adrienne LaFrance, "The Weird Familiarity of 100-Year-Old Feminism Memes," *Atlantic*, October 26, 2016, http://www.theatlantic.com/technology/archive/2016/10/pepe-the-anti-suffrage-frog/505406/.

50. Adrienne La France, "Predictions of a Presidentess," *Atlantic*, November 1, 2016, https://www.theatlantic.com/technology/archive/2016/11/predictions-of-a-presidentess/505982/.

51. Emily Crockett, "Why Some Feminists Are Conflicted about Hillary Clinton's Historic Candidacy," *Vox*, August 22, 2016, http://www.vox.com/2016/8/22/12370784/hillary-clinton-woman-president-feminists-conflicted.

52. Ana Stevenson and Kristin Allukian, "The Illustration, the Image, and the Archive: Feminist Digital Humanities Approaches to Caricatures and Cartoons of Woman Activists and Authors, 1850–1920"(paper presented at Women's History in the Digital World Conference, May 21–22, 2015, Bryn Mawr College, IL).

53. Limor Shifman and Dafna Lemish, "Between Feminism and Fun(ny)mism: Analysing Gender in Popular Internet Humor," *Information, Communication & Society* 13, no. 6 (2010): 883, 886–87.

Chapter Ten

THE IMPOSSIBILITIES OF HILLARY CLINTON AS A SELF-MADE WOMAN

Joanna Weiss

My mother always hated Hillary Clinton. Partly, that was politics—they don't agree on much—but the animosity also felt personal. For years, I chalked it up to generational angst: They both came of age in the 1960s, when women faced limited career choices and diminished expectations. Hillary was proof of what a smart, competent woman could accomplish, given the right opportunities.

The trouble, from my mother's standpoint: Those opportunities started with a husband.

And one lesson from the 2016 campaign was that it wasn't only boomers who felt this way. The summer before the election, I interviewed millennial women about Clinton, picking at the social dynamics that, to them, made her historic candidacy feel ho-hum.[1] Whether they were ambivalent or adored her, many brought up the same regret. They'd been raised to believe that girls could do anything, independent of boys. So to them, it would have been a diminishment—an unfortunate asterisk—if the first woman president had started as First Lady.

Never mind that Hillary Rodham was a prominent college valedictorian before she met Bill Clinton—and, as plenty of endorsements noted,[2] more qualified for the presidency, based on résumé alone, than perhaps any candidate ever. She never fully claimed an independent identity. Some of that was self-inflicted; the Clinton Foundation, a morally challenged maelstrom of influence and power, was a constant issue in the campaign, a reminder of Bill and Hillary's intertwined paths.

But Hillary also ran up against a particular interpretation of our American myth of meritocracy. As a politician, you get special points for seeming cleanly self-made. Even if you're rich, you rifle through the leaves of the family tree to pluck out a coal miner or a mail carrier or bartender, whose wholesome American spirit was the start of it all. For all of her accomplishments, Hillary seemed an exception to the ideal.

In actuality, American politics is thick with patrilineage. Sons take advantage of the family name and the family connections. Daughters do too: See Nancy Pelosi and Liz Cheney. Some second- and third-generation politicians turn out to be competent leaders, even great ones. Some face complaints and complications; think of the constant pop psychoanalysis of George W. Bush. Still, few question a child's moral standing to run for office in the first place.

But wives are different. And being the wife of a high-ranking American politician, even a wife with a career of her own, remains a peculiar condition. She's both put on a pedestal and diminished—at how many rubber-chicken dinners does the male politician graciously thank his wife for her support, then move on to the main event? And of course, she's called on to be character witness if scandal breaks out.

As First Lady in the 1990s, with unhidden political goals of her own, Hillary had to navigate new terrain. *Vanity Fair* called her "the first working mother in the White House, the first unapologetic feminist";[3] and her problem wasn't her competency, per se, but her need to cross back and forth from one realm to another. Comedians joked about her emasculated husband. Magazines scrutinized her fashion sense. When she tried to tackle health care, many complained that she lacked the standing to shepherd through a major government program. Again and again, she had to assume the ceremonial role of scandal-plagued wife.

When she finally ran for the US Senate in 2000—the first-ever First Lady to seek political office—you could have seen it as the ultimate act of making lemonade from lemons, or as a sign of unswerving determination—an eye on the goal, despite the indignities along the way. But to my mother, and many others of her generation, it felt like moral compromise: ambition above integrity.

In 2016, as voters scrutinized Clinton's campaign and her character, "ambition" was among her liabilities. When her campaign struggled with a clear, coherent message, critics fell back on the notion that she was running because she *wanted* to, and bold enough to presume that she should. In one focus group, assembled by the Republican strategist Frank Luntz two months before the election, voters assumed she was willing to do anything to win.[4] (Donald Trump was ambitious too, but no one seemed to mind.)

From younger generations, meanwhile, came the opposite critique:[5] By following Bill through his own career—and tacitly endorsing his political positions along the way—she hadn't been ambitious enough.

Which was she? It seems a false choice, particularly in the context of a modern marriage, in which turns are taken and accomplishments are celebrated by both partners. One of the pleasures of imagining Clinton as president was the prospect of seeing the old Clinton partnership in a new context. It had already begun, as Bill Clinton—an actual rags-to-riches man of polarizing ambition—traveled the country playing the customary role of the political wife. He did it, most strikingly, at the Democratic National Convention, in that short-lived time when it seemed that the Clintons were likely to return to the White House. He gave a prime-time speech about his wife. Cameras often caught him gazing on from the family box with a look of unalloyed pride. It didn't feel like penance—more like loyalty and partnership.

To various generations, it should have been a powerful message.

Notes

1. Joanna Weiss, "Why My Daughter Isn't Excited About Hillary," *Politico Magazine*, August 2, 2016, http://www.politico.com/magazine/story/2016/08/hillary-clinton-2016-feminist-214133.

2. Editorial Board, "Hillary Clinton for President," *New York Times*, September 24, 2016, https://www.nytimes.com/2016/09/25/opinion/sunday/hillary-clinton-for-president.html.

3. Margaret Carlson, "Looking Back at Hillary's First 100 Days as First Lady," *Vanity Fair*, June 1993, http://www.vanityfair.com/news/1993/06/hillary-clinton-first-lady-first-100-days.

4. Clare Foran, "The Curse of Hillary Clinton's Ambition," *Atlantic*, September 17, 2016, https://www.theatlantic.com/politics/archive/2016/09/clinton-trust-sexism/500489/.

5. Molly Roberts, "Why Millennials Are Yawning at the Likely First Female Major-Party Nominee for President," *Washington Post*, June 7, 2016, https://www.washingtonpost.com/opinions/why-millennials-are-yawning-at-the-likely-first-female-major-party-nominee-for-president/2016/06/07/11de9428-2cee-11e6-b5db-e9bc84a2c8e4_story.html?utm_term=.0b73f6a95efc.

Part Three

Baking Cookies and Grabbing Pussies

Misogyny and Sexual Politics

Chapter Eleven

THE WOMAN THEY LOVE TO HATE

Hillary Clinton and the Evangelicals

Mark Ward Sr.

"I suppose I could have stayed home, baked cookies, and had teas."[1] Those twelve words convey why, in voting for president, evangelical women found Hillary Clinton's feminism more disruptive to their "family values" than Donald Trump's infamous boast of touching women's genitals without their consent.[2] The sentence, uttered in 1992 when Clinton was queried by reporters on being the unconventional political wife of presidential candidate Bill Clinton, put her forever on the "wrong" side of the culture wars. More than two decades later, Christian author Rachel Held Evans reported, "I was at a Christian apologetics conference, and every time her name would come up, everyone would boo. A friend of mine said, 'Christians aren't allowed to say "bitch," but they make an exception for Hillary.'"[3]

Many politicians and public figures champion causes from reproductive rights to marriage equality that the Christian Right opposes. Why does the evangelical movement, a community of faith with which one in four adults identifies, single out Clinton?[4] Church historian Randall Balmer grew up in the evangelical subculture and affirms that the movement's politics of resentment start with "Clinton in particular, and [then] feminism in general."[5] Christian conservatives, he explains, see themselves as "a persecuted minority perpetually under siege at the hands of Communists, Hollywood, liberals, homosexuals, feminists, and Hillary Rodham Clinton."[6] As such, Clinton "has come to embody everything that politically conservative evangelicals fear: a woman who is intelligent, articulate, independent—in other words, out of control."[7]

But why do evangelicals value controlled gender relationships? The key is the Bible. When asked what source they trusted for spiritual guidance, whether the Bible or personal experience, 73 percent of evangelicals surveyed answered the Bible, versus 49 percent of mainline Protestants and 37 percent of Roman Catholics.[8] Personal Bible reading is practiced at least weekly by 63 percent of evangelicals, compared to 30 percent of mainline Protestants and 25 percent of Catholics.[9] Forty-four percent of evangelicals attend weekly Bible study or prayer groups, while only 19 percent of mainline Protestants and 17 percent of Catholics do so.[10] Thus, evangelical gender ideology begins with the Scriptures. For evangelicals, gender essentialism and male leadership are ordained in Genesis and established through a "household code" laid down in the New Testament.[11] Though men should rule considerately, wives must obey their husbands, children their fathers, slaves their masters. This code of ordered, hierarchical relationships was the basis of morality in antiquity and its adoption by late-first-century Christians was a "tradeoff for greater acceptance by Roman society."[12] Today this premodern code is taught in churches and enacted in families because evangelicals regard the Bible as divinely inspired for all time, not culture-bound for a given historical moment.

By the standard of the patriarchal New Testament household code, Clinton's seeming put-down of domesticity marked her as out of control. And once that impression took hold among evangelicals, her subsequent public statements were filtered through that prism: Did she say during her husband's 1992 presidential campaign, "I'm not sitting here like some little woman standing by my man, like Tammy Wynette"?[13] Then she is an elitist who is belittling wifely loyalty. Did she say in her 1995 speech to the United Nations Fourth World Conference on Women that "women's rights are human rights"?[14] Then she is elevating female independence to a basic right. Did she entitle her bestselling 1995 book *It Takes a Village* (to raise a child)?[15] Then she is attacking the traditional nuclear family. Did she dismiss her husband's 1998 impeachment over his affair with a White House intern as a "vast right-wing conspiracy"?[16] Then she is enabling his adultery and putting politics above morality. Despite the evident irony of ultimately supporting the morally flawed Trump, these now-famous sound bites remained firmly lodged in evangelical memory and shaped the movement's conclusion that Clinton's 2016 candidacy presented the greater threat to its conservative values.[17]

After Hillary Clinton left the White House and went on to serve as a US senator and secretary of state, she authored the memoirs *Living History* in 2003 and *Hard Choices* in 2014.[18] Because the books were seen as positioning her for a presidential run, they also launched a cottage industry of anti-Hillary books that were widely discussed in evangelical media. The "electronic church" did not go away after the televangelist scandals of the 1980s. After the landmark Telecommunications Act of 1996 ended restrictions on how many stations broadcasters could own, media deregulation gave rise to evangelical media conglomerates that now dominate an industry of more than 3,000 religious radio stations and a dozen religious television networks.[19] The anti-Hillary drumbeat began in 1999 with *Hell to Pay: The Unfolding Story of Hillary Rodham Clinton* by former federal prosecutor Barbara Olsen, and then ramped up with 2004's *Rewriting History* by disaffected former Clinton aide Dick Morris and 2005's *The Truth about Hillary* by independent journalist Edward Klein. All received airplay in evangelical media because their depictions of Hillary as sinister, secretive, and shrewish reinforced the existing evangelical narrative.[20] By the 2016 election cycle, the ground was prepared for a flood of anti-Hillary books, typified by Klein's *Unlikable: The Problem with Hillary* and *Guilty as Sin*—both released by a conservative publisher that had recently been acquired by the largest evangelical media conglomerate.[21]

Thus, when candidate Clinton declared that "you could put half of Trump's supporters into what I call the basket of deplorables," evangelicals, who are historically sensitive to being cast as ignorant social pariahs, interpreted the remark as lumping them with the "racist, sexist, homophobic, xenophobic, Islamophobic—you name it."[22] Who, they responded, is Hillary to judge us? What about her own ethical lapses? Eager to report any negative story, evangelical talk shows widely circulated the charge that Clinton channeled dead spirits—based on a report in journalist Bob Woodward's 1996 book, *The Choice*, that as First Lady she held imaginary White House conversations with Eleanor Roosevelt.[23] Feminism was bad enough, but witchcraft?[24] To evangelicals, Hillary was indeed out of control.

A Brief History of Evangelicals and Gender

Preservation of traditional gender roles has been a cultural casus belli for American evangelicals from the nineteenth century to the present. Seen in this light, antipathy to Hillary Clinton fits a two-hundred-year stream of historical continuity. During the late nineteenth and early twentieth centuries, recounts historian Betty DeBerg, "An inerrant Bible was the major weapon fielded in the fundamentalist battle for the conventions of the Victorian separate-spheres [gender] ideology."[25] Following the Scopes "Monkey Trial" of 1925 and resultant public retreat of fundamentalism, the movement concentrated on building its own subculture. Evangelical women of the 1930s and 1940s, observes historian Margaret Lamberts Bendroth, were recruited as religious schoolteachers and missionaries with the understanding that their callings were secondary to those of men. Yet by the postwar 1950s and 1960s, evangelicals responded to a desire for stability amidst rapid social change by reemphasizing the cult of feminine domesticity.[26]

When the New Christian Right emerged in the 1970s and 1980s, its culture war against "unisex" feminism further hardened the evangelical ideology of gender essentialism. The era's battles between feminists and social conservatives over the Equal Rights Amendment (sent by Congress in 1972 to the states, where its ratification ultimately stalled), abortion (legalized nationwide by the 1973 *Roe v. Wade* Supreme Court ruling), and gay rights (which became an evangelical cause célèbre after Christian singer Anita Bryant campaigned against a 1977 Dade County, Florida, ordinance barring antigay discrimination) received intense media coverage. Yet historians agree that a different issue—education—ultimately politicized evangelicals. After a series of Supreme Court decisions in the 1960s disallowed official prayers and Bible readings in public schools, evangelicals turned in the 1970s to developing their own alternative education system. Over the decade, church-run day schools opened at an average rate of two per day and enrolled nearly a million children.[27] Then in 1978, the Internal Revenue Service ruled these schools were de facto "white flight" academies and threatened to end their tax exemptions. Believing the agency unfairly misread their religious purpose, evangelicals protested what they viewed as a violation of their religious freedom.[28] A leading conservative organizer later recalled that "what galvanized the Christian community was not abortion, school prayer, or the ERA . . . [but] Jimmy Carter's intervention against the Christian schools . . . [because] suddenly it dawned on them that they were not going to be able to be left alone to teach their children as they pleased."[29] Among other concerns about public education—teaching evolution, adopting "revisionist" history textbooks, using the "look-say" method of reading instruction rather than phonics—church schools enabled evangelical parents to opt their children out of "value-neutral" sex education and instead pass along their own essentialist ideology regarding sex, marriage, and gender differences.[30]

In time, however, as feminist gains and liberalized sexual mores became mainstream, evangelicals needed to offer a satisfying alternative. Since the 1990s they have developed a rhetoric of "complementarianism." Its key doctrine is stated by the Council on Biblical Manhood and Womanhood, whose mission "is to set forth the teachings of the Bible about the complementary differences between men and women, created equally in the image of God, because these teachings are essential for obedience to Scripture and for the health of the family and the church." Founded in 1987, the group holds that the New Testament household code is vital for today: "If families do not structure their homes properly, in disobedience to the teachings of Ephesians 5, 1 Peter 3, and Colossians 3, then they will not have the proper foundation from which to withstand the temptations of the devil and the various onslaughts of the world."[31]

Examples of complementarian rhetoric in evangelical popular culture are rife. Historian Virginia Lieson Brereton surveyed conversion-story literature and concluded that evangelicals "employed the genre to affirm the conventional notion of marriage and the subordinate role of women within marriage."[32] Anthropologist John Bartkowski surveyed books on marriage by bestselling evangelical authors and found that gender essentialism is by far the majority position.[33] And media scholar Deborah Clark Vance listened daily for nine months to a major-city evangelical network radio station and observed:

> The Bible is used to support the notion of essentialist gender roles and argue that the respective behaviors of women and men are driven by their biology.... Male speakers and callers routinely described their struggles with "headship" or wisely fulfilling their role as head of the family.... Women speakers and callers agreed they are called to respect male headship . . . [and] invariably testified how they came to see God's wisdom in creating women and men to find satisfaction in their "different but equal" roles.[34]

A paradox of complementarian ideology is that it frames female submission as empowering, and many evangelical women genuinely experience it that way. Informally, observed sociologist James Ault, though "positions of formal authority are reserved, according to the patriarchal model, for men . . . organizational strength is built through family ties sustained, by and large, by women."[35] At a formal level, religion scholar Brenda Brasher discovered, sexual polarity allows "women's ministries" to operate as virtual "shadow" churches that "provide women with a counterfoil to male dominance in congregational life."[36] Ethnographer R. Marie Griffith discovered that "the women themselves claim the doctrine of submission leads both to freedom and transformation" and regard their "voluntary submission to divine authority . . . [as] a bold surrender, an act of assuming a crucial role God has called women to play."[37] By contrast, reported sociologist Sally Gallagher, evangelicals maintain that abandoning the household code would leave men rudderless and even dangerous, while leaving women bereft of love, security, and respect.[38]

The Woman Evangelicals Love to Hate

Complementarianism captured evangelical popular imagination with the 1991 publication of *Recovering Biblical Manhood and Womanhood*, an edited volume featuring more than twenty conservative evangelical scholars that is much praised in the evangelical community.[39] That complementarianism had taken root was affirmed in a sociological survey, conducted between 1995 and 1997, of more than 2,700 evangelical churchgoers. Only a minority held to unqualified male headship; most resorted to complementarianism to reconcile the New Testament household code with contemporary ideals of equality. As Christian Smith reported, "A more common approach—one which holds perhaps the greatest potential to legitimate male-privileged marriage through the rhetoric of equality—was to contend that husband and wife are equal in value and spiritual importance, but are *functionally* different."[40]

At this same time, Hillary Clinton burst onto the national political stage. Her 1992 statement that "I suppose I could have stayed home, baked cookies, and had teas" came at the right political moment to furnish evangelicals the perfect foil for their new complementarian ideology. That same year, the Christian Coalition, founded by televangelist Pat Robertson, was entering the height of its political influence. The group spent $10 million on political action in 1992, claimed a quarter of a million members, helped write that year's Republican Party platform, trained candidates and volunteers, and distributed millions of "Family Values Voter Guides" at churches nationwide. The coalition "did not just back the Republican Party. In collaboration with other conservative Christian groups, it *became* the Republican Party."[41] One of those other groups, Concerned Women for America, in 1992 claimed 573,000 members—if true, more than the feminist National Organization for Women—and a budget of $10 million. The year 1992 was also the political moment when presidential candidate Pat Buchanan electrified the Republican National Convention with his "culture war" speech. Among other dire warnings, he proclaimed: "'Elect me, and you get two for the price of one,' Mr. Clinton says of his lawyer-spouse. And what does Hillary believe? Well, Hillary believes that 12-year-olds should have a right to sue their parents, and she has compared marriage as an institution to slavery—and life on an Indian reservation. Well, speak for yourself, Hillary. Friends, this is radical feminism."[42]

The political moment when Hillary Clinton retorted, "I suppose I could have stayed home," was the same moment when Republican vice president Dan Quayle called out the television sitcom *Murphy Brown*. After the show's title character decided to conceive and raise a child out of wedlock, Quayle decried her "poverty of values." In a 1992 speech, he exclaimed, "It doesn't help matters when prime-time TV has Murphy Brown—a character who supposedly epitomizes today's intelligent, highly paid, professional woman—mocking the importance of fathers, by bearing a child alone, and calling it just another 'lifestyle choice.'"[43] As the "mommy wars" escalated, Clinton's *It Takes a Village* found its way into 1996 Republican presidential candidate Bob Dole's nomination acceptance speech: "And after the virtual devastation of the American family, the rock upon which this country was founded, we are told that it takes a village, that is collective, and thus the state, to raise a child. . . . I am here to tell you it does not take a village to raise a child. It takes a family to raise a child."[44]

Antipathy to Clinton was cemented during her husband's term as president, a period many evangelicals associate with the undoing of the Reagan Revolution and loss of the culture wars. "Hillary Clinton represents more than one liberal politician. It was the Clinton legacy and the place it had in the culture wars," recalls Karen Swallow Prior, now a professor at evangelical Liberty University.[45] Thus, when Bill Clinton's 1998 sex scandal broke and Hillary publicly blamed not her husband but a "vast right-wing conspiracy," evangelicals interpreted the sound bite as shifting responsibility and thus excusing sexual immorality. For that reason, Prior recounts, "she was viewed as an enabler." Adds Karen Beaty, a former managing editor of the evangelical *Christianity Today* magazine, "Hillary is still associated with her husband's affairs and held in contempt for her husband's behavior, even though you would think a woman staying with her husband would be praised."[46]

Evangelical reaction to Clinton illustrates a truth of persuasion theory: a person, once reduced to inflammatory sound bites, may be rejected out of hand. Seen in context, her statement about "baking cookies" prefaced a desire to "fulfill my profession which I entered before my husband was in public life." Many evangelical women have followed the same path. Likewise, her 1992 statement, "I'm not sitting here like some little woman standing by my man, like Tammy Wynette," could resonate with evangelical women if they also heard Clinton's explanation that "I'm sitting here because I love him, and I respect him, and I honor what he's been through and what we've been through together." Instead, the more inflammatory sound bites lodged in evangelical memory until "Hillary" became the symbol of a woman out of control, the arch-transgressor of the biblical household code. When that happened, evangelicals stopped processing what Clinton actually said. Rather, her symbolism has since functioned as a "peripheral cue" that shuts off active cognition and prompts immediate rejection of her message.[47] "She's not submissive, she's not sexy, she's not properly maternal," explains historian Kristin Du Mez. "Even without saying anything, she's a symbol of many of the things evangelicals have come to stand against."[48]

An irony of this impasse is that Clinton is an active Methodist and Sunday school teacher who attended weekly prayer breakfasts as a US senator and has spoken openly of her faith. Yet her mainline Protestantism stems from a moral universe in which Jesus's resurrection is a symbol of how the downtrodden can overcome the powerful rather than, as in the evangelical worldview, a vicarious sacrifice for the sins of humanity. A further, yet more hopeful, irony is that ordinary evangelical couples find admonitions to obey the New Testament household code, though clear from the pulpit, less straightforward in actual married life. In a three-year field study, Bartkowski interviewed husbands and wives at a large evangelical church. Many wives reconstructed "submission" as a choice rather than an imperative, leaving room for negotiation in marital power relations. Mutual discussion of decisions was expected. In uncommon cases when consensus could not be reached, wives voluntarily ceded final say to their husbands as a matter of expediency. For their part, husbands were aware of cultural disapproval for patriarchy and qualified their "headship" with professions not to abuse their authority but to sacrificially love their wives and welcome them as full partners. Bartkowski concluded: "[Although] essentialist rhetoric figures prominently into the construction of gender in [the] congregation . . . the general commitment to masculine-feminine difference is . . . peppered with caveats . . . [that] allow members of [the church] to retain their commitment to the general rule of gender difference while accounting for the numerous exceptions to this rule."[49]

Finally, if 81 percent of 2016 evangelical voters supported Donald Trump, then 19 percent supported other candidates—including 16 percent who voted for Clinton.[50] In fact, evangelicals engaged in thoroughgoing debate over the wisdom of tying themselves to Trump.[51] Ultimately, four in five pulled the lever for the Republican—though according to one poll, more than a third of white evangelical Protestants (35 percent) supported the twice-divorced casino owner primarily because "he is not Clinton," a response that topped "his policy positions" (34 percent), "he will bring change" (26 percent), and "he tells it like it is" (19 percent).[52] The angst was felt even by Wayne Grudem, coeditor of *Recovering Biblical Manhood and Womanhood*, who first endorsed Trump, then unendorsed him after revelations that the billionaire had bragged about sexually assaulting women, but in the end reendorsed him.[53] For many evangelicals, the decision came down to a feeling that Clinton "is personally responsible for babies being aborted," says Deborah Fikes, a former board member of the National Association of Evangelicals. After endorsing Clinton, Fikes reports, "I was told that I was supporting a daughter of Satan and that I had the blood of 60 million babies on my hands."[54] Yet many dissenters, like Fikes, agreed with Russell Moore, president of the Ethics and Religious Liberty Commission of the Southern Baptist Convention, who wrote: "Evangelical leaders have said that, for the sake of the 'lesser of two evils,' one should stand with someone who not only characterizes sexual decadence and misogyny, brokers in cruelty and nativism, and displays a crazed public and private temperament—but who glories in these things. Some of the very people who warned us about moral relativism and situational ethics now ask us to become moral relativists for the sake of an election."[55]

To Moore and others, the deep irony of the 2016 presidential election is that Christian Right leaders, who once said "character matters" and called for Bill Clinton's impeachment, seemingly changed their tune for the sake of political power as they urged evangelicals to overlook Trump's immoral behavior. "Evangelical Christians became politically active in the 1980s," cautioned Moore, "in an attempt to beat back the corrupting influence of crass, secular, and materialistic culture. Now *they* have become corrupted as they seek to retain political influence—to the detriment of both our politics and their religious communities."[56]

As *Washington Post* religion reporter Sarah Pulliam Bailey noted, "This election cycle has exposed underlying divisions within Christianity as a whole, but especially among evangelicals," who vigorously debated whether a vote for Donald Trump meant choosing the "lesser of two evils" or compromising the movement's values.[57] The quandary was best captured for Southern Baptist leader Moore when a woman queried him about the tolerance among evangelical Christians for the divisive rhetoric that the Trump candidacy injected into the nation's politics. She then lamented, "I've spent all my life saying church is going to be a place where you can go [for refuge] when you face this sort of thing."[58] Yet perhaps the deepest irony is that, in exacting its revenge on Hillary Clinton, the evangelical movement itself has fundamentally changed. "If Donald Trump has done anything," Moore states, "he has snuffed out the [old-guard] Religious Right" by laying bare the corruption of its ideals. The future of the evangelical movement, he believes, instead lies in "younger, multiethnic, gospel-centered Christians" who are motivated by global and community outreach and "not by the doctrinally vacuous resentment over a lost regime of nominal, cultural 'Christian America.'"[59]

Notes

1. See, for example, Mary Elizabeth Williams, "Hillary Clinton's Decisive Triumph over Cookie Baking and 'Stand by Your Man,'" *Salon*, July 29, 2016, http://www.salon.com/2016/07/29/hillary_clintons_decisive_triumph_over_cookie_baking_and_stand_by_your_man.

2. "Access Hollywood Archival Footage Reveals Vulgar Trump Comments from 2005," *Access Hollywood*, October 7, 2016, http://www.accessonline.com/articles/access-hollywood-archival-footage-reveals-vulgar-trump-comments-2005/.

3. Sarah Pulliam Bailey, "The Deep Disgust for Hillary Clinton That Drives So Many Evangelicals to Support Trump," *Washington Post*, October 19, 2016, https://www.washingtonpost.com/news/acts-of-faith/wp/2016/10/09/the-deep-disgust-for-hillary-clinton-that-drives-so-many-evangelicals-to-support-trump/.

4. Pew Research Center, *America's Changing Religious Landscape* (Washington, DC: Pew Research Center, 2015), http://assets.pewresearch.org/wp-content/uploads/sites/11/2015/05/RLS-08-26-full-report.pdf. According to Pew's 2014 U.S. Religious Landscape Survey of 35,000 adults, the median age of evangelicals is forty-nine years; 55 percent are women and 45 percent men; 76 percent are non-Hispanic whites; 55 percent are married; and 49 percent live in the South, 22 percent in the Midwest, 20 percent in the West, and 9 percent in the Northeast.

5. Randall Balmer, *Blessed Assurance: A History of Evangelicalism in America* (Boston: Beacon Press, 1999), 88.

6. Ibid., 109.

7. Ibid., 99.

8. Cited in Corwin E. Smidt, *American Evangelicals Today* (Lanham, MD: Rowman & Littlefield, 2013), 93.

9. Pew Research Center, *U.S. Public Becoming Less Religious* (Washington, DC: Pew Research Center, 2015), http://assets.pewresearch.org/wp-content/uploads/sites/11/2015/11/201.11.03_RLS_II_full_report.pdf.

10. Ibid.

11. On gender essentialism and male leadership, see Gen. 2:18–24, 3:16; cf. 1 Tim. 3:11–15; on the household code, see Col. 3:18–4:1, Eph. 5:22–6:9, 1 Pet. 2:18–3:7.

12. L. Michael White, *From Jesus to Christianity* (New York: HarperCollins, 2004), 276.

13. Williams, "Hillary Clinton's Decisive Triumph."

14. Hillary Rodham Clinton, "Remarks to the U.N. 4th World Conference on Women Plenary Session" (delivered September 5, 1995, Beijing, China), *American Rhetoric*, http://www.americanrhetoric.com/speeches/hillaryclintonbeijingspeech.htm.

15. Hillary Rodham Clinton, *It Takes a Village: And Other Lessons Children Teach Us* (New York: Simon & Schuster, 1995).

16. See, for example, Philip Bump, "Hillary Clinton Dusts Off the 'Vast Right-wing Conspiracy' Charge," *Washington Post*, July 8, 2015, https://www.washingtonpost.com/news/the-fix/wp/2015/07/08/is-the-vast-right-wing-conspiracy-to-blame-for-hillary-clintons-falling-honesty-rating.

17. How Christian Right media messages in support of Donald Trump influenced local congregations is examined in Mark Ward Sr., "The Dangers of Getting What You Wished For: What Do You Say to Evangelicals?," in *Constructing Narratives in Response to Trump's Election: How Various Populations Make Sense of an Unexpected Victory*, ed. Shing-Ling S. Chen, Nicole Allaire, and Zhoujun Joyce Chen (Lanham, MD: Lexington Books, 2018), 61–81.

18. Hillary Rodham Clinton, *Living History* (New York: Simon & Schuster, 2003); Hillary Rodham Clinton, *Hard Choices* (New York: Simon & Schuster, 2014).

19. Mark Ward Sr., "Dark Preachers: The Impact of Radio Consolidation on Independent Religious Syndicators," *Journal of Media and Religion* 8, no. 2 (2009): 79–96; Mark Ward Sr., "Consolidating the Gospel: The Impact of the 1996 Telecommunications Act on Religious Radio Ownership," *Journal of Media and Religion* 11, no. 1 (2012): 11–30; Mark Ward Sr., "Digital Religion and Media Economics: Concentration and Convergence in the Electronic Church," *Journal of Religion, Media, and Digital Culture* 7, no. 1 (2018): 90–120.

20. Barbara Olson, *Hell to Pay: The Unfolding Story of Hillary Rodham Clinton* (Washington, DC: Regnery, 1999); Dick Morris and Eileen McGann, *Rewriting History* (New York: Regan, 2004); Edward Klein, *The Truth about Hillary: What She Knew, When She Knew It, and How Far She'll Go to Become President* (New York: Sentinel, 2005).

21. Edward Klein, *Unlikable: The Problem with Hillary* (Washington, DC: Regnery, 2015); Edward Klein, *Guilty as Sin: Uncovering New Evidence of Corruption and How Hillary Clinton and the Democrats Derailed the FBI Investigation* (Washington, DC: Regnery, 2016). Regnery Publishing was acquired in 2014 by Salem Media Group.

22. See, for example, Domenico Montanaro, "Hillary Clinton's 'Basket of Deplorables' in Full Context of This Ugly Campaign," NPR, September 10, 2016, http://www.npr.org/2016/09/10/493427601/hillary-clintons-basket-of-deplorables-in-full-context-of-this-ugly-campaign. The actual quotation is, "You know, to just be grossly generalistic, you could put half of Trump's supporters into what I call the basket of deplorables. Right? The racist, sexist, homophobic, xenophobic, Islamophobic—you name it. . . . Now some of those folks, they are irredeemable, but thankfully they are not America." On evangelicals' historic sensitivity to being characterized as ignorant, see, for example, Edward J. Larson, *Summer for the Gods: The Scopes Trial and America's Continuing Debate over Science and Religion* (New York: Basic Books, 1997). On reaction to the "deplorables" statement, see

Todd Starnes, *The Deplorables' Guide to Making America Great Again* (Lake Mary, FL: FrontLine, 2017).

23. Bob Woodward, *The Choice: Inside the Clinton White House* (New York: Simon & Schuster, 1996).

24. See, for example, Jan Markell, "An Abomination unto the Lord," *Oliver Tree Ministries*, October 15, 2016, https://www.olivetreeviews.org/component/k2/item/11451-an-abomination-to-the-lord.

25. Betty A. DeBerg, *Ungodly Women: Gender and the First Wave of American Fundamentalism*, 2nd ed. (Macon, GA: Mercer University Press, 2000), 128.

26. Margaret Lamberts Bendroth, *Fundamentalism and Gender, 1875 to the Present* (New Haven, CT: Yale University Press, 1993), 81.

27. Joseph Crespino, "Civil Rights and the Religious Right," in *Rightward Bound: Making America Conservative in the 1970s*, ed. Bruce J. Schulman and Julian E. Zelizer (Cambridge, MA: Harvard University Press, 2008), 100.

28. The argument that segregation initially animated the Religious Right is made in Randall Balmer, "The Real Origins of the Religious Right," *Politico Magazine*, May 27, 2014, https://www.politico.com/magazine/story/2014/05/religious-right-real-origins-107133?o=0. However, religious motives are dominant in two classic field studies of Christian schools: Alan Peshkin, *God's Choice: The Total World of a Fundamentalist Christian School* (Chicago: University of Chicago Press, 1986); Susan D. Rose, *Keeping Them Out of the Hands of Satan: Evangelical Schooling in America* (New York: Routledge, 1988). Peshkin surveyed students and found large majorities supported housing integration and white responsibility to end racial discrimination (332).

29. Quoted in William Martin, *With God on Our Side: The Rise of the Religious Right in America* (New York: Broadway, 1996), 183.

30. See, for example, Keith B. Richburg, "Education Official Attacks 'Value-Neutral' Curriculum," *Washington Post*, September 6, 1985, https://www.washingtonpost.com/archive/politics/1985/09/06/education-official-attacks-value-neutral-curriculum/7aec8386-bbc5-42f4-939c-3ed5271019f7.

31. Council on Biblical Manhood and Womanhood, "Mission & Vision," accessed May 30, 2017, http://cbmw.org/about/mission-vision.

32. Virginia Lieson Brereton, *From Sin to Salvation: Stories of Women's Conversions, 1800 to the Present* (Bloomington: Indiana University Press, 1991), 89.

33. John P. Bartkowski, *Remaking the Godly Marriage: Gender Negotiation in Evangelical Families* (New Brunswick, NJ: Rutgers University Press, 2001).

34. Deborah Clark Vance, "The Flesh and the Spirit: Communicating Evangelical Identity via 'Christian Radio,'" in *The Electronic Church in the Digital Age: Cultural Impacts of Evangelical Mass Media*, vol. 1, ed. Mark Ward Sr. (Santa Barbara, CA: Praeger, 2016), 39–40.

35. James M. Ault Jr., *Spirit and Flesh: Life in a Fundamentalist Baptist Church* (New York: Knopf, 2004), 316.

36. Brenda E. Brasher, *Godly Women: Fundamentalism and Female Power* (New Brunswick, NJ: Rutgers University Press, 1998), 64.

37. R. Marie Griffith, *God's Daughters: Evangelical Women and the Power of Submission* (Berkeley: University of California Press, 1997), 179, 199.

38. Sally K. Gallagher, *Evangelical Identity and Gendered Family Life* (New Brunswick, NJ: Rutgers University Press, 2003).

39. John Piper and Wayne Grudem, eds., *Recovering Biblical Manhood and Womanhood: A Response to Evangelical Feminism* (Wheaton, IL: Crossway, 1991).

40. Christian Smith, *Christian America? What Evangelicals Really Want* (Berkeley: University of California Press, 2000), 173; emphasis in original.

41. Allan J. Lichtman, *White Protestant Nation: The Rise of the American Conservative Movement* (New York: Atlantic Monthly Press, 2008), 399; emphasis in original.

42. Patrick J. Buchanan, "1992 Republican National Convention Speech," August 17, 1992, http://buchanan.org/blog/1992-republican-national-convention-speech-148.

43. Dan Quayle, "Address to the Commonwealth Club of California," May 19, 1992, http://www.vicepresidentdanquayle.com/speeches_Standing Firm_CCC_3.html.

44. Robert Dole, "Text of Robert Dole's Speech to the Republican National Convention," August 15, 1996, CNN.com, http://www.cnn.com/ALLPOLITICS/1996/conventions/san.diego/transcripts/0815/dole.fdch.shtml.

45. Bailey, "Deep Disgust for Hillary Clinton."

46. Ibid.

47. Richard E. Petty and John T. Cacioppo, "The Elaboration Likelihood Model of Persuasion," in *Advances in Experimental Social Psychology*, vol. 19, ed. Leonard Berkowitz (Orlando, FL: Academic Press, 1986), 197–253.

48. Bailey, "Deep Disgust for Hillary Clinton."

49. Bartkowski, *Remaking the Godly Marriage*, 165.

50. Gregory A. Smith and Jessica Martinez, "How the Faithful Voted: A Preliminary 2016 Analysis," *Pew Research Center*, November 9, 2017, http://www.pewresearch.org/fact-tank/2016/11/09/how-the-faithful-voted-a-preliminary-2016-analysis.

51. See, for example, Sarah Pulliam Bailey, "Why Some Fear This Election's Lasting Damage to American Christianity," *Washington Post*, November 9, 2016, https://www.washingtonpost.com/news/acts-of-faith/wp/2016/11/09/why-some-fear-this-elections-lasting-damage-to-american-christianity.

52. Gregory A. Smith, "Many Evangelicals Favor Trump Because He Is Not Clinton," *Pew Research Center*, September 23, 2016, http://www.pewresearch.org/fact-tank/2016/09/23/many-evangelicals-favor-trump-because-he-is-not-clinton.

53. Ken Shepherd, "Theologian Wayne Grudem, Who Briefly Recanted His Endorsement, Back on the Trump Train," *Washington Times*, October 20, 2016, http://www.washingtontimes.com/news/2016/oct/20/theologian-wayne-grudem-who-briefly-recanted-his-e.

54. Bailey, "Deep Disgust for Hillary Clinton."

55. Russell Moore, "If Donald Trump Has Done Anything, He Has Snuffed Out the Religious Right," *Washington Post*, October 9, 2016, https://www.washingtonpost.com/news/acts-of-faith/wp/2016/10/09/if-donald-trump-has-done-anything-he-has-snuffed-out-the-religious-right.

56. Ibid.

57. Bailey, "Why Some Fear."

58. Ibid.

59. Moore, "If Trump Has Done Anything."

Chapter Twelve

"LOCKER ROOM TALK"
AS "SMALL POTATOES"

Media, Women of the GOP, and
the 2016 Presidential Election

Jiyoung Lee, Carol M. Liebler, and Neal J. Powless

There is little question that the 2016 US presidential election was highly contentious and polarizing. When all was said and done, Donald Trump had not only won the Electoral College, but enjoyed 88 percent of Republican women's votes and 52 percent of white women's vote, continuing a trend found in previous presidential elections.[1] With Democrats selecting Hillary Clinton as the first woman major-party presidential nominee, and Republicans nominating Donald Trump with his history of sexist attitudes and behaviors, the question arises as to how Republican women navigated the gendered terrain that the campaign presented. Were they drawn toward Clinton because she was a woman or did they hold party affiliation dear? Alternatively, despite party affiliation did they push away from Trump because of his past, and feel a tug toward a woman candidate?

Through the lens of feminist standpoint theory, this chapter investigates how women of the GOP experienced each candidate, and how the media, candidates, and party each helped to formulate their opinions. We hope to contribute to a better understanding of the dynamics of Trump's victory over Clinton by seeking out and giving voice to the perspectives of Republican women in this election.

Researchers have discussed the discrimination women politicians encounter in the male-dominated political field, especially focusing on Hillary Clinton. In 2008 Clinton was reported in a more negative way than other candidates,[2] labeling her a nontraditional woman obsessed with political power and thereby stepping out of an acceptable role.[3]

Much less is known, however, about how Republican women specifically view Clinton as a woman and as a politician, or what they made of the Republican nominee, Donald Trump.

Gender-Related Theories

Due to traditional gender expectations, women in leadership roles tend to be negatively evaluated compared to men in the same positions.[4] For example, whereas women are associated with friendliness, men are thought to be independent.[5] Role congruity theory,[6] an extension of social role theory,[7] explains how these expectations become problematic.[8] If a woman in high power behaves in an agentic way, which violates a traditional role, people tend to discredit her. Such negative evaluations are aggravated when women exhibit agentic leadership styles in masculine-dominated fields such as politics or military.[9] Thus, women who strive to be a prototypical politician can be caught in a double bind, such that enacting agentic behaviors can make them respected but not liked. In contrast, exhibiting communal behaviors can have the effect of making them liked but not respected as a politician.[10]

Gender-role conflict theory provides further explanation of how traditional gender roles are maintained, suggesting that role conflicts occur when women face contradicting gender roles.[11] In the political arena, such conflicts from contradicting gender roles can be shown among voters. The term "baseline gender preference" indicates that voters tend to have a preference for a woman or man candidate who is in accordance with gender stereotypes.[12]

In relation to the 2016 presidential election, these gender theories raise the question of how Republican women felt toward Clinton and Trump as candidates, and as a woman and man, respectively. Thus, the main goal of our study is to examine Republican women's normative expectations of Clinton and Trump in relation to gender. If Republican women held hostile attitudes toward Clinton while placing little importance on Trump's sexual harassment/abuse allegations, they might have assumed that Clinton violated women's traditional gender roles whereas Trump followed male ones. Sexual harassment and sexism are congruent with gender role stereotyping,[13] such that Republicans who internalized traditional gender norms may have granted Trump considerable leeway in his behaviors. Gender role stereotyping may also have heightened hostility toward Clinton because of the assumption that Clinton does not fit into the traditional characteristics of womanhood. Indeed, past media coverage had described Clinton as a nontraditional woman who subverted her femininity earlier in her career.[14]

Biased Perceptions of Media Portrayals

Republican claims that media are biased toward the Democrats (i.e., supportive of Hillary Clinton)[15] can be explained by *the hostile media effect*, which argues that partisans see a news report as slanted toward the opposing side. For example, empirical evidence of a hostile media effect shows that both pro-Israeli and pro-Arab partisans evaluated the same news coverage as being slanted toward the "other" side.[16] Psychological mechanisms—selective recall (paying more attention to dissimilar opinion), selective categorization (classifying information that they receive as opponents' information), and different standards (positing one's opinions as more accurate than the opposing one's)—have been noted as underlying factors of the hostile media effect.[17]

Past presidential election research has revealed the hostile media effect. In the 1980 election, for example, most Americans (66 percent) perceived media coverage about presidential candidates as impartial, but for those who perceived bias in media, most of them (89 percent) tended to presume the coverage was in opposition to candidates whom they supported.[18] In a similar study, according to 2008 US presidential election polls, opponents of Obama and supporters of McCain perceived that the election polls had a bias in favor of Obama but were unfavorable to McCain.[19] Thus the public's "distrust [of media] is more likely to be a situational response, stemming from involvement with issues and groups."[20] Based on social judgment theory, partisans will be more likely to refute message content than nonpartisans who have low levels of interest in politics.[21]

Research Questions

Based on the above literature, we developed three research questions for this study. We investigate these three questions using the lens of feminist standpoint theory (discussed below).

How did Republican women perceive Hillary Clinton and Donald Trump in relation to gender roles and performance?

What meaning and subtext do Republican women find in media portrayals of Hillary Clinton, and how might these be different from those of Donald Trump?

How are gender, political orientation, and perceptions of media coverage of the two presidential candidates interrelated?

Method

This study employed an in-depth interviews methodology. To recruit participants, we first sent a recruitment email to acquaintances. We asked them to recommend Republican women they knew, using a purposive snowball sampling method. The qualitative interview at the heart of this study "attempts to understand the world from the subjects' points of view, to unfold the meaning of their experiences, to uncover their lived world prior to scientific explanations."[22]

Our sample included twenty-one self-identified Republican women, ranging in age from eighteen to fifty-eight years old. Participant occupations were varied and included, for example, a political blogger, former researcher, at-home mother, surgical nurse, doctoral student, administrator, college student, accountant, senior sustainability consultant, and retired special education teacher.

To understand how these Republican women navigated the gender issues of the 2016 presidential campaign, we apply feminist standpoint theory, which argues that "women's historical situation of subordination within a system of gender hierarchy creates conditions for them to see the operations of the male-as-norm."[23]

We conducted semistructured interviews from October 14 to November 7, 2016, the day before the election. We held the interviews prior to the presidential election so that its outcome did not bias participant perceptions. The interviews, which were conducted by two doctoral students residing in New York, were either face-to-face or on the phone and ranged from twenty-two to forty-nine minutes. All participants were white (twenty) with the exception of one Native American. According to CNN exit poll data, 52 percent of white women and 88 percent of Republican women voted for Trump,[24] thereby indicating that our sample is a particularly relevant one. Participants' residencies included New York, Missouri, Michigan, and Illinois.

Interviews focused on such topics as the importance of politics in participants' lives, how they personally felt about Hillary Clinton as a woman and her purported ethical issues such as using a personal email account for business conducted as secretary of state; how they felt about allegations that Donald Trump had committed sexual harassment and assault and tax fraud; and how they evaluated media coverage of the candidates and whether they perceived coverage to exhibit gender bias. For example, we asked the interviewees questions such as "How important is politics in your life?" "How much concern do you have regarding the presidential election?" "Despite your political ideology, how do you feel about Clinton, particularly as a woman?" "What do you think of unethical issues in relation to Clinton? What of Trump?" "Do you feel media coverage of Clinton's purported unethical issues are reported in an unbiased and objective way? Why or why not?" and "How do you feel about the media reports on Trump's sexual harassment and assault allegations?"

We transcribed all interviews and used descriptive coding to discover dominant themes. Interview participants are referred to with pseudonyms here, to protect their privacy. Our analysis resulted in four main themes, elaborated on below.

Wanted: A Traditional Woman

This theme revealed the social expectations and actions of women in politics. These societal expectations of traditional womanhood create the lens through which Republican women have viewed Clinton and evaluated her actions as well as visual appearance. The views of the Republican women we interviewed largely reflected and reinforced a baseline gender preference as they took Clinton to task for how she dressed and looked. Collectively they expressed that she did not represent what a woman should be: always smiling, wearing a skirt and heels.

Emily, a forty-eight-year-old accountant, felt strongly that a woman, in this case Clinton, should dress in a traditionally feminine manner consisting of a skirt and heels: "So yes, it is sexist, it is still. But is it wrong? We might have the first woman president but does she look like a woman, no. She's dressing like a man for crying out loud, with her man suit." Emily added that Clinton has taken on male dominant traits of dress and speaking in order to survive in a male-dominated political world: "She acts like a man, she looks like a man, she doesn't act like a lady and that's the truth because it's [politics] a man's world." So although Emily recognized that Clinton may be facing a double bind, she condemned her response to it.

For fifty-four-year-old Ann, it was Clinton's facial expressions that troubled her. "When Hillary talks, I feel it she is a very angry woman. Like her face. Her facial expression. She's like . . . They are always saying that Donald is angry but I see [it] on her." What is telling in both of these examples is that they echoed criticisms of Clinton found in the popular press during the presidential campaign.[25] Therefore, although the women interviewees criticized the news media (a phenomenon we discuss below), it appears their perceptions may have been at least partially framed by them.

This perception is not limited to appearance alone. A fifty-three-year-old homemaker took great offense to one Clinton comment in particular—one that aired March 26, 1992, on ABC's *Nightline*[26]—because it challenged traditional gender roles: "And she was asked, in an interview, I believe it was about why she chose the career path that she did. And she said: 'What did you want me to do? Stay home and bake cookies all day?' And that was an insult to myself."

Others took Clinton to task for what they perceived she had *not* said, and this, too, had gendered implications. For example, said one participant: "We all have things that we're sorry for. Hillary never even said 'Yes, I breached my computer and got rid of those emails and I'm very sorry.'" Here, Clinton is called out for not apologizing when the participant perceived she should have. Notably, women apologize more than men and are more likely to feel an apology is warranted,[27] so Clinton was thought to be particularly egregious in this regard as she was a woman perceived to transgress this norm. Clinton in fact had apologized in an interview with CNN for the email scandal by saying that "there are no excuses. I want people to know that the decision to have a single account was mine. I take responsibility for it. I apologize for it," showing genuine contrition.[28]

Hostile Media: A Clinton Bias?

Not only did our participants criticize Clinton herself; they also took the media to task for what they perceived was favoring a woman candidate. In the second presidential debate, Trump raised the issue that the media were biased by questioning how they treated Clinton.[29] This claim seemed to resonate with the women we interviewed, as their comments mirrored Trump's debate rhetoric, and a concern with media bias seemed to outweigh any concerns they may have had at how he appeared to treat women.

Participants' criticisms included their disapproval of major networks such as CNN, ABC, CBS, NBC, and even FOX, as well as friends' social media posts. Alana, an eighteen-year-old college student, explained how she saw the differences in media reports of Clinton and Trump: "I think the media is excited about, once they have something about Trump that is negative. They find it really easy to go against him. Rather than Hillary, they report on her but it's like just factual reporting. But with Trump, I think they give excuses to hate him."

Diana, a thirty-eight-year-old political blogger, put it this way: "Grossly underreported it [Clinton's unethical issues]. Absolutely nothing about Wikileaks from my evening news, well very very little." Wikileaks is a reference to the released email dump that included derogatory comments made by Clinton campaign senior officials regarding minority organizations and religious communities. Diana's comment echoed Trump's own claims that the information was damaging but the media underreported it.[30]

The women in this study expressed a deep concern that media coverage was slanted in favor of a female candidate, and they didn't like it. Sally, a forty-year-old sustainability consultant, noted, "I think that the media is trying to portray him in a bad light so that women almost have to vote for Hillary by default." Not only does Sally push back against the idea that as a woman she should automatically support a woman for president; she attributes motivation on the part of the news media for trying to make her do so.

Some participants went further, asserting that Democrats paid off the media. In this case, interviewees theorized that where the money was coming from influenced what types of stories were covered, mirroring Trump's campaign rhetoric on the strong relations between Clinton's campaign and media.[31] A forty-two-year-old jewelry stylist had this to say about network media outlets: "They all, the majority of them support Hillary, they support the Democratic side. Who they're giving their money to, who they are getting their money from."

Unanimously, these Republican women agreed that Donald Trump is not the ideal man or presidential candidate, as reflected in forty-nine-year-old Victoria's comment: "They both have ethical problems so I cannot weigh. . . . I have a strike against them because of ethical issues." In some cases, participants felt Trump's past indiscretions were serious, but in order to justify their support of him, they continued to maintain that Clinton was no better and that her ethical choices were left unaddressed by the media. Kary, a forty-nine-year-old small business owner, dismissed any concerns about Donald Trump by pointing at Clinton: "I mean he's done some stupid stuff but it's blown way out of the water. And I just think that things Hillary has gotten by with you know, with friends from people in high places is sort of swept under the rug." The women's views went beyond local and national news or what they saw on social media, to what they observed during the presidential debates. Indeed, the concern and distrust of the media was pervasive. One woman summed up what the majority of these interviews uncovered: "They tend to support in favor of the more liberal platform of the Democratic side in this particular election. I think that the favorable images and coverage of Hillary Clinton has far outweighed those of Donald Trump. I don't think that there's a fair and equal balance of issues covered."

To sum up, the participants in this study tended to perceive media coverage as in favor of the liberal side and biased against the conservatives, which is in line with the hostile media effect.[32] Particularly interesting was that although they acknowledged unethical issues of both candidates, they applied a much harsher standard to media coverage of Clinton than that of Trump, stating that media are biased favorably toward the liberal viewpoint.

It's a Man's World

In a patriarchal society, white male privilege affords many luxuries when exposed to the public eye. Donald Trump was not only known for his role on *The Apprentice*, but also as a businessman who is very often willing to do whatever it takes to close a deal. Indeed, Trump claimed that he had learned at a young age that he had an aptitude for success, which he attributed to genetic design.[33]

The societal acceptance of white male privilege seemed to be reflected among the opinions of the women we interviewed. Ethical choices when made by any other man of a different stature might not have been so forgivable; but Donald Trump was given a pass for his deeds. Take, for example, Diana, the political blogger: "Locker room talk which happens . . . it's not appropriate, unacceptable. . . . However, it's just small potatoes compared to Hillary. And what she is done is putting national security at risk by using her server and the FBI has totally—ah, totally walked away from their, responsibility . . . another example of corruption."

Others seemed to assume a "boys will be boys" mentality when speaking of Trump. According to Donna, "Well, I think he is just a child, and I don't know, I'm sure that you know he was on a television show. So, I mean he is just a . . . he has always been in that way. I don't know that he will ever change." Another participant put it this way: "I, um, at this point I'm not as concerned about Trump. The way he talks about women. Because that everything happened like 10 years ago." This lowering of expectations exemplifies the ability to look past the behavior of a white man and to attribute misdeeds to his gender, or the passing of time.

Consistent with white male privilege was the apparent blindness that some respondents had toward the Republican candidate. When Ali, a sixty-seven-year-old special education teacher, was discussing

Trump's history of bankruptcy and his manipulation of laws regarding his taxes, she said he was simply taking advantage of the tax system like any other American would. She noted, "I'm not, not really happy um, with either of their unethicalness." Yet she continued, "Um, I don't know, to me at this point I haven't seen proof of Donald Trump doing unethical things."

The women of this study were able to look past Trump's inappropriate comments (e.g., locker-room talk) in large part because society always has, which is congruent with the argument that Trump's words are commonly spoken among ordinary men when they talk with other men.[34] For Ali, the sixty-seven-year-old retired teacher, it is the compilation of a lifetime of experiences: "We know that locker-room talk exists. We know that the loopholes are out there. We know that [heckling] whistles are out there. We know that the looks are out there. We know that some of the gestures are out there. Are we happy about it? No. Do we live with it? Yes. And that's the way I'm taking this."

Ali reinforces the notion that such locker-room talk, however undesirable, is taken for granted in our ordinary lives; therefore, we need to leave such talk as "men's only spaces with other guys" who want to affirm their masculinities.[35] Ann, who works at a church, expects people to act in a moral way, in line with her religious beliefs. Such expectations of other people motivated her to look at the conduct and behavior of both candidates. She said Trump's locker-room talk was difficult to hear, but Trump's public apology led her to support him:

> I think if we took videos of all of us in our lifetime . . . we say lot of things. He did come up and apologize for that. They haven't put anything out there in the last five years. I think God has been grooming him for this last 10 years. And that [the *Access Hollywood* video of Trump's locker-room talk in 2005 obtained by the *Washington Post*] was what 13 years ago? It's disappointing to hear that man talks that way, but I am not going to take a vote away from him. He came publicly and said "Yes, it was wrong and I am sorry for that."

However, the lingering issue surrounding "locker-room talk" is that Trump has not apologized for the actions that the words described; rather, he apologized for saying the words recorded on tape. At the second presidential debate he stated only that it was wrong to say crude things about women: "I apologize for those words. But it is things that people say. . . . Certainly I'm not proud of it. But this is locker room talk."[36] Trump therefore did not distinguish between his words and his actions; nor did the women in our study.

Depoliticizing Gender

Many participants found the presidential election to be more focused on mudslinging than on policies related to immigration, health care, and the economy. For example, Kary, a forty-nine-year-old small business owner, said: "I wish they [the two presidential candidates] would talk more in the debate about the talking points and talk more about policy." Similarly, a twenty-two-year-old online columnist and political science major opined that the presidential debates had diverted attention from discussing policy to who could make the other look worse, and she included gender in the mix of unworthy topics: "I think this election has focused on everything but policies. I think that, you know, gender has been brought up a lot. You know the ethical issue like her emails, her track record, his talking about women like him, his every day, his tax returns, his business dealings, his 'wall' . . . [are] of secondary importance."

Indeed, Laura, a fifty-nine-year-old retired nurse practitioner, reflects the sentiments of a number of participants in expressing that gender was irrelevant to the presidential election: "I want it between two individuals. I don't care if they are black, white, purple, male, female, whatever, I want it between the candidates themselves and not just because one is female or one is male. I would rather it be based on knowledge and ability."

Thus, while most participants wanted to know more about both candidates' policies, they did not perceive gender as relevant to that discussion. This orientation is a clear dismissal of the Clinton campaign's effort to frame health care, immigration, and foreign policy as "women's issues"—in other words, as having clear implications for women's lives.[37] Our participants simply did not see themselves reflected in Clinton, whether it be her policies or her femininity. So, while they made it clear that they did not vote based on gender,[38] they depoliticized gender-related topics, especially those related to sexual harassment and assault, as being outside the scope of a political campaign and therefore unworthy of attention.

"Locker-Room Talk" as "Small Potatoes"

This study explored gender in relation to the 2016 presidential campaign from the perspective of Republican women. Interviews with twenty-one women suggest a strong dislike of Clinton, at least partially a result of a perception that she transgresses traditional gender expectations. In addition, participants believed the media were biased in favor of Clinton, which consequently contributed to their dislike of her. Meanwhile, most of the Republican women interviewed did not place much emphasis on Trump's "locker-room talk," or other such behaviors related to alleged sexual assault and harassment, seemingly finding his comments congruent with expected male behavior. Indeed, our interview subjects appeared to sidestep allegations of sexual harassment and assault, providing a rationale that they were unrelated to issues surrounding US policy.

Such findings can be explained by role congruity and other gender-related theories: the Republican women studied here stuck to the traditional gender norms for men and women. Men play the "breadwinner" role and are task oriented, while women play the "caretaker" role and are relationship oriented.[39]

Interestingly, our participants did not perceive that Clinton shared any commonalities with them—even though one might expect that as women or mothers they could conceivably share similar experiences and struggles. Rather, they faulted Clinton because they felt she did not behave in a traditional and appropriate way. At the same time, Trump was largely given a pass because his behaviors *were* congruent with expected male behavior; or at least they aligned with expectations for a white, upper-class male. Such findings are in line with baseline gender preference since the women in our study compared Clinton's and Trump's behaviors and appearances to those of traditional women and men, respectively.[40]

Notably, the women in our study seemed unaware of the privilege they granted Trump, which is in line with aspects of feminist standpoint theory: women internalize male-oriented norms, because of hegemonic masculinity and a gendered hierarchy.[41] The Republican women interviewed here tended to accept hegemonic perceptions of traditional gender roles. They considered "locker-room talk" as "small potatoes." To them, such behavior was normalized as they accepted the notion that men objectify and sexualize women. Furthermore, participants held traditional standards for women, as seen in their perceptions toward Clinton's appearance and career, which they openly criticized for transgressing traditional femininity. Thus, the perceptions discovered here were socially situated within the patriarchal system of US politics and gender relations more broadly.

Our study also offers evidence for the hostile media effect. The Republican women in our sample maintained that media portrayals of Trump's sexual harassment issues were exaggerated and negative on purpose in order to increase women's support for Clinton. According to participants, allegations against Trump were insignificant (in actuality) and were purposefully overrepresented by media, while Clinton's unethical behavior went underreported. Therefore, data from this study support the explanation that Republican women tended to resent the news media as they perceived reports leaned favorably toward their opponent. This tendency is illustrative of the hostile media phenomenon.[42]

There is much conjecture and analysis as to why Trump won the 2016 presidential election.[43] Our study leads us to conclude that party, traditional gender expectations, and perceptions of news coverage all contributed to keeping glass ceilings and locker rooms intact.

Notes

1. "Election 2016, Exit Polls," CNN.com, November 23, 2016, http://www.cnn.com/election/results/exit-polls.

2. Regina G. Lawrence and Melody Rose, "Bringing Out the Hook," *Political Research Quarterly* 64, no. 4 (2011): 870–83, https://doi.org/10.1177/1065912910376390.

3. Janis L. Edwards and Huey-Rong Chen, "The First Lady/First Wife in Editorial Cartoons: Rhetorical Visions through Gendered Lenses," *Women's Studies in Communication* 23, no. 3 (2000): 367–91, https://doi.org/10.1080/07491409.2000.11735774; Erica Scharrer and Kim Bissell, "Overcoming Traditional Boundaries: The Role of Political Activity in Media Coverage of First Ladies," *Journal of Women, Politics & Policy* 21, no. 1 (2000): 55–83, https://doi.org/10.1080/1554477x.2000.9970897.

4. Alice H. Eagly and Linda L. Carli, *Through the Labyrinth: The Truth about How Women Become Leaders* (Boston: Harvard Business School Press, 2008); Alice H. Eagly, Mona G. Makhijani, and Bruce G. Klonsky, "Gender and the Evaluation of Leaders: A Meta-analysis," *Psychological Bulletin* 111, no. 1 (1992): 3–22, https://doi.org/10.1037//0033-2909.111.1.3; Laurie A. Rudman and Peter Glick, "Prescriptive Gender Stereotypes and Backlash toward Agentic Women," *Journal of Social Issues* 57, no. 4 (2001): 743–62, https://doi.org/10.1111/0022-4537.00239.

5. Eagly, Makhijani, and Klonsky, "Gender and the Evaluation of Leaders"; Rudman and Glick, "Prescriptive Gender Stereotypes."

6. Alice H. Eagly and Steven J. Karau, "Role Congruity Theory of Prejudice toward Female Leaders," *Psychological Review* 109, no. 3 (2002): 573–98, https://doi.org/10.1037/0033-295x.109.3.573.

7. Eagly, Makhijani, and Klonsky, "Gender and the Evaluation of Leaders"; Alice H. Eagly, Mary C. Johannesen-Schmidt, and Marloes L. Van Engen, "Transformational, Transactional, and Laissez-Faire Leadership Styles: A Meta-analysis Comparing Women and Men," *Psychological Bulletin* 129, no. 4 (2003): 569–91, https://doi.org/10.1037/0033-2909.129.4.569.

8. Alice H. Eagly, Wendy Wood, and Amanda B. Diekman, "Social Role Theory of Sex Differences and Similarities: A Current Appraisal," in *Developmental Social Psychology of Gender*, ed. Thomas Eckes and Hanns M. Trautner (Mahway, NJ: Lawrence Erlbaum Associates, 2000), 123–74.

9. Daria A. Bakina, "Power, Likeability, and Perception: Evaluating Men and Women in High and Low Power Positions" (PhD diss., Syracuse University, 2013).

10. Rudman and Glick, "Prescriptive Gender Stereotypes."

11. George H. Sage and Sheryl Loudermilk, "The Female Athlete and Role Conflict," *Research Quarterly. American Alliance for Health, Physical Education, Recreation and Dance* 50, no. 1 (1979): 88–96.

12. Kira Sanbonmatsu, "Gender Stereotypes and Vote Choice," *American Journal of Political Science* 46, no. 1 (2002): 20–34.

13. Janet T. Spence and Robert L Helmreich, *Masculinity and Femininity: Their Psychological Dimensions, Correlates, and Antecedents* (Austin: University of Texas Press, 1979).

14. Dianne G. Bystrom, Lori Melton McKinnon, and Carole Chaney, "First Ladies and the Fourth Estate: Media Coverage of Hillary Clinton and Elizabeth Dole in the 1996 Presidential Election," in *The Electronic Election: Perspectives on the 1996 Campaign Communication*, ed. Lynda L. Kaid and Dianne Bystrom (Thousand Oaks, CA: Sage, 1999), 105–22; Scharrer and Bissell, "Overcoming Traditional Boundaries," 55–83.

15. Michael Grynbaum, "CNN's Coverage of Trump Was Biased, Presidential Candidates' Aides Say," *New York Times*, December 1, 2016, http://www.nytimes.com/2016/12/01/business/media/trump-cnns-coverage-biased-presidential-candidates-aides-say.html?_r=1.

16. Robert P. Vallone, Lee Ross, and Mark R Lepper, "The Hostile Media Phenomenon: Biased Perception and Perceptions of Media Bias in Coverage of the Beirut Massacre," *Journal of Personality and Social Psychology* 49, no. 3 (1985): 577.

17. Roger Giner-Sorolla and Shelly Chaiken, "The Causes of Hostile Media Judgments," *Journal of Experimental Social Psychology* 30, no. 2 (1994): 165–80; Albert C. Gunther and Janice L Liebhart, "Broad Reach or Biased Source? Decomposing the Hostile Media Effect," *Journal of Communication* 56, no. 3 (2006): 449–66.; Vallone, Ross, and Lepper, "Hostile Media Phenomenon," 577.

18. Robert Vallone, Lee Ross, and Mark Lepper, "Perceptions of Media Bias in a Presidential Election" (Stanford University, typescript, 1981).

19. Ran Wei, Stella C Chia, and Ven-Hwei Lo, "Third-Person Effect and Hostile Media Perception Influences on Voter Attitudes toward Polls in the 2008 US Presidential Election," *International Journal of Public Opinion Research* 23, no. 2 (2011): 169–90.

20. Albert C. Gunther, "Biased Press or Biased Public? Attitudes toward Media Coverage of Social Groups," *Public Opinion Quarterly* 56, no. 2 (1992): 147.

21. Muzafer Sherif and Carl I. Hovland, *Social Judgment: Assimilation and Contrast Effects in Communication and Attitude Change* (New Haven, CT: Yale University Press, 1961).

22. Steinar Kvale and Svend Brinkman, *InterViews: Learning the Craft of Qualitative Research Interviewing* (Thousand Oaks, CA: Sage, 2015), 3.

23. Annica Kronsell, "Gendered Practices in Institutions of Hegemonic Masculinity: Reflections from Feminist Standpoint Theory," *International Feminist Journal of Politics* 7, no. 2 (2005): 280–98.

24. "Election 2016, Exit Polls," CNN.com.

25. James Allsup, "RIGGED: Leaked Emails Reveal How Media Is Rigging Polls for Hillary," *Liberty Conservative*, October 23, 2016, http://www.thelibertyconservative.com/rigged-leaked-emails-reveal-media-rigging-polls-hil; Editorial, "Clinton Email Scandal: Hillary's Hypocrisy and Media's Bias Revealed," *Investor's Business Daily*, October 10, 2016, http://www.investors.com/politics/editorials/clinton-email-scandal-hillarys-hypocrisy-and-medias-bias-revealed/; Joe Tacoplno, "Emails Show Hillary Has the Media in Her Pocket," *New York Post*, October 12, 2016, http://nypost.com/2016/10/12/emails-show-hillary-has-the-media-in-her-pocket/.

26. Gregory Krieg, "12 Quotes from Hillary Clinton Show Her Remarkable Defiance," *Mic*, April 22, 2015, https://mic.com/articles/116152/12-quotes-from-hillary-clinton-show-her-remarkable-defiance#.h7YW9ilDh.

27. Karina Schumann and Michael Ross, "Why Women Apologize More Than Men: Gender Differences in Thresholds for Perceiving Offensive Behavior," *Psychological Science* 21, no. 11 (2010): 1649–55.

28. Chris Cillizza, "Hillary Clinton Just Gave Her Best Answer on the Email Controversy. By Far," *Washington Post*, August 25, 2016, https://www.washingtonpost.com/news/the-fix/wp/2016/08/25/hillary-clinton-just-gave-her-best-answer-on-the-email-controversy-by-far/?utm_term=.f6102d28aaa4.

29. Cynthia Littleton, "Donald Trump Suggests Debate Moderators Favored Hillary Clinton," *Variety*, October 9, 2016, http://variety.com/2016/tv/news/donald-trump-hillary-clinton-debate-anderson-cooper-martha-raddatz-1201883531/.

30. Alex Nitzberg, "Biased Media Coverage of Trump and Clinton Scandals," Accuracy in Media, October 21, 2016, http://www.aim.org/on-target-blog/biased-media-coverage-of-trump-clinton-scandals/.

31. Howard Kurtz, "Clinton Raising Money on Media 'Bias,' a New Rallying Cry on the Left," Fox News, September 12, 2016, http://www.foxnews.com/politics/2016/09/12/clinton-raising-money-on-media-bias-new-rallying-cry-on-left.html.

32. Richard M. Perloff, "A Three-Decade Retrospective on the Hostile Media Effect," *Mass Communication and Society* 18 (2015): 701–29.

33. Caroline Mortimer, "Donald Trump Believes He Has Superior Genes, Biographer Claims: Republican Nominee Follows 'Racehorse Theory' of Genetics," *Independent*, September 30, 2016, http://www.

independent.co.uk/news/world/americas/donald-trump-president-superior-genes-pbs-documentary-eugenics-a7338821.html.

34. Shaun R. Harper, "Many Men Talk Like Donald Trump in Private. And Only Other Men Can Stop Them," *Washington Post*, October 8, 2016, https://www.washingtonpost.com/posteverything/wp/2016/10/08/many-men-talk-like-donald-trump-in-private-and-only-other-men-can-stop-them/?utm_term=.f09ce3430f72.

35. Ibid.

36. "Transcript of the Second Debate," *New York Times*, October 10, 2016, https://www.nytimes.com/2016/10/10/us/politics/transcript-second-debate.html.

37. Suzanne Nossel, "A Feminist Foreign Policy: Hillary Clinton's Hard Choices," *Foreign Affairs*, February 15, 2016, https://www.foreignaffairs.com/reviews/review-essay/2016-02-15/feminist-foreign-policy.

38. Angelina Chapin, "I'm Not with Her': Why Women Are Wary of Hillary Clinton," *Guardian*, May 23, 2016, https://www.theguardian.com/us-news/2016/may/23/women-female-voters-us-election-hillary-clinton.

39. Gary N. Powell and Kimberly A. Eddleston, "Linking Family-to-Business Enrichment and Support to Entrepreneurial Success: Do Female and Male Entrepreneurs Experience Different Outcomes?," *Journal of Business Venturing* 28, no. 2 (2013): 261–80.

40. Sanbonmatsu, "Gender Stereotypes and Vote Choice."

41. Kronsell, "Gendered Practices in Institutions."

42. Vallone, Ross, and Lepper, "Hostile Media Phenomenon," 577.

43. Anthony Zurcher, "US Election 2016 Results: Five reasons Donald Trump Won," *BBC News*, November 9, 2016, http://www.bbc.com/news/election-us-2016-37918303.

Chapter Thirteen

"I'M NOT VOTING FOR *HER*"

Internalized Misogyny, Feminism, and Gender Consciousness in the 2016 Election

Pamela Aronson

"I'm not voting for *her*."

—A middle-aged, female, registered Democrat,
as told to the author in a get-out-the-vote call
in Michigan on November 8, 2016.

The 2016 election was surprising in many respects. Preelection polls consistently predicted a popular and electoral win for Hillary Clinton.[1] With the presence on the ballot of the first female major-party presidential candidate, there were many expectations that women would vote for Clinton in large numbers. According to exit polls, women of color did, in fact, follow this pattern: among this demographic, 81 percent of those with no college degree and 77 percent of those with a college degree voted for Clinton.[2] As predicted, the majority of men (52 percent overall and 62 percent of white men) reported voting for Trump. What pollsters failed to predict, however, was the voting behavior of white women, 52 percent of whom voted for Donald Trump. When considering educational background, these numbers are even more striking: among white women, 61 percent of those without a college degree and 44 percent of those with a college degree voted for Trump.[3] Rural white women also disproportionately supported Trump.[4] However, despite nearly evenly split voter identification, a majority of white women have been voting Republican for president for the past 60 years, with the exception of only two presidential contests.[5] One possible reason for inaccurate polls in 2016 is "shy Trumpers" who were not honest about their voting plans.[6] Exit polls revealed that 18 percent of voters held an unfavorable view of *both* candidates and that these votes went disproportionately to Trump.[7] There were also a large number of Obama supporters who simply did not vote in 2016. These figures raise questions not only about white women's voting behavior, but also about gender consciousness and how women view other women in leadership positions.

As I will argue, internalized misogyny, gender consciousness, and feminist consciousness all influenced women's voting behavior and activism in the election. Gender consciousness is an awareness of women's political and social interests and makes salient the status of women *as women.*[8] Gender consciousness is distinct from feminist consciousness, which is an awareness and critique of gender inequalities and patriarchy.[9] Feminist consciousness differs from feminist identity because not all women who are critical of gender inequalities take on the identity of "feminist."[10] Historically, women of color and working-class women were excluded from the second wave women's movement and many have argued that the movement does not address their concerns.[11] As a result, some of these women have rejected a feminist identity while still exhibiting feminist consciousness. Nearly all women (whether feminist or not) have internalized the misogyny of our culture. Although this type of bias against women can operate even among those who consider themselves to be feminists, internalized misogyny can produce a barrier to gender or feminist consciousness. In the case of the election, the notion of a woman being elected as president seemed to repel many women, especially white women. Internalized misogyny, and the inability of the Clinton campaign to overcome it by fully activating and mobilizing gender and feminist consciousness, contributed to Trump's victory over Clinton.

Internalized Misogyny

Most women have internalized the misogyny of our culture in one way or another. Although related to sexism, which is discrimination against someone as a result of their sex, misogyny represents a disdain for women. Internalized misogyny, which can take the form of unconscious bias, results from living in a patriarchal society. Because subtle gender inequalities are pervasive, even people who identify as feminists may find themselves unconsciously preferring male leadership.

While the public is generally supportive of a woman running for president, not everyone supports this notion. In 2011 a Gallup poll asked, "If your party nominated a woman for president, would you vote for her if she were qualified for the job?" and 95 percent agreed, with minimal gender differences in responses.[12] However, a related question, asking, "Do you think the voters of this country are ready to elect a woman president, or don't you think so?" produced only 78 percent agreeing that voters were "ready."[13] A Pew Research Center study revealed that roughly equal numbers (three-quarters) of both men and women agree that "women and men make equally good political leaders."[14] Yet 31 percent of both men and women in recent years agreed that "most men are better suited emotionally for politics than are most women."[15] Despite widespread support for women in politics, even a small percentage withholding approval and voting accordingly could tip the balance in a close election.

Some scholars argue that survey respondents exaggerate support for a female president because they do not want to violate social rhetoric favoring equality. To counter these effects, political scientist Matthew Streb and colleagues asked about views toward a female president alongside other political issues (including "gasoline prices . . . going up" and "large corporations polluting the environment"). They found that slightly more than a quarter of both men and women were "angry or upset" about the possibility of a female president.[16] Some research has found that women voters exhibit a greater ambivalence toward female candidates than do men and that white women have a stronger implicit gender bias than both men and women of color.[17] In one study, women who believed that more women should hold elected office were *not* more likely to vote for a female candidate than other women, while men who held this same belief were significantly more likely to vote for a female Democrat than other male voters.[18]

Women candidates face a no-win situation: many voters view them negatively if they are portrayed by the media as violating gender stereotypes or if they are portrayed as too nurturing and sensitive.[19] The former is the case for Clinton, who has been criticized for having qualities that are not viewed negatively when perceived in male politicians, including being ambitious and strong.[20] Before the 2008 election, psychologists David Paul and Jessi Smith found that a candidate's gender had a larger impact on candidate preference than either the gender of the voter or their party affiliation. In hypothetical head-to-head matchups, the three male candidates always beat the female candidates (Hillary Clinton and Elizabeth Dole) and voters were much more likely to "defect" from a female to a male candidate.[21] Considering evaluations of Clinton in particular, psychologists Blair Vandegrift and Alexander Czopp found that "women may be demonstrating internalization of gender bias," as they rated a male Clinton supporter as "more competent and less annoying" than a female Clinton supporter.[22] Men did not express the same bias against female Clinton supporters.

While social class discontent and racism undoubtedly influenced the 2016 election, particularly Trump's support among working-class whites in Rust Belt states, we cannot understand the outcome without also considering misogyny and internalized misogyny.[23] As the first female major-party presidential nominee, Clinton could not escape gender issues. Journalist Nina Burleigh said that Trump "ran against all of that, glorying in unapologetic, unreconstructed macho."[24]

Although people have strong opinions about Clinton, who has been in the public eye for many years, there were many instances of blatant misogyny during the election. For example, when referring to reporter Megyn Kelly, who asked him during a Republican primary debate about his negative comments about women, Trump implied that she was menstruating, saying: "You could see there was blood coming out of her eyes, blood coming out of her, wherever."[25] Trump interrupted Clinton over fifty times in the first general election debate (versus her interrupting him eleven times) and thirty-seven times in the third debate (versus her interrupting him nine times).[26] At Trump rallies, it was common to see misogynistic campaign materials, such as T-shirts with the slogan "Trump That Bitch" or pins with the slogan "Finally Someone with Balls."[27] Journalist Peter Beinart argued that it is fear of men's subordination to women that drives male misogyny, as evidenced in the fact that typical comments about Clinton did not "explain the intensity of this opposition."[28] Some women supported this perspective. For example, one Trump supporter was seen wearing a T-shirt with the words "Trump can grab this," with an arrow pointing toward her vagina.[29]

Conservative commentator David Brooks pointed out that Trump's misogyny "takes economic anxiety and turns it into sexual hostility. He effectively tells men: You may be struggling, but at least you're better than women, Mexicans and Muslims."[30] Yet these messages were also directed at women voters. As sociologist Daniel Farber and his colleagues state, Trump "projected a hegemonic masculinity, continuously denigrating strong and popular woman figures. He liked to warn white America, and white women in particular, that they were in danger. Only he, the authoritarian Great White Male, could protect them from people of color, immigrants, terrorists, Muslims, and the Chinese."[31]

A study by political scientist Carly Wayne and her colleagues found that, even when controlling for party identification, ideology, authoritarianism, and ethnocentrism, sexism was strongly correlated with supporting Trump. Although most commentators assume that fear drives these views, researchers found that anger served to increase the impact of sexism on Trump support. These researchers argue that the "dominant narrative in this election—about 'fearful authoritarians' who are resentful of immigrants and other minorities—misses out on a crucial dynamic of this campaign, namely, sexism."[32]

Misogyny and internalized misogyny are not always overt and often operate in subtle ways. In particular, Clinton was judged more harshly than Trump for similar actions. Perhaps the single most influential event in determining the election's outcome was the release of a letter to congressional committee chairs by James Comey, the director of the FBI, on October 28, just days before the election. The letter, which was leaked and immediately reported by the several news media organizations, stated that Comey was investigating a set of newly discovered emails for possible mishandling of classified information. The letter defied Justice Department policy that no public statements should be made about politically sensitive investigations in the two-month period prior to an election.[33] Although difficult to verify given the nature of FBI investigations, it appears that an investigation of the Trump campaign (and its involvement with Russia in election interference) was also ongoing at that time yet remained unannounced.[34] As journalist Adele Stan points out, Trump "certainly benefited from the selective application of this policy."[35] Although it cannot be confirmed, Stan attributed this disparity to misogyny: "Everyone knows that women are duplicitous. Everyone knows that women lie. . . . Comey's reopened investigation [of Clinton] advanced that very idea."[36] Poll numbers reveal that Comey's letter may have been one of the most influential events in the election's outcome. The day before the announcement (October 27), polls predicted a win for Clinton. FiveThirtyEight, a polling aggregation website, reported that Clinton had an 82.2 percent chance of winning and concluded that the "race hasn't fundamentally changed all that much, and Clinton remains in a strong position."[37] By November 4, the same organization reported that Clinton's chance of winning had fallen to 64.5 percent, a drop of nearly 18 percent.

Interviews with voters in January 2017 further revealed that 53 percent of those who voted for Obama in 2012 and Trump in 2016 said that their vote was one "*against* Clinton" rather than "*for* Trump."[38] Similarly, 36 percent of "drop-off voters" (those who voted for Obama in 2012 but did not vote in 2016) reported that they decided not to vote in advance of Election Day for reasons akin to "I did not like either candidate."[39] Although misogyny was obviously not the only factor in voters' dislike of Clinton as a candidate, these findings may suggest a hidden, and perhaps unconscious, level of misogyny among both male and female voters.

Some women internalize the misogyny of our culture in order to fit within our patriarchal society. As journalist Rebecca Solnit states, it makes sense for women to support Trump if their husbands and other male family members are voting for him. Distinguishing between feminists and those who embrace misogyny, she says, "To be a feminist, you have to believe in your equality and rights, which can make your life unpleasant and dangerous if you live in a marriage, a family, a community, a church, a state that does not agree with you about this."[40] Similarly, Burleigh remarked that the "'Trump factor' not only frightened women; it quieted them. . . . [M]any women simply kept things 'smooth' by not speaking up."[41] Psychologist Jen Kim points out that internalized misogyny may be present for women who are dependent on men because "inequality is easier" than challenging patriarchal arrangements.[42] This may especially be the case for working-class women with lower levels of education, as they have fewer resources and may be more financially dependent on men.[43] In their examination of support for a woman president prior to the 2016 election, Erika Falk and Kate Kenski found that voters with lower levels of education were less likely to support a woman candidate than those with higher levels of education.[44] This finding is consistent with previous research that found that feminist consciousness more readily develops in contexts where there is institutionalized support of feminism, such as in college, while "having the space to think about political issues such as feminism may be a luxury" that some women simply "cannot afford."[45]

In sum, women from all types of backgrounds internalize misogyny, as it represents the dominant narrative in American culture. The Trump campaign was able to tap into these perspectives, particularly among white women. Because the election was so close (with less than 80,000 votes in three states tipping the electoral vote in Trump's favor), internalized misogyny must be considered as a decisive factor in influencing the outcome.[46]

Gender Consciousness, Feminism, and the Election

Gender consciousness—women's awareness of their interests as women—can take conservative or progressive forms or can simultaneously embrace and subvert traditional gender norms.[47] In contrast, feminist consciousness is an awareness and critique of gender inequalities and patriarchy.[48] It is distinct from feminist identity, as some women reject gender inequality but do not necessarily call themselves feminists.[49] For example, women of color may emphasize racial and class oppression over gender oppression, making racial consciousness more salient and politicized than feminist consciousness.[50] Although the meaning of "feminist" is complex, about 23 percent of women in the United States identify as such.[51] In order for gender consciousness, feminist consciousness, or feminist identity to influence voting behavior, it must be both activated and mobilized. Activation occurs when gender becomes a noticeable identity to women voters. Mobilization occurs when these voters actually participate in the political process.

There were a number of flashpoints when gender and/or feminist consciousness became salient for many women during the 2016 presidential election campaign. The most notable of these was the release of the infamous 2005 videotaped conversation with Billy Bush of *Access Hollywood*, in which Trump bragged about kissing and groping women without their consent. The subsequent social media explosion after the tape's release illustrated the activation of gender consciousness.

When the *Access Hollywood* story first hit the airwaves in early October, news organizations emphasized the vulgar aspects of Trump's words, yet at the outset they did not call his stated behavior sexual assault. For example, the *Washington Post* article that broke the story stated that Trump "bragged in vulgar terms about kissing, groping and trying to have sex with women."[52] In response, Trump released a video dismissing his comments as "locker-room talk." However, Dawn Laguens, the executive vice president of the Planned Parenthood Action Fund, was one of the first public figures who began to change this narrative in a *New York Times* interview: "What Trump described in these tapes amounts to sexual assault."[53] Laguens's analysis prompted many news sources to shift their language from terms such as "vulgar" to "sexual assault."[54] Three days after the tape was released, a *New York Times* editorial by Amanda Taub described this behavior as "all-too common" and linked it with broader gender inequalities: "This kind of behavior isn't just offensive; it also imposes real costs on women. The burden of avoiding and enduring sexual harassment and assault results, over time, in lost opportunities and less favorable outcomes for girls and women."[55] The linguistic reframing of this event toward women's bodily integrity illustrates a movement toward gender consciousness, while its framing in terms of larger gender inequalities illustrates feminist consciousness.

Although many of those responsible for shifting the cultural understanding of this event are probably feminists, others who spoke out utilized a gender consciousness frame. Republican Senator Kelly Ayotte stated: "I am a mom and an American first, and I cannot and will not support a candidate for president who brags about degrading and assaulting women."[56] Here, we see an awareness of the importance of bodily integrity as a woman but not a concern about systematic gender inequalities and patriarchy.

Soon after the tape was leaked, Kelly Oxford, a Canadian novelist and screenwriter, sent out a request: "Women: tweet me your first assaults" (@kellyoxford, October 7, 2016). In the next fourteen hours, at a minimum of fifty per minute, Oxford received stories from women about their first experiences of being sexually assaulted.[57] This was followed by an explosion on social media of women's reports of sexual assault, with 8 million women responding.[58] In addition, the weekend after the clip was released, "calls to the telephone hotline of the Rape, Abuse and Incest National Network increased 35 percent."[59] The "secret" Facebook page "Pantsuit Nation" was formed on October 20, and it continued the national conversation about sexual assault with its explicit mission being to "harness the power of collective storytelling to drive social and political change."[60] The outpouring of sexual assault survival accounts in the news and on social media suggests the activation of gender and/or feminist consciousness. That is, many women became aware that their interests *as women* ran contrary to Trump's candidacy, and some linked this awareness with systematic inequalities and patriarchy.

How did Clinton respond to gender-relevant issues in her campaign? As previously discussed, women candidates are in a no-win situation: if they emphasize gender, perhaps making gender consciousness salient, they risk appearing "weak," whereas if they emphasize "masculine" characteristics, they are seen as cold and unfeeling.[61] It appears that the Clinton campaign sought to balance this contradiction. In its efforts to appeal broadly, the campaign simultaneously "played" and downplayed what Trump referred to as "the woman card." In terms of highlighting gender, after Trump mocked Clinton's use of her gender, Clinton's campaign website released a webpage that sarcastically listed some of the "perks that your Woman Card gets you," including lower wages and no family leave.[62] Similarly, during the first debate, Clinton directly confronted Trump's sexism, saying that Trump "is a man who has called women pigs, slobs, and dogs, and someone who has said pregnancy is an inconvenience to employers, who has said women don't deserve equal pay unless they do as good a job as men." She went on to discuss Trump's racist and sexist attack on Alicia Machado, a former Miss Universe.[63]

Although Clinton's advertisements both highlighted and downplayed gender, it appears that the campaign could have done more to mobilize the gender consciousness of women voters, particularly after the release of the *Access Hollywood* tape, when gender was perhaps the most salient for many women voters. For example, the campaign released at least two advertisements that sought to highlight Trump's misogyny, yet they were not aired as frequently as other ads.

The advertisement called "Mirrors" shows girls looking at themselves in a mirror while a voice-over with Trump's voice replays his negative statements about women, including words like "slob" and "pig." Another ad highlights Trump's disparaging and insulting comments toward women and ends with an admission that he "can't say" whether or not he treats women with respect. Although the latter was the ninth-most-shown ad during the campaign overall, it was not aired at all between October 8 (which was the day after the *Access Hollywood* tape was released) and October 30.[64] After October 30, it was only shown 96 times.[65] In comparison, my analysis reveals that the third-most-aired ad, "Trump can't be trusted with nuclear weapons," was shown over 2,000 times between October 8 and the election.[66] Although an analysis of campaign strategy is beyond the scope of this chapter, the frequency and timing of the "Mirrors" ad's airing suggest that it was shown only very minimally after the *Access Hollywood* tape release. This does not seem coincidental. Perhaps the campaign feared turning off voters by emphasizing gender issues too much. Or perhaps the campaign did not want to draw attention to Trump's October accusations that Bill Clinton sexually assaulted women and that Hillary Clinton played a role in silencing them.[67] Regardless, it is worth asking whether the *Access Hollywood* revelation represented a missed opportunity that could have more effectively activated and mobilized the gender and feminist consciousness of women voters. Thus, reflecting the double bind of many women candidates, it appears that the Clinton campaign sought to both tap gender and feminist consciousness and simultaneously downplay the importance of gender.

Although the 2016 election result has been attributed in large part to racism and social class discontent, particularly the surprising vote of working-class whites in Rust Belt states, we cannot understand the outcome without also considering internalized misogyny among white women, especially rural women and those without a college degree. According to exit polls, these women disproportionately supported Trump, suggesting that their gender and feminist consciousnesses were not activated or mobilized. Rather, exit polls and news reports suggest that gender was less salient than other issues in determining the voting behavior of some white women. Similar to findings that feminist identities develop most readily in contexts where there is institutionalized support of feminism, there was more support among educated women.[68] Women of color, who have historically been less likely to identify as feminists, were far more likely to vote for Clinton than white women, suggesting that the intersection of gender and racial identities is a key in understanding the election outcome. The outpouring of survival accounts in the news and on social media in response to Trump's bragging about sexual assault suggests that support for a woman candidate can be linked directly to gender and feminist consciousness, although the Clinton campaign did not fully capitalize on this issue.

The 2016 election offers important lessons for future elections with women candidates. First, we are likely to continue to see the use of misogyny—both subtle and blatant—as a campaign strategy. We are also likely to see internalized misogyny on the part of women voters who are confronted with women candidates for top political offices. Finding a way to combat internalized misogyny should be an important component of future campaign strategy. Finally, campaigns should recognize that it is particularly important for gender and feminist consciousness to be fully activated and mobilized rather than assuming support on Election Day. Future campaigns need to devote significant resources toward this concern in order for a female candidate to "shatter that highest, hardest glass ceiling."[69]

Notes

1. I would like to thank the following people, who all contributed insights or read drafts of this work: Ronald Aronson, Georgina Hickey, Maureen Linker, Todd Paxton, Pat Smith, and Jackie Vansant.

Andrew Mercer, "Why 2016 Election Polls Missed Their Mark," Pew Research Center, November 9, 2016, http://www.pewresearch.org/fact-tank/2016/11/09/why-2016-election-polls-missed-their-mark/.

2. "The 2016 Election Exit Polls," *Washington Post*, November 29, 2016, https://www.washingtonpost.com/graphics/politics/2016-election/exit-polls/.

3. "2016 Election, Exit Polls," CNN.com, November 23, 2016, http://www.cnn.com/election/results/exit-polls.

4. Rich Morin, "Behind Trump's Win in Rural White America: Women Joined Men in Backing Him," Pew Research Center, November 17, 2016, http://www.pewresearch.org/fact-tank/2016/11/17/behind-trumps-win-in-rural-white-america-women-joined-men-in-backing-him/.

5. Vanessa Williams, "What's Wrong with White Women Voters? Here's the Problem with That Question," *Washington Post*, December 22, 2017, https://www.washingtonpost.com/news/post-nation/wp/2017/12/22/whats-wrong-with-white-women-voters-heres-the-problem-with-that-question/?utm_term=.dc0fe011f8a1.

6. Mercer, "Why 2016 Election Polls Missed."

7. "2016 Election, Exit Polls," CNN.com.

8. Myra Marx Ferree and Beth B. Hess, *Controversy & Coalition: The New Feminist Movement across Three Decades of Change*, 2nd ed. (New York: Twayne Publishers, 1994).

9. Pamela Aronson, "The Dynamics and Causes of Gender and Feminist Consciousness and Feminist Identities," in *The Oxford Handbook of U.S. Women's Social Movement Activism*, ed. Holly McCammon, Lee Ann Banaszak, Verta Taylor, and Jo Reger (Oxford: Oxford University Press, 2017): 335–53.

10. Ibid.

11. Patricia Hill Collins, *Black Feminist Thought: Knowledge, Consciousness and the Politics of Empowerment* (New York: Routledge, 1991).

12. Roper Center for Public Opinion Research, Cornell University, "Madame President: Changing Attitudes about a Woman President," accessed July 23, 2017, https://ropercenter.cornell.edu/changing-attitudes-about-a-woman-president/.

13. Ibid.

14. D'Vera Cohn, "Americans' Views of Women as Political Leaders Differ by Gender," Pew Research Center, May 19, 2016, http://www.pewresearch.org/fact-tank/2016/05/19/americans-views-of-women-as-political-leaders-differ-by-gender/.

15. Kathleen Dolan and Timothy Lynch, "Making the Connection? Attitudes about Women in Politics and Voting for Women Candidates," *Politics, Groups, and Identities* 3, no. 1 (2015): 111–32.

16. Matthew J. Streb, Barbara Burrell, Brian Frederick, and Michael A. Genovese, "Social Desirability Effects and Support for a Female American President," *Public Opinion Quarterly* 72, no. 1 (2008): 76–89.

17. Carl Bialik, "How Unconscious Sexism Could Help Explain Trump's Win," FiveThirtyEight.com, January 21, 2017, https://fivethirtyeight.com/features/how-unconscious-sexism-could-help-explain-trumps-win/; Jesse Singal, "Maybe Clinton Lost Because of Implicit Sexism, but a Test Can't Prove It," *New York Magazine*, January 24, 2017, http://nymag.com/scienceofus/2017/01/there-are-problems-with-the-gender-bias-iat-too.html.

18. Dolan and Lynch, "Making the Connection?"

19. Caitlin E. Dwyer, Daniel Stevens, John L. Sullivan, and Barbara Allen, "Racism, Sexism, and Candidate Evaluations in the 2008 U.S. Presidential Election," *Analyses of Social Issues and Public Policy* 9, no. 1 (2009): 223–40; Sarah Burns, Lindsay Eberhardt, and Jennifer L. Merolla, "What Is the Difference between a Hockey Mom and a Pit Bull? Presentations of Palin and Gender Stereotypes in the 2008 Presidential Election," *Political Research Quarterly* 66, no. 3 (2013): 687–701.

20. Dwyer et al., "Racism, Sexism, and Candidate Evaluations"; Lindsey Meeks, "All the Gender That's Fit to Print: How the *New York Times* Covered Hillary Clinton and Sarah Palin in 2008," *Journalism & Mass Communication Quarterly* 90, no. 3 (2013): 520–39; Janis L. Edwards and C. Austin McDonald II, "Reading Hillary and Sarah: Contradictions of Feminism and Representation in the 2008 Campaign Political Cartoons," *American Behavioral Scientist* 54, no. 3 (2010): 313–29; Philo C. Wasburn and Mara

H. Wasburn, "Media Coverage of Women in Politics: The Curious Case of Sarah Palin," *Media, Culture & Society* 33, no. 7 (2011): 1027–41.

21. David Paul and Jessi L. Smith, "Subtle Sexism? Examining Vote Preferences When Women Run against Men for the Presidency," *Journal of Women, Politics & Policy* 29, no. 4 (2008): 451–76.

22. Blair E. Vandegrift and Alexander M. Czopp, "In to Win? Intergroup Processes and the Effectiveness of Male versus Female Endorsements for Hillary Clinton," *Journal of Women, Politics & Policy* 32, no. 3 (2011): 92.

23. "2016 Election, Exit Polls," CNN.com.

24. Nina Burleigh, "The Presidential Election Was a Referendum on Gender and Women Lost," *Newsweek*, November 14, 2016, http://www.newsweek.com/2016/11/18/hillary-clinton-presidential-election-voter-gender-gap-520579.html.

25. Paola Chavez, Veronica Stracqualursi, and Meghan Keneally, "A History of the Donald Trump–Megyn Kelly Feud," ABCNews.com, October 26, 2016, http://abcnews.go.com/Politics/history-donald-trump-megyn-kelly-feud/story?id=36526503.

26. Chris Wilson, "Donald Trump Interrupted Hillary Clinton and Lester Holt 55 Times in the First Presidential Debate," *Time*, September 27, 2016, http://time.com/4509790/donald-trump-debate-interruptions/; Claire Landsbaum, "Donald Trump Interrupted Hillary Clinton 37 Times during Last Night's Debate," *New York Magazine*, October 20, 2016, http://nymag.com/thecut/2016/10/trump-interrupted-clinton-37-times-in-final-debate.html.

27. Peter Beinart, "Fear of a Female President," *Atlantic*, October, 2016, https://www.theatlantic.com/magazine/archive/2016/10/fear-of-a-female-president/497564/.

28. Ibid.

29. Lindsey Ellefson, "People Are Losing It Over a Woman Whose Shirt Says Trump Can Grab Her . . . You Know," Mediaite.com, October 14, 2016, http://www.mediaite.com/online/people-are-losing-it-over-a-woman-whose-shirt-says-trump-can-grab-her-you-know/.

30. David Brooks, "The Sexual Politics of 2016," *New York Times*, March 29, 2016, https://www.nytimes.com/2016/03/29/opinion/the-sexual-politics-of-2016.html?_r=0.

31. Daniel Faber, Jennie Stephens, Victor Wallis, Roger Gottlieb, Charles Levenstein, Patrick CoatarPeter, and the Boston Editorial Group of CNS, "Trump's Electoral Triumph: Class, Race, Gender, and the Hegemony of the Polluter-Industrial Complex," *Capitalism Nature Socialism* 28, no. 1 (2017): 6. See Joshua D. Martin's chapter in this volume, as well, on Trump's fear-mongering about Mexican rapists; and Carly Wayne, Nicholas Valentino, and Marzia Oceno, "How Sexism Drives Support for Donald Trump," *Washington Post*, October 23, 2016, http://www.washingtonpost.com/news/monkey-cage/wp/2016/10/23/how-sexism-drives-support-for-donald-trump/?utm_term=.4c2118d29643.

32. Wayne, Valentino, and Oceno, "How Sexism Drives Support."

33. Adele Stan, "Did Misogyny Drive Comey's Subversion of Presidential Campaign?," *American Prospect,* May 3, 2017, http://prospect.org/article/did-misogyny-drive-comey%E2%80%99s-subversion-presidential-campaign.

34. Eugene Kiely, "Timeline of Russia Investigation," Factcheck.org, posted June 7, 2017 (accessed August 10, 2017), http://www.factcheck.org/2017/06/timeline-russia-investigation/.

35. Stan, "Did Misogyny Drive Comey's Subversion."

36. Ibid.

37. "Who Will Win the Presidency?," FiveThirtyEight.com, November 8, 2016, https://projects.fivethirtyeight.com/2016-election-forecast/; Nate Silver, "Election Update: The Polls Disagree, and That's OK," FiveThirtyEight.com, October 27, 2016, https://fivethirtyeight.com/features/election-update-the-polls-disagree-and-thats-ok/.

38. Global Strategy Group and Garin Hart Yang, "Post-Election Research: Persuadable and Drop-off Voters," Priorities USA, April 2017, https://www.washingtonpost.com/r/2010-2019/WashingtonPost/2017/05/01/Editorial-Opinion/Graphics/Post-election_Research_Deck.pdf.

39. Ibid.

40. Rebecca Solnit, "From Lying to Leering," *London Review of Books* 39, no. 2 (January 19, 2017): 3–7, https://www.lrb.co.uk/v39/n02/rebecca-solnit/from-lying-to-leering.

41. Burleigh, "Presidential Election Was a Referendum."

42. Jen Kim, "Are Female Misogynists on the Rise? An Exploration of How the Trump Campaign Encourages Women to Hate Women," *Psychology Today,* October 25, 2016, https://www.psychologytoday.com/blog/valley-girl-brain/201610/are-female-misogynists-the-rise.

43. Johanna Brenner, *Women and Politics of Class* (New York: Monthly Review Press, 2000).

44. Erika Falk and Kate Kenski, "Sexism versus Partisanship: A New Look at the Question of Whether America Is Ready for a Woman President," *Sex Roles* 54, nos. 7–8 (2006): 413–28.

45. Pamela Aronson, "Feminists or 'Postfeminists'? Young Women's Attitudes toward Feminism and Gender Relations," *Gender & Society* 17, no. 6 (2003): 919.

46. Philip Bump, "Donald Trump Will Be President Thanks to 80,000 People in Three States," *Washington Post,* December 1, 2016, https://www.washingtonpost.com/news/the-fix/wp/2016/12/01/donald-trump-will-be-president-thanks-to-80000-people-in-three-states/?utm_term=.d91589077e48.

47. Aronson, "Dynamics and Causes."

48. Ibid.

49. Ibid.

50. Esther Ngan-Ling Chow, "The Development of Feminist Consciousness among Asian American Women," *Gender & Society* 1, no. 3 (1987): 284–99; Andrea Hunter and Sherrill Sellers, "Feminist Attitudes among African American Women and Men," *Gender & Society* 12, no. 1 (1998): 81–99.

51. Emily Swanson, "Poll: Few Identify as Feminists, but Most Believe in Equality of Sexes," *Huffington Post*, April 16, 2013, http://www.huffingtonpost.com/2013/04/16/feminism-poll_n_3094917.html.

52. David A. Fahrenthold, "Trump Recorded Having Extremely Lewd Conversation about Women in 2005," *Washington Post*, October 8, 2016, https://www.washingtonpost.com/politics/trump-recorded-having-extremely-lewd-conversation-about-women-in-2005/2016/10/07/3b9ce776-8cb4-11e6-bf8a-3d26847eeed4_story.html?utm_term=.73ea1a4faf5e.

53. Alexander Burns, Maggie Haberman, and Jonathan Martin, "Donald Trump Apology Caps Day of Outrage over Lewd Tape," *New York Times*, October 7, 2016, https://www.nytimes.com/2016/10/08/us/politics/donald-trump-women.html?_r=0.

54. Christine Hauser and Jonah Engel Bromwich, "From 'Locker Room Talk' to 'Muslims Report Stuff': The Internet Strikes Back," *New York Times*, October 10, 2016, https://www.nytimes.com/2016/10/11/us/politics/from-locker-room-talk-to-muslims-report-stuff-the-internet-strikes-back.html?_r=0.

55. Amanda Taub, "Special Tax on Women: Trump Tape Is a Reminder of the Cost of Harassment," *New York Times*, October 10, 2016, https://www.nytimes.com/2016/10/11/business/a-special-tax-on-women-trump-tape-is-a-reminder-of-the-cost-of-harassment.html.

56. Rachel Wellford, "Here's the List of GOP Responses to Trump's Vulgar Comments about Groping Women," *PBS Newshour*, October 7, 2016, http://www.pbs.org/newshour/rundown/headline-republicans-react-trump-comments-objectifying-women/.

57. Hauser and Bromwich, "From 'Locker Room Talk.'"

58. Burleigh, "Presidential Election Was a Referendum."

59. Ibid.

60. "Pantsuit Nation—Public" Facebook page, https://www.facebook.com/pg/pantsuitnation11.8/about/?ref=page_internal.

61. Dwyer et al., "Racism, Sexism, and Candidate Evaluations"; Meeks, "All the Gender That's Fit"; Edwards and McDonald, "Reading Hillary and Sarah"; Wasburn and Wasburn, "Media Coverage of Women."

62. Logan Anderson, "This Is What an Official Hillary for America 'Woman Card' Gets You," Hillary for America, April 30, 2016, https://www.hillaryclinton.com/feed/what-official-hillary-america-woman-card-gets-you/.

63. Politico staff, "Full Transcript: First Presidential Debate," Politico.com, September 27, 2016, http://www.politico.com/story/2016/09/full-transcript-first-2016-presidential-debate-228761.

64. Linda Qui, "10 Most Aired Political Ads, Fact-Checked," Politifact, November 3, 2016, http://www.politifact.com/truth-o-meter/article/2016/nov/03/10-most-aired-political-ads-fact-checked/.

65. Ibid.

66. Ibid.

67. Jon Greenberg, "Trump Says Clinton Viciously Attacked Those Who Charged Abuse by Bill," Politifact, October 10, 2016, http://www.politifact.com/truth-o-meter/statements/2016/oct/10/donald-trump/donald-trump-says-hillary-clinton-viciously-attack/.

68. Aronson, "Feminists or 'Postfeminists'?"

69. Hillary Clinton, "Hillary Clinton's Concession Speech (Full Text)," CNN.com, November 9, 2016, http://www.cnn.com/2016/11/09/politics/hillary-clinton-concession-speech/index.html.

Chapter Fourteen

CONFRONTING "BIMBO ERUPTIONS" AND THE LEGACY OF BILL CLINTON'S SCANDAL

Slut-Shaming and the 2016 Presidential Campaigns

Leora Tanenbaum

The time was ripe for a cultural conversation about the sexual double standard—popularly referred to in recent years as "slut-shaming." During the second presidential debate, one month before the election, Hillary Clinton had the chance to confront Donald Trump about his sexual objectification of women and the manner in which he upheld a sexual double standard. But Clinton remained silent—most likely to protect her husband's political legacy as well as her own. She allowed an opportunity to educate Americans about slut-shaming to pass by. And it is possible that she lost the election as a result.

The Slut-Shaming Landscape in the Fall of 2016

To understand how important that moment was, we need to remember what was at stake in the months leading up to the election. The sexual double standard—the mindset that boys will be boys, and girls will be sluts—was deeply entrenched. Trump had made it clear that in his opinion, women's primary value came from being sexually desirable—yet paradoxically, he devalued women whom he considered sexually desirable; he also devalued women whom he judged insufficiently sexually desirable, including his political opponent. Some of his supporters agreed with this worldview, shouting, "Hillary is a whore!" and "Tramp!" at his political rallies.[1]

A serious, thoughtful conversation about slut-shaming was, and remains, necessary because this mindset props up sexual assault. If a woman is sexually assaulted, she must either secretly want it—or she has done something to deserve it, the thinking goes. Slut-shaming protects sexual assaulters. It was not surprising that when Fox News chief executive Roger Ailes was forced out of the network in July 2016 due to allegations that he had sexually harassed multiple women, Trump hired him as a campaign adviser. Trump explained that he felt "very badly" for Ailes, "a very, very good person," and that "I can tell you that some of the women who are complaining, I know how much he's helped them."[2]

On October 7, 2016, the *Washington Post* released a 2005 *Access Hollywood* recording of Trump saying it was acceptable to grab women by their genitals against their will. Thousands of women loudly said #NotOkay on social media, sharing their own stories of sexual assault online and with reporters.[3] Trump discredited the women who had accused him of groping or kissing them against their will by calling them "horrible, horrible liars," adding that one of them could not be telling the truth because, as he said, "Look at her."[4] Several weeks before, Trump had made a false accusation that Alicia Machado, the former Miss Universe whom Hillary Clinton had praised, had appeared in a "sex tape."[5] (Clinton had noted that Trump had demeaned Machado for gaining weight and called the Latina pageant winner "Miss Housekeeping" when he was an executive producer of the pageant.) After the debate, he dismissed Hillary Clinton by saying he "wasn't impressed" by her backside.[6]

But Trump was not the only candidate who had participated in slut-shaming. Hillary Clinton also participated in this sexist behavior, when her husband, Bill Clinton, was the governor of Arkansas and campaigned for the presidency himself, though quietly and for political reasons that campaign strategists believed were necessary. In 1992 Betsey Wright, chief of staff to Governor Bill Clinton, was given the task—with Hillary Clinton's support and approval—of dealing with accusations of his infidelity. Wright famously referred to women's accusations of affairs with Bill Clinton as "bimbo eruptions."[7]

When a *New York Times* reporter asked Wright in October 2016 to comment on this chapter of Hillary Clinton's political history, Wright responded that discussing these events was "dredging up irrelevant slime from the past."[8] Yet this history in fact was relevant, and Trump shrewdly seized on it for his advantage. Hillary Clinton should have acknowledged what she did in 1992. She erred when she glossed over her own past complicity in perpetuating one of the worst stereotypes about women: that being sexually active means lacking credibility and

character. Had she owned up to her own behavior in the "bimbo eruptions" chapter of her life, she could have confronted Trump on his
egregiously sexist assumptions, demonstrating that she had evolved
since the 1990s to become a significant champion for women. Remaining silent, however, meant she did not have the moral authority to call
him out.

Bill Clinton's 1992 Presidential Campaign

In January 1992, several weeks before the New Hampshire primary,
a nightclub singer and Arkansas state employee named Gennifer
Flowers claimed in a paid interview with a tabloid magazine that she
and the governor, Bill Clinton, who was running for president of the
United States, had had an affair lasting more than a decade.[9] Her allegation was dangerous to Clinton's presidential bid because an extramarital sexual liaison, even a consensual one, was perceived as deadly
to any rising politician. Indeed, in the previous presidential campaign
of 1988, Democratic front-runner Gary Hart dropped out because of
speculations that he had an affair with Donna Rice, memorably photo-
graphed sitting on his lap on a yacht named *Monkey Business*.[10]

Bill Clinton admitted that Flowers was a "friendly acquaintance"
but denied the affair in an interview on *60 Minutes*, aired immediately following the Super Bowl—the most media exposure he had
had at that point, with an audience estimated to be 50 million. When
pressed by interviewer Steve Kroft, he refused to state outright that he
had ever had an extramarital affair, yet he "acknowledged wrongdoing" and admitted to "causing pain in my marriage." Hillary Clinton,
who sat next to her husband during the interview, said that it wasn't
right that they were expected to reveal personal details to the public,
adding, "I think it's real dangerous in this country if we don't have
some zone of privacy for everybody. . . . You know, I'm not sitting here,
some little woman standing by my man like Tammy Wynette. I'm sitting here because I love him, and I respect him and I honor what he's
been through and what we've been through together. And you know, if
that's not enough for people, then, heck, don't vote for him."[11]

At a news conference the next day, Flowers played excerpts of
phone calls she had taped with Bill Clinton to back up her claim that
they had a close relationship. In one excerpt, she joked about his sexual abilities, though he didn't respond.[12]

Flowers may not have been the only woman with whom Bill Clinton had an affair. A former Arkansas state employee, Larry Nichols,
who held a grudge against the governor, had alleged publicly that Bill

Clinton had extramarital affairs with a number of women. The day before the *60 Minutes* interview, Nichols admitted that his actions were politically motivated—though he didn't retract his allegation that the governor was involved with other women.[13]

Several weeks later, Hillary Clinton and a small group of campaign aides decided to become more aggressive in discrediting women who claimed they had had sexual encounters with Bill Clinton and hired a hard-hitting private investigator, Jack Palladino.[14] Flowers later reported that the investigator had reached out to her former boyfriends and others to "get them to say things like I was sexually active" and that the stories he collected were used to characterize her as a "bimbo" and a "pathological liar." Bill Clinton admitted in 1998 that he and Flowers indeed had had a sexual relationship.[15]

It remains unclear how deeply Hillary Clinton was involved in the efforts to destroy Flowers's reputation. James Carville, Bill Clinton's top campaign strategist, along with two lawyers who worked on his presidential campaign, told the *New York Times* in 2016 that she had not been involved. However, another campaign aide said that she discussed and approved hiring Palladino.[16] We know that she discredited Flowers by referring to her as "some failed cabaret singer who doesn't even have much of a résumé to fall back on" on national television on the program *Primetime Live*.[17] She told the journalist Gail Sheehy, who was profiling her at the time for *Vanity Fair*, that if she had the chance to cross-examine Flowers, "I would crucify her."[18]

Did Hillary Clinton engage in slut-shaming? Yes. She either directly coordinated efforts to ruin Flowers's reputation or indirectly enabled these efforts. We know now that Flowers was telling the truth, and even in 1992, her story was credible given Bill Clinton's public admission that he had been involved in "wrongdoing" and causing "pain in my marriage" in the past as well as the audiotapes Flowers had recorded, the authenticity of which were never denied.

Hillary Clinton could have responded instead by repeating her *60 Minutes* message that the matter was a private one between herself and her husband. Even if she truly believed that Flowers had fabricated the claim that she was having an affair with Bill Clinton, digging into her sexual past was not necessary. It also was not relevant or even logical, since if Flowers had had a number of sexual partners in the past, this did not rule out the possibility that she was a sexual partner of Bill Clinton.

The women's rights lawyer Gloria Allred, who was a convention delegate for Hillary Clinton during her 2016 presidential bid, told the *New York Times* she does not approve of these tactics. "Most people are not nuns, and most people aren't Girl Scouts. That doesn't mean they're not telling the truth." Regarding Hillary Clinton's involvement in hiring Palladino, Allred said, "If Hillary signed off on a private investigator, let's call it a minus." But "it wouldn't change my support for her because there are so many pluses for her."[19] Hillary Clinton, in other words, has been an advocate for many but not all women.

Of course, Bill Clinton won the 1992 presidential election despite these "bimbo eruptions." But during his presidency, several other women came forward with sexual allegations—in these instances claiming that he had assaulted or propositioned them. In 1994, at a press conference organized by a politically conservative organization, Paula Jones, an Arkansas state worker, accused Bill Clinton of having made an unwanted sexual advance during his presidential campaign in 1991. Several years later, Juanita Broaddrick accused Bill Clinton of having raped her in 1978 when he was the attorney general of Arkansas and she was a state employee, and Kathleen Willey accused him of assault when he was president in 1993 and she was a volunteer aide working in the White House.

In these matters, we do not have a record of Hillary Clinton having said anything publicly about the women.[20] Jones told the *New York Times* in 2016 that "they sent out people to dig up trash on me," but we don't know if the "trash" was connected with her sexual history, affiliation with a politically right-wing organization, or something else, and we don't know that Hillary Clinton was involved.[21] We also do not know whether or not these accusations are true. It is possible that some, all, or none of the accusations were politically motivated—though in the wake of the #MeToo movement, some feminist commentators are reevaluating the accusations and raising the possibility that they may have merit.[22]

Hillary Clinton's 2016 Presidential Campaign

Against this historical backdrop, Donald Trump seized an opportunity to deflect attention away from his own mistreatment of women and to chip away at Hillary Clinton's feminist credentials. He told Fox News in January 2016 that Hillary Clinton is "not a victim. She was an enabler. . . . Some of these women have been destroyed, and Hillary worked with" her husband, he said.[23]

This was a dramatic change of opinion for Trump; in 1998, he had called Paula Jones and the other women who had accused Bill Clinton of assault "terrible people" and "a really unattractive group."[24] Now, however, it was politically expedient for him to side with them.

On the evening of the second presidential debate, which took place two days after the *Access Hollywood* tape was released, Trump held a press conference with Paula Jones, Kathleen Willey, Juanita Broaddrick, and Kathy Shelton (who had been raped at age twelve by a man Hillary Clinton legally defended) and invited them as his guests to attend the debate. "Hillary Clinton attacked those women and attacked them viciously," he said that evening.[25]

We have no evidence that Hillary Clinton had "attacked" these women. Most likely, she chose not to correct Trump on this point because she knew her moral standing on the issue of defending women against slut-shaming had been weakened due to her involvement, whether peripheral or direct, in slandering Flowers in 1992. Defending her husband was also problematic because she could have been perceived as denigrating the claims of all women who say they have been assaulted. Trump saw this weak spot and shrewdly managed to pivot attention away from his own slut-shaming behavior by making accusations against both Clintons. Backed into a corner, she responded during the debate only by quoting Michelle Obama, saying, "When they go low, we go high."[26]

But what if instead she had acknowledged that she is and was a product of her time—a woman born in 1947 who grew up in an era when girls and women were divided into two categories—"good" girls, on the one hand; and "tramps," "bimbos," or "sluts," on the other— and no one questioned this division? What if she had pointed out that she had internalized the message that boys will be boys, and girls will be sluts? What if she had noted that earlier in her life she was guilty of implicit sexist bias, just as so many of us harbor implicit racial bias, which she rightly described during the first presidential candidate debate as a "problem for everyone, not just police"?[27]

Hillary Clinton missed an opportunity to educate Americans that many people unconsciously call up sexist stereotypes about sexually active women as deviant and even disgusting, that many of us are socially conditioned to believe this is natural and true, and that we must interrupt this sexist attitude.

She could and should have used herself as a living example—to admit her flaws and to show that her behavior over two decades ago may not be forgivable, but it is understandable. She could and should have seized the moment to contrast her attitudes about women and sexuality with those of her opponent, a man who unrepentantly makes crude, hateful comments about women's appearance and sexuality. She could and should have demonstrated that she had evolved; the proof is her commitment to protecting and expanding reproductive rights, promoting equal pay, and protecting women on college campuses from sexual assault.

This lost opportunity had ramifications not only for Hillary Clinton's campaign but for us all. Examining her past in addition to Donald Trump's could have helped us disrupt the normalization of slut-shaming by placing it in historical context, allowing us to understand how far we have come—and how much farther we still must go.

Notes

1. Ashley Parker, Nick Corasaniti, and Erica Bernstein, "Voices from Donald Trump's Rallies, Uncensored," *New York Times*, August 3, 2016, https://www.nytimes.com/2016/08/04/us/politics/donald-trump-supporters.html?_r=0.

2. Adam Edelman and Leonard Greene, "Donald Trump Still Fan of Former Fox CEO Roger Ailes; Disbelieves Sexual Harassment Charges," *New York Daily News,* July 24, 2016, http://www.nydailynews.com/news/politics/trump-disbelieves-sexual-harassment-charges-roger-ailes-article-1.2724178.

3. Amy B. Wang, "'This Is Rape Culture': After Trump Video, Thousands of Women Share Sexual Assault Stories," *Washington Post,* October 8, 2016, https://www.washingtonpost.com/news/wonk/wp/2016/10/08/this-is-rape-culture-after-trump-video-thousands-of-women-share-sexual-assault-stories/?utm_term=.f8bf6af61f6a; Jonathan Mahler, "For Many Women, Trump's 'Locker Room Talk' Brings Memories of Abuse," *New York Times*, October 10, 2016, https://www.nytimes.com/2016/10/11/us/politics/sexual-assault-survivor-reaction.html.

4. Sean Sullivan, "Trump Launches Deeply Personal Attacks against Female Accusers, Calling Them 'Horrible, Horrible Liars,'" *Washington Post*, October 13, 2016, https://www.washingtonpost.com/news/post-politics/wp/2016/10/13/trump-launches-deeply-personal-attacks-against-women-accusers-calling-them-horrible-horrible-liars/?utm_term=.a3593953ab0f.

5 "Tessa Berenson, "Donald Trump Urges Followers to Check Out Alicia Machado's 'Sex Tape,'" *Time*, September 30, 2016, http://time.com/4514358/donald-trump-alicia-machado-feud/.

6. Daniella Diaz, "Trump: I 'Wasn't Impressed' When Clinton Walked in Front of Me at Debate," CNN.com, October 15, 2016, http://www.cnn.com/2016/10/14/politics/donald-trump-hillary-clinton-appearance-debate/.

7. Ibid.

8. Megan Twohey, "How Hillary Clinton Grappled with Bill Clinton's Infidelity, and His Accusers," *New York Times*, October 2, 2016, https://

www.nytimes.com/2016/10/03/us/politics/hillary-bill-clinton-women. html.

9. Ibid.

10. Matt Bai, "How Gary Hart's Downfall Forever Changed American Politics," *New York Times*, September 18, 2014, https://www.nytimes. com/2014/09/21/magazine/how-gary-harts-downfall-forever-changed-american-politics.html?_r=0.

11. Gwen Ifill, "The 1992 Campaign: Media; Clinton Defends His Privacy and Says the Press Intruded," *New York Times*, January 27, 1992, http:// www.nytimes.com/1992/01/27/us/the-1992-campaign-media-clinton-defends-his-privacy-and-says-the-press-intruded.html; Michael Kruse, "The TV Interview That Haunts Hillary Clinton," *Politico Magazine*, September 23, 2016, http://www.politico.com/magazine/story/2016/09/hillary-clinton-2016-60-minutes-1992-214275.

12. Gwen Ifill, "The 1992 Campaign: Democrats; Clinton Attempts to Ignore Rumors," *New York Times*, January 28, 1992, http://www.nytimes. com/1992/01/28/us/the-1992-campaign-democrats-clinton-attempts-to-ignore-rumors.html.

13. Ifill, "Clinton Defends His Privacy."

14. Twohey, "How Hillary Clinton Grappled."

15. Ibid.

16. Ibid.

17. Kruse, "TV Interview That Haunts"; Steven A. Holmes and Lisa Rose, "Reality Check: Did Hillary Clinton Attack Her Husband's Accusers?," CNN.com, October 12, 2016, http://www.cnn.com/2016/10/11/politics/hillary-clinton-donald-trump-bill-clinton-accusers/.

18. Gail Sheehy, "The Women Who Should Love Hillary Clinton," *New York Times*, January 29, 2016, https://www.nytimes.com/2016/01/31/opinion/campaign-stops/why-dont-boomer-women-like-hillary-clinton. html.

19. Twohey, "How Hillary Clinton Grappled."

20. Holmes and Rose, "Reality Check."

21. Twohey, "How Hillary Clinton Grappled."

22. Michelle Goldberg, "I Believe Juanita," *New York Times*, November 13, 2017, https://www.nytimes.com/2017/11/13/opinion/juanita-broaddrick-bill-clinton.html.

23. "Donald Trump Talks Ted Cruz, Gun Control and the Clintons," Fox News, January 10, 2016, http://www.foxnews.com/transcript/2016/01/10/donald-trump-talks-ted-cruz-gun-control-and-clintons-denis-mcdonough-previews.html.

24. Justin Baragona, "Back in 1998, Trump Called Bill Clinton's Accusers 'Terrible' and 'A Really Unattractive Group,'" *Mediaite*, October 9, 2016, http://www.mediaite.com/election-2016/back-in-1998-trump-called-bill-clintons-accusers-terrible-and-a-really-unattractive-group/.

25. Charlotte Alter, "Donald Trump Highlighted Bill Clinton's Accusers at Debate," *Time*, October 9, 2016, http://time.com/4341892/presidential-debate-donald-trump-bill-clinton/; Holmes and Rose, "Reality Check."

26. NBC News, "Clinton's Response: 'When They Go Low, We Go High,'" October 10, 2016, http://www.nbcnews.com/card/clintons-response-when-they-go-low-we-go-high-n663036.

27. Daniel A. Yudkin and Jay van Bavel, "The Roots of Implicit Bias," *New York Times*, December 9, 2016, https://www.nytimes.com/2016/12/09/opinion/sunday/the-roots-of-implicit-bias.html.

Chapter Fifteen

HOW TO TURN A BERNIE BRO INTO A RUSSIAN BOT

Steve Almond

L ike a lot of Americans, my twenty-two-year-old friend John began the 2016 presidential campaign as a passionate supporter of Bernie Sanders and the progressive cause. During family gatherings, he spoke eloquently, if quietly, about income inequality, single-payer health care, and a livable wage.

By Election Day, John had become a full-fledged Hillary hater, an angry young man who posted fake news stories about Clinton online, trolled family members, and greeted the election of Donald Trump with a strange elation.

To understand what happened here requires an understanding of how two historical forces collided during the 2016 election: Cold War–style Russian propaganda and old-fashioned American misogyny. Because John's radical shift in perspective was, in fact, engineered— both from outside America and from within his own psyche.

We now know that Russian operatives, acting on orders from the Kremlin, bombarded guys like John with anti-Clinton agitprop throughout the campaign.[1]

This effort was part of what the *New York Times* called, back in 2015, "the biggest trolling operation in history," one aimed at decimating "the utility of the Internet as a democratic space."[2] It was also, in essence, the new face of an old tradition: Soviet espionage, which had evolved from double agents to cyber warfare.

When people hear allegations of cyber warfare, they envision high-tech operatives hacking into secure government servers. But the Russians recognized that American democracy in the Internet era was

Portions of this essay appeared originally in Steve Almond, *Bad Stories: What the Hell Just Happened to Our Country* (Pasadena, CA: Red Hen Press, 2018), and are reprinted here by permission of the author.

vulnerable to a far more humble approach. They could "hack" Bernie supporters simply by posting propaganda on their Facebook pages, websites, and forums.

The Russians targeted Bernie believers because they evinced the same basic attitudes as Trump voters: contempt for the establishment and Clinton. Wikileaks released 19,000 Russian-hacked emails on the eve of Democratic National Convention specifically to promote the notion that Clinton and the Democratic establishment had jobbed Bernie.[3]

It appears that the Russians made a calculated bet that a guy like John, if sufficiently goaded, would shift from an agenda driven by progressive goals to one driven by animus toward Clinton.

I saw this shift play out in real time.

As summer 2016 turned to fall, Bernie Sanders campaigned for Clinton and openly implored his followers to reject Trump. Yet John did not post any articles critical of Trump. Nor did he draw attention to GOP voter-suppression efforts.

Instead, John's Facebook page began to include more and more memes and articles vilifying Clinton. These items came from far-right websites, Romanian fake news farms, even a website affiliated with the Syrian dictator Bashar al-Assad.

Taken together, John's posts composed a kind of ideologically incoherent gumbo in which the main ingredients were disinformation and distrust of authority in general, and Clinton in particular—the same stew Trump dished out daily at his rallies.

And John didn't just opine on social media. He also participated in various online chats, circulating these same links, while bantering with friends and relatives. Here, too, his logic was tough to follow. "This country can't survive another Clinton presidency," he wrote to his chat group, most of whom happened to be female Clinton supporters.

And: "Clinton will lead us into war."

And: "She'll create a corporatist controlled police state."

When another member of his chat group asked John about the potential dangers of electing Trump, he replied, "Why are you stuck on fear mongering?"

John insisted he wanted to vote for someone he believed in, not the lesser of two evils. He promoted himself as the epitome of righteous idealism. But his logic was that of a fatalist. The system was rigged beyond repair. Platforms and policies were bullshit. "A vote for hillary is a vote for trump," John wrote my wife a few weeks before the election.

This is how you knew he wasn't a person of color, or a Muslim, or an immigrant.

On the morning after the election, John asked his mother—a Clinton volunteer who had spent much of election night in tears—whether it was weird that he was happy about the result.

When I heard about this comment, something clicked in my mind. I began to realize that John had an emotional agenda far more powerful than his political one. Early in the campaign, he'd been full of talk about social justice and reforming the two-party system. But his digital footprint made it clear that he was far more interested in trashing Hillary and agitating her voters. This was why he'd sent provocative messages to female Clinton supporters such as my wife. He was trolling them, just like he'd trolled his mother the day after the election.

And why was that?

Because John wasn't just a thwarted crusader. He was, more fundamentally, a high school graduate who was stuck living in his mom's house, a guy who worked a low-wage job, amid the multinational zillionaires, in Silicon Valley.

In this sense, he was part of a larger generational cohort: alienated young men who went online to find the power they couldn't experience IRL ("in real life"), often by spouting misogynistic invective.

Am I suggesting that my sweet friend John would do such a thing? No. I don't think he would. But I do think the nomination of our nation's first major-party female candidate roused a strain of misogyny that has always been endemic to the American spirit.

For every young woman who paid tribute to the suffragists during the campaign, there was a young man like John, angrily dependent on a woman at home, intimidated and unmanned by ambitious women in the workplace, disempowered by the globalized economy and ready to blame feminism for his self-doubt.

Hillary Clinton—with her "corporate" pantsuits and her staid policy talk—made an ideal target for this isotopic ire. After all, she had spent her entire public life absorbing abuse, mostly at the hands of men.

Maybe the Russia-backed operatives who targeted Bernie supporters knew this. Maybe they recognized that beneath America's rippling banner of gender equality there was a bottomless pit of unreconstructed chauvinism, one that they could exploit to turn guys like my friend into bots.

Or maybe—like the self-professed sexual predator they helped elect—they just got lucky.

Notes

1. Ryan Grim and Jason Cherkis, "Bernie Sanders' Campaign Faced a Fake News Tsunami: Where Did It Come From?," *Huffington Post,* March 13, 2017, http://www.huffingtonpost.com/entry/bernie-sanders-fake-news-russia_us_58c34d97e4b0ed71826cdb36.

2. Adrian Chen, "The Agency," *New York Times,* June 2, 2015, https://www.nytimes.com/2015/06/07/magazine/the-agency.html?_r=0.

3. Tom Hamburger and Karen Tumulty, "Hacked Emails Are Posted Online as Democrats' Convention Nears," *Washington Post,* July 22, 2016, https://www.washingtonpost.com/politics/2016/07/22/117f0574-504f-11e6-a422-83ab49ed5e6a_story.html?utm_term=.11221df633cf.

Part Four

Election Day

Rewriting Past and Future

Chapter Sixteen

#WOMENCANSTOPTRUMP

Intimate Publics in the Twitterverse

Gina Masullo Chen and Kelsey N. Whipple

The 2016 US presidential election stands out for many reasons. It was the first time a female candidate, Hillary Clinton, topped the ballot from a major political party. It followed a campaign unrivaled for vitriolic discourse by her opponent, Donald J. Trump.[1] In the months leading up to the election, the polls largely showed support for a Clinton win, but it looked to be a squeaker.[2] Women who were galvanized by Clinton's candidacy used social media to mark the significance of the historic election. One popular way of doing this was through the use of gendered hashtags—keywords with a phone's number or pound sign used to categorize posts on social networking sites such as Twitter. People used #ImWithHer and #ShesWithUs—and sometimes, #GirlIGuessImWithHer—to support Clinton, the Democratic candidate.[3] They used hashtags including #WomenCanStopTrump and #PantsuitNation to oppose her Republican ballot mate.[4] They highlighted the importance of women and women's issues by using #HerStory, #TheFutureIsFemale, #DedicateYourVoteToAWoman, and the many versions of #ForMyDaughter, #ForMyMother, and so on.[5] For many women, the hashtags became a rallying cry that exemplified the political power of gathering together—#StrongerTogether—online for a common cause.

Invoking these hashtags allowed women to express their voting intentions, share their political ideology, and, often, express disapproval of Trump's behavior toward women and his positions on women's issues. Throughout the 2016 election cycle, Trump's public missteps regarding women, both historical and ongoing, were so numerous that one newspaper in the United Kingdom created a running "Trump sexism tracker."[6] He verbally attacked women during the campaign, including Megyn Kelly, who was a Fox News anchor at the time; comedian Rosie O'Donnell; and Carly Fiorina, a Republican primary opponent.[7] He called Clinton a "nasty woman" during the final presidential debate on live television, and this accusation led to the #NastyWomen hashtag going viral on social media and appearing on protest signs across the country.[8] Revelations about Trump's past behavior also surfaced in campaign coverage and ignited new public furor. One example was Trump's mocking of international beauty queen Alicia Machado in the late 1990s by calling her "Miss Piggy" because she had gained weight and "Miss Housekeeping" because she is Latina. Clinton brought up these incidents during a debate with Trump.[9] Another was a newly leaked video from 2005 that showed Trump boasting about "grab[bing] 'em [women] by the pussy."[10] This action, too, led to hashtag activism: #NotMyPussy, #ThisPussyGrabsBack, and the like. It was a popular time for hashtag feminism and for hashtags in general.[11]

This chapter aims to explore this seminal moment in women's political history by qualitatively analyzing 1,493 tweets—with the hashtag #WomenCanStopTrump—posted on Twitter before and after the November 8, 2016, presidential election, which Trump won in a surprising twist of fate. We chose this hashtag, out of the many that relate to this topic, because it provides a telling example of how some women gathered to support Clinton and stop Trump. Once their hopes of a Clinton win were dashed, they continued to rally around the hashtag to resist the new president. We begin by briefly exploring hashtag feminism as a concept. Then we draw on critical theorist Lauren Berlant's concept of "intimate publics"—defined as the emotional experience of feeling political together—to understand how this election fomented a digital movement for female empowerment in the United States, despite the outcome of the presidential contest.[12] This concept of intimate publics is akin to communication scholar Zizi Papacharissi's idea of "affective publics," which describes how people mobilize in online networks through expressions of sentiment.[13] Next, we explore four major themes that surfaced in the tweets before offering larger statements about what these examples indicate about women's empowerment.

Hashtag Feminism

Since the first hashtag appeared on Twitter in 2007, hashtags have been used to foster social change and give voice to people from marginalized groups. For example, activists across several countries in the Middle East and North Africa used hashtags to organize, such as during the series of popular uprisings in 2010 called the Arab Spring.[14] More recently, hashtags have been used to give voice to movements as divergent as a battle against femicide in Turkey and the Black Lives Matter movement in the United States.[15] Specifically in relation to feminism, the use of hashtags has become a powerful tool that has earned the name *hashtag feminism*. For example, #YesAllWomen sprang up in May 2014 in response to a killing spree in California in which the shooter claimed he was retaliating against women who had rejected his sexual advances.[16] #YesAllWomen was used to demonstrate that sexism, misogyny, and hate against females is widespread. Use of the hashtag became a "feminist meme event," which is "a form of feminist media event that references not only an external event, but itself becomes a reference point."[17] Thus, the hashtag offered a "critical counter narrative to dominant gender discourses that present male harassment as either not serious . . . or somehow unusual or untypical."[18] Similarly, hashtags have been used to fight efforts to trivialize the rape of an African American teenager and combat stereotypes about Latinas and Asian women.[19] Yet hashtag feminism has its critics, who suggest online engagement can foster an illusion of solidarity that does little to provide real empowerment or change.[20] Critics also suggest that the American feminist movement's historic focus on the white middle-class experience can be reinforced through hashtags that leave out diverse voices.[21] We acknowledge these limitations. However, we embrace hashtag feminism as a way to understand women's sense of digital "we-ness" or camaraderie online, where they envision themselves as part of a larger, more powerful group.[22]

Intimate Publics

Berlant's concept of intimate publics illustrates how strangers may feel a sense of connection with each other through the affective—or emotional—experience of being political together.[23] As people publicly share feelings on Twitter, hashtags can help them stand together and be counted in a "collectively shaped identity."[24] The way this works is that heightened emotions about a specific topic, such as the election, draw people into politics. Hashtags, such as #WomenCanStopTrump, expose people to others' opinions on the topic and permit them to rebroadcast or represent these views as their own.[25] Thus, women who were not politically active before were emboldened by the example of more activist women. In addition, people who feel politically impotent on their own can draw strength from others' voices. These intimate publics make a "shared atmosphere something palpable" and powerful.[26] #WomenCanStopTrump, therefore, exemplifies a fundamental shift in how the public communicates politically, through the engaging power of social media sites such as Twitter.[27]

Based on this literature and theoretical framework, we pose the following research questions to answer through our analysis: Why did women use the #WomenCanStopTrump hashtag and what role—if any—did it play in their sense of feeling political together? Did their use of the hashtag foster intimate publics of political agency, and, if so, how did this operate?

Our Analysis

To create the sample for our analysis, we used computer software to collect 44,338 tweets in English that used the #WomenCanStopTrump hashtag from October through December 2016.[28] We then narrowed our time range to the two weeks before and after the election, focused only on tweets sent by females, and removed retweets from the sample. This left us with 1,493 original tweets using the #WomenCanStopTrump hashtag across four weeks. Our qualitative analysis involved becoming familiar with the tweets by reading the entire sample multiple times until common themes emerged. Both researchers performed this analysis independently, and then compared commonalities between the themes each found to provide a fuller picture. This type of analysis relies on uncovering underlying or latent meaning in text, rather than focusing solely on facts or literal meaning.[29] Our goal was to understand the discourse in which these tweets operate, so that we could reveal their implied meaning and make broader inferences about how women use hashtags to rally together.[30] All grammatical and spelling errors have been retained in quoted tweets, and Twitter handles are reported as they appeared on Twitter.

Speaking through Tweets

Overall in our data, four major themes surfaced that reveal how women used the #WomenCanStopTrump hashtag and how it bonded them politically, answering both our research questions. The most dominant theme was how the hashtag drew women together in intimate or affective publics, through a shared sense of political agency and calls to action that grew increasingly frenzied, as women realized their plan to stop Trump would not be achieved on election night. We call this theme One Voice because the term crystallizes the camaraderie women felt and the emotion and empowerment that fomented through this connection. We dubbed our second theme Trump's Sexploits because it focused strongly on his affronts to women and how this rendered him unfit for the presidency, according to the women who used the hashtag. The third theme we found was Amplified Agency. This theme demonstrated the importance of women acting together to take advantage of their civic power during a time of political polarity and the ways in which they held each other accountable regarding that responsibility. And finally, we examined the ways in which the #WomenCanStopTrump hashtag encouraged women to Make the Personal Public through sharing private emotions or details to express authenticity and forge relationships in the intimate publics connected by the hashtag.

One Voice

Tweets that exhibited the theme One Voice included a variety of calls to action, urging other women to vote, march, rally, or simply add the #WomenCanStopTrump hashtag to their profiles as a sign of solidarity. "If voting with my vag means keeping these loons from the [White House], find me a pen I'll figure it out," tweeted @sarahsettgo on November 8, 2016, explicitly using the vagina as a political symbol. In doing so, the tweet reclaimed a phrase that had been used to demean women.[31] Another message, from @satnettv on November 1, "Women Let your Voice be Heard in the Silence of your Vote you have the Ultimate Power #WomenCanStopTrump #GoVote," was typical of tweets showing this theme. Another example is this tweet from @easttown-Dems on November 3: "Women voters are not a special interest group; women are the majority!" Sometimes, this theme described people's response to the act of voting for Clinton, such as "I feel 'cleansed'! I voted," as @loisjost tweeted on October 25. Many pointed to the potency of women acting in concert. For example, @hilgaines tweeted on October 29: "On Nov. 9th we'll be able to say 'remember when women saved the world?' Yeah, you're welcome!" These tweets illustrate how hashtags may create a collective digital space that unites people around a shared interest or belief.[32]

It is notable that tweets frequently contained hashtags celebrating racial diversity (e.g., #LatinaPower or #BlackVotes) or overt statements that showed the #WomenCanStopTrump hashtag resonated particularly with women of color. For example, @maysapet tweeted on November 1: "#WomenCanStopTrump If this doesn't move U 2 TEARS, U R not human. first generation PROUD American, Latina. #vote." The tweet linked to a Clinton ad that featured the father of Humayan Khan, an American soldier born in Pakistan who died fending off a suicide bomber. The tweet celebrates the immigrant experience, while tying it to Latina female agency. The intersectionality apparent in these tweets is important because it demonstrates the reality that women of color voted overwhelmingly for Clinton. According to exit polls reported by CNN, Clinton won 43 percent of the white female vote, while she accrued 94 percent of the African American female vote and 64 percent of the Latina vote.[33] Although our sample did not enable us to assess the race of all women using the #WomenCanStop-Trump hashtag, many tweets contained references to race that suggested women of color were using the hashtag to rally in an intimate public.[34] In this way, the hashtag became a form of "signifyin'," which invites an audience and establishes the boundaries of an organically formed online community.[35]

Trump's Sexploits

The theme Trump's Sexploits depicted how women were hurt by the fact that a major-party presidential candidate had such a misogynistic past. Tweets referenced claims women had made against Trump for sexual abuse and his diatribe against Machado, the former Miss Universe winner, about her weight and ethnicity.[36] Debbie's (@DebYNYer) tweet on October 25 in response to another tweet illustrates this: "@ VaTxn Rape/sex assault isn't 'lusty appetite.' It's a crime. We 'gals' are making our statement @ the polls." The tweets clearly showed that women saw Trump's sexual failings as invalidating him as a presidential hopeful. "It really isn't enough to say that DJT is unfit as a presidential nominee," tweeted Renée Mountain Passage (@MountainPassage) on October 31, 2016. "He isn't fit as a man." These tweets depicted a palpable moment in the campaign, as women realized his sexploits did not nullify his chances of winning with many voters. For example, @Caroline_Muir tweeted on October 28: "I have discovered that my country should be called 'United States of Misogyny.'" Tweets belonging to this theme also contrasted Trump with Clinton, who was vilified throughout the campaign for her use of a private email server while she was secretary of state and for deleting 30,000 emails on her private computer.[37] Clinton was cleared of wrongdoing; however, the scandal haunted her campaign. Tweets demonstrated women's consternation with the seemingly inflated impact of the emails, compared with the many accusations against Trump, which included child rape, sexual assault, fraud and racketeering, and collusion with Russia.[38] "Keep it real, emails or child rapist, sexual predator, fraud, racist, Russian loving con," tweeted Karen Goodwin (@jkgood1) on October 30, 2016, exemplifying this theme. Collectively, these tweets depicted a potent rage at what these Twitter users saw as society's view that assaults against women were unimportant. Their anger suggested these women saw this as an affront to womanhood in general. The women seemed to be asking: If sexploits do not nullify a presidential candidate's bid, what does that say about the value of women in society?

Amplified Agency

One of the most popular ideas expressed using this hashtag was demonstrated in a tweet on October 31, from Emily's List (@emilyslist), a pro-choice political action committee in Washington, DC: "If women vote together, we will decide who the next president will be." This belief was echoed throughout the tweets in our sample and exemplified in the very text of the hashtag, #WomenCanStopTrump. It's worth noting that this belief continued to appear in tweets even after the election. The Emily's List tweet, in particular, illustrates the degree to which women expressed agency over the political process and held each other accountable for claiming and taking advantage of that agency. The idea expressed here is that power was in their hands, and they were responsible for wielding that power en masse. "We have to fight to keep our world save [*sic*] from evil," is how Taslima Ahmad (@taslima_ahmad) framed her political responsibility in a tweet on November 9. At the same time, Laurie Voss (@laurie_voss) warned followers away from apathy on October 25: "A vote is a horrible thing to waste." This appeal to women to join together is reminiscent of what the suffragists expected when women gained the right to vote with approval of the Nineteenth Amendment to the Constitution, but in reality, women voters in the 2016 election did not vote as a group. Class, race, religion, and geographic region divided them.

Because the sample included two weeks before the election and two weeks after it, this time span allowed us to explore changes in hashtag usage over time. Even after Trump's win, women used the #WomenCanStopTrump hashtag to call themselves and others to action to speak out against Trump and his political positions. In one example, a tweet shared a link promoting the Women's March in Washington, DC, which was one of hundreds of events organized to stand up against Trump after his inauguration. The tweet announced, "I'm going! Anyone else? Just booked our flights from CA. Let our voices be heard!" (@jkgood1, November 17, 2016). Others echoed this action with similar tweets, such as @weezeramb's on November 12, "I'm planning on going. Are you?" By continuing to apply the hashtag to their tweets after the election, these women extended its life cycle and attempted to continue their movement's momentum. Rather than give up in the face of the reality that women had indeed *not* stopped Trump, these hashtag users seemed to gain agency from the loss.

They converted the hashtag into a call for more action, including signing a petition appealing to the Electoral College to vote against Trump when it finalized election results in December. "Electoral College CAN Make Hillary Clinton President on December 19," wrote Maysa-Maria Peterson (@maysapet) in a tweet on November 11, linking to a Change.org petition to that effect. Twitter users continued to urge people to change their Twitter profile pictures to include the hashtag, as they had before the election. They also advocated support for civic and humanitarian groups, such as the American Civil Liberties Union (ACLU), to thwart Trump's policies. In a show of intimate togetherness, women used this hashtag and others to console each other about the election results, encouraging each other to keep the faith. For example, when one hashtag user reported she woke up with a broken heart on November 9, @spadekgj10 responded, "Just remember what you do & who you are is an inspiration to women despite was has happened." These tweets suggested an unwillingness to let "what has happened"—the reality that Trump won—detract from the political momentum of American woman claiming and wielding political agency as a group.

Making the Personal Public

Another way this hashtag cemented political togetherness on social media was through the women's expression of personal details to connect with other women and make their voices heard. "#Election2016 is full of fear. #Election2008 was full of hope" is how @RubinBuijserd on November 8 summarized the differences between Trump's election and that of his predecessor, President Barack Obama. Both before and after the election, women used the hashtag in tweets mourning the nation's lack of gender equality and bemoaning the freedoms they feared they might lose during Trump's administration. Mary Walden (@MaryWalden13) on October 25 shared her fear that "Trump is so dangerous, not just to US but to the entire planet" while others expressed heartbreak. "Oh dear pray the world is safe," tweeted @ paceprojectuk on Election Day. "Grieving and vulnerable and looking at art and poetry and the fight in us all," tweeted @YYJPoetry the morning after the election. Fear was a common issue, as women both expressed it and urged others to leave it behind. "Don't Let WeakAss TrumpClone PussyGrabbers Scare U," wrote @DarwunStJames, on November 3.

Personal feelings proved a popular basis of many tweets, with @Liviapolise asking her followers on November 1, "How does he [Trump] make you feel?" Many women shared intimate details about their lives and grounded their tweets in these elements. For example, @EmmaEdenRamos wrote on October 26, "I'm a gay, half Mexican woman," before summarizing her recent donation to Clinton's campaign. Others identified as undocumented immigrants, as mothers, as victims of sexual violence, and as other categories of people threatened by Trump's candidacy, in order to appeal to followers to support Clinton. These details served to strengthen the political pleas of Twitter users by increasing their authenticity while also amplifying the sense of intimacy that pervaded the affective publics created by the shared use of the #WomenCanStopTrump hashtag.

Our data showed that the #WomenCanStopTrump hashtag proved a largely positive galvanizing feminist moment on social media, a realm regularly analyzed as being comprised of "gendered, oppressive technologies" with little safe space for women.[39] Instead, it allowed women to "feel their way into politics" and assemble themselves in empowering political publics that did not disband even when the focus of their efforts—to defeat Trump—fell short.[40] Certainly, the Internet in many forms, from blog posts to tweets, has always offered ways for people to gather with other like-minded souls.[41] Yet, our analysis showed that the use of this hashtag could strengthen these efforts because it made it easier for women to find others with similar views. We find it notable that the women did not abandon the hashtag when their political aim was dashed. Instead, they built on the agency that the hashtag had fostered. Will these women eventually obtain the political power they seek by obstructing Trump's policies or even thwarting his reelection in 2020? That is uncertain. However, we believe that does not mean their actions were for nothing. Papacharissi argues that online affective publics should not be judged "as forces that bring about change, do activism, or enact impact."[42] Instead, she suggests their value lies in "presenting people with environments of a social nature, supporting interactions that are aligned with particular cultural ethos."[43] We agree. As seen in this example, the uniting of women with a shared digital voice can improve our society and these women's experiences regardless of whether they achieve every aim they seek. However, certainly not every online community improves society, as research has shown that 20 percent of online discourse is mired in vitriol.[44]

Our view is not only positive. Dozens of the tweets with the #WomenCanStopTrump hashtag contained content that belied that message and instead degraded Clinton, applauded Trump, or mocked

Clinton's supporters. As one such tweet from @tbmo on November 19 read: "Thanks feminists for rallying behind #WomenCanStopTrump. Your plans always #Backfire spectacularly, and so did this one!" While the frequency of these tweets, which we call "countertweets," was less pronounced than our other themes, we feel it is important to note. These countertweets suggest that Trump's supporters were attempting to co-opt the #WomenCanStopTrump hashtag for their own goals, much as feminists have reclaimed negative hashtags for their own empowerment.[45] These countertweets also suggest that the protective bubble of agency that formed through this hashtag was so powerful that naysayers attempted to burst it. Why attack something that has no value? Yet, our analysis strongly showed that they did not accomplish this goal. The hashtag, and the women who tweeted it, did not lose power. In fact, the women supporters may have been emboldened by defeat. The hashtag effectively created a "virtual space where victims of inequality can co-exist together in a space that acknowledges their pain, narrative, and isolation."[46] And, like other feminist hashtags before it, #WomenCanStopTrump provided a "critical counter-narrative" to tropes of oppression and misogyny that can too easily flourish online and offline.[47]

Notes

1. Jake Novak, "Trump vs. Clinton: Why This Election Could Be the Nastiest in History," CNBC.com, May 3, 2016, http://www.cnbc.com/2016/05/03/trump-vs-clinton-why-this-election-could-be-the-nastiest-in-history-commentary.html.

2. Nate Silver, "Election Update: Don't Ignore the Polls— Clinton Leads, but It's a Close Race," FiveThirtyEight.com, November 6, 2016, https://fivethirtyeight.com/features/election-update-dont-ignore-the-polls-clinton-leads-but-its-a-close-race/.

3. Anna Merod, "With #GirlIGuessImWithHer, Some Clinton Voters Show Their Reluctant Support," MSNBC.com, June 9, 2016, http://www.msnbc.com/msnbc/girliguessimwithher-some-clinton-voters-show-their-reluctant-support; Heather Schwedel, "You're Nobody If You Didn't Wear a Pantsuit to the Polls," *Slate*, November 8, 2016, http://www.slate.com/blogs/xx_factor/2016/11/08/hillary_clinton_supporters_wore_pantsuits_to_the_polls.html; Madeline Stone, "Hillary Clinton Supporters Are Wearing Pantsuits to the Polls Because of a Viral Facebook Group," *Business Insider*, November 8, 2016, http://www.businessinsider.com/pantsuit-nation-viral-facebook-group-2016-11; Marie Solis, "On Election Day, People Are Celebrating Women with #DedicateYourVoteTo AWoman," *Mic*, November 8, 2016, https://mic.com/articles/158839/

on-election-day-people-are-celebrating-women-with-dedicate-your-vote-to-awoman.

4. Schwedel, "You're Nobody."

5. Anna Merod, "With #GirlIGuessImWithHer, Some Clinton Voters Show Their Reluctant Support," MSNBC.com, June 9, 2016, http://www.msnbc.com/msnbc/girliguessimwithher-some-clinton-voters-show-their-reluctant-support; Stone, "Hillary Clinton Supporters"; Solis, "On Election Day."

6. Claire Cohen, "Donald Trump Sexism Tracker: Every Offensive Comment in One Place," *Telegraph*, July 14, 2017, http://www.telegraph.co.uk/women/politics/donald-trump-sexism-tracker-every-offensive-comment-in-one-place/.

7. Ibid.

8. Daniellea Diaz, "Trump Calls Clinton 'a Nasty Woman,'" CNN.com, October, 20, 2016, http://www.cnn.com/2016/10/19/politics/donald-trump-hillary-clinton-nasty-woman/.

9. Scott Horsley, "Trump Again Attacks Former Miss Universe," NPR, September 30, 2016, http://www.npr.org/2016/09/30/496050913/trump-again-attacks-miss-universe-contestant.

10. "Transcript: Donald Trump's Taped Comments about Women," *New York Times*, October 8, 2016, https://www.nytimes.com/2016/10/08/us/donald-trump-tape-transcript.html?_r=0.

11. Melissa Gira Grant, "Is Hillary's Hashtag-Friendly Feminism All That Stands between Us and the Apocalypse?," *Village Voice*, July 20, 2016, http://www.villagevoice.com/news/is-hillarys-hashtag-friendly-feminism-all-that-stands-between-us-and-the-apocalypse-8876469.

12. Lauren Berlant, *Cruel Optimism* (Durham, NC: Duke University Press, 2011), 224.

13. Zizi Papacharissi, *Affective Publics* (New York: Oxford University Press, 2015).

14. Nahed Eltantawny and Julie B. West, "Social Media in the Egyptian Revolution: Reconsidering Resource Mobilization Theory," *International Journal of Communication* 5 (2011): 1207–24.

15. Rüstem Ertuğ Altinay, "There's a Massacre of Women: Violence against Women, Feminist Activism, and Hashtags in Turkey," *Feminist Media Studies* 14, no. 6 (2014): 1102–3; Gina Masullo Chen, "Social Media: From Digital Divide to Empowerment," in *The Routledge Companion to Media and Race*, ed. Christopher P. Campbell (New York: Routledge, 2017), 117–25.

16. Samantha Thrift, "#YesAllWomen as Feminist Meme Event," *Feminist Media Studies* 14, no. 6 (2014): 1090–92; Bernadette Barker-Plummer and Dave Barker-Plummer, "Hashtag Feminist, Digital Media, and New Dynamics of Social Change: A Case Study of #YesAllWomen," in *Social Media and Politics: A New Way to Participate in the Political Process*, ed. Glenn W. Richardson Jr. (Santa Barbara, CA: Praeger, 2017), 79–96.

17. Thrift, "#YesAllWomen as Feminist Meme Event," 1091.

18. B. Barker-Plummer and Barker-Plummer, "Hashtag Feminism," 91.

19. Sherri Williams, "Digital Defense: Black Feminists Resist Violence with Hashtag Activism," *Feminist Media Studies* 15, no. 2 (2015): 341–44; Tanisha Love Ramirez and Carolina Moreno, "#LatinasAreNot Going to Stand for Stereotypes, This Hashtag Proves It," *Huffington Post*, November 6, 2015, http://www.huffingtonpost.com/entry/latinasarenot-going-to-stand-for-stereotypes-and-this-hashtag-proves-it_us_563cd6ece4b0307f2cad295c; Casey Capachi, "Suey Park: Asian American Women Are #NotYourAsianSidekick," *Washington Post*, December 17, 2013, https://www.washingtonpost.com/blogs/she-the-people/wp/2013/12/17/suey-park-asian-american-women-are-notyourasiansidekick/?utm_term=.b540f01e9dd0.

20. Jodi Dean, *Democracy and Other Neoliberal Fantasies: Communicative Capitalism and Left Politics* (Durham, NC: Duke University Press, 2009); Yu-Hao Lee and Gary Hsieh, "Does Slacktivism Hurt Activism? The Effect of Moral Balancing and Consistency on Online Activism," *Proceedings of the CHI 2013: Changing Perspectives*, April 27–May 2, 2013, Paris, France; Tavia Nyong'o, "Queer African and the Fantasy of Virtual Participation," *Women's Studies Quarterly* 40, no. 1 (2012): 40–63.

21. Shenila Khoja-Moolji, "Becoming 'Intimate Publics': Exploring the Affective Intensities of Hashtag Feminism," *Feminist Media Studies* 15, no. 2 (2015): 347–50.

22. Leda Cooks, Mari Castaneda Paredes, and Erica Scharrer, "There's 'O Place' Like Home: Searching for Community on Oprah.com," in *Women and Everyday Uses of the Internet: Agency & Identity*, ed. Mia Consalvo and Susanna Paasonen (New York: Peter Lang, 2002); Gina Masullo Chen, "Tweet This: A Uses and Gratifications Perspective on How Active Twitter Users Gratify a Need to Connect with Others," *Computers in Human Behavior* 27 (2011): 755–62.

23. Berlant, *Cruel Optimism.*

24. Papacharissi, *Affective Publics*, 117.

25. Papacharissi, *Affective Publics.*

26. Berlant, *Cruel Optimism*, 16.

27. Jason Gainous and Kevin M. Wagner, *Tweeting to Power: The Social Media Revolution in American Politics* (New York: Oxford University Press, 2014).

28. Scraping was conducted using Crimson Hexagon, a computer coding software that allows analysis of all publicly available Twitter posts.

29. Elfriede Fürsich, "In Defense of Textual Analysis," *Journalism Studies* 10 (2009): 238–52.

30. Kent Lindkvist, "Approaches to Textual Analysis," in *Advances in Content Analysis*, ed. Karl Erik Rosengren (Beverly Hills, CA: Sage, 1981), 23–41; Donald G. McTavish and Ellen B. Pirro, "Contextual Content Analysis," *Quality & Quantity* 24 (1990): 245–65.

31. Korin Miller, "Why the Phrase 'Voting with Your Vagina' Is Not OK," Yahoo.com, February 2, 2016, https://www.yahoo.com/beauty/voting-with-your-vagina-155833380.html.

32. Khoja-Moolji, "Becoming 'Intimate Publics.'"

33. "2016 Exit Polls," CNN.com, November 23, 2016, http://edition.cnn.com/election/results/exit-polls.

34. Berlant, *Cruel Optimism.*

35. André Brock, "From the Blackhand Side: Twitter as a Cultural Conversation," *Journal of Broadcasting & Electronic Media* 56, no. 4 (2012): 539.

36. Horsley, "Trump Attacks Former Miss Universe."

37. Alicia Parlapiano, "What We Know about the Investigation into Hillary Clinton's Private Email Server," *New York Times*, October 28, 2016, https://www.nytimes.com/interactive/2016/05/27/us/politics/what-we-know-about-hillary-clintons-private-email-server.html?_r=0.

38. Rory Carroll, "Woman Accusing Trump of Raping Her at 13 Cancels Her Plan to Go Public," *Guardian*, November 3, 2016, https://www.theguardian.com/us-news/2016/nov/02/donald-trump-rape-lawsuit-13-year-old-cancels-public-event; Adam Entrous, Ellen Nakashima, and Greg Miller, "Secret CIA Assessment Says Russia Was Trying to Help Trump Win White House," *Washington Post*, December 9, 2016, https://www.washingtonpost.com/world/national-security/obama-orders-review-of-russian-hacking-during-presidential-campaign/2016/12/09/31d6b300-be2a-11e6-94ac-3d324840106c_story.html?utm_term=.e589066144fe.

39. Elisa Tate, "Challenging Women's Digital Agency: The Frequency of Slut Shaming in Social Media," *iJournal: Graduate Student Journal of the Faculty of Information* 1, no. 1 (2016): n.p.

40. Papacharissi, *Affective Publics*, 118.

41. Chen, "Tweet This"; Cooks, Paredes, and Scharrer, "There's 'O Place' Like Home."

42. Papacharissi, *Affective Publics*, 121.

43. Ibid.

44. Gina Masullo Chen, *Online Incivility and Public Debate: Nasty Talk* (New York: Palgrave Macmillan, 2017); Kevin Coe, Kate Kenski, and Stephen A. Rains, "Online and Uncivil? Patterns and Determinants of Incivility in Newspaper Website Comments," *Journal of Communication* 64 (2014): 658–79.

45. Williams, "Digital Defense."

46. Kitsy Dixon, "Feminist Online Identity: Analyzing the Presence of Hashtag Feminism," *Journal of Arts and Humanities* 3, no. 7 (2014): 34–40.

47. Barker-Plummer and Barker-Plummer, "Hashtag Feminist," 91.

Chapter Seventeen

A RENAISSANCE OF FEMINIST RITUAL

Susan B. Anthony's
Gravesite on Election Day

Christine A. Kray

Rochester, New York, November 8, 2016. It was one of those unforgettably splendid fall days in Upstate—the leaves on the trees had turned brilliant shades of gold, orange, and red, and held fast to their branches, resisting gravity and decay, creating a delightful canopy that celebrated nature's artistry. It was unseasonably warm, the sun was bright, and after voting, I drove to the historic Mount Hope Cemetery to document, as an anthropologist, what I expected to be a sizable crowd of visitors at women's rights activist Susan B. Anthony's grave. By the time I arrived, at 9:15 a.m., and clambered up the cobblestone path, a long line had formed and people had already been waiting more than an hour just for the opportunity to put their "I Voted" stickers on her headstone and leave other tokens of gratitude. As a steady stream of visitors came throughout the day—an estimated 8,000–12,000 people—the wait grew to two hours, even after it started raining in the evening, until the cemetery gates closed at 9:00 p.m., at which time polling stations were closing up and down the eastern seaboard.[1]

Cultural anthropologists use a combination of research methods to understand the complexity and dynamism of sociocultural phenomena. My research for this chapter included: standardized interviews of open-ended questions with fifty-four people who visited Susan B. Anthony's gravesite on Election Day (thirty-one interviews on Election Day itself and twenty-three over the three weeks following the election); ethnographic observations at the cemetery on Election Day and the next morning; interviews with three people whose photos of the sticker ritual attracted national attention prior to Election Day; and consultation of news related to Anthony's grave since 2014. I asked open-ended questions in the interviews to encourage people to talk about what was most important to them, so I could understand the meanings and motivations of their gravesite visits.[2]

Interviews that I conducted with Election Day cemetery visitors on that day and in the weeks to follow revealed that those visits were an embodied expression of an upsurge in feminist sentiment. While there was no highly visible mass women's movement in the United States at the beginning of the campaign season, events of the campaigns triggered a sense among many that the status and rights of women were fragile and threatened within the political system, and that protective action was urgently needed. On Election Day, the physical act of paying homage, of showing gratitude to the historic women's rights activist, was a way, literally and symbolically, of taking a stand in support of people's rights. Moreover, the ritual action was not just on behalf of women—the cemetery visitors generally nested women's rights within a broader framework of respect for the individual. They linked their feminism to support for the dignity of people of color, LGBTQ people, immigrants, religious minorities, and people with disabilities. That broader, intersectional, and inclusive feminist vision became articulated more clearly across the nation in the wake of a Trump victory. This chapter concludes with reflections on the creation of rituals and authenticity in the twenty-first century.

Commemoration

Susan B. Anthony (1820–1906) is probably the most famous women's rights activist in United States history. An indefatigable organizer and orator, Anthony formed a partnership with writer Elizabeth Cady Stanton beginning in 1851 that became the backbone of the women's rights movement for the next half century. In part through her own editorial collaboration with Stanton and Matilda Joslyn Gage on the first four volumes of *History of Woman Suffrage*, Anthony has become enshrined as the country's leading women's suffragist, overshadowing the legacies of her many collaborators.[3] She was the first woman featured on any US currency, the one-dollar coin minted in 1979, and appeared on a US postal stamp twice (in 1936 and 1955).[4]

Residents of her hometown have long looked to Anthony's grave as a tangible symbol of voting rights, especially women's suffrage. For many years, both on her birthday and on election days, city residents have visited her grave, leaving flowers, letters, and pebbles.[5] At some point prior to 2014, a few people independently came up with the idea of placing the "I Voted" lapel sticker they received at the polling booth on her gravestone. On Election Day in 2014, Rochester resident Brianne Wojtesta imagined that she could symbolically place her sticker on Anthony's lapel by placing it on the stone. She explained to me, "Susan B. Anthony couldn't vote, but she was pivotal in a long line of women working tirelessly for voting rights, from [abolitionist] Sarah Grimké to [civil rights activist] Mary Church Terrell and beyond. Giving her my 'I Voted' sticker felt like a fitting way to show gratitude for these foremothers by letting her participate in the privilege of voting."[6]

On Facebook, Brianne shared her photo of the gravestone with two stickers, and a friend suggested that they start the "Thank You Susan B. Anthony" Facebook group to encourage the practice.[7] The practice was reported by the local ABC affiliate and, through the *Huffington Post* it received national attention for the first time.[8] One of Brianne's friends, Greta Page-Mann, explained to me that her reaction upon seeing the photo was, "This is epically cool!" and every Election Day since then (whether local, state, primary, or national) she has visited Anthony's grave, and has a "beautiful, meditative moment" giving thanks for the right to vote. She added, "We have come so far. We have so much more to do. But it is just being in that moment of gratitude."

A Buzz Created

Neither local nor national news covered the sticker ritual in 2015, but attention to the ritual exploded in 2016—boosted by social media, national news, the Clinton campaign, and Rochester's mayor. On April 19, Greta visited Anthony's grave after voting in the New York state primary, and she saw the greatest number of stickers that she had ever seen, twenty-eight, near cemetery closing time. Her photograph of the grave posted on Facebook went viral, and articles about the sticker ritual appeared the following day (April 20) in *Smithsonian Magazine, Huffington Post*, the *Washington Post*, the *New York Times*, *USA Today*, Buzzfeed, and Bustle.com.[9] That same day, the treasury secretary announced that the back of the new ten-dollar bill would feature women's suffragist leaders Anthony, Stanton, and Sojourner Truth— all New York State residents.[10] The combined local and national focus on the suffragist legacy in Hillary Clinton's adopted home state may have planted the seed for a campaign strategy.

On June 7, when Clinton clinched the Democratic nomination, she wore a cream-colored jacket at her victory speech. She called the night "historic," acknowledged the 1848 Seneca Falls Convention on women's rights, and noted that her mother was born on the day that Congress voted in favor of the Nineteenth Amendment.[11] The next day, Rochester residents Mari Tsuchiya and her husband went to Anthony's grave to leave flowers; their photo of the grave (also featuring tokens left by others) went viral on Facebook and was picked up by ABC News and NPR.[12] Mari explained to me that Clinton's speech inspired her visit; having grown up in Japan, where women did not gain the right to vote until 1945, she was especially appreciative of suffrage activists.

On July 27, during the Democratic National Convention, Rochester's first female and second African American mayor, Lovely Warren, wrote a public letter to Anthony letting her know that for the first time a woman received the presidential nomination from a major party, and thanking her "for paving the way." A photo of the letter was circulated widely, as it was set up on a sandwich board next to the grave, posted to the city's Facebook page and also its Twitter account with the tweet, "Stop by #ROC's Mt. Hope Cemetery to sign Mayor Warren's thank you letter to Susan B. Anthony" (@CityRochesterNY); it was then shared and retweeted tens of thousands of times.[13]

In the final weeks before the election, national attention became ever more fixated on gender issues and suffragist legacies. On November 5, a CNN video that was viewed millions of times highlighted the sticker ritual, featuring interviews with Mayor Warren and Greta Page-Mann. The mayor showed Anthony commemorative stickers made by her office, bearing Anthony's photo and reading "I voted today because of women like her"; the mayor invited people to visit the grave on Election Day, leave their "I Voted" sticker on the gravestone or on sandwich boards that the city would set up next to the gravestone, and take home the commemorative sticker.[14] Local news featured a driving tour of Rochester's suffragist sites, including the gravesite, the locked ballot box on Main Street where Anthony and fourteen other women voted illegally in 1872, the Susan B. Anthony Museum and House (with discounted Election Day tours), and the Susan B. Anthony Square with its "Let's Have Tea" sculpture of Anthony and Frederick Douglass, the famed abolitionist and statesman.[15] The city announced that the cemetery would stay open late on Election Day so that people could visit the grave after work and voting.

Collective Effervescence

"Festive," "exciting," "thrilling," "joyous," and "peaceful" were words that cemetery visitors used to describe the mood that day. Although people stood in line for an hour to two hours for less than one minute at the gravesite, none seemed to mind. Visitors deposited a small

17.1. One of an estimated 8,000–12,000 pilgrims to Susan B. Anthony's grave, Mount Hope Cemetery, Rochester, NY, Election Day, 2016. Photo: Max Schulte. From Rochester Democrat and Chronicle, November 8, 2016. © 2016 Gannett-Community Publishing. All rights reserved. Used by permission and protected by the copyright laws of the United States. The printing, copying, redistribution, or retransmission of this content without express written permission is prohibited.

mountain of flowers, thank-you notes, famous Anthony quotations, a glass jar representing the "glass ceiling" to be broken, candles, photos of Anthony and of Clinton, a Halloween pumpkin carved with Hillary's "H" logo, a miniature white pantsuit, balloons, Clinton memorabilia, a copy of the US Constitution, and feminist Betty Friedan's *The Second Stage*. Gravesite photos of the sticker ritual were shared immediately on Facebook and Twitter. By my estimate, 90 percent of the visitors were women and children. Young children were running around, playing with leaves and twigs. Many visitors wore pantsuits, were dressed all in white, or wore buttons and T-shirts with themes of women's empowerment, including the reappropriated Trump slur "Nasty Woman," or Clinton's candidacy. Mayor Warren gave a speech thanking Anthony for her work on behalf of women's rights. Around 11:00 a.m., a drum circle formed, its steady rhythms intensifying the sense of sacredness. At noon, women representing the Susan B. Anthony Institute for Gender, Sexuality, and Women's Studies at the University of Rochester, along with Congresswoman Louise Slaughter, read the 1848 Seneca Falls Declaration of Sentiments at the grave.

The local ABC affiliate's Facebook page hosted a live video feed of the gravesite; it received over 4 million views plus comments by viewers around the world.[16] Strangers struck up conversation in line, and new friendships formed; strangers hugged one another, and many cried tears of joy in anticipation of a Clinton victory. A drizzling rain began around 7:00 p.m., but hundreds remained in line, undeterred. One woman remarked that she stayed for several hours, well into the evening, not wanting to leave. She said, "You had a feeling that you were part of something truly special." When the cemetery gates closed at 9:00 p.m., the stone was completely blanketed in stickers, with only Anthony's name peeking through, and an overflow of stickers covered her sister Mary's gravestone, the two sandwich boards, and cemetery signs pointing to Anthony's location. My colleague Michael Brown and I agreed that the event was a textbook example of the "collective effervescence," or joy in unity, that sociologist Émile Durkheim described for rituals in which people gather in veneration of symbols that represent them as a group and reaffirm their shared values.[17]

So, what were those shared values? There might be little correspondence between what a historical person did in the past and how they are commemorated in the present, so why were people drawn to Anthony on that day?

One thought gnawed at me. When I arrived at the cemetery in the morning and opened Facebook to "check in" at the location, an opinion piece came across my Newsfeed entitled "Before You Put an 'I Voted' Sticker on Susan B. Anthony's Grave, Remember She Was a Racist."[18] I wondered if any in the crowd before me had heard that claim before or seen that same article. Although Anthony had labored for many years in abolitionist activism, some of the abolitionists and women's rights activists who had collaborated prior to the Civil War disagreed over the proposed Fifteenth Amendment to the Constitution, as it promised to extend suffrage to black men, but not to any women. Anthony, Stanton, and Sojourner Truth, among others, felt betrayed by the men with whom they had long worked. Bitter words were exchanged, and for a time, Anthony and Stanton accepted funding from a racist Democrat in order to publish their women's suffragist newspaper.[19] (See Michael Brown's chapter in this volume for more on this topic.) During the six hours when I was at the cemetery on Election Day, I estimated that only about 5 percent of those present were African American, while according to 2010 census data, 15.2 percent of Monroe County's and 42 percent of Rochester's population is African American.[20] Awareness of that conflict may have contributed to low African American attendance at the gravesite on Election Day, despite Mayor Warren's encouragement. This troubled history rendered it all the more important that I try to understand how the visitors at the cemetery saw Anthony.

A Symbol of Rights Activism

Those whom I interviewed saw Anthony as a symbol of women's rights activism, a reminder of the struggles that women have faced historically, and for most, a symbol of the ongoing struggle for women's equality as well. Many emphasized that she epitomized a broader struggle for human rights, representative democracy, and human dignity.

When I asked people what Susan B. Anthony represented to them, common descriptors were "brave," "courageous," "strong," "tenacious," "a fighter," and "an American hero." A Planned Parenthood educator said that Anthony signifies "breaking the glass ceiling, freedom, voting, being awesome." Interviewees commented on how Anthony went up against a male-dominated society, at a time when women had very few independent rights, that she was ridiculed and harangued as she traveled the country alone giving speeches, risked imprisonment for voting illegally, and dedicated her life's work to securing rights for others. One said, "She stands for everything I believe in as a human being and as a woman and being treated equally and fairly, but having to fight for it on top of that, just because you're a woman." Older women stressed how much Anthony meant to them because they had endured severe inequalities and witnessed women's struggles for equality and respect. Several women talked about how they experience sexism in the workplace, underscoring how "there is still so much work to be done."

None of the interviewees indicated any awareness of Anthony's racist statements. To the contrary, they saw Anthony as a symbol of human rights and equality, more broadly. An obstetrician said that Anthony represents "just the very essence of progressive values and equality." A few interviewees commented that they were lesbian or gay or had LGBTQ family members and that inspired their visit. One gay man said, "She's a champion of civil rights and equality that trickled down not just to women but to gay people." One deaf woman appreciated Anthony because she "was always fighting for human rights. We're doing it now, fighting for our language rights. . . . It's about justice." One woman, now in her eighties, who has worked as a volunteer at the Susan B. Anthony Museum and House for years, discussed Anthony's abolitionist work and her friendship with Frederick Douglass, saying Anthony represents not just women's rights, but "human rights." All of the interviewees who identified themselves as immigrants or children of immigrants indicated that they visited that day because they cherished voting as a privilege.

A "Historic" Day

Although I did not ask interviewees' views on the candidates, most readily offered that information. Their comments, plus visitors' clothing, memorabilia, and gifts for Anthony indicated that the visitors were overwhelmingly Clinton voters.[21] The mood at the cemetery was celebratory in part because opinion polls predicted a Clinton win and in part because people were happy to be surrounded by like-minded voters on what they thought was a "historic" occasion—the election of the first female president. Many interviewees made special efforts to visit the cemetery with their children and/or their parents, especially their mothers, in order to "participate in history together." Some parents had kept their children out of school, so that they could enter the voting booth or fill in the bubbles on the ballot form and together vote for the first female president.

Most stressed that they voted for Clinton because of her qualifications, not because of her gender, but that, nonetheless, it was exciting to think that a woman might be elected president because it would symbolize what women could achieve. When asked, "If Clinton wins, will people see that as a victory for women?," most said yes, but qualified it in some way, as two women said that the issue was unimportant, and three commented that men might see a woman's victory as a setback for them.

Overwhelmingly, the interviewees supported Clinton in part because they saw her as someone who would defend the status and rights of women. Some remarked how Clinton's difficulty in the race exposed widespread sexism, and one remarked, "That there is somebody who is completely unqualified—it is crazy that he could be so close!"

He Who Shall Not Be Named

For those whom I interviewed, Donald Trump inspired dread. Opinions expressed about him were universally negative. When people began talking about Trump, they avoided using his name, perhaps because the thought of him made them uncomfortable. Several expressed shock about Trump's sexual misconduct, one saying, "He's a sexual predator!," and another decrying "Trump's past and the groping and the filthy language."

Slightly more than half of interviewees used the words "misogyny," "misogynistic," or "sexist" when referring to Trump, saying that his behaviors demonstrated objectification of and lack of respect for women. One woman said, "We teach our kids not to act the way he does." Three people used some version of the "picking off a scab" (or "lifting up a rock") metaphor, saying that misogyny had been lying quietly under the surface, but Trump's openness about it encouraged others to speak and act similarly.

Many viewed Trump as a threat to the rights and social standing of a variety of marginalized people, not just women. Five interviewees used some version of the "picking off a scab" metaphor to suggest that the Trump-Pence campaign had sanctioned racism, religious bigotry, and homophobia. Others talked about how Trump's aggressiveness (e.g., encouraging violence against protestors and promising to "lock her [Clinton] up!") was unsettling and that they felt he was empowering others to be aggressive, rude, and bigoted.[22] Others worried about "my grandson who is biracial," "my autistic son," and "my husband who is Hispanic."

The Morning After

Early in the morning on November 9, Trump was declared the winner in a surprising electoral upset. The Susan B. Anthony Museum and House previously had planned a gravesite gathering for 8:00 a.m.—presumably in anticipation of a Clinton victory—but by the time I arrived at the cemetery at 8:45 a.m., the small group had disbanded. The rain had continued throughout the night, soaking, discoloring, and wrinkling the stickers, letters, and flowers that had been deposited the day before. The wind had scattered many items. A note with Anthony's words "Failure is impossible" lay on the ground. The temperature had dropped twenty degrees from the day before, the sky was overcast, and gusts of wind brought on shivers. The somber weather matched the moods of the gravesite visitors who came by throughout the morning in groups of one or two.

When I arrived at the grave, one young, thin man was standing alone, crouching over, protecting himself against the wind. We stood silently together. He broke the silence, "Last year, I was attacked . . ." He had been the victim of a homophobic hate crime. He worried what Trump's victory portended, explaining, "Trump is setting an example with all of his hate. Will other people think it's okay to hate? Will he do anything to stop them?" Another woman said, "I came to apologize to her [Anthony]. I feel like we let her down." Another said that Trump reminded her of the decades of abuse she endured at the hands of her husband. She said, "Trump is an example for future men that it's okay to treat women this way." When she heard the election results, she said, "My heart broke, it sank into my stomach, my head exploded with, 'This can't possibly be real.'" Throughout the morning, strangers hugged one another and cried.

The Values of the Nation

After Election Day, interviewees reported an existential crisis. They felt that the country around them had changed, that what they thought were "American values" were not the ones that guided voters at the polls. In particular, respect for individuals regardless of gender, race, religion, sexuality, disability, or national origin appeared to have lost hold. Words they used were "devastating," "horrifying," "shock," "tragedy," "distraught," "incomprehensible," "heartbroken," "sucker-punched," "disgust," and "trauma." One woman said, "I was heartbroken. I cried for days. . . . I feel sad and scared." Another said, "The day after, I could hardly walk because I felt like gravity had been shifted under my feet. I really felt physically out of balance. What I mean is that all of my concepts of right and wrong were upended." An Asian immigrant said that as he watched the election results come in, "I felt more yellow. . . . I felt really out of place. . . . [T]his country didn't want me. It felt like a statement that this was a white country." One woman who had been in a café across from the World Trade Center on 9/11 said that the feeling of life-altering betrayal and devastation that she felt on that day was the same that she felt on November 9. She perceived that the world had changed around her, and decidedly for the worst.

Interviewees saw Trump's victory as a setback for women, one calling it "an assault on women." One woman added, "This is a huge setback. And this has nothing to do with Hillary losing. This has to do with women *and* men voting for a person who can walk into a room and brag about grabbing women by their you-know-what. And objectifying women—his own daughter. . . . And I'm frustrated by the fact that people are calling this a women's issue. This is not a women's issue. This is a people's issue, anyone who has a family. Do you want your son to treat people that way?" Interviewees expressed concern that a conservative appointment to the Supreme Court by Trump would erode reproductive rights, that Trump would not appoint women to high governmental positions, nor aggressively prosecute sexual offenders.

Interviewees stressed that Trump was a threat to a variety of people, not just women. One woman said, "I can't fathom that the United

States of America has so many people that are okay with a racist, sexist person, someone who preaches hate, bigotry, and intolerance." Another said, "This is a setback for anyone who is not a straight, white male." One woman who works with disabled children said, "I can't believe people voted for a jerk who makes fun of people with disabilities."[23] Another said, "I am Jewish and my daughter is gay. There was a lot of stuff simmering before this, but I think things will be even less hospitable." One summarized, "A lot of people got their civil liberties revoked on November 8. A lot of people near and dear to my heart."

Something New and Something (Very) Old

The convergence at Anthony's gravesite on Election Day was clearly a physical manifestation of a surge in feminist sentiment in November 2016. Generally speaking, the cemetery visitors wanted to defend women's and others' civil rights, and their electoral support for Clinton and their invocation of Anthony's memory expressed that in tandem. Rituals oblige participants to act in ways that communicate symbolic and solemn messages about themselves, their social relationships, and the values they hold as sacred. The ritual actions taken on that day were standing in line, kneeling at the gravesite, sharing a symbol of their vote (the sticker) with someone identified as a moral forebear, and sharing their photos with social media networks. Through their actions, the visitors were declaring, "I count. I follow in the line of feminist activists such as Susan B. Anthony. I am taking a stand for women and others who are under threat today."

One abiding question in anthropology concerns how new rituals are created and spread. Clearly, the advent of digital photography, Facebook, Twitter, and digital news delivery on social media made it possible for a very small-scale, local ritual practice to grow very quickly into an event with thousands of participants and millions of social media observers. Yet awareness in and of itself does not provide motivation to participate. Introducing a new ritual is risky because, as religious studies scholar Catherine Bell notes, "rituals tend to present themselves as the unchanging, time-honored customs of an enduring community."[24] New rituals risk being rejected as inauthentic, foolish, or cynical. All of the Election Day 2016 cemetery visitors I interviewed said that was the first time they had participated in the sticker ritual. What about the ritual, therefore, helped it seem authentic and thus valid and meaningful for them?

Something new (social media) and something very old (the gravestone) were paired elements of the sticker ritual that secured its authenticity on that day. The Anthony sticker ritual reveals that the spread of a ritual requires both a desire for participation in a group and also a correspondence of form and meaning. *Desire for participation in a group* emerged out of the campaign season, as Trump's ascendance led many Rochesterians to conclude that what they considered to be the bedrock premise of American democracy—equal rights— was under attack and required coordinated public defense. Through group participation, the ritual participants took a stand in support of equal rights, and reenergized one another for subsequent political action. The coparticipants served as witnesses to the ritual performance that thereby became a vow, a social contract, a commitment to the defense of equal rights. Similarly, the sharing of photos on social media was not inconsequential, but rather the means by which ritual participants converted their social media contacts into witnesses, who would remember the commitments symbolically expressed.

Regarding ritual time depth, Bell notes that not all rituals must be seen as rooted in tradition; in fact, radical and revolutionary moments call for rituals that are self-consciously new in form and content.[25] What matters is a *correspondence of form and meaning*. The sticker ritual was not radical in form, but built on a longer US tradition of leaving gifts at gravesites, and the tradition in Rochester of visiting Anthony's grave on Election Day. Applying the "I Voted" sticker was a simple addition to a preexisting ritual, and as such, it could appeal to those who wanted to tap into something deep and abiding.

Indeed, the gravestone was central in the sticker ritual, not just as a locus of action, but as a repository of symbolic meaning. Gravestones symbolize time depth, the connection between past and present. They are firm, durable, grounded, embedded, ancient, sacred—even if weathered and worn by the elements. Gravestones persist. The gravesite of a famous social activist was the ideal meeting ground for feminists who wanted to take a public stand in support of values that they considered to be ancient and nonnegotiable—the dignity and rights of the individual. The gravestone became a magnetic lodestone of ritual action on Election Day because its formal qualities aligned with the motivations of the cemetery visitors.

The participation of thousands of people in the sticker ritual shows that they felt drawn to an event that tied together past and present ceremoniously. If political elections encourage people to reflect on their values and the values of the nation, the 2016 presidential election certainly did. Many cemetery goers felt that what was at stake were not just run-of-the-mill matters of tax and trade policies, but the very rights of citizens and democracy itself. Susan B. Anthony, as a person who dedicated her life to fighting for citizens' rights through abolitionist and women's rights activism, seemed, to many Rochesterians, the right hero for the day.

Notes

1. The estimated number of visitors is found in Steve Orr, "Susan B. Anthony's Grave a Sad Place Two Days after Election," *USA Today*, November 10, 2016, https://www.usatoday.com/story/news/politics/elections/2016/11/10/susan-b-anthonys-grave-after-election/93615030/.

2. The questions asked were:

a) Is this your first time visiting Susan B. Anthony's gravesite on election day?

b) How did you first get the idea to come here today?

c) Why did you want to come here today?

d) What does Susan B. Anthony represent to you?

e) Some people have saved their "I Voted" stickers to place them on the gravestone. Were you planning on doing that? (If so, what does it mean to you?)

f) Did you come alone or with others?

g) Were you planning on doing anything else here, like visit any other graves?

j) What do you think Anthony might say about this presidential election?

k) What do you think Anthony might say about women's place in US society today?

l) If Hillary Clinton wins the election, will people see that as a victory for women, or is it more complicated than that?

In postelection interviews, I also asked, "What was your reaction to the election results?" I am very grateful to Michael Brown for interviewing four of the cemetery visitors.

3. Ann D. Gordon, "Knowing Susan B. Anthony: The Stories We Tell of a Life," in *Susan B. Anthony and the Struggle for Equal Rights*, ed. Christine L. Ridarsky and Mary M. Huth (Rochester, NY: University of Rochester Press, 2012), 201–34; Lisa Tetrault, "We Shall Be Remembered: Susan B. Anthony and the Politics of Writing History," in *Susan B. Anthony and the Struggle for Equal Rights*, ed. Ridarsky and Huth, 15–58; Lisa Tetrault, *The Myth of Seneca Falls: Memory and the Women's Suffrage Movement*, 1848–1898 (Chapel Hill: University of North Carolina Press, 2015).

4. "Leaving Their Stamp on History," National Women's History Museum, accessed June 21, 2017, https://www.nwhm.org/online-exhibits/stamps/anthony.html.

5. Caurie Putnam, "Best Use Ever for Your 'I Voted Today' Sticker," *Huffington Post*, December 6, 2017, http://www.huffingtonpost.com/

caurie-putnam/best-use-ever-for-your-i-_b_6109042.html?utm_hp_ref=women.

6. With their permission, I use the actual names of Brianne Wojtesta, Greta Page-Mann, and Mari Tsuchiya. The names of all other interviewees are withheld, to protect their privacy.

7. "Thank You Susan B. Anthony" Facebook page, http://www.facebook.com/Thankyoususanbanthony/.

8. Putnam, "Best Use Ever."

9. Erin Blakemore, "Why Women Bring Their 'I Voted' Stickers to Susan B. Anthony's Grave," Smithsonian.com, April 20, 2016, http://www.smithsonianmag.com/smart-news/why-women-bring-their-i-voted-stickers-susan-b-anthonys-grave-180958847/; Colby Itkowitz, "Susan B. Anthony Would Be Proud to See Her Grave Covered with New Yorkers' 'I Voted' Stickers," *Washington Post*, April 20, 2016, http://www.washingtonpost.com/news/inspired-life/wp/2016/04/20/new-york-voters-decorated-susan-b-anthonys-grave-with-their-i-voted-stickers/?utm_term=.02a3775312c0; Emma Lord, "This Image of Susan B. Anthony's Grave during the New York Primary Is Iconic," *Bustle*, April 20, 2016, http://www.bustle.com/articles/155832-this-image-of-susan-b-anthonys-grave-during-the-new-york-primary-is-iconic; Hinda Mandell, "Harriet T. and Susan B. Together Again," *USA Today*, April 20, 2016, http://www.usatoday.com/story/opinion/2016/04/20/harriet-tubman-20-bill-susan-b-anthony-womens-suffrage-i-voted-stickers-column/83298124/; Alana Horowitz Satlin, "New Yorkers' Tribute to Susan B. Anthony Says Everything about Why Voting Matters," *Huffington Post*, April 20, 2016, http://www.huffingtonpost.com/entry/susan-b-anthony-tribute-i-voted_us_57172d62e4b06f35cb712dcd; Women in the World staff, "Why Is Susan B. Anthony's Gravestone Covered in Stickers?," *New York Times Live*, April 21, 2016, http://nytlive.nytimes.com/womenintheworld/2016/04/21/why-is-susan-b-anthonys-gravestone-covered-in-stickers/; Krystie Lee Yandoli, "Voters Placed Their 'I Voted' Sticker on Susan B. Anthony's Grave," *Buzzfeed*, http://www.buzzfeed.com/krystieyandoli/voters-honored-susan-b-anthony-by-placing-their-i-voted-stic?utm_term=.ed9ge3aejL#.xmKvMq3M5R.

10. Ana Swanson and Abby Ohlheiser, "Harriet Tubman to Appear on $20 Bill, While Andrew Jackson Remains on $10 Bill," *Washington Post*, April 20, 2016, http://www.washingtonpost.com/news/wonk/wp/2016/04/20/u-s-to-keep-hamilton-on-front-of-10-bill-put-portrait-of-harriet-tubman-on-20-bill/?utm_term=.eada28c489e7.

11. Katie Reilly, "Read Hillary Clinton's Historic Victory Speech as Presumptive Democratic Nominee," *Time*, June 8, 2016, http://time.com/4361099/hillary-clinton-nominee-speech-transcript/.

12. Jennifer Hansler, "News of Clinton's Historic Nomination Reaches Susan B. Anthony," ABCNews.com, June 8, 2016, http://abcnews.go.com/Politics/news-clintons-historic-nomination-reaches-susan-anthony/story?id=39712117; Michel Martin, "Cemetery Visitors Honor Pioneer

Susan B. Anthony after Clinton Makes History," NPR, June 11, 2016, http://www.npr.org/2016/06/11/481703102/cemetery-visitors-honor-pioneer-susan-b-anthony-after-clinton-makes-history.

13. City of Rochester, NY—Mayor's Office, "Susan B. Anthony Thank You Letter," Facebook photo, July 27, 2016, https://www.facebook.com/CityofRochesterNY/photos/a.10153755994962621.1073741938.11419265
2620/10153755995067621/?type=3&theater.

14. "'I Voted' Stickers Put on Susan B. Anthony's Grave," CNN.com, video, November 5, 2016, http://www.cnn.com/videos/us/2016/11/04/people-are-leaving-i-voted-stickers-on-susan-b-anthonys-grave-orig-tc.cnn.

15. Tina MacIntyre-Yee, "Take Election Day Tour to Honor Susan B. Anthony," *Democrat & Chronicle*, video, November 6, 2016, http://www.democratandchronicle.com/videos/news/politics/elections/2016/11/06/93298178/.

16. News 8 WROC Rochester, "Live Broadcast: Susan B. Anthony Being Honored," video, November 8, 2016, https://www.facebook.com/News8WROC/videos/10155359367104386/?hc_ref=PAGES_TIMELINE.

17. Émile Durkheim, *The Elementary Forms of the Religious Life*, trans. Joseph Ward Swain (London: George Allen & Unwin, 1915), 216.

18. Claire Lampen, "Before You Put an 'I Voted' Sticker on Susan B. Anthony's Grave, Remember She Was a Racist," *Mic*, November 8, 2016, http://mic.com/articles/158856/before-you-put-an-i-voted-sticker-on-susan-b-anthony-s-grave-remember-she-was-a-racist#.BYMXtLB0r.

19. Kathleen Barry, *Susan B. Anthony: A Biography of a Singular Feminist* (New York: New York University Press, 1988), 164–94; Ellen Carol DuBois, ed., *Elizabeth Cady Stanton, Susan B. Anthony: Correspondence, Writings, Speeches* (New York: Schocken Books, 1981), 88–94; Carol Faulkner, *Lucretia Mott's Heresy: Abolition and Women's Rights in Nineteenth-Century America* (Philadelphia: University of Pennsylvania Press, 2011), 188–96; Laura E. Free, "'To Bury the Black Man and the Woman in the Citizen': The American Equal Rights Association and the New York State Constitutional Convention of 1867," in *Susan B. Anthony and the Struggle for Equal Rights*, ed. Christine L. Ridarsky and Mary M. Huth (Rochester, NY: University of Rochester Press, 2012), 59–85.

20. United States Census Bureau, "Quick Facts: Monroe County, New York," Census.gov, accessed April 13, 2017, http://www.census.gov/quickfacts/table/BZA010214/36055.

21. Not all interviewees were enthusiastic Clinton supporters, however; some voted for Bernie Sanders in the primary and were tempted to vote for Jill Stein (Green Party), but voted for Clinton in part to thwart Trump. Only one interviewee voted for a third-party candidate (Libertarian). To my knowledge, none voted for Trump.

22. See Alan Rappeport and Maggie Haberman, "For Donald Trump, 'Get 'Em Out' Is the New 'You're Fired,'" *New York Times*, March 13, 2016, http://www.nytimes.com/2016/03/14/us/politics/

donald-trump-security.html; see also Jeremy Diamond, "Trump on 'Lock Her Up' Chant: 'I'm Starting to Agree,'" CNN.com, July 29, 2016, http://www.cnn.com/2016/07/29/politics/donald-trump-lock-her-up/.

23. "Trump Mocks Reporter with Disability," CNN.com, November 25, 2015, https://www.cnn.com/videos/tv/2015/11/26/donald-trump-mocks-reporter-with-disability-berman-sot-ac.cnn.

24. Catherine Bell, *Ritual: Perspectives and Dimensions*, 1997; reprint with new foreword (Oxford: Oxford University Press, 2009), 210. See also David I. Kertzer, *Ritual, Politics, and Power* (New Haven, CT: Yale University Press, 1988), 12.

25. Bell, *Ritual*, 223–41.

Chapter Eighteen

BIRTHING FAMILY NARRATIVE AND BABY ON ELECTION DAY

Hinda Mandell

My water broke in the afternoon on Election Day. My due date was only a week away but I was still somehow surprised by this dramatic development. Two weeks prior, my husband and I settled on the baby's name. He was going to be Eddie.

I just didn't expect him to be Election Day Eddie.

Yet what could be more perfect and more fitting than the fulfillment of my progeny's liberal destiny? I spent the morning of Election Day in 2016 with thousands of others at Mount Hope Cemetery in Rochester, New York, visiting the gravesite of Susan B. Anthony—the matriarch of the Nineteenth Amendment—on the day when I felt certain that America would elect its first woman president.

A sense of unadulterated hope, celebration, and excitement clung to the air. I ran into my daughter's dentist at the cemetery. With evidence that our prowoman ideologies aligned, I felt validated in how much I already liked her. We hugged, beaming from ear to ear at what would surely be a remarkable day. The baby twirled in utero.

I came relatively late to the Hillary Clinton bandwagon. I voted for Bernie Sanders in the New York primary, lured by his seductive messages on income equality and racial justice. But there was also a chauvinism to some of his rabid supporters that I found unsettling, and I lost patience with his campaign when he prolonged his concession in June 2016 to Clinton as the Democratic heir apparent. Once Clinton clinched the nomination that summer, I stepped up a ritual I had begun that spring—immediately following the primary. I paid regular visits to the gravesite of Susan B. Anthony, drawn to photo documenting the tokens left behind. It felt important, encountering living history, to chronicle the types of mementos that thankful visitors wanted to share with the woman who wrote the Nineteenth Amendment but never lived to witness its impact. "You are an awesome, inspirational individual," read one letter left at the grave that I saw during a visit in August 2016. The letter was signed by "Berry," in preteen handwriting. "Thank you for getting females to the point where we can vote. Your family must be so proud. I hope that somewhere along the lines of history we are family."

I too felt a kinship to this historic legend—not in the familial sense but through connection of purpose. But more than anything, I was astounded by her dogged perseverance for a cause that met barrier upon obstacle during her lifetime. What was it like, I wondered, to commit oneself so entirely to a cause but not be able to see it bear fruit?

My curiosity was also piqued by the left-behind mementos, their existence an intriguing mystery. On the morning after the first presidential debate between Clinton and Donald Trump—in September 2016—I found a key and a hair elastic left on her grave. Someone had also built a Zen-like rock sculpture. Then the morning following the second presidential debate in October, others left dozens of hard candies wrapped in cellophane, acorns, and a pencil. The ants were already claiming the candies as their own.

I became so transfixed by the woman herself lying beneath this simple and unassuming tombstone that I brought visitors. I helped my three-year-old daughter sign her name to a thank-you placard that the city of Rochester set up honoring Susan B. Anthony once Clinton secured her party's nomination for president in July 2016. Shortly thereafter, when my mom drove in from Boston, she left a beaded necklace on top of the grave. My aunts, visiting from Washington, DC, pushed a Hillary Clinton lawn sign into the grass. My pregnant belly added a personal sense of urgency to this historical moment. The excitement that voters might elect this country's first woman president—buoyed by every major poll affirming her certain lead—coincided with my own eagerness to meet my baby boy, entering the world during what would surely be a new era.

I liked to think my body was growing a baby-boy feminist and that he would make his debut into a world that normalized women's empowerment and female power, and that slowly saw the dissolution of mansplaining, sexism, and disregard—both physical and emotional—for women.

At least, that was *supposed* to be his story. And I had no qualms about my eager embrace of this top-down narrative where I selected, massaged, and folded his (*supposed-to*) story into my view of historic events.

So on November 8, Election Day, as it became clear that I was going into labor, I embraced a narrative of my not-yet-born son that was dripping in progressive ideals. A baby conceived during the presidency of our first African American president would be born on the day the first American woman was elected to the highest office in the land. This was "kumbaya" as manifest destiny.

Imagine my surprise when Eddie burst into the world just as election results appeared to reveal that night that it was Donald Trump, and not Hillary Clinton, who would emerge as the victor. How was I to make sense of Eddie's birth if the intended narrative didn't fit? And worse yet, could this baby boy—a symbol of innocence and purity, a babe incapable of misdeed or ill intent—embody bad luck?

"It is a commonplace to note that human beings both live and tell stories about their living," writes narrative inquiry theorist Jean Clandinin.[1] She adds: "The truth about stories is that's all we are."[2]

Was my baby going to rob *me* of my "perfect" birth story? After all, at the same hour that my son entered this world—a baby named after his great uncle who fought fascism as an American soldier during World War II—it became clear that the forty-fifth president of the United States would be one who leveraged "alt-right" ideals of white nationalism for his political ascendancy.[3] But what wouldn't occur to me—until months after his birth when Eddie's distinct personality would begin to crystallize—is that babies aren't narratives. They're people. However, since it would take months to get to know my baby, and fall deeply in love with him, a supposed-to narrative was all I had to cling to in the immediate aftermath of his birth.

Hours after Eddie's birth, I was taken by wheelchair to the hospital recovery room. There I was able to compartmentalize the relief I felt at holding my son, the sheer exquisiteness of the moment, from the disbelief that we would soon see a living symbol of crass, alpha, white male dominance enter the White House. Eddie's story, the one I constructed for him in the hours leading up to his birth, evaporated before me. I knew in my bones I had been foolish to think I could control the narrative I wanted for my son. But I desperately wanted to. What the cosmos didn't grasp is that liberal activism and fighting tyranny is not only part of Eddie's DNA, it's the reason that he and I are alive. Our existence is predicated on our relatives fighting and escaping fascism and bigotry.

I grew up listening to the stories of family members' liberal activism. Collectively, these stories defined our family as a proud line of liberal activists. My grandmother was among the first organizers to desegregate her school district in Malverne, New York, following the *Brown v. Board of Education* decision in 1954. My father was an early member of the New Left activist group Students for a Democratic Society (SDS) in the 1960s, considered "the largest and most influential radical student organization" of its time.[4] And my aunt was a member of the radical left in the 1970s. But there are two overarching events that tell the story of our existence. The first is the Holocaust. The second is the civil rights movement in America. The first story involves my maternal grandfather in 1940s Panama; the second, my father in 1960s Louisiana.

My grandfather, a Jew, fled Poland in 1939 on the last train carrying civilians out of the country just as the German army invaded. In fact, members of the Polish army stopped the train to seize all able-bodied young men to fight the invasion, but my grandfather hid under a seat—his baby-faced cousin sat on top—and he was able to evade capture. Grandpa Martin fled Poland to join his wife's family in Panama, but he left behind his wife as planned—she stayed in Poland to take care of her elderly mother recovering from hip surgery. The two women would ultimately perish in the Treblinka death camp, along with Martin's entire family. Yet he would not know this until the war ended. What he did know is that letters sent home from Panama were never answered.

As Martin waited out the war in Panama, working as a tailor, he wrote letters not just to family overseas but also to US president Franklin Delano Roosevelt. A stranger in a strange land, Martin was desperate to take action against the Nazis who were responsible for the murder of his family. (Martin's brother, Moshe, was a resistance fighter who blew up German munitions trains in Poland, but he was ultimately shot and killed during a mission.) So Martin wrote to President Roosevelt asking to join American Allied forces in Europe so he could kill Nazis.

"To his excellency the President of the United States," he began his missive. "I as a Polish citizen . . . would like with all my heart to join the U.S. Armed Forces. I am now 29 years old (born on Feb. 18, 1914) and served with the Polish Army until 1938. I already have applied in the zone but I have been refused. I should like very much to fight side by side with the American boys against our common enemy. It will be an honor for me if and when the chance is given me to swear allegiance and loyalty the U.S. Army."[5]

The president wrote back, according to family memory, kindly thanking him for his sincere interest, but said only US citizens were permitted to join the army.

A generation later, and on the other side of the family, there is the story of my father. He was a member of the civil rights group the Student Non-Violent Coordinating Committee in the early 1960s, and then joined SDS at the University of Chicago, where he became editor of the group's newsletter by the mid-'60s. That's how he met the civil rights activist Jesse Jackson, who invited my dad in the summer of 1968 to join in the march along Highway 66 in Louisiana. The march commemorated the assassination of Medgar Evers, the social justice activist, the year before. My dad made his way to Louisiana, from Mexico, via bus. Yet he contracted a wretched stomach illness in Mexico that left him practically incapacitated by the side of the road once he descended from the bus nearby his Shreveport destination. It was not long before the local cops pulled over to question this worse-for-wear outsider, a man in his mid-twenties, no doubt unshowered and scruffy, and certainly a beatnik in appearance, who was sleeping on the side of the road and clearly ill. This was not the welcome my dad had hoped for in the South still reeling from Jim Crow.

"You're not here for this Nigger march, are you, boy?" the sheriff's patrolmen asked my dad. "Get in the back."

My father climbed into the patrol car as instructed, and his charges drove the car down a dirt road. They told him to get out. My dad's brain was firing on all cylinders. He knew how these stories typically ended, so he strapped on his rucksack before exiting the police cruiser, hoping that it could temper a bullet to the back. But they didn't shoot.

As soon as the cruiser pulled out of sight, my dad said he ran like the dickens into a nearby wooded area. And then he lay down in the brush, hiding from any vigilantes who might come to attack a northern, white, Jewish kid protesting their culture's mistreatment and abuse of blacks. It wasn't too long before a truck carrying a crew of white locals, with gun racks bolted to the top of the vehicle, drove down that dirt road. No doubt they were in search of my father. But they never found him. He hitched a ride from a US postal worker and caught the first bus he could heading north, but not before taking a swig of some strong "juice" on offer from a cluster of townsfolk in downtown Shreveport—no doubt a welcome balm for his ailing stomach and nerves.

These two stories—my grandpa's escape from Nazi Europe and my father's escape from a still-segregated South—are among the cornerstones of my family legacy. I've long felt privileged to be born into a clan fighting for progressive ideals and justice. Yet the inheritance was also a privilege because I never jeopardized my own safety—nor risked annihilation or assassination—because of who I was or what I believed. Instead, I used these stories to burnish my credentials as a white, Jewish liberal at dinner parties with like-minded friends. And these stories paid dividends as entertainment currency. No doubt, I had the benefit of inheriting a legacy on the "right side of history" born through pain and sacrifice, but which caused me no suffering.

The skin-tearing brutality of childbirth, with the catharsis of bringing life into the world as an act of love and anguish, became my own political activism project. Soon after Eddie's birth, when I juggled feverish news consumption with anxiety over my son's adjustment to life outside the womb, I found myself concocting—again—an altered narrative that would reclaim his progressive roots and erase his arrival as a bad omen, coinciding—as it did—with not only the continuation, but the acceleration, of white male supremacy that had the added "bonus" of rampant nativist xenophobia. In my reclamation, Eddie would have the perfect story if he ever decided to run for elected office: *Born on the day Trump was elected, I know that we need to fight for what's good and just and equitable. . . .* But it didn't take much of a cognitive leap for me to quickly realize that if baby Eddie grew into a man with conservative views, his birth story would also provide an appealing narrative for an election bid as well.

What is clear to me now is that Eddie's birth on Election Day—and the subsequent chaos and stress of his newborn months, along with my own body's healing and progression from pregnant to postpartum to physical normalcy—is tangled up in the trauma of the election. I have embodied the suffering of Donald J. Trump's election through the distress of childbirth. My physical healing from labor and delivery, as well as my corporeal challenges in the initial months after birth, are inextricably tied to Trump's admission into the West Wing. With fingers sticky from formula and spit-up, I'd scroll through news accounts on my phone during late-night feedings. There is no way for me to separate Eddie's birth from Trump's election. In fact, when our pediatrician came to meet Eddie at the hospital, he was not yet twenty-four hours old, and she was herself in shock from the previous night's election. She said in disbelief that her grown son didn't want to bring children into a world that saw Trump elected president. And there lay Eddie, part of this first cohort of babies in this bleak world.

While I wanted Eddie's story to be tied to women's ascension in the political sphere, I did my best after his birth to consecrate his arrival as a fight for justice and an intolerance to hate. It's no coincidence that our first family outing, one week after his birth, was to the gravesite of Susan B. Anthony, where we had paid our respects hours before I went into labor a week prior. Next to a crumpled "I Voted" sticker at the base of her grave, lay a brown stone decorated with the markings of a black Sharpie. The words read: "People who live under glass ceilings should throw stones." The Women's March on Washington was just a nascent idea at that moment in mid-November. But that stone alone signaled the emergence of a resistance, and Eddie would be there from the beginning, along for the ride.

Notes

1. D. Jean Clandinin, "Narrative Inquiry: A Methodology for Studying Lived Experience," *Research Studies in Music Education* 27, no. 1 (2006): 44.

2. Ibid., 51.

3. On the alt-right see "Alternative Right," Southern Poverty Law Center, accessed August 1, 2017, https://www.splcenter.org/fighting-hate/extremist-files/ideology/alternative-right. On the alt-right and Trump's campaign, see Will Rahn, "Steve Bannon and the Alt-Right: A Primer," CBS News, August 19, 2016, http://www.cbsnews.com/news/steve-bannon-and-the-alt-right-a-primer/.

4. "Students for a Democratic Society (SDS) Archives and Resources," accessed June 24, 2017, http://www.sds-1960s.org/. Also consider James Miller, *Democracy Is in the Streets: From Port Huron to the Siege of Chicago* (Cambridge, MA: Harvard University Press, 1987).

5. Martin Waysdorf (Mordka Wajsdorf) to Franklin Delano Roosevelt, Panama, November 15, 1943 (unpublished letter, in the author's possession).

Chapter Nineteen

LEFT BEHIND

Rachel Parsons

It's December 2016, and I am back home in Michigan. The house smells of urine: there is not always someone home to let the dog out, and my mom forgoes strong detergent on my father's soiled bedding to avoid irritating his skin. An artificial Christmas tree stands proudly in the family room, next to the TV and in front of the fireplace. Four senior-class pictures rest above the mantle—my siblings and I immortalized at age eighteen—next to an old family portrait and pictures of our childhood dogs, now dead. Matthew still lives at home, helping with my disabled father's care while the rest of us pursue lives in different cities.

I'm in the kitchen rummaging through the shelves. My mother went shopping and the pantry is full: chocolate pudding cups, Tostitos Scoops, instant oatmeal, Cheerios, Diet Coke, lunch meat, and a twelve-pack of Bud Light Lime-a-Ritas. I pour a bowl of dry cereal and dig in.

We moved into this house when I was seven. My mom worked the day shift, and my sister and I watched our brothers after school. She would call us multiple times a day: *What are you doing? Are the doors locked? Is the meat on the counter? Where's Matt? Well, you better find him!*

My dad worked late nights as an accountant. In the evenings, my mother shuttled us around to dance lessons and basketball practice. Dinner was fast-food or a box-prepared meal washed down with off-brand pop. My mother often ended the night on the couch, dozing to the television, reading a trashy novel, or drinking wine in the dark.

She sits next to me now and grimaces at my dry cereal. *Is that gonna be enough to eat?* I nod. She picks out a Cheerio and pops it in her mouth. *Nice to have you home, Rachie.* She stares off into space, chewing

---

A version of this essay appeared in the online publication *Guernica* as "My Mother's Secret Ballot," on January 29, 2018.

slowly. Her cheeks are peeling slightly, and red patches line the side of her face. Her eczema acts up during periods of extreme stress or fatigue; she stopped trying to cover it up with makeup years ago.

Thanks, Ma. Glad I can be here.

Everything OK with you?

I pause, considering the last six weeks since the election. A few days after Trump's upset, my father was rushed to the ER with aphasia and a high fever: a consequence of his multiple sclerosis. He almost didn't make it. Now, he's in rehab at the same nursing home where my mom is head social worker.

Not great, actually, I replied. *I wish Dad wasn't dying and Trump wasn't elected president.*

She sucks her teeth and looks at me out of the corner of her eye. *Give it a rest, OK? Everyone's got problems, not just you.*

I shrug and go back to eating my Cheerios.

Two days before the election, I called home. My friends in New York City, where I live, weren't worried about a Trump victory, but I was not so sure. I grew up in a white suburb of southeast Michigan, one of the most segregated regions in the country. Detroit lies at its center, a city built for 2 million in the heyday of the automotive industry. Despite recent gentrification efforts, it is two-thirds empty—vacant lots, abandoned buildings, decaying streets. Beauty lives in its communities, in embedded pockets, but wealth is mostly located outside the city borders. I knew that there—in my America—anything was possible.

My mother wouldn't discuss her general-election choices with me, though she had been forthcoming when she backed Bernie Sanders in the Democratic primary. This time, she bristled at my information-gathering attempts. My face flushed with anger as I realized what this meant.

We argued over the phone. Her response—like in other moments when she doesn't know what to say—was to laugh.

Stop laughing! I can't deal with you right now. Jesus, Ma, what did you do?

I exercised my constitutional right to vote without getting harassed by my daughter.

Her claims of harassment astounded me. I sat in my Brooklyn apartment, listening to her tell me, her queer daughter, why she voted for a man with a track record of misogyny and close alliances with the most vehemently anti-LGBTQ elements in our society. Her claiming victimization in this way made me think of Trump himself.

I soon gave up. *I'm gonna go, Ma. I don't know when I'm going to be able to talk to you again.*

Ok, Rachie, whatever you need. Love you.

Macomb County borders Detroit on the infamous 8 Mile Road. Clinton Township, Macomb County, one of about 30 cities in the county, is where I spent my childhood. A town of subdivisions, strip malls, and gas stations, it is like thousands of suburbs across America. A mix of middle- and working-class communities, Macomb County oscillates between red and blue. As the third-largest county in Michigan—after Wayne County, home of Detroit, and Oakland County, its wealthy, mostly white neighbor to the west—the vote here decided the state election for Trump, with 53.6 percent of the ballots designating him as our next president. Back in March, Sanders had won the state's Democratic primary. The people here wanted something different; it didn't seem to matter to them what that looked like.

My mother grew up in the nearby working-class town of Jackson, home of the state's first prison. Since it closed in 1934, it has become a tourist attraction. The current prison—which is split into different sites throughout town—is the third-largest employer in the city, hiring three times as many people as the school system.

Jackson is also the birthplace of the Republican Party. Despite Michigan going blue since the early 1990s, Jackson County has remained loyal to its roots and voted Republican in all but one of the last nine elections: Obama's first in 2008.

My mother, though, grew up in a Democratic household of second-generation Polish immigrants. To them, American political parties were simple: Republicans were for the rich, and Democrats were for everyone else. As they moved between working-class and working-poor status, it was clear which team they were on.

My mother's father worked in the gear and forge manufacturing division of the Clark Equipment Company. Her mother pitched in as a factory worker and bus driver. This went against her husband's wishes, but he relented when his layoffs became more frequent. The household was consumed with the act of staying alive: looking for work, arguing about money, going to Mass, waiting in the breadline.

By the time my mom reached ninth grade, things turned around. Her dad had saved up the money for a two-bedroom home. *He bought it with cash*, my mother would say with pride. Within two years, though, alcohol, stress, and physical labor took its toll. My grandfather died of a heart attack in the family kitchen.

My mother became the first person in her family to earn a college degree. Her deceased father's Social Security benefits paid her tuition at Michigan State. There she met my dad. After they settled in Clinton Township, her family harassed her about leaving them behind and starting a new life.

Politics were not given robust attention in my house. Even though my mother had been raised in a family of Democrats, like many white families in Clinton Township, my parents were de facto Republicans. They weren't tied to the party ideologically, but the Democrats represented something to them that they were not. My parents weren't anti-intellectual—they were college educated—but they did not identify with the East Coast liberal establishment. And despite my mother's working-class childhood, her queer daughter, and now-disabled husband, she did not see herself as part of any marginalized group, the people the Democrats claimed to be fighting for.

As I came into my own politically, my mother's electoral choices vexed me. She's not a bigot who wants to ban Muslims; she's a pragmatic Catholic who believes people should worship however they choose. She doesn't want to dismantle gay rights and send us to conversion therapy; she's a PFLAG mom who welcomes my partners to all family gatherings. She doesn't want to cast out immigrants; she thinks all people deserve a safe place to raise children.

My mother doesn't see herself as political. Her worldview doesn't expand much outside of her own orbit. The world is big, unpredictable, and complex. It all seems to go on around her, whether she participates or not.

So what motivated her to vote for Trump? In a phone conversation a few months after the presidential election, she described Michigan during the 1980s, when the state unemployment rate was at 16.8 percent. *When you guys were little, it was rough,* she said. *So many people lost their jobs all at once. I mean. God. It was awful.*

Back then, nearly everyone was connected to the auto industry in some way. Things reached a crisis point when GM, Ford, and Chrysler all gutted their workforce. People wanted someone to blame. Scapegoating fingers pointed everywhere: at corporations, politicians, and Japanese manufacturers. Claims of Japanese workers taking American jobs were tinged with racist overtones leftover from World War II.

Companies across the state folded, including my grandfather's once thriving equipment plant and the parts suppliers where my father worked. My dad experienced a series of layoffs. In between, he worked as a gas station attendant, a grocery store clerk, and a door-to-door vacuum salesman.

I remembered all this while my mother and I talked. There were years when she got our holiday meal from our church. She thanked the woman in the office, graciously accepting what she and my dad were unable to provide. Once we reached the car, she silently wiped away tears of embarrassment, remaining silent long past the time we arrived home.

Through all of this, my mother became angry. She had left her family to find her own way, trying to achieve economic stability. She had done everything right: earned a college degree; married up; got a white-collar job; mortgaged a house in the suburbs; put her kids in piano and dance lessons. She had followed all the rules, but was still precariously perched on the edge.

When my mother looks out at the world, she sees an increasingly smaller place for herself. During the 2016 presidential campaign, though, she glimpsed an opportunity for economic improvement. On the phone, my mother explained that Trump was going to put America back to work. *He is a businessman, Rachel. He says he will create jobs. People deserve a chance to make their lives better.* She paused a minute. *I know he's an ass, but there's good in everyone, ya know?*

I am sitting with all she shared. I think back to my mother filling out her ballot, and how she must have felt. She is the sole breadwinner. Most of her children have moved up and out, like she's always planned. She stays behind, managing the chores, my father's care, and the finances. Her vote, then, was an expression of anger and longing, but also her hope that someone might finally be coming back, now, for her.

I visit home the week before Trump's inauguration. My father's been in and out of the hospital. My mom is exhausted from toil and worry.

We sit on the couch next to my father's hospital bed in the living room. It is dusk, but no one's turned on any lamps. The TV light flickers, reflecting off my dad's glasses. My mom is playing on her iPhone. She's discovered memes and shows me one of a wet cat with large eyes, looking horrified. The caption: *It's great. Everything's just great.* She laughs and posts it on Facebook.

The country is about to change. I am wondering, as we sit quietly in the dark, how the resistance will look, and what part I will play. My mother's worried if she can afford the mortgage and my father's care. My dad is resting, taking part in journeys the two of us don't understand. We don't know what's coming, but right now, the surface is still. Uncertainty and fear, though, roil underneath.

Chapter Twenty

THIS IS VIENNA

Parents of Transgender Children from Pride to Survival in the Aftermath of the 2016 Election

Sally Campbell Galman

They ask why didn't you run away before? Before the borders were closed? Before the trap snapped shut?

—Primo Levi

The 2016 US presidential election dramatically disrupted the lives of many Americans, but this was particularly pronounced for transgender children and their families. In particular, it created a change in how they historicized their individual experience and that of their struggle for acceptance and legal protections. The experiences highlighted in this chapter come from an ongoing ethnographic study of young transgender children's experiences in school, family, and peer life in the United States. Prior to the election, they drew encouragement and hope from comparisons with the LGBTQ, women's rights, and civil rights movements and their associated victories; these comparisons emphasized pride, visibility, and trans rights as human rights, and appealed to the American progressive moral compass. However, when Donald Trump won the 2016 election, parents and children radically scaled back these emphases on pride, liberation, visibility, and appeals to progress, replacing them with a focus on survival and safety. Further, instead of identifying with progressive movements' histories of struggle and victory, parents began identifying with the histories of the victims of Nazism. These comparisons spoke especially to participants' feelings of running out of time, and of confusion and urgency. Said one mother, "I don't know what to do, but I feel like time is running out. . . . What if this is Vienna?"—which is to say, what if this is the moment of a great shift in vulnerability, after which things would get unimaginably worse? Like the Austrian Jews who awoke to the shock of *Kristallnacht* in 1938 and had to decide what actions to take, these families were faced with determining how to plan for unimaginable futures in a suddenly unrecognizable country.

The Viennese Jews faced gradually escalating anti-Semitic harassment and violence, beginning immediately before the Anschluss, or joining of Austria and Germany, and continuing in intensity as the Nazis attempted to push as many Jewish Austrians as possible to emigrate. Nonetheless, survivors and witnesses describe the *Kristallnacht* events and deportations as sudden and unbelievable. Those who could pay to do so, or could find international aid and sponsorship, may have tried to leave, but others did not, either because it was not financially possible, or they were restricted in some other way, or because they had to weigh the cost and potential devastation of leaving homes and businesses and extended networks of family and friends to start over completely elsewhere. As Primo Levi wrote, the question of leaving was complicated by practical financial and immigration concerns as well as deeper psychological ties to home and homeland that made leaving "before the trap snapped shut" unrealistic no matter how terrifying the escalation of hate.[1] I am sure the Viennese Jews tried to gauge the depths of Nazi threats, and like the families in this study immediately after the election, I can imagine many of them asking, "How bad can it get?" and contemplating the complexity of knowing what to do under these terrifying new circumstances.

This chapter does not make the case that transgender children and their families in 2017 were akin to the victims of the Holocaust. What this chapter is about, rather, is the use of historical memory. By first identifying with the histories of largely successful liberation and human rights struggles, these participants looked to history for inspiration and encouragement toward an eventual victory, however seemingly insurmountable the obstacles. Then subsequently aligning their experience with the Holocaust was an exercise in what Susan Opotow calls "negative memory."[2] Writing from museum studies, she describes how "negative memory" is a radically different kind of doing history: "Historical museums promote the remembrance of events and people by presenting evidence-based narratives of the past. A subset of these museums, museums of negative memory (or museums of conscience) focus on historical trauma. Instead of celebrating achievements of the past, they memorialize histories of marginalization, injustice, violence, and violations of human rights."[3] While I am not writing in the museum context, the construct of "negative memory" is nonetheless a powerful way to frame the shift experienced by these families: from claiming a history of hope to claiming a history of trauma.

Study Background

Data were collected before, during, and after the 2016 US presidential election, beginning in mid-2015. The study itself was open ended and discovery oriented, and ultimately involved over fifty children aged three through ten and their families in diverse political contexts across the United States. Data collection involved multiple semistructured ethnographic interviews with parents and teachers, artifact collection, and a range of task-based methods with children, in addition to participant observation across contexts over an eighteen-month period. Most of the parents, but not all, belonged to private Facebook and other social media groups, and communicated with me via email, telephone, or in person at playgroups and social gatherings.

As per the nature of ethnographic research, I developed close relationships with children and their families that deepened throughout the data collection period. Of particular importance to these analyses is reflection on and bracketing of one's researcher subjectivity and role. While acceptable standards of ethnographic fieldwork "hygiene"—standards of distance and the management of subjectivity and researcher bias—were followed, it would have been unethical to assume a neutral and uninvolved stance in light of what participants endured. Finally, this meant being open with participants and critically reflective of my own experience as the parent of a transgender child. This required significant critical reflection throughout.

Before: "Children of Stonewall"

Prior to the election, families and children alike drew from a range of positive historical memories including the LGBTQ, women's, and civil rights movements, and very much saw their historical experience as a natural outgrowth of this historical trajectory. Affiliation with the history of LGBTQ Pride movements is not surprising (one child said, "I'm in LGBTQ—I'm the T!") but was marked and pronounced before the election and nearly absent afterward. Even families from more conservative backgrounds referenced this historical movement's strategy of visibility and pride. One parent put a picture of gay rights' activist Harvey Milk (1930–78) on her Facebook page, and explained that this was because Milk was "about pride, and putting yourself out there, and coming out—because if someone knows you, and then knows that your cute little kid is trans, then that is one person they know who is trans, and one person they will remember and speak up for the next time they hear some transphobic bullshit."

Positive memory included a range of progressive American movements. One mother said that she took inspiration from the visibility strategies in the women's suffrage movement, and how women "got out in the streets to show people that they were there, everywhere, as their sisters and wives and mothers." One mother even contextualized and defanged local Trump supporters' rage as similar to that of southern whites in the 1960s: "The world was changing for the better, and those people couldn't bear it—but the end of their way of thinking had come. This is just like that."

Many parents noted with pride that the United States had been a leader in human rights in recent years, and they had confidence that with enough visibility the "arc of the moral universe" would continue to bend toward inevitable justice.[4] It was only, they affirmed, a matter of time: the arrival of increased acceptance and legal protection was a function of their and their children's activism and courage and the relentless march of progress as a function of the appeal to American progressivism. Their protests were described as joyous. They attended Pride parades and celebrations and proudly affiliated with that movement, very much seeing their children as the "children of Stonewall," a reference to the historic tipping point of the gay rights movement in 1969 at the Stonewall Inn in New York City.

Cities flew the transgender flag, and children had their photos taken underneath its billowing blue, pink, and white stripes. Families flew that same flag from their homes and cars, and children proudly displayed rainbow and transgender pride buttons on their school backpacks. Children watched transgender teen activist Jazz Jennings on TV and read about trans character Melissa's triumph in the children's novel *George*.[5] The meteoric popular media and positive political visibility that began the summer of 2015 was taken as evidence that visibility worked and was confirmation, to many, that their strategies of both "coming out" and achieving public support were going in the right direction. The Obama administration had moved swiftly to insure appropriate and affirming bathroom and locker-room access in schools under Title IX, to protect transgender children from bullying and make schools gender affirming. So-called "bathroom bills," which criminalize the use of a restroom that does not match the gender on one's birth certificate, were rapidly withering under legal and social scrutiny. A transgender teen successfully sued his school district over restroom access, and the case was on its way to the Supreme Court.[6] As descendants of successful progressive movements of the past, positive memory promised eventual victory.

Positive memory persisted, even though participants felt uniquely vulnerable and targeted by preelection campaign trail rhetoric. In addition to everyday political activities, such as bringing their children to marches and on door-to-door canvasses, many of these families felt that they had to speak explicitly to their children about what the election could mean. "I had to actually explain to my six-year-old what a rapist was," said one mother, "Because Trump was recorded talking about how all Mexicans were rapists and drug dealers."[7] Other parents described worrying that transphobic, violent Trump supporters would take Trump's words literally and act out; This was hardly an unfounded fear, as more than once individuals acted on Trump campaign rhetoric to excuse acts of targeted violence.[8]

Study participants also reported that during the months leading up to the election the general atmosphere of peer acceptance was punctuated with the odd threat, such as one participant in Florida who was told by a second-grade classmate, "My dad says that when Trump wins he is going to kill all the transgender people." The child took these threats seriously. Study parents minimized these as the last gasps of the old regime, and bemoaned having to assure their children that "this won't happen, that Trump won't win, and that everything is going to be fine." Most believed until the very last moment that this would be the case.

Impact: "Groping in the Dark"

When Donald Trump won the election, participant parents and children were, without exception, surprised and horror-struck. Most parents described feeling physically sick, and many frightened children stayed home from school. Families immediately scaled back pride, visibility, and positive memory talk. Instead of drawing inspiration from histories of progressive movements, they referenced the perceived warnings of negative memory, in particular the Holocaust, as a new strategy of historical sense making and self-preservation. As mentioned above, when asked why she was planning and acting so quickly, in this case mobilizing passports for her family, a mother responded with the only semirhetorical question, "What if this is Vienna?" The urge to be prepared for even the unimaginable, and to heed the worst-case scenarios of history, weighed heavily on families. To say that they were afraid is an understatement.

When I asked this mother to elaborate, she said that whereas yesterday she was counting on a "pride party in the streets to celebrate," she now wanted to be ready for the tidal wave of hate Trump's campaign trail rhetoric had portended. Like others, her negative memory comparisons were somber and reflective: She had always wondered why Jewish people in Nazi Europe did not flee in advance of the coming destruction. "Now I feel like I understand. They couldn't know." She continued,

> But we do. We can look back at history and know. Like when the people in Vienna woke up and saw Hitler was coming and they didn't know what to do and were just there hoping it would all be okay and in the back of their minds . . . Who knows what they knew? I wish they all had panicked and picked up and left, but . . . —I feel like this is Vienna. Like we know it is not going to be okay but we can't imagine how bad it is going to get, and leaving, well, leaving is complicated but the clock is ticking.

Many parents used metaphors like this—the clock ticking, the noose tightening, the door closing—to express their fearful and urgent need to do *something*, despite not knowing what constituted the path to safety. Parents on social media began immediately posting links focused on planning, about legal steps transgender children and their families should urgently take for protection, from wills to name and gender changes, to passport requirements.[9] Several families posted Werner Weinberg's 1982 essay, "Why I Did Not Leave Nazi Germany in Time" and another article with advice for packing a "go bag" to leave the country quickly if necessary.[10] While a few guffawed, another parent wrote, "If we have learned anything it is that anything we think can't happen here can and probably will." This parent, who, like so many others, had acted swiftly in the days following the election to begin changing their child's legal name and gender and accruing the necessary travel documents, also began packing a "go bag" full of clothes, medication, and cash. "I thought I would never do this crazy stuff," she says, "but better safe than sorry. Who knows if this will even be enough." Frantic, possibly futile planning for new, unseen but doubtlessly dark outcomes under the heavy warning of history was what characterized the shift to negative memory.

It is important to acknowledge that the days and weeks that followed the election were marked by a breathtaking increase in reported hate crimes.[11] One parent said she felt like this was a "shock and awe or blitzkrieg-type approach—we are literally being bombed back into our houses. I want to say that making us hide will be enough for them, but I am sure it is only the beginning." Another said, "It's everywhere—somebody put swastikas on this guy's garage, and someone put these horrible notes on people's cars in the parking lot that says nasty stuff [about gay and lesbian people] and my kid gets it and he is terrified. And so am I." It is also important to note that Nazi and Holocaust imagery were actively employed by some Trump supporters during this period, and that these uses were intended to terrify. One family of a transgender girl in the study received hate mail crowing that they would be "exterminated" once Trump "came to power." Another child living in a small New England town woke up the day after the election to find "Gas the Jews" among other anti-Semitic, racist, and homophobic slogans, spray-painted twenty feet high on a mountainside near his house. Still others experienced graffiti on their homes and cars, leaflets from neo-Nazi and other hate groups left on windshields, derogatory emails, rocks thrown through windows, angry shouts from passing vehicles, and for some of the children, an uptick in school bullying including at least one physical assault.

Parents described being torn between contradictory parenting tasks: remaining calm and projecting normalcy to soothe terrified children, while also frantically preparing and planning for the possible worst. In conversations and on social media, parents and families of transgender children worked quickly to move forward with affirming name and gender changes for their children, obtain prescriptions for hormones and blockers, and inquire about legal futures. Parents felt responsible for making an array of complicated medical, legal, and social decisions for unpredictable and unknown futures. When asked where this drive came from, parents uniformly expressed that they had been advised by professionals and peers that they had no time to lose in safeguarding their child to the greatest extent possible before the new administration made it difficult to do so. While early in the campaign Trump had claimed that he would "fight for" LGBTQ people, as when he tweeted, "Thank you to the LGBT community! I will fight for you while Hillary brings in more people that will threaten your freedoms and beliefs" (@realDonaldTrump, June 14, 2016), study participants never believed that he would actually do so once elected to office. This was clear from comparing the Democratic and Republican National Conventions; the DNC welcomed the country's first openly transgender convention speaker and the largest contingent of transgender delegates in history.[12] Meanwhile the RNC adopted a vigorously anti-LGBTQ party platform that supported medically dangerous conversion therapy, and prominently positioned speakers who enthusiastically degraded transgender protections as "meaningless," "empty," and "politically correct" rhetoric.[13]

Some parents feared that Trump's political partnership with former Indiana governor Mike Pence, whose homophobic/transphobic stance was widely documented, would lead to myriad new, unimagined legal difficulties for individuals whose birth certificates did not match their affirmed gender.[14] Still others were worried that the new administration, which wasted no time filling cabinet positions with anti-LGBTQ activists, would make it impossible for their children to make legal changes down the road.[15] Groups of parents pooled knowledge and resources, supporting one another through often-byzantine legal channels. Parents asked not just about how to change names and gender, but also how to make special wills for what should happen to minor transgender children should they die because, as one said, "We want it to protect our child as much as possible, and keep them safe from our unsupportive family." These were new legal challenges, as parents must imagine the most horrible possible outcomes and eventualities in order to feel prepared. So, it is not unsurprising that a drive to imagine and prepare for the worst outcome would invite negative memory in general and reflections on the Holocaust in particular.

Some children went back in the closet. One parent said she felt like she was just "sucking everything in and hiding"—a big change from the pride and visibility rhetoric from before. In interviews, mothers in particular felt intense responsibility to "save" their children, as if they were responsible for the ultimate outcomes of the unthinkable political reality. "If I don't do the right thing," one mother said, "my child could be in danger. But I don't know what the right thing is. It seemed like just yesterday everything was going to be okay and now we are groping in the dark." Another mother wrote, "We have a small window to do everything we can to keep our kids as safe as we can. But we don't know what to do. I feel responsible for things I can't predict or understand. How bad do you think it will get?" Another mother responded, "Well, you know it's bad when you have to ask that question. Don't wait for the answer. Get out."

Aftermath: Persistence

By late March 2017, use of negative memory in everyday conversation in person and on social media had lightened somewhat. On the one hand, the November–February level of terror and frantic activity could not possibly be sustained. On the other, the powerful drive to normalize and create a livable, less reactive routine determined a politically muted everyday tone among some families, at least in the presence of their children.

20.1. Transgender rights protest sign, 2017.

It is important to emphasize that while jolted and frightened, families were not at any time cowed, nor were they less brave in their fight for their children's rights and safety. As was famously said of Senator Elizabeth Warren, they "persisted."[16] While some made choices to scale back some efforts, most continued to visibly support their children and engage in different levels of activism. Nonetheless, the overall temperature had changed. One mother and her transgender daughter attended the Women's March in DC on January 21, the day after Trump's inauguration, and while she said it was inspiring and rejuvenating, and "reminded me of the times from before," things had darkened. She said, "I actually wrote my name and cell phone number and my daughter's date of birth on her arm in Sharpie marker in case there were problems or we got tear-gassed or shot or separated, something like that." She shook her head. "I didn't tell her what it was for and drew a little flower too, you know, to make it less scary. . . . It was fine but it crossed my mind."

Other kinds of activism lost their humming undercurrent of hope. For example, in February 2017, parents of transgender children nationwide, including several study participants, signed a letter to the new president imploring him not to take away their children's hard-won legal protections, to no avail. "It felt like trying to bargain with Hitler," said one mother after signing. "Writing that nice letter all please-and-thank-you. Because no matter how emotional or convincing your argument is, he isn't listening. I think he enjoys crushing us. I think he probably ripped that letter up and laughed." As this mother predicted, their letter came to naught and Obama-era federal protections for transgender children were rolled back almost immediately.[17] The Trump administration had appointed what one *Boston Globe* opinion writer called "a who's who of homophobia" to his cabinet.[18] Gavin Grimm's publicized Supreme Court case was sent back to the lower courts.[19] Neil Gorsuch was confirmed to the Supreme Court despite a "disturbing record" on LGBTQ rights.[20] At one point in late March 2017, the federal government removed proposed questions related to LGBTQ people from the 2020 Census.[21] State-level bathroom bills sprouted like weeds.[22] Said one father, "The hits just keep on coming."

Before the election, transgender children and their families felt that they at least had a sympathetic government, and could use the courts and other civic tools to make the world a better place for their children. Negative memory and Holocaust comparisons may be the result of a need for historical exemplars to understand, plan for, and navigate a new reality in which this was no longer true. The actions of the Trump administration and Republican-led Congress seem deliberate and unrestrained. One parent commented that she remembered reading about how the Nazis seemed to "delight in hurting people" and how this mirrored their own experience. "They know we can't do anything about anything," she wrote, describing her first grader's experience in their small southern town. "It's like they enjoy it":

> They had a spelling competition at another school in the district. Eliza was supposed to be participating, and was really looking for-

ward to it. So I called the school and asked if they had a staff or gender-neutral restroom near the gym (where the performance is being held) since they don't allow Eliza to use the girls' restroom [because she is transgender]. The person I spoke to said there is no gender-neutral or staff restroom available at the event because they will be locked. I asked if they could be unlocked. She laughed and told me to have my child use the boys' bathroom.

The parent added, "She laughed at me. She laughed at my child. It's like the people who do horrible things and say 'This is Trump country now!' . . . And my child is seven years old. Didn't the Nazis make old Jewish men scrub the ground, and laughed and made them cut off their beards just to be cruel, because there would be no consequences under Hitler? It's like that. That's how I feel."

The Whole World Is Watching

Persistence under negative memory reframed activism. While many continued to participate in large-scale protests, others constructed the everyday as a form of protest: "Little things—making lunch, sending my kid to school with the same note every single day—*Chris has permission to use the boys' bathroom*—reading my kid a story in bed each night, doing the shopping, loving my child, it's all a way to show them that we are here to stay." Providing loving, visible support became political. As another mother said, "That is courage too." She continued,

> I read somewhere that the bravest of them all were the mothers of little children. If they had abandoned their babies and toddlers when they got off the trains at the gas chambers they could have gone to work in the camps and maybe survived, but they didn't. They went quietly, smiling to calm down these little tiny kids, holding their hands, to accompany their children, to be there for them, to make whatever was coming as not scary as possible for those little ones. And if that isn't bravery I don't know what is. I don't think anyone is going to, like, *kill* us, but just keeping going and propping up and loving my child—even if the future is hopeless—I think I'm brave for just doing that.

Six-year-old Deziree wrote a letter to the Federal Court of Appeals for help when her historically uncooperative school district, emboldened by the Trump win, refused to allow her to use the girls' bathroom. Her letter went viral.[23] Other people picked up the concern, and hundreds wrote the school district to apply pressure. As Dezi's mother said, "We are never going to be safe. But now the district knows that the world is watching."

Interestingly, this phrase returns us to LGBTQ activism. The phrase "the whole world is watching," chanted by ACT UP activists while the Reagan administration ignored the AIDS crisis, wasn't a deliberate connection to ACT UP or its strategies, but this strategy and others from ACT UP could prove useful for engaging a hostile government.[24] This pattern of historicizing was already present among the handful of gay- and lesbian-headed families in the study, many of whom are old enough to have participated in late 1980s and early 1990s AIDS-crisis activism.

When asked why they made this particular comparison, many participating gay and/or lesbian parents wondered if they were perhaps less fazed by the election than were straight parents: "We already have the language and mind-set for resistance from coming up in that [earlier] era." They described already having the experience of lifelong marginalization already in place, and belonging to a community of marginalized people that enables positive memory even in the context of continued persecution. Most (but not all) straight parents had, for the most part, limited language for this experience, and this may be one reason why they historicized their experience in the strongest terms possible—the Holocaust as "archetype of barbarism"—to reflect their feelings of vulnerability and desperation.[25]

Conclusion: On Comparison and Memory

There is a tendency among American activists and politicians alike to make clumsy and insensitive Holocaust/Hitler analogies in the pursuit of attention.[26] All study participants would agree that public comparison with the Holocaust trivializes the Nazi genocide and desecrates the memory of its victims, and would not place their fears and suffering on that par. They made their comparisons in private, worried conversations, as they looked to history for instruction and tried to understand their own perceived upheaval and danger.

It is important to emphasize that this comparison was private; it was not employed to publicly aggrandize or add historical gravitas to families' predicaments in any way. It was employed to fill the spaces left behind by positive memory and provide instruction and motivation. "I don't think I would have had the strength to get [name changes, passports, and other legal protections] done," said one parent, "if I wasn't so scared, and so aware of how bad things could get." One mother, admittedly a shy and quiet person, found her voice to email an uncooperative school and to be vocal at school committee meetings and elected officials' offices. "I never could have done this before," she said. "But now the gloves are off." As political scientist Claire Jean Kim also observes, "When activists and authors evoke these analogies inter-nally, within movement circles, they may produce a positive effect of strengthening activists' shared identity and commitment."[27]

If anything, the postelection proliferation of hate speech target-ing the study population is proof that transgender children need pro-tection. All the families and children in this study occupy a complex and paradoxically vulnerable location. They are categorically different from the heroes of ACT UP and other activists because they must bal-ance the work of confrontation and activism with the work of caring for and insulating children from the same hostile government they must confront. Indeed, as they have pointed out several times, the safety of children must take precedence over visibility politics, and activism. In this way, many express being immobilized, and return to the Holocaust and negative memory. However, as transgender children and their families continue to develop community in the context of Trump-era marginalization, new ways of historicizing experience might bring renewed hope.

Notes

1. Primo Levi, *The Drowned and the Saved*, reprint edition (New York: Vintage, 1989), 163. This study was generously supported by the Spencer Foundation.

2. Susan Opotow, "Historicizing Injustice: The Museum of Memory and Human Rights, Santiago, Chile," *Journal of Social Issues* 71, no. 2 (June 2015): 229–43, https://doi.org/10.1111/josi.12107.

3. Ibid., 229.

4. The phrase "arc of the moral universe," commonly used by study par-ticipants, is attributed in its quoted form to Martin Luther King Jr. (1965) during the march from Selma: "How long? Not long because the arc of the moral universe is long, but it bends toward justice. How long? Not long." Martin Luther King Jr., "Our God Is Marching On!," speech delivered March 25, 1965, Montgomery, AL, Martin Luther King, Jr. Research and Education Institute, Stanford University, https://kinginstitute.stanford.edu/our-god-marching.

5. Alex Gino, *George* (New York: Scholastic Press, 2015).

6. "Title IX Protections for Transgender Students," FindLaw.com, accessed August 9, 2017, http://education.findlaw.com/discrimination-harassment-at-school/title-ix-protections-for-transgender-students.html.

7. David A. Graham, "Is Running for President Donald Trump's Worst Business Decision Yet?," *Atlantic*, July 2, 2015, https://www.theatlantic.com/business/archive/2015/07/donald-trump-bad-businessman/397517/.

8. Adrian Walker, "'Passionate' Trump Fans behind Homeless Man's Beating?," *Boston Globe*, August 21, 2015, https://www.bostonglobe.com/metro/2015/08/20/after-two-brothers-allegedly-beat-homeless-man-one-them-admiringly-quote-donald-trump-deporting-illegals/I4NXR-3Dr7litLi2NB4f9TN/story.html.

9. Jeff Brady, "Transgender Americans Race to Finish Paperwork before Trump Administration," NPR, December 17, 2016, http://www.npr.org/2016/12/17/503753624/transgender-americans-race-to-finish-paperwork-before-trump-administration.

10. Werner Weinberg, "Why I Did Not Leave Nazi Germany in Time," *Christian Century*, March 21, 1982, 4; Deanna Pan, "She's 10 Years Old, and She's Transgender: Her Parents Are More Scared Than Ever," *Post and Courier*, March 26, 2017, http://www.postandcourier.com/news/she-s-years-old-and-she-s-transgender-her-parents/article_9d86cc6e-0e4a-11e7-99e0-6f529d1bc11a.html.

11. "Ten Days After: Harassment and Intimidation in the Aftermath of the Election," Southern Poverty Law Center, November 29, 2016, http://www.splcenter.org/20161129/ten-days-after-harassment-and-intimidation-aftermath-election.

12. P. R. Lockhart, "A Transgender Woman Just Made History at the Democratic National Convention," *Mother Jones*, July 28, 2016, http://www.motherjones.com/politics/2016/07/transgender-woman-makes-history-democratic-national-convention/.

13. David Badash, "Tony Perkins Successfully Introduces Plank Supporting Anti-LGBT Conversion Therapy into GOP Platform," *New Civil Rights Movement*, July 11, 2016, http://www.thenewcivilrightsmovement.com/davidbadash/tony_perkins_successfully_introduces_plank_supporting_anti_lgbt_conversion_therapy_into_gop_platform; David S. Cloud and Christine Mai-Duc, "Retired Army Gen. Michael Flynn Delivers Fiery Speech to Emptying Convention Hall (VIDEO)," *Los Angeles Times*, July 20, 2016, http://www.latimes.com/nation/politics/trailguide/la-na-republican-convention-2016-live-passed-over-as-vice-presidential-pick-1468897531-htmlstory.html.

14. On Mike Pence's record on LGBTQ issues, see Michelangelo Signorile, "Mike Pence's Blatant Anti-LGBT Extremism Completely Ignored in Debate," *Huffington Post*, October 5, 2016, http://www.huffingtonpost.com/michelangelo-signorile/mike-pences-blatant-anti-lgbt-extremism-completely-ignored-in-debate_b_12353590.html. At this writing, these early fears have been at least partially validated. See Jesse Mechanic, "7 Anti-LGBTQ Moves the Trump Administration Has Made Already," *Huffington Post*, July 27, 2017, http://www.huffingtonpost.com/entry/7-anti-lgbtq-moves-the-trump-administration-has-made_us_597a0dc9e4b0c69ef7052638.

15. Michelangelo Signorile, "Trump's Cabinet: A Who's Who of Homophobia," *Boston Globe*, December 15, 2016, https://www.bostonglobe.

com/opinion/2016/12/15/trump-cabinet-who-who-homophobia/9UDr8 MnXIQAxjO369qzT0J/story.html.

16. Amy B. Wang, "'Nevertheless, She Persisted' Becomes New Battle Cry after McConnell Silences Elizabeth Warren," *Washington Post*, February 8, 2017, http://www.washingtonpost.com/news/the-fix/wp/2017/02/08/ nevertheless-she-persisted-becomes-new-battle-cry-after-mcconnell-silences-elizabeth-warren/.

17. Jeremy W. Peters, Jo Becker, and Julie Hirschfeld Davis, "Trump Rescinds Rules on Bathrooms for Transgender Students," *New York Times*, February 22, 2017, http://www.nytimes.com/2017/02/22/us/politics/ devos-sessions-transgender-students-rights.html.

18. Signorile, "Trump's Cabinet."

19. Robert Barnes, "Supreme Court Sends Virginia Transgender Case Back to Lower Court," *Washington Post*, March 6, 2017, http://www. washingtonpost.com/politics/courts_law/supreme-court-sends-trans-gender-case-back-to-lower-court/2017/03/06/0fc98c62-027a-11e7-b9fa-ed727b644a0b_story.html.

20. Mark Joseph Stern, "Neil Gorsuch's Disturbing Record on LGBTQ Rights," *Slate*, February 1, 2017, http://www.slate.com/blogs/outward/ 2017/02/01/neil_gorsuch_s_disturbing_record_on_lgbtq_rights.html.

21. Mary Emily O'Hara, "LGBTQ Americans Will Not Be Counted in the 2020 U.S. Census after All," NBC News, last revised March 29, 2017, http://www.nbcnews.com/feature/nbc-out/lgbtq-americans-won-t-be-counted-2020-u-s-census-n739911.

22. Lucy Westcott, "The Eight States That Could Enact 'Bathroom Bills' This Year," *Newsweek*, January 6, 2017, http://www.newsweek.com/ states-bathroom-bill-transgender-2017-legislation-texas-539567.

23. Rose Kennedy, "A 6-Year-Old Transgender Girl in Knoxville Writes a Letter to the U.S. District Court of Appeals," *Knoxville Mercury*, March 29, 2017, http://www.knoxmercury.com/2017/03/29/6-year-old-transgender-girl-knoxville-writes-letter-u-s-district-court-appeals/.

24. On ACT UP activism, see *How to Survive a Plague*, directed by David France (2012; New York: Public Square Films, Ninety Thousand Words).

25. On the "archetype of barbarism," see Peter Novick, *The Holocaust in American Life* (New York: Mariner Books, 2000), 255.

26. Alan Mintz, *Popular Culture and the Shaping of Holocaust Memory in America* (Seattle: University of Washington Press, 2001).

27. Claire Jean Kim, "Moral Extensionism or Racist Exploitation? The Use of Holocaust and Slavery Analogies in the Animal Liberation Movement," *New Political Science* 33, no. 3 (2011): 332, https://doi.org/10.1080 /07393148.2011.592021.

Chapter Twenty-One

TRIUMPH OF THE CONSTITUTION

American Muslims and Religious Liberty

Asma T. Uddin

Of the many worrisome aspects of the campaign rhetoric during the 2016 presidential election, one theme stood out as dominant: minorities are bad and scary, and the scariest of them all are Muslims. The proposed solution time and again was to curtail Muslims' civil rights. In October 2015, when asked what his solution to ISIS was, Donald Trump advocated shutting down mosques where suspected terrorists were thought to operate.[1] In November Trump praised the surveillance program imposed by the New York Police Department on its local Muslim community.[2] And in December the now most notorious suggestion: a "total and complete shutdown of Muslims entering the United States until our country's representatives can figure out what is going on."[3]

The insistence that Islam is a threat and Muslims must be controlled was not without consequences. The year 2015 saw a 67 percent increase over 2014 in attacks against Muslims, including "257 reports of assaults, attacks on mosques and other hate crimes."[4] It was the biggest surge in hate crimes overall in that year.[5] And one of Trump's first moves in office was to sign an executive order imposing a travel ban from select Muslim-majority states—a move he explained as necessary for national security.

From the rhetoric to the hate crimes to the policy proposals, anti-Muslim aspects of American culture were gaining ground. On the evening of the day after the elections (November 9), I found myself overcome with dread. Muslim friends reported on social media that longtime friends were suddenly turning on them. A Christian friend found a note on her car warning her to leave her Muslim boyfriend. A Catholic friend, with whom I had shared an interfaith connection, suddenly posted on my Facebook page that "America is a Judeo-Christian country. Anyone who doesn't agree with Judeo-Christian values should leave the country." I could not help but feel that the America I had known had just been a facade. Overwhelmed with fear, I broke down in tears.

But yet, just earlier that day, I had delivered a talk at Duke University on the topic of "religious liberty for religious minorities in the U.S." My legal work over the past eight years defending the religious liberty of believers of every faith gave me a unique vantage point on the present threat. I assured those assembled that the US Constitution would prevail. Our jurisprudence provides robust religious liberty protections for all, even—in fact, *especially*—minorities. The Constitution is the special tool for those society would not otherwise protect, those whose beliefs and practices may be idiosyncratic or misunderstood.

The message I had delivered to others had to also be my way out of hopelessness and fear. America has seen worse, but the Constitution's religious liberty protections have helped the nation overcome many of its mistakes, heal, and move forward.

For example, my work has involved challenging legislative remnants of an era in American history rife with anti-Catholic animus. These remnants include antireligious garb statutes that prohibit public school teachers from wearing religious garb while teaching; scholars have found evidence the statutes targeted Catholic nuns in particular.[6]

Another example is state constitutional provisions that prohibit any money raised through taxes to be "under the control of any religious sect" or given to "sectarian" entities.[7] "Sect" and "sectarian" were, at the time of enactment, code for "Catholics." The goal was to prevent secure public funding for parochial schools; Catholic schools were seen as inculcating a dangerous ideology, one that espoused loyalty to the Catholic hierarchy instead of the American government.[8]

The anti-Catholic sentiment led to the formation of the Know-Nothing Party in the mid-1850s. Party members "were sworn to do everything in their power to 'remove all foreigners, aliens, or Roman Catholics from office' and to refrain from appointing Catholics to positions of power."[9] Violence was also a common weapon. For example, during the August 1854 elections, riotous Know-Nothing mobs in St. Louis ransacked Catholic homes, drove residents out of their homes, and destroyed their property.[10]

Members of the Church of Latter-Day Saints (Mormons) have also faced extreme violence because their beliefs were considered "contemptible gibberish."[11] In 1836, for example, over thirty Mormons were killed or wounded in the Hawn's Mill Massacre. Victims of the massacre included men, women, and children—including one child whose head was blown off by a musket. And the worst part? These acts of violence were legal. Just days prior to the massacre, Missouri governor Lilburn Boggs issued Executive Order 44, requiring that Mormons be "exterminated or driven from the state."[12]

The various episodes of persecution—anti-Catholic, anti-Mormon, and anti-Muslim—have much in common. Like Catholics in nineteenth-century America, Muslims today are deemed allegiant to a foreign, threatening ideology. Like Mormons and Catholics of the past, American Muslims today are seen as espousing values antithetical to American ideals. They have been portrayed as wanting to take over the government.[13] And, where still in force, the antireligious garb statutes once motivated by anti-Catholic animus are now used against Muslim teachers in headscarves.[14]

Yet despite this heinous history, America has shown progress, and constitutional ideals of religious liberty have been critical to that forward movement. Catholics and Mormons not only no longer face widespread persecution, but their religious liberty is largely secure. And even in today's troubled climate, President Trump's campaign rhetoric was used to hold the first two versions of his travel ban unconstitutional, while a third, pared-down version that included some non-Muslim-majority countries was upheld by the Supreme Court.[15]

While there continue to be challenges, what matters is that we have strong, protective precedent. America goes through its ups and downs; Americans may fear the unknown and experience deep anxiety. But in the end, America's principles prevail. We go from persecuting a group to being its staunchest defenders; indeed, as a religious liberty attorney, I have been devoted to that defense. In the era of Trump, this is what I hold on to.

Notes

1. Sarah Pulliam Bailey, "Donald Trump Says He Would Consider Closing Down Some Mosques in the U.S.," *Washington Post*, October 21, 2015, http://www.washingtonpost.com/news/acts-of-faith/wp/2015/10/21/donald-trump-says-he-would-consider-closing-down-some-mosques-in-the-u-s/?utm_term=.a1aa071f6e82.

2. Maggie Haberman, "Donald Trump Calls for Surveillance of 'Certain Mosques' and a Syrian Refugee Database," *New York Times*, November 21, 2015, http://www.nytimes.com/2015/11/22/us/politics/donald-trump-syrian-muslims-surveillance.html.

3. Jessica Taylor, "Trump Calls for 'Total and Complete Shutdown of Muslims Entering' U.S.," NPR, December 7, 2015, http://www.

npr.org/2015/12/07/458836388/trump-calls-for-total-and-complete-shutdown-of-muslims-entering-u-s.

4. Eric Lichtblau, "U.S. Hate Crimes Surge 6%, Fueled by Attacks on Muslims," *New York Times*, November 14, 2006, https://www.nytimes.com/2016/11/15/us/politics/fbi-hate-crimes-muslims.html?_r=0.

5. Ibid.

6. Caitlin S. Kerr, "Teachers' Religious Garb as an Instrument for Globalization in Education," *Indiana Journal of Global Legal Studies* 18 (2011): 550.

7. Portions of this paper have been taken from the author's legal brief: Amicus Curiae of the Becket Fund for Religious Liberty in Support of Appellant, Trinity Lutheran Church of Columbia, Inc. v. Pauley, 788 F.2d 779 (8th Cir.) (No. 14-1382), http://s3.amazonaws.com/becketpdf/Blaine-Amicus-Brief-FINAL.pdf.

8. William Barnaby Faherty, *The St. Louis Irish: An Unmatched Celtic Community* (St. Louis: Missouri Historical Society Press, 2001), 62.

9. Meir Katz, "The State of Blaine: A Closer Look at the Blaine Amendments and Their Modern Application," *Engage: Journal of the Federalist Society for Law & Public Policy Studies* 12 (2011): 112.

10. William Hyde, *Encyclopedia of the History of St. Louis*, vol. 4 (New York: Southern History Co., 1899), 1917.

11. Leonard J. Arrington and Davis Bitton, *The Mormon Experience: A History of the Latter-Day Saints*, 2nd ed. (Urbana: University of Illinois Press, 1992), 47.

12. Hannah Smith, "My View: Obama's Speech at Mosque and Religious Freedom," *Deseret News*, February 14, 2016, http://www.deseretnews.com/article/865647693/My-view-Obamas-speech-at-mosque-and-religious-freedom.html.

13. For examples see Leo Hohmann, "Poll: Most U.S. Muslims Would Trade Constitution for Shariah," *World Net Daily*, September 24, 2015, http://www.wnd.com/2015/09/poll-most-u-s-muslims-would-trade-constitution-for-shariah/.

14. United States v. Bd. of Educ. for Sch. Dist. of Philadelphia, 911 F.2d 882 (3d Cir. 1990).

15. Int'l Refugee Assistance Project v. Trump, 2017 WL 2273306 (4th Cir. 2017); Washington v. Trump, 847 F.2d 1151 (9th Cir. 2017); Adam Liptak, "Supreme Court Allows Trump Travel Ban to Take Effect," *New York Times*, December 4, 2017, https://www.nytimes.com/2017/12/04/us/politics/trump-travel-ban-supreme-court.html.

Part Five

The Future Is Female (?)

Critical Reflections and Feminist Futures

Chapter Twenty-Two

"WHEN THEY GO LOW, WE GO HIGH"

African American Women Torchbearers for Democracy and the 2016 Democratic National Convention

De Anna J. Reese and Delia C. Gillis

> We are the backbones of our churches, organizations, communities, and political party. We are the "willing workers." We are the Mothers of the Movement. We are the group with the highest level of voter participation of any demographic group in America. We are the enthusiastic delegates and community leaders waving placards and chanting "Yes we can!" on the floor of Philadelphia's Wells Fargo Center.
>
> —Ginger McNight-Chavers, African American author

Among the many messages the 2016 presidential election cycle sent, one remains abundantly clear. At the end of the day, the most qualified presidential candidate in history could still lose to a man who through word and deed is unapologetic about making America hate again.[1] These misogynistic messages were not lost on Black women who have spent a lifetime defending their names and bodies against similar attacks. As public figures, delegates, and voters, Black women supported Hillary Clinton because, of the two major candidates, they believed she was the only one to push forward progressive change on jobs, health care, and education—issues important not only to Black women, but to all Americans. By crafting a message of unity, mutual respect, and optimism during the 2016 Democratic National Convention (DNC) in Philadelphia, African American women joined their foremothers whose patriotism and understanding of American democratic ideals began long before they formally earned the right to vote.

Through examining the contributions and the message of Black women organizers for the Clinton-Kaine campaign during the forty-seventh Democratic National Convention in Philadelphia July 25–28, 2016, this chapter explores how Black women's stand "with her" was an outgrowth of their lifelong commitment to race, gender, and class-based equality. It will also discuss why Clinton's campaign message at the 2016 DNC—one of hope, compassion, and inclusion—remains important postelection, and why "going high" and refusing to normalize bigotry allows us to find common ground, work together, and move our nation forward.

On July 25, 2016, Stephanie Rawlings Blake called to order the Democrats' forty-seventh national convention. She replaced Chairperson Debbie Wasserman Schultz, who resigned from her position at the Democratic National Committee following the release of nearly 20,000 emails from a WikiLeaks hack that showed an attempt to derail Senator Bernie Sanders from becoming the Democratic presidential nominee.[2] Blake, the mayor of Baltimore, was one of several Black women who led the convention, taking charge of the top jobs that kept the massive gathering with an estimated 50,000 in attendance on schedule and on message.[3]

The first time African American women held the highest-ranking and most prominent spots for a major national political party—convention CEO, convention chair, and interim chair of the committee—this completed a seismic shift from a Democratic Party that before the 1930s had historically championed states' rights, territorial expansion, slavery, the KKK, and Jim Crow. Who could have predicted that only a half century since the passage of the 1965 Voting Rights Act, Black women's talent and political savvy, which had once been silenced and trivialized, would be welcomed by a party splintered by scandal and division?

Having served as attorney, governor's wife, First Lady, senator, secretary of state, presidential candidate and nominee, Hillary Clinton was, according to President Obama, the "most qualified" person to potentially serve as president of the United States.[4] Her decades of public service, leadership skills, and willingness to address social justice issues including living-wage jobs, affordable health care, college accessibility, and criminal justice reform, were among the reasons 94 percent of Black women voted for Clinton in the 2016 election.[5]

Representing the Clinton "firewall" in the 2016 primaries, Black women's support for the Democratic Party has been especially significant in recent elections. In 2008 the voter turnout rate among eligible Black female voters increased 5.1 percentage points, from 63.7 percent in 2004 to 68.8 percent. Among all racial, ethnic, and gender groups, this was the first time Black women had the highest voter turnout rate. Four years later, more than 70 percent of eligible Black women voted in the 2012 presidential election, outvoting white women (65.6 percent), white men (62.6 percent), and Black men (61.4 percent).[6] The past systemic exclusion of African Americans from the franchise explains why many Black women (78 percent in one online poll) feel such a strong responsibility to vote.[7] Of equal importance is what journalist Esther Armah refers to as Black women's "emotional labor," the weight and phenomenal support of their lifelong legacy in nation building, movement building, and electoral politics. In the last presidential election, it was this "labor," Armah argues, that "lifted the DNC from confusion and controversy to optimism and committed engagement."[8]

Black women have a long history of political engagement in the United States, operating in both formal and informal arenas. As slaves and free women, they circulated petitions, wrote letters and poems, and participated in antislavery and self-help organizations. After the Civil War, many Black women willfully influenced the direction of a husband's or father's vote even if unable to cast their own ballot. As participants in mass meetings, parades, and rallies across the nation, Black women took seriously their responsibility to educate the community on issues, raise funds for candidates, and register voters. These examples illustrate the ways in which Black women understood the vote, and by extension the political work that accompanied it, as a collective and not an individual enterprise.[9]

Two activists whose involvement within the Democratic Party profoundly shaped the message of inclusion and mutual respect later developed by conference organizers at the 2016 DNC were Fannie Lou Hamer and Shirley Chisholm. Among the most celebrated of all civil rights movement heroines, Hamer (1917–77) was not only instrumental in challenging the systemic discrimination against African Americans in the Democratic Party in her day, she played an integral role in expanding their future participation and representation as party leaders and delegates. A founder of the Mississippi Freedom Democratic Party (MFDP) in 1964, Hamer made a televised address during the 1964 DNC in Atlantic City in which she and others challenged the seating of the all-white prosegregation Mississippi delegation. That same year, Hamer ran unsuccessfully for Congress. Her loss was in part due to the national Democratic Party's refusal to include her name on the ballot. Contesting the party's discriminatory policies, Hamer's tireless efforts on behalf of the poor and disenfranchised demonstrated her exceptional leadership and ability to encourage a national dialogue on the limits of American democracy.[10]

While Hillary Clinton's nomination as the first female presidential candidate for a major party is historic, it was Shirley Chisholm (1924–2005) who paved the way for both this milestone and the Obama presidency. During her decades-long political career, Chisholm, the educator and community activist who later became the first Black woman elected to the House of Representatives and a founding member of both the Congressional Black Caucus and the Congressional Women's Caucus, became the first Black woman in US history to run for a major-party presidential nomination in 1972.[11] A realistic and grounded political thinker, Chisholm admitted that her run for the presidency, "despite hopeless odds, [was] to demonstrate sheer will and refusal to accept the status quo."[12] Refusing to be silenced, even by some feminists who blatantly dismissed her, Chisholm served in the House for fourteen years under the slogan "unbought and unbossed," during which time she was a staunch advocate for progressive issues.

While the two are dramatically different in background, there are similarities regarding the treatment of Chisholm and Clinton in politics. Both experienced blatant sexism in their run for the presidency, with Trump labeling Hillary Clinton "a nasty woman" and Chisholm described by a Black politician in 1972 as "that little black matriarch who goes around messing things up."[13] However, unlike Clinton, whose political and financial capital made possible her presidential bids in 2008 and 2016, Chisholm's resources during her 1972 run were scant at best. A feminist who supported the social welfare programs of the Great Society, Chisholm paid close attention to shaping policy, plotting tactics, and lobbying lawmakers to create opportunities for women and children.[14] She was also a trailblazer who broke through racial and gender barriers, carrying forward a vision centered on full access and participation for all in American life. This vision was precisely what Black female organizers relayed in their message to the nation during the 2016 DNC.

Convention CEO Leah Daughtry, permanent chair Marcia Fudge, and interim chairperson Donna Brazile proved critical in developing an agenda and tone at the convention aimed at representing the nation's growing diversity while shoring up support for the Clinton nomination. This message not only served to complement the Clinton-Kaine campaign slogan of "Stronger Together," it culminated in the rallying slogan of "When they go low, we go high," delivered in the powerful speech by First Lady Michelle Obama.[15]

As chief executive officer, Rev. Daughtry was the lead strategist, event manager, and problem solver of the convention. Having grown up in Shirley Chisholm's district in Brooklyn, New York, Daughtry had managed the 2008 Democratic National Convention in Denver and is the first person in Democratic Party history to lead the convention twice.[16] A veteran of Bill Clinton's 1992 transition team, she worked at the Labor Department during his first administration and later created Faith in Action, the Democratic Party's outreach to faith communities. In her promise to deliver "the most diverse and the most forward-looking convention that we've had in recent history," Daughtry acknowledged that to do so meant honoring the legacy of Hamer and Chisholm, both of whom waged a lifetime struggle to include underrepresented people in the political process.[17] She credits growing up in "Miss C's" district with helping inspire her own political work. Daughtry also explained how the boldness and courage of Hamer, whose 1964 testimony before the DNC Credentials Committee sparked her own interest to do progressive work:

> It means everything for me to serve as the CEO of a convention that would not even seat her [Hamer]. I stand there on the opening night and hold the gavel in a hall that I oversee, in a process that I put together, and I just think of Ms. Hamer, because even though she didn't know my name Ms. Hamer was thinking of me. I just want to do a good job, because I want her to look over that edge of heaven and say, "That's why I did it. That's why. I knew we had the capacity and the talent to be everything America says we can't be. All we needed was an open door."[18]

Acknowledging the honor she, too, felt as permanent chair, Marcia Fudge led with integrity while asserting control over the convention. An ardent supporter of a quality education for all children, Fudge came to Congress in 2008 as the US representative for the 11th Congressional District of Ohio, and went on to chair the Congressional Black Caucus from 2012 to 2014.[19] On July 25, Fudge promised a "different kind" of convention than what many had witnessed in Cleveland, at the Republican National Convention. This was no easy task, especially on the first night when loud boos and chants rung out during an opening prayer and persisted throughout the DNC's early moments. Fudge managed to quickly make her presence and authority known, stating: "There are many of you that do not know me in this room; but let me say to you . . . I intend to be fair; I want to hear the varying opinions here. I'm going to be respectful of you, and I want you to be respectful of me. We're all Democrats and we need to act like it; let's do it."[20]

When asked later how she interpreted the crowd's noise, Fudge said, "It was kind of surreal." She continued, "I just believe in common courtesy. It just came to mind that I needed to say something. If I didn't, it probably would have gone on for four days. Really after that, you could feel a difference in the tone."[21] Unfortunately, the tone may have changed but the disruptions did not. Even as Fudge spoke of lifting one another up "regardless of race, religion, and sexual orientation,"[22] repeated boos from Sanders supporters revealed the chasm within the ranks of the Democratic Party—a divide left unbridged on Election Day.

In fall 2016, the release of hacked Wikileaks emails revealed that Donna Brazile gave one primary debate question to Clinton while serving as a CNN contributor.[23] However, this does not negate the importance of her role in boosting support for Clinton's nomination, calming Bernie supporters, and attempting to unify the party. The former chair of the DNC's Voting Rights Institute and the interim Democratic National Committee chair following the resignation of Wasserman Schultz, Brazile is a political stalwart. With a penchant for politics that began as a child in New Orleans and matured through her work on the presidential campaigns of many Democratic candidates, Brazile became the first African American to manage a major-party presidential campaign, that of Al Gore in 2000.[24] She also maintained long-standing ties to the Clinton family, including her role as Bill Clinton's campaign adviser in 1992 and 1996, and a relationship with Hillary going back more than thirty years.

At the convention, Brazile spoke convincingly of her initial impressions of Hillary Clinton; namely, her resolve, commitment, and genuine interest in the lives of children when the two first met at the Children's Defense Fund in 1981. Brazile commented that what she saw in Clinton was "a woman who didn't mess around," who followed the path of her idol Marian Wright Edelman, and who had a passion for improving the lives of children, especially girls, through early childhood education and health care. Brazile noted that as First Lady, Clinton had helped to win health care coverage for more than 8 million children.[25] Moreover, the Clinton she knew kept working when no one watched, making a difference "for the voiceless among us."[26]

While these heartfelt sentiments garnered some applause, they were not enough to bridge the deep mistrust and resentment toward Clinton even at the convention. Described by one adviser as "the most famous woman who no one truly knows,"[27] Hillary's enigmatic personality, political missteps, and the sexism she faced both subtle and blatant contributed to her uneven reception.[28] But before it was over, the 2016 DNC witnessed an abundance of powerful speeches by women including Elizabeth Warren, US senator from Massachusetts; Gabrielle Giffords, former congresswoman from Arizona and shooting survivor; Karla Ortiz, American daughter of undocumented parents; Christine Leinonen, mother of a 2016 Orlando LGBTQ nightclub massacre victim; actress Eva Longoria; stand-up comedian Sarah Silverman; and Sarah McBride, who became the first transgender person to speak at a major-party convention. McBride argued that despite recent advances in LGBTQ rights, the fight for equality must continue and that it was Clinton who "understands the urgency of our fight."[29] Her well-spoken words were among those that resonated with the Black community, especially Black women, who understood that Hillary's promotion and advocacy on the real issues affecting working and middle-class families, like gun violence, made her the best choice for president.

The issue of gun violence took center stage when nine women connected by the tragic deaths of their children—known as Mothers of the Movement (MOTM)—announced their support for Clinton, as she was the only major-party candidate to address the loss of life by gun violence and racially charged incidents with law enforcement. Adorned with bright red rose corsages, these mothers addressed the convention floor in response to the sustained and increasingly visible violence against Black communities that had fueled the Black Lives Matter movement. After a standing ovation, several spoke about the most painful event of their lives. Sharing their stories, each reflected on how their lives had changed and why they chose to endorse Clinton, a candidate they claimed was unafraid to say, "Black lives matter" and address the need for police reform. Among them was Geneva Veal-Reed, the mother of twenty-eight-year-old Sandra Bland, who allegedly hung herself in a Texas jail in 2015, three days after being arrested during a traffic stop. Reflecting on why Clinton was her choice, Veal-Reed stated, "So many of our children [are] gone but not forgotten. . . . I'm here with Hillary Clinton because she is a leader and a mother who will say our children's names. Hillary knows that when a young Black life is cut short, it's not just a personal loss. It is a national loss. It is a loss that diminishes all of us."[30]

Sybrina Fulton, the mother of slain Florida teen Trayvon Martin, added that Clinton was passionate and understanding enough to support mothers who lost children to gun violence by leading the fight for commonsense gun control and presenting a solid plan to address the divides between the police and Black communities. She reminded the audience, "This isn't about being politically correct . . . [It] is about saving our children."[31] Such comments reflect Clinton's long history of support of children, including an invitation she extended during the primaries to the MOTM to tell their stories with hopes of reaching out to undecided voters and developing a plan of action.

The carefully orchestrated vision of teamwork and inclusion promoted by Daughtry, Fudge, and Brazile greatly benefited Clinton at the convention, but the most striking boost came from the outstanding speech made by First Lady Michelle Obama. In what some said was a "defining moment" for Clinton at the convention, Obama lent credence to why Trump was ill-suited for the presidency. Explaining that, as First Lady, she realized that "our time in the White House would form the foundation for who [my daughters] would become," Obama described how she and her husband had tried to guide their daughters through the spotlight, stating: "We urge them to ignore those who question their father's citizenship or faith. . . . We insist that the hateful language they hear from public figures on TV does not represent the true spirit of this country. . . . We explain that when someone is cruel or acts like a bully, you don't stoop to their level. No, our motto is, when they go low, we go high."[32]

Reflecting on the way she and the president raised the First Daughters, Obama spoke about them in a way that touched on multiple subjects at once, including the ongoing struggle of race relations and the historic moment for women, underscoring throughout her speech the DNC's message of choosing "love over hate."[33] The latter, she said, was the duty of responsible parents who understand that children mimic what they see and that parents should be the first role models for their children. Acknowledging the great influence the future president would have over the course of our children's lives in coming years, she highlighted why she supported Clinton, commending her on "her lifelong devotion to our nation's children" evidenced by "decades spent doing the relentless, thankless work to actually make a difference in their lives . . . advocating for kids with disabilities as a young lawyer, fighting for children's health care as a first lady, and for quality child care in the Senate." She also described the personality attributes of a good president; one who is "steady," "measured," and "well-informed," implicitly contrasting Donald Trump's noted impulsiveness.[34]

With reference to the African proverb of "the village" necessary to keep our children safe and the ongoing challenges women face attempting to crack the "highest and hardest" glass ceiling, Obama powerfully articulated that "going high" meant far more than to refrain attacking a political opponent. Instead, it meant reframing the election's focus on why a Clinton presidency represented the best of our democratic ideals—the promise to develop one's full potential and to work together to improve the lives of all. In doing so, Obama singlehandedly embodied the enduring role of Black women as "torchbearers for democracy," a role in which Black women understand the "big picture" and high stakes of ensuring equality of opportunity for everyone, not just a privileged few. In interviews after the convention, Clinton gave high praise for Mrs. Obama's remarks, reiterating that she, too, believed in the values of diversity, respect, and kindness and what they offer to heal and repair the nation postelection.[35]

First Lady Michelle Obama's soul-stirring speech left an indelible mark on what Clinton tried to accomplish in the final weeks before the election—an attempt to move the needle from one of fear and mistrust to one of inclusion. For Black women, this meant voting for Clinton not merely because she was the "lesser of two evils," but for her legacy of substantively addressing issues that impact working families, including affordable health care, criminal justice reform, living-wage jobs, and college affordability.[36] The most reliable and solid voting bloc for the Democratic Party, Black women supported Hillary Clinton in larger numbers than any other group. Despite a jobless rate that rose to 8.9 percent in 2015, the highest percentage among any female demographic in the nation,[37] Black women turned out on behalf of the Clinton-Kaine campaign in numbers (10.1 million) closely resembling those that helped elect President Obama in 2012 (10.4 million) and 2008 (9.4 million).[38]

Black women's sense of pragmatism had dictated that they support the candidate they believed would most likely earn the party's nomination, which made standing "with her" a natural fit for some, and the only choice for others. But what was less understood from the outset was to what extent a feminist "sisterhood" would unite women across race and class. What has become clear is that misogyny made some voters, including many white women, receptive to claims that Clinton was dishonest and untrustworthy, while believing Trump's promises to improve the economic and social standing of white, native-born Americans.[39] As legal scholar Kimberlé Crenshaw commented after the election, "If we [had] 'intersectionalled' better we would have understood how the votes happened. We would have been able to anticipate white women's votes, for example, because it has to do with patriarchy more than the 'women'-ness of those voters."[40] By this she meant that while Clinton won a higher percentage of votes from women overall, had we understood how class-based politics fueled racialized narratives about the Other, we would have been less surprised by the voting patterns of middle-class white women, many of whom voted Republican, were unsold on gender-based appeals, and despite the horribly offensive and sexist rhetoric and behavior of their party's nominee, felt he best represented their interests.[41]

While Clinton's loss in the 2016 presidential election remains painful in light of the new administration's rollback of Obama-era policies and revolving-door appointments to end government as we know it, it does not diminish or make obsolete the message and the values incorporated into her platform at the DNC. The idea of "Stronger

Together"—emphasizing cooperation over division, understanding over fear and anger, and globalism over extreme nationalism—is not back-door tribalism, but an opportunity to build on the democratic ideals that in theory unite us as Americans. As torchbearers for democracy, Black women understand that elections are bigger than the candidates who run for office. For many, supporting Clinton meant promoting someone who had real ideas, not tweets, on how to further a just and better world where all people, not just those with exorbitant wealth, family connections, and white skin privilege have a seat at the table. And of equal importance, ideas about ways to work out our differences in a spirit of compromise that do not intentionally set out to diminish, silence, and hurt one another. These are the values Mrs. Obama spoke of in the phrase "when they go low, we go high," and they are also the ones that inspired other important election night victories for women, including Kamala Harris's, who became only the second Black female to serve in the US Senate, and nine Black female judges in Jefferson County, Alabama.[42]

Vowing a different kind of convention than the Republican one in Cleveland, Daughtry, Fudge, Brazile and others showed how diversity and inclusion work across gender, class, and race by assembling a broad range of voices, including but not limited to teachers, DREAMers, military families, civil rights leaders, activists, government officials, and entertainers—all attempting to showcase the best of what America offers and what the nation stood to gain under a unified effort to elect a president who would have worked to ensure increased opportunity and life chances for all. In turn, they understood how working together and respecting difference is not a weakness, but the first step in moving us toward to a more perfect union.

Notes

1. Epigraph: Ginger McKnight-Chavers, "Who Runs the World of the Democratic Convention? Black Women," *Blue Nation Review*, July 28, 2016, http://bluenationreview.com/who-runs-the-world-of-the-democratic-convention-black-women/.

Trump's comments during the 2016 election cycle encouraged both hatred and violence. From banning Muslims to building walls, Trump initially accused Mexican immigrants of "bringing drugs and crime" and committing rape. See *Washington Post* staff, "Full Text: Donald Trump Announces a Presidential Bid," June 16, 2015, https://www.washingtonpost.com/news/post-politics/wp/2015/06/16/full-text-donald-trump-announces-a-presidential-bid/?utm_term=.18c0fc3b41f7; and Michael Finnegan and

Noah Bierman, "Trump's Endorsement of Violence Reaches New Level: He May Pay Legal Fees for Assault Suspect," *Los Angeles Times*, March 13, 2016, http://www.latimes.com/politics/la-na-trump-campaign-protests-20160 313-story.html.

2. Jasmine Ellis, "Black Women Take over Top Spots for Democratic Convention," *USA Today*, July 26, 2016, https://www.usatoday.com/story/news/politics/elections/2016/07/26/black-women-take-over-top-spots-democratic-convention/87565302.

3. Donavan Harrell, "DNC by the Numbers," Politico.com, July 26, 2016, http://www.politico.com/story/2016/07/dnc-by-the-numbers-226037.

4. Charlotte Alter, "Now What?," *Time*, November 21, 2016, 43. On July 27, 2016, President Obama made the case for Hillary Clinton's qualifications for the presidency. For an excerpt from his remarks at the 47th DNC, see Associated Press, "Obama: Clinton Most Qualified Candidate Ever," YouTube.com, video, https://www.youtube.com/watch?v=7w5x0NiUtOg.

5. "Election 2016, Exit Polls," CNN.com, November 23, 2016, http://www.cnn.com/election/results/exit-polls; Donna M. Owens, "Vote," *Essence*, November 2015, 98.

6. Kelly Ditmar and Glynda Carr, "Black Women Voters by the Numbers," *Huffington Post*, December 6, 2017, http://www.huffingtonpost.com/kelly-dittmar/black-women-voters-by-the_b_9389330.html. For more information on the African American vote from 2008 to 2016, see Roper Center for Public Opinion Research, "How Groups Voted in 2016," Cornell University, all accessed August 11, 2017: https://ropercenter.cornell.edu/polls/us-elections/how-groups-voted/groups-voted-2016/; https://ropercenter.cornell.edu/polls/us-elections/how-groups-voted/how-groups-voted-2012/; and https://ropercenter.cornell.edu/polls/us-elections/how-groups-voted/how-groups-voted-2008/.

7. Owens, "Vote," 98.

8. Esther Armah, "Black Women's Emotional Labor Saved the Democratic National Convention," *Ebony*, August 12, 2016, http://www.ebony.com/news-views/black-women-dnc#axzz4gyDUWaKT.

9. Elsa Barkley Brown, "Negotiating and Transforming the Public Sphere: African American Political Life in the Transition from Slavery to Freedom," *Public Culture* 7, no. 1 (1994): 107–46.

10. Linda Reed, "Fannie Lou Hamer," in *Black Women in America: An Historical Encyclopedia*, vol. 2, *M–Z*, ed. Darlene Clark Hine, Elsa Barkley Brown, and Rosalyn Terborg-Penn (Bloomington: Indiana University Press, 1993), 518.

11. Danny Lewis, "44 Years Ago, Shirley Chisholm Became the First Black Woman to Run for President," Smithsonian.com, January 29, 2016, http://www.smithsonianmag.com/smart-news/44-years-ago-shirley-chisholm-became-the-first-black-woman-to-run-for-president-180957975/. See also Barbara Winslow's chapter in this volume.

12. Barbara Winslow, *Shirley Chisholm: Catalyst for Change* (Boulder, CO: West View Press, 2014), 97.

13. Ibid., 98.

14. Philip Elliott and David Von Drehle, "The Hardest One to Know," *Time*, August 1, 2016, 37.

15. Michelle Obama, "When They Go Low, We Go High," YouTube.com, video, July 25, 2016, https://www.youtube.com/watch?v=mu_hCThhzWU.

16. The House of the Lord Church, "The National Board of Elders: Leah D. Daughtry," accessed July 16, 2017, http://www.holc.org/our-leadership/national-board-of-elders/leah-d-daughtry/.

17. Valerie Wardlaw, "African American Women Make History at Democratic National Convention," *Los Angeles Sentinel*, August 3, 2016, https://lasentinel.net/african-american-women-make-history-at-democratic-national-convention.html.

18. Melissa Harris Perry, "CEO of the DNC: This Will Be an Inclusive Convention; the Reverend Leah D. Daughtry on What to Expect in Philadelphia This Week," *Elle*, July 25, 2016, http://www.elle.com/culture/career-politics/news/a38077/leah-daughtry-ceo-of-the-dnc/.

19. "Biography," Congresswoman Marcia L. Fudge, accessed March 11, 2017, https://fudge.house.gov/biography1/.

20. "Rep. Marcia Fudge Speaks over Cheers and Boos at the 2016 Democratic National Convention," PBS NewsHour, July 25, 2016, https://www.youtube.com/watch?v=wxMpSdHATOU.

21. Henry J. Gomez, "Marcia Fudge Reflects on Her Big Democratic National Convention Moment: Q&A," Cleveland.com, August 2, 2016, http://www.cleveland.com/open/index.ssf/2016/08/marcia_fudge_reflects_on_her_b.html.

22. "Rep. Fudge Speaks over Cheers."

23. During the spring and fall of 2016, WikiLeaks released a series of hacked emails from Clinton campaign chairman John Podesta. In October 2016 a hacked WikiLeaks email was released exposing that Brazile, a CNN contributor, provided Clinton with at least one question in advance prior to a Democratic primary debate against Bernie Sanders. For more information see Donna Brazile, "Donna Brazile: Russian DNC Narrative Played Out Exactly as They Hoped," *Time*, March 17, 2017, http://time.com/4705515/donna-brazile-russia-emails-clinton/.

See also Brazile's controversial but revealing account of the 2016 election and missteps by the Clinton campaign in *Hacks: The Inside Story of the Break-ins and Breakdowns that Put Donald Trump in the White House* (New York: Hachette Press, 2017).

24. "Donna Brazile to Lead DNC after Chair Resigns," *New Journal and Guide*, accessed July 28, 2017, http://thenewjournalandguide.com/2016/07/28/donna-brazile-to-lead-dnc-after-chair-resigns/.

25. The Hill staff, "FULL SPEECH: Donna Brazile Revs Up Crowd in Philadelphia," *Hill*, July 26, 2016, http://thehill.com/blogs/pundits-blog/presidential-campaign/289353-full-speech-donna-brazile-revs-up-crowd-in.

26. Ibid.

27. Elliott and Von Drehle, "Hardest One to Know," 37.

28. Ibid., 34; Rebecca Onion, "Bad News: We're Sexist: New Data Show How Sexism Played a Role in Donald Trump's Election," *Slate*, June 7, 2017, http://www.slate.com/articles/double_x/doublex/2017/06/new_research_on_role_of_sexism_in_2016_election.html.

29. P. R. Lockhart, "A Transgender Woman Just Made History at the Democratic National Convention," *Mother Jones*, July 28, 2016, http://www.motherjones.com/politics/2016/07/transgender-woman-makes-history-democratic-national-convention.

30. Christina Coleman, "Mothers of the Movement Endorse Hillary Clinton in Emotional Address," *News One*, July 27, 2016, https://newsone.com/3491466/mothers-of-the-movement-dnc-2016/.

31. Ibid.

32. "Transcript: Read Michelle Obama's Full Speech from the 2016 DNC," *Washington Post*, July 26, 2016, https://www.washingtonpost.com/news/post-politics/wp/2016/07/26/transcript-read-michelle-obamas-full-speech-from-the-2016-dnc/?utm_term=.27a096d82c3c.

33. Ibid.

34. Ibid.

35. See, for example, "Clinton Praises Michelle Obama: 'Is There Anyone More Inspiring?'" NBC News, October 27, 2016, http://www.nbcnews.com/video/clinton-praises-michelle-obama-is-there-anyone-more-inspiring-795102275915.

36. Donna M. Owens, "Black Women Sound Off," *Essence*, November 2016, 64.

37. Owens, "Vote," 97.

38. Center for American Women And Politics (CAWP), "Gender Differences in Voter Turnout," Eagleton Institute of Politics, Rutgers University, July 20, 2017, http://www.cawp.rutgers.edu/sites/default/files/resources/genderdiff.pdf.

39. Stephanie Schwartz, "Why Do Voters Say Hillary Clinton Is Untrustworthy?," *National Memo*, March 28, 2016, http://www.nationalmemo.com/why-do-voters-say-hillary-clinton-is-untrustworthy/.

40. Laura Flanders, "No Single-Issue Politics, Only Intersectionality: An Interview with Kimberlé Crenshaw," *Truthout*, May 8, 2017, http://www.truth-out.org/opinion/item/40498-no-single-issue-politics-only-intersectionality-an-interview-with-kimberle-crenshaw.

41. Kristine Phillips, "Tina Fey Tells College-Educated White Women Who Voted for Trump: 'You Can't Look Away,'" *Washington Post*, April 1, 2017, https://www.washingtonpost.com/news/arts-and-entertainment/

wp/2017/04/01/tiny-fey-tells-college-educated-white-women-who-voted-for-trump-you-cant-look-away/?utm_term=.96b58d5a16e5.

42. Tanasia Kenney, "Alabama County Elects 9 Black Women Judges," *Atlanta Black Star*, November 15, 2016, http://atlantablackstar.com/2016/11/15/jefferson-county-alabama-appoints-9-beautiful-black-female-judges/. Following Trump's election, Black women, once again, showed their remarkable consistency as a voting bloc in securing the victory of Democrat Doug Jones in the December 2017 special election against Republican Roy Moore to fill the Senate seat vacated by Jeff Sessions in Alabama. Unmoved by serious claims of child molestation and sexual misconduct, two-thirds of white women, or 63 percent, including those with college degrees, voted for Roy Moore while a whopping 98 percent of Black women gave Jones their votes. The shocking upset in the Bible-belt state was largely the result of a massive turnout among African American voters, especially black women who appreciated his platform and Jones's successful prosecution of Klansmen who murdered four young girls in the infamous 1963 Birmingham church bombing. For more information see Scott Clement and Emily Guskin (graphics by Darla Cameron), "Exit Poll Results: How Different Groups Voted in Alabama," *Washington Post*, December 13, 2017, https://www.washingtonpost.com/graphics/2017/politics/alabama-exit-polls/?utm_term=.1e334fb04fe2; and DeNeen L. Brown, "Long before Sinking Roy Moore's Candidacy, Black Women in Alabama Were a Force for Change," *Washington Post*, December 16, 2017, https://www.washingtonpost.com/news/retropolis/wp/2017/12/16/long-before-sinking-roy-moore s-candidacy-black-women-in-alabama-have-been-a force/?utm_term=.94de997185aa. See also DeNeen L. Brown, "Doug Jones Triumphs in an Alabama Senate Race That Conjured a Deadly Church Bombing," *Washington Post*, March 11, 2018, https://www.washingtonpost.com/news/retropolis/wp/2017/11/09/an-alabama-senate-race-conjures-the-awful-1963-church-bombing-that-killed-4-black-girls/?utm_term=.978c95685b49.

Chapter Twenty-Three

AMNESIA AND POLITICS IN THE
MOUNT HOPE CEMETERY

Toward a Critical History
of Race and Gender

Katie Terezakis

Introduction: A Rhizomic Trail

The graves of Susan B. Anthony and Frederick Douglass are near neighbors at Mount Hope Cemetery in Rochester, New York. To walk from one to the other, you climb and descend rambling slopes, moving around an ancient esker, now a paved driving lane, and formerly the road that native Seneca people used to travel between Lake Ontario and the Bristol Hills. Along the way, reading any given inscription might bring a jolt of recognition, so crowded is the place with luminaries and supporting actors. Most days, you will find yourself nearly alone but for the urban wildlife, in a vast settling garden undisturbed by its historical standing. As Mount Hope sits atop retired catacombs and moves with the bustle of groundhog burrows, so too within the story of Mount Hope, active recesses are as likely to be found as they are to be found sealed over. The history we customarily acknowledge in Mount Hope is a sprout, sustained by unseen networks. This essay is about one of them: the lines between Anthony and Douglass and their political causes, which extended into the dynamics at work in the 2016 presidential election, and into the social and political activities that have followed it. More specifically, I will focus on the racial inequality Douglass and Anthony confronted, which lives on in our institutions, our appreciation of American history, and our tools of theoretical analysis. I utilize Friedrich Nietzsche's juxtaposition of three modes of interpreting history—*monumental, antiquarian,* and *critical*—to argue that the 2016 election and the predicaments in American social and political life that it laid bare indicate our need for a renewed critical history, as Nietzsche understood it and as Douglass practiced it, and for a racially relevant intersectional politics.

The story of Anthony and Douglass's friendship includes Douglass's support of women's rights conventions, including in Seneca Falls in 1848, where his defense of the resolution for women's suffrage helped secure its inclusion in the convention's program. This story remembers that Anthony and Douglass were allies when he died, having just spent an afternoon together. Less discussed is the record of Anthony's indignation at the possibility that black men would win suffrage before white women and their consequent falling-out over the Fifteenth Amendment.[1] In 1869 in her newspaper, the *Revolution*, Anthony argued that cosuffragist Lucy Stone was damaging the cause with "her cry of the Negro's hour"; Anthony called it "both wrong and insulting to the intelligence of the age." In that same issue, Anthony included a transliterated (alleged) quote, under the title "Sound Argument" from a "Negro Preacher of the Gospel," that was made to sound both barely literate and dangerously antiwoman.[2] The imputation was furthered by Anthony's closest ally, Elizabeth Cady Stanton, who in arguing against the Fifteenth Amendment claimed that men of the "lower order" or "Sambos" would prove especially cruel rulers if granted voting rights before women.[3]

We might continue to debate, as Anthony and Douglass did, the political strategies motivating the rhetoric, but the fact remains that within the suffragist and women's causes, we find pointed divides between black women who fought against both sexism and the active practice of lynching—for example, Ida B. Wells—and their white suffragist contemporaries, such as Frances E. Willard, president of the Woman's Christian Temperance Union. Willard smeared Wells in the press for publicizing an antilynching campaign, and in response to that campaign, Willard insisted that blacks were uncontrollable drunks who threatened the lives of white families when not kept in check.[4] Anthony's statements were never as venomous as Willard's, but the overtly antiblack elements of her suffragist movement belong to her story and to her relationship with Douglass. In the full telling, antislavery and antiracist politics connect with divisions of the progressive movement that proved ready to bud with antiblack discrimination.

Here I wish to reintroduce an image that fixes this collection: the grave of Anthony, freshly affixed with stickers proclaiming "I Voted" on Election Day—a ritual encouraged by Rochester mayor Lovely Warren, who is African American.[5] The image redoubles, with people visiting Anthony's grave by the thousands on the day before and of the 2016 election, and then fewer people, still gathering on the day after Hillary Clinton's loss to Donald Trump. I would like to consider the sticker ritual at the Anthony gravesite as a living node we can connect, for orientation, with other key points, before reconsidering the ritual itself. For more clarity, the nexus I wish to consider is not just the place or the timing of the stickering ritual; it includes the tombs of both Anthony and Douglass and the line (or trailing path) between them. I take this nodal path as a figure of Douglass and Anthony's relationship and the affiliation of their political movements.

I gather these images together here at the outset because they suggest the tangle of action that brought abolitionism in contact with women's suffrage and with the forms of racism that attended legalized slavery, Jim Crow, and white supremacy as well as progressive liberal paradigms. Frederick Douglass drove himself with an urgency that was unprecedented and remains unmatched. He taught himself how to read and how to fight; he reimagined himself a man when his possessors tried intently to break him; he met arguments in favor of slavery and pretenses for segregation with some of the most lucid arguments in our intellectual tradition; and he evaluated with far-reaching discernment invitations to inhabit more violent as well as more docile territories within his movement.[6] At the same time, antiblack racism, or more specifically, *white supremacy* was robust in Douglass's lifetime as it is today; a legion whose offshoots take on new lives, even where a parent bulb has been cut. Like the image of the rhizome introduced by philosopher Gilles Deleuze, we find an active plurality of racial coordinates within the American project, rather than a single root to our racial legacy.[7] White supremacy as well as black (and other) liberation movements are multiplicities that become defined from outside surface planes, even as they regenerate in subterranean linkages. While this metaphor suggests that we cannot simply weed racism out of the culture in which it is so well established, it also points to how intersectional liberation movements can outcreate, outconnect, and outterritorialize it.

A Fragmentary Recent History:
The Internecine and the Intersectional

Among all other snarls, racism courses most aggressively through the networks of American history but is among the least studied in contemporary moral and political theory.[8] Unacknowledged, racializing practices thrive in our sociopolitical system; the life and work of Anthony, of women's suffrage, modern feminism, or of the presidential bid of

Hillary Clinton prove fruitful sites for investigating these practices. But how could racism simultaneously be invisible or deniable and so ubiquitous? Philosopher Christopher J. Lebron argues that despite a set of decent political commitments, the United States suffers from the national version of bad moral character.[9] The nation's hypocrisy and ambivalence regarding its black population is so habituated that it has become dispositional. The greatest impediment to reversing the bad habits that give rise to bad character is denial that they exist. In the United States, we find not just denial, but well-established *disavowal*— the refusal even to recognize the object of stress. Disavowal is fundamental dishonesty, posing as innocence. "What gets me about the United States," feminist Audre Lorde wrote, "is that it pretends to be honest and therefore has so little room to move toward hope."[10] In the United States, disavowal often cuts a historical figure. The relatively recent existence of chattel slavery and Jim Crow is undeniable, but we cast them into an arc in which all past crimes have been redeemed— current inequities in wealth, access to resources such as health care and education, or criminal sentencing notwithstanding. Our memorial culture reinforces disavowal and the ubiquitous invisibility of racism and white supremacy. Let us continue to look for examples at Anthony and Douglass's former hometown.

Rochester's 2016 racial demographics, according to the Census Bureau, include a population of 41 percent black or African American, 16 percent Hispanic or Latino, and 43 percent white, but visitors to Anthony's grave on the days surrounding the 2016 election appeared to be predominantly white.[11] In Rochester and nationally, the maltreatment of blacks by police was constantly in the news: 2016 brought to attention Justice Department reports on systematic racism in the police departments of Baltimore, Maryland, and Ferguson, Missouri.[12] In 2016 we saw video recordings of the deaths of Philando Castile, Alton Sterling, and Terence Crutcher; they also came to represent the 258 black people who were killed by police in 2016, thirty-nine of them unarmed.[13] The killings were in the news in part through the efforts of the Black Lives Matter (BLM) movement, which began in 2012 with a social media post, responding to the postmortem condemnation of Trayvon Martin and the exoneration of his killer. BLM quickly coalesced into a rallying vision for groups staging protests, lobbying legislators, and challenging news reports; in addition, it inspired both racialized backlash and intramural co-opting.[14] When a BLM rally responding to the deaths of Philando Castile and Alton Sterling took place in downtown Rochester in July of 2016, marchers, predominantly black, were met with police in riot gear, who arrested seventy-four of them.[15] News of the rally began spreading nationally when it became clear that police had arrested only the two black (but no white) reporters covering the event,[16] and as firsthand commentaries and video recording were shared, showing the rough treatment of peaceable attendees, including the tackling and arrest of a black woman as she was being interviewed.[17] Following the event, the Rochester Association of Black Journalists accused Rochester police of bias against blacks.[18]

For some, the July 2016 escalation recalled July 1964, when Rochester erupted into days of so-called race riots that shocked its white residents, in spite of the fact that African Americans had for years attempted to address their segregation in crumbling neighborhoods where rat bites were common, the overt refusal of local companies to employ them in any but menial jobs, and policing tactics that including the threat of dog bites. The final spark for rioting was police brutality, including reports that a police dog bit a child.[19]

During his campaign, Trump was faulted for displaying racial bias, which he denied.[20] Openly racist organizations, such as the Ku Klux Klan and the American Nazi Party, embraced him. The KKK's foremost newspaper, the *Crusader*, devoted its November issue to his celebration and defense. Its former leader, David Duke, as well as a representative of the American Nazi Party, affirmed that their constituency would support Trump as an opportunity to restore white nationalism and to expand their base among less resolute right-wing voters.[21] Trump's campaign officially condemned the KKK and the *Crusader*, but when pressed in person to reject Duke, Trump declined.[22] In July 2016, Trump told Bill O'Reilly of Fox News that Black Lives Matter had "certainly in certain instances" led to the recent assassinations of police officers and had been "essentially calling death to the police"; he added that when elected, he would consider talking "to the attorney general about it or do something."[23] Although right-partisan pundits had declared America a *postracial* society immediately upon Barack Obama's election in 2009, in 2016 racial division in the country still looked substantial. In a recent report, political scientists Brian Schaffner, Matthew MacWilliams, and Tatishe Nteta demonstrate how voters' affirmation of racist and sexist ideologies correlated closely with their votes for Trump.[24]

A racial strain also opened within the moderate and overtly Democratic vote during the organization of the postinauguration Women's March on Washington, when some white feminists responded with incomprehension and denunciation (some pulling out of the event entirely) to black women's concerns about their representation within the march's organizing committees, as well as about an approach to protest activities that could otherwise pose exceptional dangers to people of color.[25] As racial divisions came up in sister marches in different cities, some recalled the 1913 Women's Suffrage Parade: for its organizing heroine, Alice Paul, had asked black women not to participate, and when they came anyway, organizers attempted to segregate them into a "black procession" at the back of the parade. Ida B. Wells and other black women refused, walking between white allies in their state delegations.[26]

What to make of the recurrent internecine conflict over race in the feminist undertaking?[27] Kimberlé Williams Crenshaw introduced the notion of *intersectionality* in 1989 to address the ways that racism and sexism interconnect in everyday life and in the legal system.[28] She writes: "The failure of feminism to interrogate race means that feminism's resistance strategies will often replicate and reinforce the subordination of people of color; likewise, the failure of antiracism to interrogate patriarchy means that antiracism will frequently reproduce the subordination of women."[29]

Early on, Crenshaw identifies the *structural intersectionality* by which we can identify a host of issues facing women who enter shelters to escape violence (e.g., educational, economic, linguistic, racial, child-care related) and the *political intersectionality* or intersectional disempowerment faced predominantly by women of color, who must split their energies between two or more, sometimes opposing, political groups. Where people cannot yet grasp the everyday consequence of intersectionality, we might expect internecine conflict stemming from an inability to discern racially imposed disadvantages and privileges. With the concept now so often cited, however, we cannot fault an intellectual confusion as much as the disavowal that stands in the way of grasping it. I'd like to address that disavowal more directly and, on the way, to gather another theoretical tool for activating the historical assemblage provided by Mount Hope.

Critical History and White Ignorance

In 1873 Nietzsche addressed his German contemporaries in *On the Uses and Disadvantages of History for Life*.[30] Every person and each people require "a certain kind of knowledge of the past," he writes, detailing how monumental, antiquarian, and critical histories suit different needs and achieve different goals.[31] Nietzsche also diagnoses a self-destructive tendency in idealizations of the past. *This* age is witnessing the disadvantageous mingling of antiquarian and monumental history, Nietzsche writes, and has indulged so long in forgetting its own unjustness that it is setting into a lifeless monument. The abuse of history sustains a political culture that can smother the personalities and deeds it monumentalizes. Against the more entrenched approaches of *monumental history* and *antiquarian history*, Nietzsche identifies *critical history* as the form that can free historical action by interrogating it, "bringing it before the tribunal," not out of righteousness or mercy, but backed by the force of "life alone, that dark, driving power that insatiably thirsts for itself"—the desire to live and to realize.

> Sometimes . . . this same life that requires forgetting demands a temporary suspension of this forgetfulness; it wants to be clear as to how unjust the existence of anything—a privilege, a caste, a dynasty, for example—is, and how greatly this thing deserves to perish. Then the past is regarded critically, then one takes the knife to its roots, then one cruelly tramples over every kind of piety. . . . Since we are the outcome of earlier generations, we are also the outcome of their aberrations, passions, and errors, and indeed of their crimes; it is not possible to free oneself wholly of this chain.[32]

Critical history is the mode of judgment practiced for emancipation, especially from the stranglehold of long-standing practices, concealed in historical fictions. Unknown to Nietzsche, in 1852 Frederick Douglass provided an example of the critical historical approach, with his Rochester speech "What to the Slave is the 4th of July?" Like Nietzsche, Douglass allows that history is only relevant where it is necessary for the present and the future.[33] Like Nietzsche, he identifies in a contemporary, idealizing historical trend the enshrining of forgetfulness and injustice, and he begins to display a different form of narrative. Unlike Nietzsche, Douglass is speaking on behalf of 3 million people who are enslaved in actual fact, and unlike Nietzsche, Douglass calls out his nation's hypocrisy to a live crowd, immediately following its most important patriotic holiday. Unlike Nietzsche, Douglass speaks from the position of one who requires critical history as a matter of life and death. Douglass presents "this day and its popular characteristics from the slave's point of view." Slaveholding, racist America, at seventy-six years of age, "is false to the past, false to the present, and solemnly binds herself to be false to the future." The Fourth of July as national celebration is an attempt to monumentalize a shared love of freedom that citizens are unwilling to share; indeed that is premised on enslavement of and contempt for others.

> Your high independence only reveals the immeasurable distance between us. . . . The rich inheritance of justice, liberty, prosperity and independence . . . is shared by you, not me. . . . To drag a man in fetters into the grand illuminated temple of liberty, and call upon

him to join you in joyous anthems, [is] inhuman mockery and sac-
rilegious irony. Do you mean citizens, to mock me, by asking me to
speak today?

Douglass goes on to call out the insincerity of demands that he
soften his tone to win support or engage in reasonable argumenta-
tion about the humanity of the enslaved. "At a time like this, scorching
irony, not convincing argument, is needed," yet Douglass provides the
arguments as well, in a critical-historical form.

He does the same in his autobiography, as when he calls out the
self-congratulatory exposure of white activists on the Underground
Railroad: "I have never approved of the very public manner in which
some of our western friends have conducted what they call the *underground railroad*, but which, I think, by their open declarations, has been
made most emphatically the *upperground railroad*. . . . I feel assured that
those open declarations are a positive evil to the slaves remaining."[34]

Nietzsche, too, notices the psychological need among "helpers" to
receive recognition for their virtue. It is part of a monumental historicizing inclination, linked with ascetic ideals.[35]

Where the monumental form becomes imperative, "the past itself
suffers *harm*: whole segments of it are forgotten, despised, and flow
away."[36] Monumental history encourages the imitation of great acts,
but it can atrophy into a "mimesis unto death" when the acts to be
copied are distorted in the form that reconstitutes them—as, in Douglass's speech, the jubilee made of the Fourth of July drowns out the
stories of blacks who contributed to American independence and of
their descendants, who are barred from it.[37]

Where monumental history urges imitation of an idealized past,
Nietzsche's antiquarian form honors the past generally and excessively.
Antiquarian history treats each element of a historical thing as precious rather than distinguishing between past horrors, banalities, and
achievements. When it becomes imperative, the antiquarian is so dedicated to transmitting stories of past greatness that it becomes blind or
hostile to what is coming into being in and native to his own time.

There are elements of monumental as well as antiquarian history
in Trump's campaign call to "Make America Great Again," and we must
notice, too, how monumental and antiquarian tendencies strain our
embrace of the friendship between Douglass and Anthony. The danger, in both cases, is adopting a form of *willful ignorance* or motivated
inattention; an unawareness that is not, like mere ignorance, a matter
of not yet knowing something. Philosopher Marilyn Frye provides the
examples of white Americans' racialized ignorance of Native American clans, of histories of Asian immigrants to America, and of African

Americans' relationships with ongoing institutional racism. Philosopher Charles Mills designates a special form of willful ignorance, *white ignorance*, to name the prevalent social cognition that tends (among both whites and people of color) to ignore or underestimate black achievements and white brutalities, to deny the existence of white privilege, and to interpret by default any new evidence to support a foundational assurance of white superiority.[38]

Claims for the postracial character of our contemporary American society, as well as any claim that black poverty is the result of indolence or poor judgment, whereas white prosperity is the result of industriousness, exhibits white ignorance in its deliberate form.[39] This is white ignorance as an attempt to make unknown and unknowable, and to encourage disavowal of, the historic record of white wealth in the United States, and to monumentalize a golden vision of the white entrepreneur or go-getter and his black inferior.

Nationally in 2013, the median white family was thirteen times wealthier than the median black family; a 2017 study showed the racial wealth gap persisting, despite controlling for marital status, college education, full-time employment, and a record of lower black than white spending (i.e., "personal responsibility and initiative").[40] Whites have more wealth accumulated, more to share with their families, and are still more institutionally supported (with opportunities such as mortgage loans and federal housing policies) to hold wealth.[41] Yet in the relatively short time from legalized slavery through Jim Crow and to the present, befuddlement has cloaked that wealth, such that it can only be seen as the result of innovation and industriousness. Mills observes:

> The editing of white memory ... enables a self-representation in which differential white privilege, and the need to correct for it, does not exist. ... The erasure of the history of Jim Crow makes it possible to represent the playing field as historically level, so that current black poverty just proves blacks' unwillingness to work. As individual memory is assisted through a larger social memory, so individual amnesia is then assisted by a larger collective amnesia.[42]

The *level historical playing field* is an image we are invited to accept in all postracial discourses, including in the common tirades charging that false claims to victimhood are made by those protesting juridical violence. It is made more subtly when we imagine out the differences between historical actors—for example, when we take the historic friendship of Douglass and Anthony as a matter of untroubled course. Here white ignorance operates as amnesia and erasure. Philosopher Alfred Frankowski writes:

> Antiblack violence may not be communicated solely in the way whites
> censor or restrict the production of memory. It may be found in how
> memory becomes distant, ineffectual, or absent even when it is repre-
> sented. Hyper-visibility sets up the conditions for a political invisibility
> rooted in a particular sense and relation to memory. . . . the history of
> black memorial culture rearranges the visible and invisible in a way that
> produces a selective, naïve, and often problematic memory. It produces
> a memory prone to amnesia resulting in a disempowering agency.[43]

Frankowski is analyzing how memory can be reconstructed into a
form of forgetting, as in memorials and a memorial approach to history that simultaneously acknowledges and denies the force of racism
and white supremacy, precisely by framing it as a relic of the past; consider, for example, Rochester's Frederick Douglass–Susan B. Anthony
Memorial Bridge. This kind of memorializing suggests that wounds
have fully healed and that the present is healthy.[44]

The problem Frankowski identifies in memorial culture runs
throughout the whole of American culture, for by eluding a critical
historical reckoning, we miss the context for mass incarceration.[45]
Though it is not yet the subject of significant public discourse, scholars and journalists have publicized the incredible incarnation rates in
the United States, much of it following from "zero tolerance" sentencing and aggressive policing exacerbated with Ronald Reagan's war on
drugs and the rise of for-profit private prisons.[46] For the critical historian, the fact that African Americans are incarcerated at five to six times
the rate of whites will not be unrelated to current disproportional burdens in black communities.[47] Nor is it unrelated to widespread convict
leasing of blacks in the first decades of the twentieth century or to the
forced labor that built, for example, the United States Steel Corpora-
tion, when blacks in huge numbers were falsely imprisoned and sent to
work in coal mines.[48] Large portions of the American black population
have been captive and at work in forced, uncompensated labor for the
whole span of our national history to date.[49]

An example of a nonamnesiac response to current, apparently progressive events is a 2013 editorial written by Crenshaw and colleagues,
"Why We Can't Celebrate."[50] The authors are addressing the Supreme
Court's decision to protect marriage equality, which came days after its
undermining of the Voting Rights Acts—a primary achievement of 1960s
civil rights activism. In the context of all Americans' relationship to state
power, the editorial asks that we question why America remains de facto
segregated and how current lawmaking will deepen that segregation.

In Douglass's old home of the city of Rochester, African Americans are three times more likely to be poor than non-Latino whites,
and are significantly more likely to be poor than African Americans

nationwide.[51] According to data from 2011 to 2015, in the city of Rochester 14 percent of white children and 50 percent of African American children live in poverty. The poverty rate for children in all groups is rising, but at a significantly higher rate for African Americans.[52] A 2017 state report judged fifteen schools to be failing in the Rochester City School District; five of these have been considered failing for the last ten years.[53]

Rochester proudly, one might say monumentally, publicizes its progressive history, but has not yet linked its more baleful lines to present distresses in a way that enacts progressive solutions. Because its more affluent, whiter residents do so well, this city with the highest extreme poverty rate in the nation among similarly sized cities also boasts suburbs that rank among the nation's best for public schools and quality of life.[54] We can imagine, then, why the softer politics of recognition would appeal to many who do well and would irritate those who do not. Bridges, statues, and street names offer reminders of our racialized history, yet they appear to be the kinds of reminders that Frankowski associates with the calcifying of cultural memory and the atmosphere of neglect that attends it.[55]

Developing upon the work of philosopher Judith Butler, Frankowski suggests that *political mourning* initiates an alternative to amnesia and white ignorance. I read the editorial "Why We Can't Celebrate" as an example of active political mourning. In both Butler and Frankowski's work, the political mourning of a traumatic past is a social practice; it is a way of taking account of how our lives have been transformed by loss.[56] Mourning can also be the way that a political community comes to question its founding conditions and its shared future, or engages in critical history.

Mourning is akin to what philosopher George Yancy calls *unsuturing*, a willingness to be *undone*, in crisis, or seriously troubled by the conditions of one's privilege, and to revise oneself through addressing them.[57] Mourning and unsuturing are healthy psychological responses to finding oneself in a time out of joint, even if one appears to be its beneficiary. Mourning and unsuturing are at the beginning of an epistemologically fair response to finding oneself operating from a state of white ignorance, and they are decent ethical responses to the Adornian insight that "wrong life cannot be lived rightly."[58]

Race Technology and the Countermemorial

We differentiate races in terms of vulnerability to the law, not only insofar as groups will be differently disciplined, but insofar as they experience the threat of being abandoned by law, for example, among border populations of migrant workers. Philosopher Falguni A. Sheth identifies three dimensions within which race functions as a technology for dividing, subduing, and reorganizing populations, and for rendering them more and less vulnerable legally.[59] The racializing of a group begins with marking some observable characteristic, but as populations are divided, that characteristic readily shifts: thus we find in recent American history the "non-whiteness" of Mediterraneans such as Italians and Greeks, of Jews, and of the Irish, and then of their becoming white vis-à-vis more unruly populations, including African Americans as well as racialized immigrants from Latin America, the Caribbean, Asia, and Africa, who are perceived as threats to the social order.[60] "Race locates something that is real," Sheth writes, "the identification of which is always shifting."[61]

In 1996 these racializing gears were at work when Hillary Clinton touted Bill Clinton's Violent Crime Control and Law Enforcement Act for its management of "super-predators" lacking in conscience and empathy, for which we might speculate reasons, but only after we "bring them to heel."[62] Much political hay has since been made of the comment, by the Trump campaign as well as the progressive left. It is the same tension Trump pressurized in 1989 with his calls for the death penalty for the "Central Park Five" and again in 2014, after they were exonerated based on DNA evidence, with Trump still insisting they had to be guilty—if not of the rape, then of something.[63] Reagan drew off the same racist sentiment by conjuring "welfare queens" and "strapping young bucks" and by lamenting the way the Voting Rights Act was humiliating the South. For now, let it suffice to note how easily underlying racist beliefs are tapped, and how readily racism flows.

Mills, as I touched on, details the ways that race acquires power, autonomy, and materiality of its own, beyond the intentions or even the antiracism of individuals. Sheth's study of the ascription of unruliness and of race as technology helps describe the legal mechanism of this transformation. Jacqueline Scott suggests that we think of racism as "the incurable symptom of a congenital disease."[64] She predicts that a primary problem of the twenty-first century will be reconceptualization of racial identity.[65] Can modern liberalism survive a self-critique of its congenitally racist past and of its coeval, segregating institutions?

We will answer for the American experiment, if we do so at all, while the current administration undercuts the legal and ideological supports of liberal democracy. Many of Trump's more intractable supporters embrace white power unapologetically, but among progressives the inheritance of American racism is no less real. By disavowing it, white liberals extend the legacy of those *upperground railroad* workers questioned by Douglass, so eager for the virtuous limelight that we are blind to how we benefit from harm. At present, we are on the verge of being undone in different senses of the word, so it is here again that the fixing image of the stickering ritual at Anthony's grave is apt. That somewhat spontaneous, somewhat authorized activity shows a haunted ambivalence: it represents our desire to honor the past and to participate on the "right side of history," and it presents the juridical and social safety of throngs of white people hastening to a public space. Connected to the tomb of Douglass, and to the relative scarceness of white liberals in equally local, equally contemporary movements for black security, it invites reckoning with our place within the intersections of power.

To affirm the aesthetic and political potential of the stickering ritual, I suggest that we consider it a *countermemorial*. Especially since World War II, countermemorials have been designed as commemorative social acts that resist the invisibility that comes with conspicuous everydayness, in order to open the question of how we will realize the legacy of our collective present.[66] Insofar as it disappears (Anthony's grave is barely visited, most days) and reappears (at politically significant moments), the stickering ritual mirrors an episodic cultural memory, and potentially, with Douglass there to remind us, it could resist schisming into easy narratives of progress. As countermemorial, the stickering ritual and the path between Anthony and Douglas provide a forum, not yet workably accessible to all, but indicative of a democratic experiment that is still entwined with its coercive, racist companion. To take on the site as countermemorial is to let be its relatively unstructured strangeness; to open up to the authentic political mourning it could initiate. Treating the memorial site as countermemorial act opens it to a renewed critical history, for monumental and antiquarian artifacts are the proper subjects of critique precisely where we have invested in them, but have not yet realized, or righted, their legacy.

The stickering ritual is an invitation to practice critical history, at a moment when—as both Nietzsche and Douglass would appreciate—many Americans are bewildered by historical amnesia and rigidly fixed on an illusion of restored national greatness. Economic, legal, and carceral injustice, all of which work by racializing while denying racism, cannot be pushed to the margins of a viable progressive political movement, nor, as specters raised by a countermemorial, should they remain phantoms of merely quiet contemplation.

Notes

1. Midge Wilson and Kathy Russel, *Divided Sisters* (New York: Anchor Books, 1996), 29–35. See also Michael J. Brown's chapter in this volume.

2. Susan B. Anthony, proprietor, *The Revolution*, February 4, 1869, vol. 3, no.5.

3. "Elizabeth Cady Stanton: A Passionate Mind," accessed July 6, 2017, https://www.albany.edu/history/digital/stanton/law.html.

4. Monee Fields-White, "The Root: How Racism Tainted Women's Suffrage," NPR, March 25, 2011, http://www.npr.org/2011/03/25/13484 9480/the-root-how-racism-tainted-womens-suffrage.

5. Chris Fien, "Mayor Lovely Warren on Trump's Immigration Ban," Youtube.com, accessed January 29, 2017, https://www.youtube.com/watch?v=GF9ZcLnZZU4, 7. See also Christine A. Kray's chapter in this volume.

6. Douglass's autobiography contains many examples: *Narrative of the Life of Frederick Douglass* (Mineola, NY: Dover Publications, 1995).

7. Gilles Deleuze and Félix Guattari, *A Thousand Plateaus: Capitalism and Schizophrenia*, trans. Brian Massumi (Minneapolis: University of Minnesota Press, 1987); see esp. 3–25.

8. For a survey see Charles W. Mills, "White Ignorance," in *Race and Epistemologies of Ignorance*, ed. Shannon Sullivan and Nancy Tuana (Albany: State University of New York Press, 2007), 11–38.

9. Christopher J. Lebron, *The Color of Our Shame: Race and Justice in Our Time* (Oxford: Oxford University Press, 2013).

10. Audre Lorde, "Trip to Russia," *Sister Outsider* (Berkeley, CA: Crossing Press/Random House, 2007), 28.

11. United States Census Bureau, accessed July 6, 2017, www.census. gov/quickfacts/table/PST045215/3663000. See also Christine A. Kray's chapter in this volume.

12. United States Department of Justice, Civil Rights Division, "Investigation of the Baltimore City Police Department," August 10, 2016, https://www.justice.gov/crt/file/883296/download; United States Department of Justice, Civil Rights Division, "Investigation of the Ferguson Police Department," March 4, 2015, https://www.justice.gov/sites/default/files/opa/press-releases/attachments/2015/03/04/ferguson_police_department_report.pdf.

13. "The Counted: People Killed by Police in the US," *Guardian*, accessed July 6, 2017, https://www.theguardian.com/us-news/ng-interactive/2015/jun/01/the-counted-police-killings-us-database; for Philando Castile see New Day, "Woman Streams Graphic Video of Boyfriend Shot by Police," CNN.com, July 7, 2016, http://www.cnn.com/videos/us/2016/07/07/graphic-video-minnesota-police-shooting-philando-castile-ryan-young-pkg-nd.cnn; for Alton Sterling see "New Video Released of Alton Sterling Shooting," CBS News, July 6, 2016, https://www.youtube.

com/watch?v=pdGXhSQvTKc; for Terence Crutcher see "Video Shows Police Shooting Unarmed Oklahoma Man Terence Crutcher," *New York Daily News*, video, September 19, 2016, https://www.youtube.com/watch?v=n9F-Bxwu3_Y.

14. Alicia Garza, "A HerStory of the #BlackLivesMatterMovement," accessed June 20, 2017, http://blacklivesmatter.com/herstory/.

15. Ryan C. Miller, "More Than 70 Arrested at Black Lives Matter Protest in Rochester," *Democrat & Chronicle*, July 9, 2016, http://www.democratandchronicle.com/story/news/2016/07/09/dozens-arrested-during-black-lives-matter-protest/86890270/.

16. Morgan Winsor, "Black Reporter's Arrest during Rochester, New York, Protest Captured on Live TV," ABCnews.com, July 9, 2016, http://abcnews.go.com/US/police-arrest-74-people-including-reporters-protest-rochester/story?id=40459279.

17. The woman, who had not been part of the event initially, and was standing and calmly facing a reporter, was subsequently charged with disorderly conduct. Shachar Peled, "NY Protester Arrested on Camera While Talking to Reporter," CNN.com, July 14, 2016, http://www.cnn.com/2016/07/14/us/ny-protester-rushed-by-police-during-interview/.

18. Todd Clausen, "Black Journalists Association Claims Bias in Detaining 2 Reporters," *Democrat & Chronicle*, July 13, 2016, http://www.democratandchronicle.com/story/news/2016/07/13/rochester-association-of-black-journalists-says-rochester-police-revealed-bias-arrest-reporters/87031928/.

19. For a recent documentary, see *July '64*, directed by Carvin Eison, produced by Chris Christopher, released February 14, 2006, http://www.pbs.org/independentlens/july64/film.html.

20. See, for example, Nicholas Kristof, "Is Trump a Racist?," *New York Times*, July 23, 2016, https://www.nytimes.com/2016/07/24/opinion/sunday/is-donald-trump-a-racist.html.

21. KKK newspaper, Trump Endorsement Issue, accessed July 6, 2017, https://www.scribd.com/document/329628320/KKK-Newspaper-Trump-Endorsement-Issue (page subsequently removed); Peter Holley, "KKK's Official Newspaper Supports Donald Trump for President," *Washington Post*, November 2, 2016, https://www.washingtonpost.com/news/post-politics/wp/2016/11/01/the-kkks-official-newspaper-has-endorsed-donald-trump-for-president/?utm_term=.49722440436b; Camila Domonoske, "Former KKK Leader David Duke Says 'Of Course' Trump Voters Are His Voters," *The Two-Way*, NPR, August 5, 2016, http://www.npr.org/sections/thetwo-way/2016/08/05/488802494/former-kkk-leader-david-duke-says-of-course-trump-voters-are-his-voters.

22. CNN's *State of the Union*, "Trump on David Duke: 'I Know Nothing about White Supremacists,'" *CNN Press Room*, February 28, 2016, http://cnnpressroom.blogs.cnn.com/2016/02/28/trump-on-david-duke-i-know-nothing-about-white-supremacists.

23. Fox News Shows, Interviews, "Donald Trump: 'We Have to Demand Law and Order,'" July 19, 2016, http://www.foxnews.com/transcript/2016/07/19/donald-trump-have-to-demand-law-and-order.html.

24. For the widespread use of term "postracial" during Obama's presidential campaign, see Daniel Schorr, "A New 'Post-Racial' Political Era in America," NPR, January 28, 2008, https://www.npr.org/templates/story/story.php?storyId=18489466. Brian F. Schaffner, Matthew MacWilliams, Tatishe Nteta, "Explaining White Polarization in the 2016 Vote for President: The Sobering Role of Racism and Sexism" (paper presented at the The U.S. Elections of 2016: Domestic and International Aspects Conference, January 8–9, 2017, IDC Herzliya Campus, https://people.umass.edu/schaffne/schaffner_et_al_IDC_conference.pdf). We now know that 52 percent of white women (and 63 percent of white men) voted for Trump. "Election 2016, Exit Polls," CNN.com, November 23, 2016, http://www.cnn.com/election/results/exit-polls. The black vote went overwhelming Democratic: over 89 percent for Clinton (94 percent of black women voted for Clinton) though some white commentators still blamed poor voter turnout among blacks for Clinton's loss. See, for example, Omri Ben-Shahar, "The Non-Voters Who Decided the Election: Trump Won Because of Lower Democratic Turnout," *Forbes*, November 17, 2016, https://www.forbes.com/sites/omribenshahar/2016/11/17/the-non-voters-who-decided-the-election-trump-won-because-of-lower-democratic-turnout/#e38de3953ab1.

25. Farah Stockman, "Women's March on Washington Opens Contentious Dialogues about Race," *New York Times,* January 9, 2017, https://www.nytimes.com/2017/01/09/us/womens-march-on-washington-opens-contentious-dialogues-about-race.html?_r=1.

26. Michelle Bernard, "Despite the Tremendous Risk, African American Women Marched for Suffrage, Too," *Washington Post*, March 3, 2013, https://www.washingtonpost.com/blogs/she-the-people/wp/2013/03/03/despite-the-tremendous-risk-african-american-women-marched-for-suffrage-too/?utm_term=.362771682251.

27. In the interest of providing a brief introductory history, I am not addressing the schisms and connections made between/within second wave feminism, womanism, and black feminism, leading up to Crenshaw's coining of *intersectionality*. For analysis see Angela Davis, *Women, Race, and Class* (New York: Random House, 1981); Layli Phillips, *The Womanist Reader* (New York: Routledge, 2006); and Patricia Hill Collins, *Black Feminist Thought: Knowledge, Consciousness, and the Politics of Empowerment* (New York: Routledge, 2000).

28. Kimberlé Williams Crenshaw, "Demarginalizing the Intersection of Race and Sex: A Black Feminist Critique of Antidiscrimination Doctrine, Feminist Theory, and Antiracist Politics," *University of Chicago Legal Forum* 140 (January 1989): 139–67; and "Mapping the Margins: Intersectionality, Identity Politics, and Violence against Women of Color," reprinted in

Critical Race Theory: The Key Writings That Formed the Movement, ed. Kimberlé Crenshaw, Neil Gotanda, Gary Peller, and Kendall Thomas (New York: New Press, 1995), 357–83.

For a more recent statement in the popular press, see Kimberlé Crenshaw, "Why Intersectionality Can't Wait," *Washington Post*, September 24, 2015, https://www.washingtonpost.com/news/in-theory/wp/2015/09/24/why-intersectionality-cant-wait/?utm_term=.affd3c22b347.

29. Crenshaw et al., *Critical Race Theory*, 360.

30. Friedrich Nietzsche, *On the Uses and Disadvantages of History for Life*, *Untimely Meditations*, ed. Daniel Breazeale, trans. R. J. Hollingdale (Cambridge: Cambridge University Press, 2016), 57–213. All quotes are from this edition.

31. Ibid., 77.

32. Ibid., 76–77.

33. "What to the Slave Is the 4th of July?," delivered July 5, 1852, in *Great Speeches by Frederick Douglass*, ed. James Daley (New York: Dover Publications, 2013). All quotes are from this edition, 33–36. A case for Douglass's employment of a critical historical approach could be made based on many of his writings, including his autobiography, *Narrative of the Life of Frederick Douglass*, along with essays such as "The Church and Prejudice" (1841), "John Brown" (1881), and "The Race Problem" (1890). Although Nietzsche does not seem to have read Douglass, a productive juxtaposition of their positions is provided by Christa Davis Acampora in "Unlikely Illuminations: Nietzsche and Frederick Douglass on Power, Struggle, and the *Aisthesis* of Freedom," in *Critical Affinities: Nietzsche and African American Thought*, ed. Jacqueline Scott and A. Todd Franklin (Albany: State University of New York Press, 2006), 175–202.

34. Douglass, *Narrative*, 60.

35. See, for examples, Friedrich Nietzsche, *On the Genealogy of Morals*, trans. Walter Kaufmann and R. J. Hollingdale (New York: Random House Vintage Books Edition, 1989), esp. section 3, as well as *Human, All Too Human*, trans. R. J. Hollingdale (Cambridge: Cambridge University Press, 1996), esp. vol. 1, section 2.

36. Nietzsche, *Uses and Disadvantages of History*, 70–71.

37. I have borrowed "mimesis unto death" from Max Horkheimer and Theodore W. Adorno, *Dialectic of Enlightenment* (New York: Continuum, 1996), 57.

38. Marilyn Frye, *The Politics of Reality: Essays in Feminist Thought* (Freedom, CA: Crossing Press, 1983); Charles Mills, *The Racial Contract* (Ithaca, NY: Cornell University Press, 1997); Mills's "White Ignorance" is the first chapter of *Race and Epistemologies of Ignorance*; in its introduction, the editors reference the works named in this note.

39. Neighboring Buffalo school board member Carl Paladino makes this claim; see Glenn Blain, "Carl Paladino Stirs Outrage with 'Stop Blaming White People Month' Meme," *New York Daily News*, March 14, 2017,

http://www.nydailynews.com/news/politics/carl-paladino-stirs-outrage-stop-blaming-white-people-meme-article-1.2997971.

40. Amy Traub, Laura Sullivan, Tatjana Meschede, and Tom Shapiro, "The Asset Value of Whiteness: Understanding the Racial Wealth Gap," *Demos*, 2017, http://www.demos.org/sites/default/files/publications/Asset%20Value%20of%20Whiteness_0.pdf.

41. For the analysis of federal housing policy, see Richard Rothstein, *The Color of Law: A Forgotten History of How Our Government Segregated America* (New York: W. W. Norton, 2017).

42. Mills, "White Ignorance," 31. Mills utilizes wealth gap data collected and analyzed by Thomas M. Shapiro, *The Hidden Cost of Being African American: How Wealth Perpetuates Inequality* (New York: Oxford University Press, 2004). George Yancy likewise analyzes "the historically contingent struts of white normative and institutional power, which would call into question such a grand gesture of white self-creation 'out of nothing,'" in his introduction to *White Self-Criticality beyond Anti-Racism*, ed. George Yancy (Lanham, MD: Lexington Books, 2015), xvi.

43. Alfred Frankowski, *The Post-Racial Limits of Memorialization* (Lanham, MD: Lexington Books, 2015), 23.

44. Ibid., 18–22.

45. Ibid., 9.

46. Michelle Alexander, *The New Jim Crow: Mass Incarceration in the Age of Color Blindness* (New York: New Press, 2010).

47. NAACP, "Criminal Justice Fact Sheet," accessed July 6, 2017, http://www.naacp.org/criminal-justice-fact-sheet/; Federal Bureau of Prisons, "Inmate Race," accessed July 6, 2017, https://www.bop.gov/about/statistics/statistics_inmate_race.jsp; Prison Policy Initiative, "Mass Incarceration: The Whole Pie 2017," accessed July 6, 2017, https://www.prisonpolicy.org/reports/pie2017.html.

48. Leon F. Litwack, *Been in the Storm So Long: The Aftermath of Slavery* (New York: Random House Vintage Books, 1979) and *Trouble in Mind* (New York: Random House Vintage Books, 1998). Douglas Blackmon, *Slavery by Another Name: The Re-Enslavement of Black Americans from the Civil War to World War II* (New York: Random House Anchor Books, 2008).

49. Lisa Guenther, *Solitary Confinement: Social Death and Its Afterlives* (Minneapolis: University of Minnesota Press, 2013).

50. Devon Carbado, Kimberlé Williams Crenshaw, and Cheryl Harris, "Why We Can't Celebrate," *Nation*, July 8, 2013, https://www.thenation.com/article/why-we-cant-celebrate/.

51. Strategic Community Intervention, LLC, prepared for ACT Rochester and The Community Foundation, *Poverty and Self-Sufficiency in the Nine-County Greater Rochester Area*, Special Update, September 2016, http://www.actrochester.org/sites/default/files/2016%20Poverty%20and%20Financial%20Self-Sufficiency%20Report.pdf, 13.

52. ACT Rochester, "Family Support: Children in Poverty, by Race/Ethnicity," Center for Governmental Research, Inc., accessed July 6, 2017, http://www.actrochester.org/children-youth/family-support/children-poverty/children-poverty-by-race-ethnicity; ACT Rochester, "Academic Achievement: Education Levels of Adults by Race/Ethnicity," Center for Governmental Research, Inc., accessed July 6, 2017, http://www.act rochester.org/education/academic-achievement/education-attainment-levels-people-25-and-older/education-levels.

53. Office of Governor Andrew M. Cuomo, Policy Office, Education Team, and Division of Budget, "The State of New York's Failing Schools, 2015 Report," https://s3.amazonaws.com/bncore/wp-content/uploads/2015/02/Cuomos-NYSFailingSchoolsReport.pdf; Ali Touhey, "State Report: 15 Rochester City Schools Are Failing," RochesterFirst.com, February 26, 2015, http://www.rochesterfirst.com/news/state-report-15-rochester-city-schools-are-failing/189243369. Independent research confirms a clear-cut correlation between low test scores and poverty (while researchers continue to disagree about the best policy for addressing the problem within struggling and failing schools). The Fiscal Policy Institute, "The State of New York 'IS' Failing Schools: New York Should Address the Major Reason Schools 'Fail'—Child Poverty," March 17, 2015, http://fiscalpolicy.org/wp-content/uploads/2015/03/Schools-and-poverty-brief-final2-031715.pdf; John M. Bacheller, "Poverty in Upstate New York Cities: Social and Educational Impacts," November 18, 2015, http://www.rockinst.org/forumsandevents/2015/Bacheller_Presentation.pdf.

54. Edward J. Doherty, "Benchmarking Rochester's Poverty: A 2015 Update and Deeper Analysis of Poverty in the City of Rochester," Rochester Area Community Foundation and ACT Rochester, http://www.act rochester.org/sites/default/files/Poverty%20Report%20Update%20 2015-0108.pdf; *US News and World Report*, Real Estate, Best Places Rankings, accessed July 6, 2017, http://realestate.usnews.com/places/new-york/rochester.

55. Frankowski, *Post-Racial Limits*, 67–69, 76.

56. Judith Butler, *Precarious Life: The Powers of Mourning and Violence* (London: Verso, 2004).

57. Yancy, introduction to *White Self-Criticality*. Yancy borrows this use of the concept of *troubling* from Judith Butler, for example in *Giving an Account of Oneself* (New York: Fordham University Press, 2005).

58. Theodor Adorno, *Minimia Moralia: Reflections from Damaged Life*, trans. E. F. N. Jephcott (New York: Verso, 1978), section 18, "Refuge for the Homeless," 39.

59. Falguni A. Sheth, *Toward a Political Philosophy of Race* (Albany: State University of New York Press, 2009), 38, 129–43.

60. Charles W. Mills makes the same observation in *From Class to Race: Essays in White Marxism and Black Radicalism* (Lanham, MD: Rowman & Littlefield, 2003), 182. Exploration of race as technology is undertaken by

Camisha Russell, *The Assisted Reproduction of Race: Thinking through Race as Reproductive Technology* (Bloomington: Indiana University Press, forthcoming 2018).

61. Sheth, *Political Philosophy of Race*, 26.

62. A video and accompanying transcript of the January 25, 1996, speech is available at https://www.c-span.org/video/?69606-1/mrs-clinton-campaign-speech. On the subsequent apology, see Jonathan Capehart, "Hillary Clinton on 'Superpredator' Remarks: 'I Shouldn't Have Used Those Words,'" *Washington Post*, February 25, 2016, https://www.washingtonpost.com/blogs/post-partisan/wp/2016/02/25/hillary-clinton-responds-to-activist-who-demanded-apology-for-superpredator-remarks/?utm_term=.f535801bd024. Clinton's supporters point to her evenhanded narrative throughout the speech and the liberal initiative of which it speaks, some denying outright the racialized language and its employment as a political dog whistle. Clinton's reference to super-predators (as well as examples from other politicians that follow) match Sheth's category of the "unruly." See Sheth, *Political Philosophy of Race*, 26–29.

63. Benjy Sarlin, "Donald Trump Says Central Park Five Are Guilty, Despite DNA Evidence," NBC News, October 7, 2016, http://www.nbcnews.com/politics/2016-election/donald-trump-says-central-park-five-are-guilty-despite-dna-n661941.

64. Quoted in Frankowski, *Post-Racial Limits*, 106. See also Jacqueline Scott, "Racial Nihilism as Racial Courage," *Graduate Faculty Philosophy Journal* 35, nos. 1–2 (2014): 297–330.

65. Jacqueline Scott, "The Price of the Ticket: A Genealogy and Revaluation on Race," in *Critical Affinities*, ed. Scott and Franklin, 149–71.

66. Frankowski studies counter-memorialists (*Post-Racial Limits*, 25–45). He presents Holocaust memorial sites as points of juxtaposition to American memorials for race-related atrocities. See also James E. Young, *The Stages of Memory* (Amherst: University of Massachusetts Press, 2016), esp. chap. 6; and Jonathan Bach, "Memory Landscapes and the Labor of the Negative in Berlin," *International Journal of Politics, Culture, and Society* 26, no. 1 (March 2013): 31–40.

Chapter Twenty-Four

BEWARE! BENEVOLENT PATRIARCHY

Election 2016 and Why No One Can Save Us but Ourselves

Jamia Wilson

From the trailblazing work of journalist, suffragist, and antilynching activist Ida B. Wells to Bree Newsom, an activist who removed the Confederate flag from South Carolina's statehouse grounds in 2015, black women have charted a long roadmap that can teach our white sisters a considerable amount about claiming freedom.

While reflecting on how black women and other women of color continue to develop and expand their political and cultural power despite high odds, I often think about Toni Morrison's wisdom that she shared in a *New York Times* interview in 1971 and reiterated in her novel *Sula*: "And she had nothing to fall back on: not maleness, not whiteness, not ladyhood, not anything. And out of the profound desolation of her reality she may very well have invented herself."[1]

Women of color have long known that no one is coming to save us. Since an entire political economy and its legacy was built on keeping black women in "our place" as the literal means of production, we've had to serve as our own saviors to survive and take ownership of our liberation.

From Election Day 2016 to President Donald Trump's deployment of the "Global Gag Rule"[2] and the "Muslim Ban," one question has plagued me: When will the weight of complicity force white women who voted for Trump to realize that they are ultimately sacrificing their own rights while they wantonly threaten mine?

As I contemplate the anxiety and racial resentment that likely drove 52 percent of white women voters to prioritize benevolent sexism's patronizing and watered-down promises of white privilege, I look to historic lessons to deeply understand their motivations for trading gender justice to protect their proximity to white male power.[3]

Although I first encountered the terms benevolent patriarchy and benevolent sexism during lively "fireside chats" with other Christian feminists, I discovered the depths of its political meaning during the 2016 election. According to these discussions, benevolent patriarchy is the idea that true liberty or spiritual absolution must be earned and granted by a patriarchal institution and/or its surrogates, and benevolent sexism is in large part a function of that belief system, which defines womanhood by placing stereotypically feminine characteristics and behaviors on a pedestal, while pressuring women and girls to conform to a narrow and confining ideal. While this phenomenon takes on many incarnations and often masks itself as altruism or chivalry as opposed to hostile or oppressive sexism, one constant remains—cisgender white maleness is centered, and everyone else is mitigated by their closeness to it, or at least compliance with its ideals.

Election 2016 and its immediate aftermath taught us that women lose when we ignore history's repeated lesson that power is taken and never freely relinquished. Through the most divisive and inflammatory election cycle of our lifetime, the 24/7 news cycle weaponized our cultural obsession with white patriarchal authority so much that it seemed to reinforce some women's implicit bias against women's leadership—including their own.

Though much attention has been paid to political science research demonstrating that voters who held hostile views toward women in June 2016 were more likely to support Trump's candidacy,[4] there's been less focus on the cyclic reality that *Vox*'s Emily Crockett explored a week after Election Day. She wrote, "benevolent sexism is supposed to protect women from hostile sexism, and hostile sexism is supposed to keep women in line with the ideals of benevolent sexism."[5]

While the media has covered what CNN pundit Van Jones described as an "economic-anxiety"-ridden "whitelash"[6] that contributed to Trump's victory, the public conversation about a backlash against feminists (or what Kellyanne Conway, counselor to the president, spins as "postfeminism") has been less prominent.

This version of sugarcoated patriarchy is fueled by celebrating paternalistic praise and rejecting women that don't conform to so-called "positive" stereotypes. Those stereotypes include unfounded ideas that render women inherently compassionate, forgiving, intuitive, or deferential to toxic masculinity. This informs how some media outlets reported that Secretary Clinton lost favor with voters because they claimed she lacked these traits in both her messaging and presentation.

I didn't believe the hype that Secretary Clinton was losing ground with some conservative and independent women voters until I saw this play out firsthand in my personal life. On October 16, 2016, like 24 million other Americans, I watched presidential candidate Donald Trump's apology video on Facebook, following the release of a recording with *Access Hollywood*'s Billy Bush in 2005 that was lewd and misogynistic.[7]

Following Trump's quick and shoddy admission of misconduct, he pivoted to a statement minimizing the egregiousness of his actions by accusing former President Bill Clinton of abusing women, and naming Hillary Clinton as an accomplice who "bullied, shamed, and intimidated his victims."[8]

I ventured into the Facebook comment section attached to Trump's apology video, hoping to see women from all walks of life condemn Trump for shirking responsibility, decry his attempt to leverage the spectacle to victim-blame his female opponent, and hold him accountable for diminishing the gravity of his actions' impact on the women he harassed. Instead, the first comment Facebook's algorithm showed me indicated that far too many women have become ambivalent or downright accepting of benevolent sexism as legitimate.

After I adjusted my glasses to make sure I was reading correctly, I noticed my former elementary school classmate's comment clearly at the top of the FB comment section of Trump's apology post. I reread in disbelief her statement of gratitude to Mr. Trump as a good example for her daughter, and for something to the effect of teaching kids "that presidential candidates can be real and tell it like it is."

I scrolled through the comment section in search of solidarity, but instead I witnessed some women hailing Trump as "honest," "sincere," and "real" by apologizing and speaking about his mistakes, while mentioning Bill Clinton's shortcomings (although he wasn't running) and calling Secretary Clinton "crooked," "deceitful," and "a liar."[9]

My mouth fell agape, as I noted that my former classmate who had previously touted the importance of equal pay and women's leadership ended her declaration of support by relegating Trump's references to "grab[bing women] . . . by the pussy" as innocuous locker-room-style talk.[10]

This telling Facebook comment is just one example of how a majority of white women voters appear to hold the belief that a more generous and benign brand of patriarchy will protect their privileges and reward them with freedoms if they are complicit with its demands. Many of the Trump supporters I encountered in the comment section of the aforementioned post perceived the media's scrutiny of his vulgar rhetoric as a distraction from what they celebrated as his commitments to protecting US borders, being tough on crime, and "putting America first." His deployment of dog-whistle politics appeared to be working, because they seemed to prioritize policies that had racist and imperialistic underpinnings but were shrouded in patriotic messaging.

The tentacles of benevolent sexism's inherent racism are rooted in history but remain present today. From the racist terrorism of the Charleston, South Carolina, church shooter Dylan Roof, who attempted to justify his violence as a crusade to "save" white women when he said to his black victims, "I have to do it. You rape our women and you're taking over our country,"[11] to Trump's references to "taking back our country"[12] by labeling Mexican immigrants as rapists and "bad hombres"[13] as a reference to protecting the virtues of (white) womanhood, benevolent sexism and patriarchy present a vision for "Making America Great Again."[14] Such a vision claims to safeguard white women's entitlement and access to safety, privilege, and protection at the cost of communities with a lot more to lose.

In the aftermath of Trump's inauguration, black women remain at the front lines of the resistance movement. Just a few examples of women-of-color elected officials who are pushing back against discriminatory policies advanced by the Trump Administration include Rep. Maxine Waters, who is leading the charge to impeach Trump,[15] and Senator Kamala Harris, who remained persistent during a Senate hearing despite being told to be "courteous."[16] Beyond Capitol Hill, black women from across the country mobilized in Washington, DC, on September 30, 2017, for the March for Black Women, part of the scheduled March for Racial Justice,"[17] and spoke truth to power from White House press briefings and beyond.[18]

Frederick Douglass warned us that "power concedes nothing without a demand. It never did, and it never will." His prophecy came true in the 2016 election, and it will again if the majority of women fail to claim their power in 2018 and beyond. Until women who continue to cash the empty promises of benevolent patriarchy's blank checks learn to share and build power without conceding it to maintain the threadbare rewards of a slightly elevated but still subjugated status, we'll keep running in place, without moving forward.

Notes

1. Toni Morrison, "What the Black Woman Thinks about Women's Lib," *New York Times Magazine*, August 22, 1971, 63.

2. United States Department of State, Office of the Spokesperson, "Protecting Life in Global Health Assistance," news release, May 15, 2017,

https://www.state.gov/r/pa/prs/ps/2017/05/270866.htm. The global "gag rule" blocks US family-planning funds, as well as State Department, USAID, and Department of Defense funding, from global health assistance programs that use non-US governmental funds to provide abortion services, counseling, and referrals, or that advocate for liberalization of abortion laws in their countries.

3. "2016 Election Results," CNN.com, November 23, 2016, http://www.cnn.com/election/results.

4. Carly Wayne, Nicholas Valentino, and Marzio Oceno, "How Sexism Drives Support for Donald Trump," *Washington Post*, October 23, 2016, https://www.washingtonpost.com/news/monkey-cage/wp/2016/10/23/how-sexism-drives-support-for-donald-trump/?utm_term=.6ba44a12e15a.

5. Emily Crockett, "Why Misogyny Won," *Vox*, November 15, 2016, https://www.vox.com/identities/2016/11/15/13571478/trump-president-sexual-assault-sexism-misogyny-won.

6. Josiah Ryan, "'This Was a Whitelash': Van Jones' Take on the Election Results," CNN.com, November 9, 2016, http://www.cnn.com/2016/11/09/politics/van-jones-results-disappointment-cnntv/index.html.

7. Donald J. Trump, "Donald J. Trump" Facebook page, video, October 7, 2016, https://www.facebook.com/DonaldTrump/videos/10157844642270725/.

8. Ibid.

9. Ibid.

10. "Transcript: Donald Trump's Taped Comments about Women," *New York Times*, October 8, 2016, https://www.nytimes.com/2016/10/08/us/donald-trump-tape-transcript.html.

11. Lisa Wade, "How 'Benevolent Sexism' Drove Dylann Roof's Racist Massacre," *Washington Post*, June 21, 2015, https://www.washingtonpost.com/posteverything/wp/2015/06/21/how-benevolent-sexism-drove-dylann-roofs-racist-massacre/?utm_term=.378c149a5f3d.

12. Dan Nowicki, "Trump to Phoenix: 'Don't Worry, We'll Take Our Country Back,'" *USA Today*, July 12, 2015, https://www.usatoday.com/story/news/politics/elections/2016/2015/07/12/donald-trump-talks-immigration-phoenix-visit/30042291/.

13. "Donald Trump: We Need to Get Out 'Bad Hombres'—CNN Video," CNN.com, October 19, 2016, https://www.cnn.com/videos/politics/2016/10/19/third-presidential-debate-trump-immigration-bad-hombres-sot.cnn.

14. Karen Tumulty, "How Donald Trump Came Up with 'Make America Great Again,'" *Washington Post*, January 18, 2017, https://www.washingtonpost.com/politics/how-donald-trump-came-up-with-make-america-great-again/2017/01/17/fb6acf5e-dbf7-11e6-ad42-f3375f271c9c_story.html?utm_term=.afca471cde1f.

15. Natasha Geiling, "Maxine Waters, Patron Saint of Resistance Politics," ThinkProgress.com, May 31, 2017, https://thinkprogress.org/maxine-waters-leads-the-resistance-2a6beb3873f8/.

16. Abby Hamblin, "Watch Kamala Harris Carry On after 'Courtesy' Lecture from Male Senator," *San Diego Union Tribune*, June 7, 2017, http://www.sandiegouniontribune.com/opinion/the-conversation/sd-kamala-harris-silenced-senate-hearing-20170607-htmlstory.html.

17. Rachel Chason, "'Let the Black Women Lead': Marches Converge on D.C. to Highlight Racial Injustice," *Washington Post*, September 30, 2017, https://www.washingtonpost.com/local/let-the-black-women-lead-marches-converge-on-dc-to-highlight-racial-injustice/2017/09/30/aa213ecc-a612-11e7-b14f-f41773cd5a14_story.html?noredirect=on&utm_term=.01f7d5cb70da.

18. Nia-Malika Henderson, "April Ryan Asked the Most Important Question of the Trump Presidency," CNN.com, March 30, 2017, http://www.cnn.com/2017/03/29/politics/april-ryan-sean-spicer-trump-presidency/index.html.

EPILOGUE

Public Memory, White Supremacy, and Reproductive Justice in the Trump Era

Tamar W. Carroll, Hinda Mandell, and Christine A. Kray

Donald Trump's surprise victory necessitated a rethinking of narratives of both self and nation, and a reimagining of the future for many feminists and others on the left. Misogyny and white nationalism, as we saw in parts 1 through 3, fueled Trump's campaign and victory; it is thus fitting that the election inspired a new, multiracial women's movement with a broad and inclusive social justice agenda. The planning of the Women's March to coincide with Trump's inauguration sparked a debate about the best methods to realize an intersectional feminism, a necessity that is dedicated to dismantling the many "systems of oppression" governing women's lives.[1] On January 21, 2017, more than 5 million people worldwide participated in 635 reported marches in the United States and at least 261 marches abroad, in "what was likely the largest single-day demonstration in recorded U.S. history." The Women's March was notable for the diversity of participants, who spanned generations and racial and ethnic groups, as well as for their numbers and geographic range.[2]

Leading up to the 2016 election and in its aftermath, many of the marchers had participated in the online "intimate publics" described by Gina Masullo Chen and Kelsey Whipple in this volume; those social media groups as well as "huddles" inspired by the Women's March itself led to the formation of hundreds of new, community-based women's groups, which dedicated themselves to involvement in local government and encouraging women to run for office in an effort to transform the American political system from the ground up.[3] In November 2017, a record number of women candidates and their grassroots supporters led the Democratic Party to a surprise upset in the Virginia House of Delegates, while Black women's high turnout and almost uniform support for Democrat Doug Jones proved decisive in Jones's December 2017 victory over Republican Roy Moore in the Alabama special election for the US Senate.[4] A year after the first Women's March, on the weekend of January 21, 2018, hundreds of thousands of protestors again marched through cities across the United States and the world, including 300,000 in Chicago and 500,000 in Los Angeles.[5] The organizers of the Women's March selected Las Vegas, in key battleground state Nevada, to launch their "Power to the Polls" rally and stated goal of registering at least 1 million voters in time for the 2018 midterm elections.[6] Nationally, a record number of women are running for US House and Senate seats in the 2018 midterms elections, with 330 Democratic and ninety-three Republican women likely to run for the House, along with fifty-two women running or likely to run for the Senate.[7]

Women's anger and determination to achieve more equitable gender relations have also manifested in the powerful #MeToo social movement against sexual harassment. In early October 2017, the *New York Times* published allegations of sexual assault and harassment by film mogul Harvey Weinstein that spanned decades, including accusations by actresses Rose McGowan and Ashley Judd.[8] The report sparked more women, many of them celebrities, to come forward with complaints against Weinstein, including Gwyneth Paltrow, Angelina Jolie, and Uma Thurman, resulting in Weinstein's termination from his company.[9] On October 15, actress Alyssa Milano urged women who had experienced sexual harassment or assault to share their stories with the hashtag #MeToo on social media, unleashing a flood of posts, including nearly a million tweets in forty-eight hours and 12 million Facebook posts, comments, and reactions in twenty-four hours by 4.7 million users, from women across all walks of life, both in the United States and internationally.[10]

The sheer volume of testimonies along with the high-publicity charges inspired women in many industries, ranging from academia to banking, comedy, media, politics, restaurants, sports, and tech also to come forward with their own charges of sexual harassment in the workplace. The #MeToo movement has resulted in news coverage of sexual harassment of, among others, hotel housekeepers, women on the assembly line at a Ford plant in Chicago, and farmworkers—all of which groups are disproportionately women of color and often in vulnerable economic circumstances.[11] However, the initial focus on female celebrities, almost all white, and the fact that Black activist Tarana Burke had coined the "Me Too" movement in 2007 to reassure young women of color that they were not alone, but was only belatedly recognized for her work, drew attention to the ways in which race and class shape women's experiences, including of workplace harassment and assault, as well as society's attention to their voices.[12]

E.1. Women wearing pussyhats lead the Second Women's March, Seneca Falls, NY, January 20, 2018. Photo: Tamar W. Carroll

E.2. "Now you've pissed off Grandma": Second Women's March, Seneca Falls, NY, January 20, 2018. Photo: Tamar W. Carroll

Indeed, as many women reacted to Trump's victory by taking action or coming out as feminists or as survivors of sexual harassment or assault, debates over whose "women's movement" they were joining intensified. Across the nation and here in Rochester, New York, contests over the past continue to animate contemporary debates about feminism. In July 2017, the Susan B. Anthony House organized VoteTilla, a weeklong celebration of the centennial of women's suffrage in New York State, which featured packet boats traveling from Seneca Falls to Rochester, culminating in the Suffragist City Parade through downtown Rochester to the Anthony home. More than 400 participants donned the suffragists' colors (white, purple, and gold) and marched in affiliation with stalwart women's organizations including the American Association of University Women and Planned Parenthood.[13] The crowd grew quiet, however, as a large contingent from Feminists Choosing Life of New York Action (FCLNY ACT) marched behind a banner featuring an image of Susan B. Anthony and the words "Celebrating 100 Years of Pro-Life Feminism: Susan B. Anthony." Creating a dramatic spectacle, about half a dozen young women wearing black leotards and with black gags tied across their mouths performed a dance at the front of the contingent, followed by women of varying ages and racial/ethnic backgrounds dressed in white wearing purple sashes with gold lettering reading "Pro-Life and Pro-Woman."[14]

Those spectators familiar with the iconography of the "abortion wars" might have been momentarily confused about the meaning of the young women's performance, as the pro-choice movement has long used gags to demonstrate against the so-called gag laws first implemented by the Reagan administration, which the Trump administration broadened, to block US foreign aid to international family planning services that provide abortion, or that provide referrals or counseling for abortion services, or that advocate for repeal of antiabortion laws.[15] Pro-choice activists have criticized the chilling effect the gag laws pose to women's reproductive freedom, and have used gags to symbolize the restriction of women's liberty, and the threat to their lives, posed by the funding bans.[16] In this case, however, the gags recalled a dispute in the planning of the 2017 Women's March. The March organizers published Unity Principles that included a reproductive rights plank that stated, "We believe in Reproductive Freedom. . . . This means open access to safe, legal, affordable abortion and birth control for all people."[17] Still, antiabortion groups applied to join the march, and were refused official recognition by the organizing team, raising the broader question of the place of antiabortion activists within a feminist movement that has long prioritized reproductive freedom as a necessary condition of women's empowerment.[18]

E.3. Feminists Choosing Life of New York Action (FCLNY ACT) march in the Suffragist City Parade, Rochester, NY, July 22, 2017. Credit: Max Schulte. From Rochester *Democrat and Chronicle*, July 22, 2017. © 2017 Gannett-Community Publishing. All rights reserved. Used by permission and protected by the copyright laws of the United States. The printing, copying, redistribution, or retransmission of this content without express written permission is prohibited.

Feminists Choosing Life of New York Action is not the first anti-abortion group to claim Susan B. Anthony as a precursor; in 1993 activist Rachel MacNair took Anthony's name for her antiabortion advocacy group, the Susan B. Anthony List, founded to counter the power of Emily's List, a political action committee that helped elect female, pro-choice Democratic candidates to office, including Hillary Clinton.[19] Feminists for Life, meanwhile, has championed Anthony's reform partner Elizabeth Cady Stanton as their pro-life historical heroine. As law professor Tracy Thomas points out, over the past two decades, anti-abortion groups have succeeded in linking their cause with feminist icons from the past. Federal antiabortion legislation bears their names, including the Susan B. Anthony and Frederick Douglass Prenatal Non-discrimination Act of 2011 and the Elizabeth Cady Stanton Pregnant and Parenting Students Services Act of 2005, while "political forums for college students popularize the notion that feminists historically opposed abortion."[20]

The Susan B. Anthony List, along with its partner super PAC Women Speak Out, report spending more than $18 million nationally in the 2016 election cycle, reaching at least 1.6 million voters with their antiabortion message through door-to-door, mail, and digital ad campaigns. According to SBA List president Marjorie Dannenfelser, "Not only did we work to turn out inconsistent pro-life voters, we identified and contacted persuadable Democrats, including Hispanics, who were horrified to learn about Hillary Clinton's support for forcing taxpayers to fund late-term abortion up until the moment of birth."[21] This characterization of Clinton's position is grossly inaccurate,[22] yet there is evidence that the Susan B. Anthony List's message succeeded, as journalists report that antiabortion activism bolstered Trump's victory.[23]

Historians of women's suffrage object to the claim that Susan B. Anthony and Elizabeth Cady Stanton were antiabortion, pointing out that neither leader ever advocated for the criminalization of abortion, and that the evidence on which antiabortion groups have based their claims is taken out of context, inaccurate, and wrongly applied to a contemporary debate whose terms have very different meanings than they did in the nineteenth century.[24] To the contrary, women's rights advocates supported voluntary motherhood and opposed what we would now call marital rape as well as criminal punishment for women for infanticide.[25] And yet the popular comedy show *Saturday Night Live* aired a January 2017 sketch in which a group of young women touring Susan B. Anthony's home encounter her ghost, who exhorts them: "Abortion is murder!"[26] Scholars' protests notwithstanding, antiabortion groups edge closer to realizing their goal of decoupling reproductive rights and feminism through their co-optation of Anthony, Stanton, and other nineteenth-century women's rights leaders.

What to make of this disjuncture between history and (newly created) public memory? Thomas, the legal scholar, argues that antiabortion advocates' counternarrative, by pairing feminist icons with antiabortion sentiment, works to "undermin[e] the prevailing feminist and legal view that a woman's right to bodily autonomy and reproductive choice is a privacy right of constitutional dimension going to the heart of gender equality." Separating abortion rights from feminism thus makes it easier to diminish or eliminate them, by weakening public support for women's reproductive autonomy. This co-optation of history and of feminism can only succeed, Thomas adds, because of a "lack of popular knowledge" about Anthony, Stanton, Douglass, and other women's rights advocates.[27] History matters, and there's a lot at stake.

Collectively, the contributors to this volume show the need for more robust and complex public understandings of American history, with a broader cast of characters that eschews hero worship while cultivating empathy. Only by wrestling with the rupture in Anthony and Douglass's friendship over the Fifteenth Amendment, for example, can we appreciate both how liberalism, the structure of the US political system, and white supremacy, so foundational to the US nation-state, work to limit social change, and thus to imagine new methods for achieving transformative justice. We might start by applying Katie Terezakis's call in chapter 23 for a renewed critical history to the state of women's reproductive health in Rochester. Responding to the history of forced sterilization of Native American, African American, and Puerto Rican women in the twentieth-century United States, women-of-color feminists have asserted that reproductive rights include not only the right to limit childbirth through abortion and birth control, but also the right to have children and to raise them in safe and healthful conditions in which they can realize their potential.[28]

For African American and Puerto Rican women in Rochester's central city, their ability to give birth to and raise healthy children is imperiled. Rochester has the highest rate of infant mortality in New York State and one of the highest in the nation—an average of 14.1 deaths per 1,000 live births from 2008 to 2010; during these years, Monroe County's white infant mortality rate averaged 3.9 while its African American rate averaged 16.[29] Black mothers are much more likely than white mothers to lose their babies before their first birthday; the deaths are caused by chronic stress, poor nutrition, and lack of access to good medical care—in other words, by poverty.[30] The danger of the "pro-life" counternarrative that Susan B. Anthony was antiabortion lies not only in the creation of a false public memory, but also in neglecting this context: the very real suffering of Black mothers in Rochester, who lose their babies at unconscionably high rates. The right-to-life movement's emphasis on outlawing abortion—in this case, miscast as a profeminist move—diverts public attention from the changes necessary for the realization of full reproductive justice, including child welfare. Given the history of racism within women's rights movements in the United States, explored in the chapters by Michael J. Brown, Katie Terezakis, and Barbara Winslow in this volume, building an inclusive movement requires attending to both the legacies of American history and the ongoing inequalities. As writer and activist Renee Bracey Sherman argues in linking the fight to eliminate racial disparity in policing and incarceration with the struggle for reproductive rights, "State violence and control, whether through racist policing, the criminal justice system or the welfare system, are all issues at the core of reproductive justice. They are fundamentally about whether you, or the state, has control over your own body and destiny. . . . Reproductive justice is about the resolve to raise our families on our own terms, safely. This is the fight for the right to life."[31]

Black women in the United States have long fought for control of their own bodies, as recent calls to take down statues of Dr. J. Marion Sims, the white man known as the "father of modern gynecology," who experimented on enslaved women without their consent or anesthesia, remind us. Just as New Orleans Mayor Mitch Landrieu argued in May 2017 that Confederate monuments in his city must be taken down because they "purposefully celebrate a fictional, sanitized Confederacy" that ignores the death and slavery, and because they were an ongoing part of the "terrorism" inflicted on Black residents under white supremacy, so, too, have community groups in East Harlem, New York, successfully argued that the Sims statue must go, as he is "a constant reminder of the silences of the black women whose bodies he operated on"—"a different form of racial terrorizing," in historian Susan Reverby's words.[32]

As monuments to white supremacy come down across the United States, we hope that space opens for an overdue recognition of Black women's many historical contributions to the United States, not least their expansive vision of social justice, chronicled by De Anna Reese, Delia Gillis, and Jamia Wilson in this volume. To move forward with building a more just future, Women's March participants will need to make use of critical history to interrogate the past and to reject false public memories, particularly those that frame white women as victims in need of protection by a patriarchal state, including the myth of the Black and Mexican rapist as well as the "pro-life" feminist, while eliding the suffering of women of color.[33] New narratives that tackle misogyny and racism head-on are necessary to activate gender consciousness and empower female voters to renounce the dangerous allure of benevolent sexism and white supremacy. As the infant mortality rates in Rochester attest, lives depend on it. As early as 1853, Douglass wrote, "Woman, however, like the colored man, will never be taken by her brother and lifted to a position. What she desires, she must fight for. With her as with us, 'Who would be free themselves must strike the blow.'"[34]

Notes

1. "Our Mission," Women's March, accessed August 1, 2017, https://www.womensmarch.com/mission.

2. Erica Chenoweth and Jeremy Pressman, "This Is What We Learned by Counting the Women's Marches," *Washington Post*, February 7, 2017,

https://www.washingtonpost.com/news/monkey-cage/wp/2017/02/07/
this-is-what-we-learned-by-counting-the-womens-marches/?utm_term=.
ca3417e73753.

3. Jodi Enda, "Donald Trump Is the Best—and Worst—Thing That's
Happened to Modern American Feminism," CNN.com, July 2017, http://
www.cnn.com/interactive/2017/politics/state/womens-movement-
donald-trump/.

4. Fenit Nirappil, "Women Hit a Record High in Virginia Legislature.
Can They Break the Boys' Club?," *Washington Post*, January 11, 2017,
https://www.washingtonpost.com/local/virginia-politics/women-hit-
a-record-high-in-virginia-legislature-can-they-break-the-boys-club/2018/
01/11/e1d5f2f4-f4aa-11e7-beb6-c8d48830c54d_story.html?utm_term=
.29ec0d390f9c; Eugene Scott, "Black Women Are Demanding More Than
a Thank You from the Democratic Party," *Washington Post*, December 14,
2017, https://www.washingtonpost.com/news/the-fix/wp/2017/12/14/
black-women-are-demanding-more-than-a-thank-you-from-the-democratic-
party/?utm_term=.0bb5b2472bde.

5. Emma Stefansky, "Women's March Dials Up Major Crowd Size Numbers across the U.S.," *Vanity Fair*, January 21, 2018, https://www.vanityfair.
com/news/2018/01/womens-march-crowd-size-numbers.

6. Chris Benderev, "On Anniversary of Women's March, a Las Vegas Rally
with a Tighter Focus: The Midterms," NPR, January 21, 2018, https://www.
npr.org/sections/thetwo-way/2018/01/21/579553749/on-anniversary-
of-womens-march-a-las-vegas-rally-with-a-tighter-focus-the-midter.

7. Rachel Wolfe, "A New Study Finds More Women Now Lean Democratic," *Vox*, March 21, 2018, https://www.vox.com/2018/3/21/17144602/
gender-gap-democrat-liberal-women.

8. Jodi Kantor and Megan Twohey, "Harvey Weinstein Paid Off Sexual Harassment Accusers for Decades," *New York Times*, October 5, 2017,
https://www.nytimes.com/2017/10/05/us/harvey-weinstein-harassment-
allegations.html.

9. Ronan Farrow, "From Aggressive Overtures to Sexual Assault: Harvey Weinstein's Accusers Tell Their Stories," *New Yorker*, October 23, 2017,
https://www.newyorker.com/news/news-desk/from-aggressive-overtures-
to-sexual-assault-harvey-weinsteins-accusers-tell-their-stories; Christen
A. Johnson and KT Hawbaker, "#MeToo: A Timeline of Events," *Chicago
Tribune*, accessed March 13, 2018, http://www.chicagotribune.com/life-
styles/ct-me-too-timeline-20171208-htmlstory.html.

10. "More Than 12M 'Me Too' Facebook Posts, Comments, Reactions
in 24 Hours," CBS News, October 17, 2017, https://www.cbsnews.com/
news/metoo-more-than-12-million-facebook-posts-comments-reactions-
24-hours/.

11. Stephanie Zacharek, Eliana Dockterman, and Haley Sweet-
land Edwards, "Time Person of the Year 2017: The Silence
Breakers," *Time*, December 18, 2017, http://time.com/time-person-of-the-

year-2017-silence-breakers/; Susan Chria and Catrin Einhorn, "How Tough Is It to Change a Culture of Harassment? Ask Women at Ford," *New York Times*, December 19, 2017, https://www.nytimes.com/interactive/2017/12/19/us/ford-chicago-sexual-harassment.html; Catrin Einhorn and Rachel Abrams, "The Tipping Equation," *New York Times*, March 12, 2018, https://www.nytimes.com/interactive/2018/03/11/business/tipping-sexual-harassment.html.

12. Gillian B. White, "The Glaring Blind Spot of the 'Me Too' Movement," *Atlantic*, November 22, 2017, https://www.theatlantic.com/entertainment/archive/2017/11/the-glaring-blind-spot-of-the-me-too-movement/546458/.

13. Caitlin Whyte, "Suffragist City Parade Celebrates Susan B. Anthony's Impact on Multiple Issues," WXXI News, July 22, 2017, http://wxxinews.org/post/suffragist-city-parade-celebrates-susan-b-anthonys-impact-multiple-issues; Patti Singer, "Thank You, Susan B., for the Right to Vote," *Democrat & Chronicle*, July 22, 2017, http://www.democratandchronicle.com/story/news/2017/07/22/thank-you-susan-b-right-vote/499579001/.

14. Photographs from the FCLNY ACT contingent at the parade are available on the group's Facebook page, accessed August 2, 2017, https://www.facebook.com/fclnyact/. In the summer of 2017, the group also sponsored a highway billboard in the city on Interstate 490 East with the message that Susan B. Anthony was against abortion. More information on the organization is available on its website, https://www.fclny.org/.

15. Nikita Biryukov, Emma Margolin, and Ari Melber, "Trump Reinstates, Broadens Reagan-Era Anti-Abortion Policy," NBC News, January 24, 2017, http://www.nbcnews.com/news/us-news/trump-reinstates-reagan-era-anti-abortion-policy-n710081.

16. See, for example, Meryl Levin's 1991 photograph of the Statue of Liberty "gagged" in a direct action protest by the New York City–based reproductive rights feminist group Women's Health Action Mobilization (WHAM!). Tamar W. Carroll, *Mobilizing New York: AIDS, Antipoverty, and Feminist Activism* (Chapel Hill: University of North Carolina Press, 2015), 2.

17. "Unity Principles," Women's March, https://www.womensmarch.com/principles/.

18. Sheryl Gay Stolberg, "Views on Abortion Strain Calls for Unity at Women's March on Washington," *New York Times*, January 18, 2017, https://www.nytimes.com/2017/01/18/us/womens-march-abortion.html; Ruth Graham, "Women's March on Washington Says No to Pro-Life Feminist Group," *Slate*, January 17, 2017, http://www.slate.com/blogs/xx_factor/2017/01/17/pro_life_feminist_group_new_wave_feminists_removed_from_women_s_march_partnership.html.

19. Ruth Graham, "How Susan B. Anthony Became a Pro-Life Heroine," *Dallas News*, May 23, 2017, https://www.dallasnews.com/opinion/commentary/2017/05/23/susan-b-anthony-became-anti-abortion-heroine.

20. Tracy A. Thomas, "Misappropriating Women's History in the Law and Politics of Abortion," *Seattle University Law Review* 36, no. 1 (2012): 1–68, quotation at 2.

21. Susan B. Anthony List, "Mobilizing the Pro-Life Vote in 2016 to Elect Donald Trump and Pro-Life Senators," press release, November 8, 2016, https://www.sba-list.org/newsroom/press-releases/mobilizing-pro-life-vote-2016-elect-donald-trump-pro-life-senators-2.

22. In the third presidential debate, Clinton voiced strong support for maintaining Roe v. Wade, which protects women's right to abortion prior to viability, as well as funding for Planned Parenthood, and stated that she supported restrictions on late-term abortions only when they include exceptions to protect the life and health of the mother. Aaron Blake, "The Final Trump-Clinton Debate Transcript, Annotated," *Washington Post*, October 19, 2016, https://www.washingtonpost.com/news/the-fix/wp/2016/10/19/the-final-trump-clinton-debate-transcript-annotated/?utm_term=.523352eeba28. This is consistent with her prior position on abortion rights. While Clinton has repeatedly stated her support for Roe v. Wade, she has stated support for restrictions on abortion after 24 weeks of pregnancy with exceptions for the life and health of the mother. Pema Levy, "Lat-Term Abortion Debate Reveals a Rift between Clinton and Sanders," *Mother Jones*, March 11, 2016, http://www.motherjones.com/politics/2016/03/hillary-clinton-late-term-abortions/.

23. Katherine Stewart, "Eighty-One Percent of White Evangelicals Voted for Donald Trump. Why?," *Nation*, November 17, 2016, https://www.thenation.com/article/eighty-one-percent-of-white-evangelicals-voted-for-donald-trump-why/.

24. Historian Cornelia Hughes Dayton writes that in early America, "abortion was understood as blameworthy because it was an extreme action, designed to hide a prior sin, sex outside of marriage, not because of concern over "the destruction of the fetus." "Taking the Trade: Abortion and Gender Relations in an Eighteenth-Century New England Village," *William and Mary Quarterly* 48, no. 1 (1991): 19–41, quotation at 23. As Janet Farrell Brodie details, prior to the late 1800s, abortions before "quickening," or fetal movement, generally occurring around four months, were not punishable under common law tradition, and those performed after quickening "might be high misdemeanors if the woman died, but not felonies." An anti–reproductive control movement led by Anthony Comstock and the American Medical Association resulted in the criminalization of both birth control and abortion in the late nineteenth century. Brodie, *Contraception and Abortion in 19th-Century America* (Ithaca, NY: Cornell University Press, 1994), 254–56. For the rise of a fetal-centric understanding of abortion in the twentieth century, see Sara Dubow, *Ourselves Unborn: A History of the Fetus in Modern America* (New York: Oxford University Press, 2011).

25. In addition to Thomas, see for example two leading scholars of Anthony, Lynn Sherr and Ann D. Gordon, "No, Susan B. Anthony and Elizabeth Cady Stanton Were Not Antiabortionists," *Time*, November 10, 2015, http://time.com/4106547/susan-b-anthony-elizabeth-cady-stanton-abortion/.

26. *Saturday Night Live*, season 42, January 14, 2017, http://www.nbc.com/saturday-night-live/video/susan-b-anthony/3454414?snl=1.

27. Thomas, "Misappropriating Women's History," 3.

28. Jennifer Nelson, *Women of Color and the Reproductive Rights Movement* (New York: New York University Press, 2003).

29. David Andreatta, "In City's History of Infant Deaths, Some See a Crisis," *Democrat and Chronicle*, September 22, 2012. In 2014 in Monroe County, while overall the infant mortality rates had improved, stark disparities persisted: African American infants had the highest rate of mortality: 10 deaths for every 1,000 live births, compared to white infants' rate of 3.6. "Child Health: Infant Mortality Rate, Race/Ethnicity, Monroe County," ACT Rochester, accessed August 4, 2017, http://www.actrochester.org/children-youth/child-health/infant-mortality-rate/infant-mortality-rate-race-ethnicity-monroe-county.

30. "Surviving Year One," *America by the Numbers*, PBS, season 1, episode 7, aired November 15, 2014, http://www.pbs.org/video/america-numbers-surviving-year-one/; Maria Hinojosa, "Babies Are Dying in Rochester at Twice the National Average. Why?," Culture of Health Blog, Robert Wood Johnson Foundation, November 7, 2014, http://www.rwjf.org/en/culture-of-health/2014/11/babies_are_dyingin.html. On the national disparities in infant and maternal mortality, see Linda Villarosa, "Why America's Black Mothers and Babies Are in a Life-or-Death Crisis," *New York Times*, April 11, 2018, https://www.nytimes.com/2018/04/11/magazine/black-mothers-babies-death-maternal-mortality.html.

31. Renee Bracey Sherman, "The Right to (Black) Life," *New York Times*, August 9, 2017, https://www.nytimes.com/2017/08/09/opinion/michael-brown-anniversary-black-mothers.html?_r=0.

32. Susan M. Reverby, "This Doctor Experimented on Slaves: It's Time to Remove or Redo His Statue," The Hastings Center Bioethics Forum Essay, August 7, 2017, http://www.thehastingscenter.org/doctor-experimented-slaves-time-remove-redo-statue/; "Mitch Landrieu's Speech on the Removal of Confederate Monuments in New Orleans," *New York Times*, May 23, 2017, https://www.nytimes.com/2017/05/23/opinion/mitch-landrieus-speech-transcript.html?mcubz=0&_r=0; Caitlin Byrd and Mary Katherine Wildeman, "Momentum Builds to Remove Statues of a Controversial Doctor in Columbia, NYC in Wake of Charlottesville," *Post and Courier*, August 16, 2017, http://www.postandcourier.com/news/momentum-builds-to-remove-statues-of-a-controversial-doctor-in/article_7912f6c8-82ad-11e7-8630-6bcbc1f52b31.html. The Sims statue was removed from Central Park in April 2018 and moved to the cemetery at which he is

buried, Green-Wood. Ginia Bellafante, "Statue of Doctor Who Did Slave Experiments Is Exiled. Its Ideas Are Not," *New York Times*, April 18, 2018, https://www.nytimes.com/2018/04/18/nyregion/sims-sculpture-green-wood-cemetery.html.

33. Making use of critical history also includes interrogating those that traffic in anti-Semitism and homophobia. Women's March organizer Tamika Mallory was criticized by many for attending a Nation of Islam keynote address by Louis Farrakhan at the February 2018 Saviours' Day conference, at which he referred to the "Satanic Jew." *The Advocate*, a prominent LGBTQ magazine and online news site, described Farrakhan in its coverage of this controversy as "a well-known homophobe, transphobe, and an anti-Semite." The Women's March co-president who was present at the speech was called upon by an onslaught of social media posts to explain her presence there, especially following a 2017 Instagram posting that featured her posing with Farrakhan, and referring to him as "GOAT," or the greatest of all time. Ariel Sobel, "Women's March Refuses to Denounce Antigay, Anti-Semitic Louis Farrakhan," *Advocate*, March 7, 2018, https://www.advocate.com/women/2018/3/07/womens-march-leader-refuses-denounce-antigay-anti-semitic-louis-farrakhan; Tamika Mallory (@tamikadmallory), "Thank God this man is still alive and doing well," Instagram, May 11, 2017, https://www.instagram.com/p/BT9wDcUBShs/?hl=en.

34. Frederick Douglass, "Some Thoughts on Woman's Rights," in *Frederick Douglass on Women's Rights*, ed. Philip S. Foner (New York: Da Capo Press, 1992), 59.

CHRONOLOGY

Note: This list of events is not comprehensive. It begins in the 1990s, when Hillary Clinton and Donald Trump's prominence on the national stage was cemented. It includes key elements of the candidates' biographies; important milestones in the 2016 election; notable behaviors and statements by the candidates that invoked or performed specific understandings of gender, race, and history; and postelection events that are the direct outgrowth or aftermath of those specific campaign-period events and promises.

1993–2001	Bill Clinton serves two terms as president of the United States, with his wife, Hillary Clinton, as First Lady.
1996	Donald Trump purchases the Miss Universe Organization, which also includes Miss USA and Miss Teen USA.
1998	President Bill Clinton is impeached by the House of Representatives for lying under oath and obstructing justice in a sexual harassment case against him, although he is acquitted by the Senate and serves out his second term in office.
1999–2000	Donald Trump runs for the Reform Party nomination for the presidency.
2001–9	Hillary Clinton serves as US senator from the state of New York, becoming the first former First Lady ever to be elected to public office in the United States.
2004	*The Apprentice*, starring Donald Trump, first airs on NBC.
2007–8	Hillary Clinton competes for the Democratic nomination for the presidency, losing to Barack Obama.
2009	*The Celebrity Apprentice*, starring Donald Trump, first airs on NBC.

2009–13   Hillary Clinton serves as US secretary of state under President Barack Obama.

2011–14   Donald Trump gains political attention by making a series of televised statements charging that President Obama was not born in the United States.

2012   Donald Trump registers his "Make America Great Again" slogan, echoing the "Let's Make America Great Again" slogan used by Ronald Reagan in his 1980 presidential campaign.

2014   The Kremlin-linked Internet Research Agency in St. Petersburg begins an operation to influence US politics through social media.

2015

April 12   Hillary Clinton announces her run for the Democratic nomination for the office of president of the United States, using the slogan "I'm with Her."

June 16   Donald Trump announces his run for the Republican nomination for the presidency, using his slogan "Make America Great Again." Referring to Mexican immigrants as criminals, rapists, and drug dealers, he introduces a plan to build a wall along the US-Mexico border.

July 1   An undocumented Mexican national and convicted felon who had been deported from the United States five times previously shoots and kills Kathryn Steinle in San Francisco. Trump says it is, "yet another example of why we must secure our border immediately. . . . This is an absolutely disgraceful situation and I am the only one that can fix it." He moves to the top of polls among contenders for the Republican nomination.

July 8   Donald Trump charges, without substantiation, that, "This man, or this animal, that shot that wonderful, that beautiful woman in San Francisco, this guy was pushed back by Mexico." "Beautiful Kate" becomes a common reference.

July 11   Echoing Richard Nixon, Donald Trump exclaims at a rally,
                 "The silent majority is back, and we're going to take our
                 country back."

July 18   Trump says of Senator John McCain (R-AZ), who had
                 been a prisoner of war in Vietnam, "He's not a war hero.
                 He's a war hero because he was captured. I like people
                 that weren't captured."

August 8   Referring to his quizzing during a Republican primary
                 debate by Fox News anchor Megyn Kelly, Donald Trump
                 says, "You could see there was blood coming out of her
                 eyes. Blood coming out of her wherever." Clare Cohen of
                 The Telegraph begins compiling her "Donald Trump Sex-
                 ism Tracker."

August 24   Trump introduces the nickname "Low Energy Jeb" for his
                 Republican challenger, former Governor Jeb Bush.

September 9   About his Republican challenger, Carly Fiorina, Trump
                 says, "Look at that face! Would anyone vote for that? Can
                 you imagine that, the face of our next president?"

September 22   The FBI reveals an ongoing review of whether Hillary
                 Clinton's use of a private email server while she served as
                 Secretary of State included messages that contained classi-
                 fied information.

September 23   In a campaign speech, Trump calls Clinton "shrill."

November 13   ISIS (Islamic State of Iraq and Syria) terrorist attacks in
                 Paris kill 130.

December 2   Islamist terror attack in San Bernardino, California, kills
                 fourteen. Trump says, "Donald J. Trump is calling for
                 a total and complete shutdown of Muslims entering the
                 United States until our country's representatives can fig-
                 ure out what the hell is going on."

2016

January 28   Senator Bernie Sanders (I-VT), Clinton's opponent in the Democratic primary race, releases an ad identifying Goldman Sachs Bank as one of the financial institutions that caused the financial crisis of 2008. The narrator says, "How does Wall Street get away with it? Millions in campaign contributions and speaking fees." The ad implicates Hillary Clinton, who was paid $675,000 by Goldman Sachs in 2013 for a series of speeches.

February 4   At a Democratic primary debate, Sanders calls on Clinton to release the transcripts of her Goldman Sachs speeches.

February 28   Trump introduces the nickname, "Little Marco," for his Republican challenger, Senator Marco Rubio (R-FL).

February 29   At a rally, Senator Rubio notes that Donald Trump has small hands, remarking, "You know what they say about men with small hands." Four days later, at a Republican primary debate, Trump says, "Look at those hands, are they small hands? . . . And [Marco] referred to my hands—if they're small, something else must be small. I guarantee you there's no problem. I guarantee."

March 13   At a town hall event in West Virginia, Hillary Clinton says, "I'm the only candidate which has a policy about how to bring economic opportunity using clean renewable energy as the key into coal country. Because we're going to put a lot of coal miners and coal companies out of business, right? And we're going to make it clear that we don't want to forget those people. . . . Now we've got to move away from coal and all the other fossil fuels, but I don't want to move away from the people who did the best they could to produce the energy that we relied on." This statement is widely interpreted as indifference to rural, working-class men.

April 17   Donald Trump introduces the nickname, "Crooked Hillary."

April 21   The Treasury Department announces that it will replace President Andrew Jackson on the twenty-dollar bill with Harriet Tubman, the African American abolitionist and leader in the Underground Railroad, positioning Tubman to become the first African American to appear on US paper currency and the first woman to do so in over a century. Trump calls the move "pure political correctness," and he says of Jackson, who owned slaves and led westward expansion through forced military campaigns and removal of Native Americans, that he "had a history of tremendous success for the country."

April 26   Trump charges Clinton with playing the "woman card," adding that, "the only card she has is the woman's card" and that "If Hillary Clinton were a man I don't think she'd get five percent of the vote."

April 27   Reacting to a Clinton speech, Trump says, "I haven't quite recovered, it's early in the morning, from her shouting that message. And I know a lot of people would say you can't say that about a woman because of course a woman doesn't shout."

May 5   At a rally in West Virginia, Trump dons a hard hat, mimics a shoveling motion, and says, "We're going to get those miners back to work. . . . We're not going to be Hillary Clinton . . . and she was talking about how she wants the mines closed and will never let them work again. . . . For those miners, get ready because you're going to be working your asses off."

May 14   The *New York Times* publishes a list of women who had accused Donald Trump of harassment, discrimination, and inappropriate sexual conduct since the 1980s.

May 23   Hillary Clinton's campaign rolls out the new "Stronger Together" slogan.

May 26   Donald Trump wins enough delegates to secure the Republican nomination.

June 7	During her victory speech after clinching the Democratic nomination, Hillary Clinton wears a cream-colored jacket, inspired by suffragists' white clothing. She calls it a "milestone—the first time in our nation's history that a woman will be a major party's nominee for president of the United States." She credits the organizers of the convention on women's rights in Seneca Falls, New York, in 1848, saying that they, "came together with the idea that women deserved equal rights, and they set it forth in . . . the Declaration of Sentiments, and it was the first time in human history that that kind of declaration occurred."
June 12	Terror attack at Pulse, a gay nightclub in Orlando, Florida, kills forty-nine. Donald Trump tweets, "Appreciate the congrats for being right on radical Islamic terrorism."
June 15	The self-styled hacker, Guccifer 2.0, begins leaking thousands of documents stolen from the Democratic National Committee, later leaking some through DCLeaks.
July 5	FBI Director James Comey announces that no criminal charges would be brought against Hillary Clinton for her private email server.
July 18–21	Republican National Convention, Cleveland, Ohio. Michael Flynn leads the crowds in chanting "Lock her up!" Trump invites on stage family members of three people killed by undocumented immigrants.
July 22	Wikileaks begins dumping tens of thousands of emails stolen from the Democratic National Committee.
July 25–28	Democratic National Convention, Philadelphia, Pennsylvania. When accepting the nomination, Hillary Clinton wears a white pantsuit. Pakistani American doctor, Khazir Khan, remembers his son, an American soldier, who was killed by a suicide bomber while on deployment in Iraq; his wife stands silently next to him. Khan asks Trump: "Have you even read the United States Constitution? I will gladly lend you my copy." Trump later responds, "I'd like

to hear his wife say something. Maybe she wasn't allowed to have anything to say."

July 31   The FBI begins an investigation into possible collusion between Donald Trump's campaign and the Russian government to sway the election in Trump's favor. Knowledge of this investigation does not become public until after the election.

August 12   Guccifer 2.0 begins leaking thousands of documents stolen from the Democratic Congressional Campaign Committee.

August 17   Trump hires as his campaign chief executive Stephen K. Bannon, the executive chair of Breitbart News, an alt-right news site.

September 9   Hillary Clinton remarks, "You know, to just be grossly generalistic, you could put half of Trump's supporters into what I call the basket of deplorables. Right? The racist, sexist, homophobic, xenophobic, Islamaphobic—you name it. And, unfortunately, there are people like that. And he has lifted them up."

September 11   Hillary Clinton stumbles at a 9/11 memorial event due to pneumonia.

September 15   Donald Trump talks about his health on the *Dr. Oz Show*, contrasting his vigor to Clinton's recent collapse.

September 26   At the first presidential debate, Trump says of Clinton, "she doesn't have the stamina." Clinton wears a red pantsuit.

October 6   DCLeaks dumps emails stolen from Capricia Marshall, a Clinton ally.

October 7   The *Access Hollywood* audio recording from 2005 is released in which Trump says about a female reporter:
                 I did try and fuck her. She was married. . . . I moved on her like a bitch. . . . She's now got the big phony tits and

everything. . . . I better use some Tic Tacs just in case I start kissing her. You know I'm automatically attracted to beautiful—I just start kissing them. It's like a magnet. Just kiss. I don't even wait. And when you're a star, they let you do it. You can do anything. Grab 'em by the pussy.

The Department of Homeland Security and the director of National Intelligence publicly warn that the Russian government was attempting to interfere in the election, including through the Wikileaks, Guccifer 2.0, and DCLeaks dumps of stolen documents.

Wikileaks begins dumping tens of thousands of documents stolen from Clinton campaign chairman John Podesta's email account, including excerpts of her Goldman Sachs speeches.

October 8–27   In addition to four accusations previously on record, thirteen women step forward to accuse Donald Trump of sexual assault or sexual misconduct. Several other women recount that when he owned the Miss Teen USA pageant, he regularly walked into the dressing room unannounced when the girls, many of whom were underage, were changing.

October 9   Just before the second presidential debate, Donald Trump hosts a Facebook live event with three women who had accused President Bill Clinton of sexual misconduct, plus a woman who claimed that Hillary Clinton attacked her credibility when Clinton served as the court-appointed defense attorney for her accused rapist in the 1970s. The four women are then seated in the debate hall as Trump's guests. When asked about the *Access Hollywood* tape, Trump calls it "locker-room talk." He remarks of Bill Clinton, "There's never been anybody in the history of politics in this nation who's been so abusive to women. . . . Hillary Clinton attacked those same women and attacked them viciously." Clinton wears a blue pantsuit.

October 10   At a rally, Trump says, "I love Wikileaks!"

October 13   #Repealthe19th hashtag trends on Twitter.

October 19   Third presidential debate. Trump uses the phrases "nasty woman" and "bad hombres." Clinton wears a white pantsuit.

October 20   Libby Chamberlain founds Pantsuit Nation, an invite-only Facebook page to support Clinton's bid by wearing pantsuits to the voting polls. It gains 2.9 million members by Election Day, rapidly becoming a space for people to share accounts of sexual harassment, assault, and discrimination against women and LGBTQ people, and to communicate support for Clinton and against Trump.

October 23   The *www.iwaited96years.com* website is created to feature women who were born before the ratification of the Nineteenth Amendment who intended to cast a ballot for the first female president.

October 28   FBI Director James Comey reveals the discovery of emails that might be relevant to the prior investigation into Clinton's private email server.

November 6   James Comey announces that the recently discovered emails yielded no new information.

November 8   Election Day; Hillary Clinton wins the popular vote by over 2.8 million people, but Donald Trump ekes out a win by securing a margin of fewer than 80,000 votes in three key swing states (Michigan, Wisconsin, and Pennsylvania), thereby clinching the electoral vote.

2017

January 6   A report from the Office of the Director of National Intelligence, ordered by President Obama, states that Russian President Vladimir Putin ordered an influence campaign aimed at ensuring Trump would win the 2016 presidential election. A publicly released version of the report notes that, "Putin and the Russian Government aspired to help President-elect Trump's chances when possible by discrediting Secretary Clinton and publicly contrasting her unfavorably to him. All three agencies agree with this judgment. CIA and FBI have high confidence in these judgements; NSA has moderate confidence."

January 20   Donald J. Trump is inaugurated as the forty-fifth president of the United States.

January 21   Women's March: more than 5 million people worldwide participate in 635 reported marches in the United States and at least 261 marches abroad.

January 25   Trump hangs a portrait of Andrew Jackson in the Oval Office.

                 Trump signs two executive orders related to immigration. The first strips federal grant money to sanctuary cities, directs the secretary of homeland security to hire 10,000 more immigration officers and to create a publicly available list of crimes committed by undocumented immigrants, and creates an office to assist victims of crimes committed by undocumented immigrants. The second order instructs the secretary of homeland security to prepare congressional budget requests for a border wall with Mexico and to hire 5,000 more Border Patrol agents, to construct facilities to hold undocumented immigrants near the Mexican border, and to detain undocumented immigrants while they await court hearings.

January 27   Trump signs an executive order suspending the entry of immigrants from seven majority-Muslim countries for ninety days, banning all refugees from entering the United States for 120 days, and indefinitely barring Syrian refugees from entering the United States.

May 9   Trump fires FBI Director James Comey, who was leading the investigation into Russian interference in the election and any possible connection with the Trump campaign.

May 17   Acting Attorney General Rod J. Rosenstein appoints former FBI director Robert S. Mueller III as special counsel to take over Comey's investigation into Russian interference in the election.

June 29   The House passes "Kate's Law," a bill inspired by Kathryn Steinle's shooting in 2015, which increases the penalties for convicted and deported aliens who reenter the United States illegally.

August 11–12   White nationalists rally at the University of Virginia in opposition to the removal of Confederate monuments throughout the country and clash with counter protestors. James Alex Fields, associated with white supremacist groups, drives his car into counterprotestors, killing one and injuring nineteen people. Trump is criticized for not denouncing white nationalism explicitly and instead condemning "hatred, bigotry, and violence on many sides."

September 5   The Trump Administration announces it will phase out Deferred Action for Childhood Arrivals (DACA), the Obama-era program that temporarily shielded from deportation 800,000 undocumented immigrants who were brought to the United States as children.

October 5   The *New York Times* publishes accusations of sexual harassment against film mogul Harvey Weinstein by actresses including Rose McGowan and Ashley Judd; this leads many other women to come forward with allegations not only against Weinstein, but against dozens of powerful men in a variety of fields, in the #MeToo social movement.

2018

January 12   The *Wall Street Journal* reports that Donald Trump's personal lawyer paid adult film actress Stormy Daniels $130,000 in October 2016, just days before the election, to deny that she had an affair with Trump in 2006.

March 20   The New York State Supreme Court allows former reality TV *Apprentice* contestant Summer Zervos's lawsuit against Donald Trump for defamation to go forward. Zervos is one of the women who, in October 2016, had accused

Trump of sexual assault, and she contends that his denial of those claims as "total lies" constitutes defamation.

Former Playboy model Karen McDougal files suit to gain the right to speak publicly about an alleged affair with Trump in 2006.

April 5   Trump reprises the specter of the Latino rapist to call for a border wall. A caravan of about one thousand Honduran migrants travels northward, fleeing violence in their home country, most seeking asylum in Mexico and some in the United States. While no news reports recorded incidences of rape perpetrated by any of the migrants, Trump says, "And remember my opening remarks at Trump Tower when I opened. Everybody said, 'Oh, he was so tough.' And I used the word 'rape.' And yesterday it came out where, this journey coming up, women are raped at levels that nobody has ever seen before."

CONTRIBUTORS

STEVE ALMOND is the author of ten books of fiction and nonfiction, most recently *Bad Stories: What the Hell Just Happened to Our Country*. His stories and essays have appeared in the *Best American Short Stories*, the Pushcart Prize, the *New York Times Magazine*, and elsewhere. He also hosts the *New York Times* podcast Dear Sugars with Cheryl Strayed.

R. BRANDON ANDERSON is a visiting assistant professor in the Department of Communication Studies at Gustavus Adolphus College in St. Peter, Minnesota. He is a rhetorician whose research centers on discourses of political and social change. Some of his prior work appears in the edited volumes *Silencing the Opposition: How the U.S. Government Suppressed Freedom of Expression during Major Crises* and *A First Amendment Profile of the Supreme Court*. He earned a PhD from the Moody College of Communication at the University of Texas at Austin.

PAMELA ARONSON is professor of sociology at the University of Michigan–Dearborn. Her research examines the differences between gender consciousness, feminist consciousness, and feminist identity; young women's attitudes toward feminism and work and family life; and gender differences in career development and higher education. She has over two dozen publications, appearing in such places as *Gender & Society*, *The Oxford Handbook of U.S. Women's Social Movement Activism*, *International Journal of Psychology*, *Critical Sociology*, *Journal of Youth Studies*, *Advances in Life Course Research*, *Journal of the Association for Research on Mothering*, *New Directions for Child and Adolescent Development*, and *Crossings to Adulthood: How Diverse Young Americans Understand and Navigate Their Lives*.

BETH L. BOSER is an assistant professor in the Department of Communication Studies at the University of Wisconsin–La Crosse. She is a rhetorical and media scholar whose research focuses on representations of gender in media, childbirth and motherhood advocacy, and political and social change discourse. Some of her prior work appears in the journal *Rhetoric & Public Affairs* and the edited volume *Mediated Moms: Contemporary Challenges to the Motherhood Myth*. She earned a PhD from the Annenberg School for Communication and Journalism at the University of Southern California.

MICHAEL J. BROWN is an assistant professor of history and a faculty affiliate of the museum studies program at Rochester Institute of Technology. An intellectual and cultural historian of the United States, Michael is also a public historian whose work focuses on the Rochester region. His current book project, *Experts, Eggheads, and Elites: Debating the Role of Intellectuals in American Political Culture, 1952–2008*, examines the polarizing figure of the intellectual in political life. Michael has been a member of the board of contributors at the *Rochester Democrat and Chronicle* and is a trustee of the Rochester Historical Society.

JANE CAPUTI is professor of Women, Gender and Sexuality Studies at Florida Atlantic University. In 2016 she was named as the Eminent Scholar of the Year by the Popular Culture Association. She is the author of several books, including *Goddesses and Monsters: Women, Myth, Power and Popular Culture*. She also has made two educational documentaries, *The Pornography of Everyday Life* and *Feed the Green: Feminist Voices for the Earth*, and currently is writing a book, *Call Your Mutha': A Deliberately Dirty-Minded Devotion to the Earth Mother*, for an Oxford University Press series on heretical thought.

TAMAR W. CARROLL is associate professor of history at Rochester Institute of Technology, where she is also affiliated with the digital humanities and social sciences, museum studies, and women's and gender studies programs. She is the author of *Mobilizing New York: AIDS, Antipoverty and Feminist Activism*. She is cocurator, with Meg Handler and Mike Kamber, of "'Whose Streets? Our Streets!': New York City, 1980–2000," an exhibition at the Bronx Documentary Center and companion multimedia website at www.whosestreets.photo. Carroll received her PhD in history at the University of Michigan and was Mellon Postdoctoral Fellow in History at Cornell University before joining the faculty at RIT.

GINA MASULLO CHEN is an assistant professor in the School of Journalism and assistant director of the Center for Media Engagement, both at the University of Texas at Austin. She spent twenty years as a newspaper reporter and editor before joining the academy. Her research focuses on the online conversation around the news with a particular interest in both uncivil debate and how gender and politics intersect in this process. She is author of *Online Incivility and Public Debate: Nasty Talk* and coeditor of *Scandal in a Digital Age*. Her research has been published in academic journals, including *Communication Research, Computers in Human Behavior, Journalism Practice, Journal of Broadcasting & Electronic Media, Mass Communication and Society, New Media & Society,* and *Newspaper Research Journal.*

SALLY CAMPBELL GALMAN is professor of child and family studies at the University of Massachusetts–Amherst. Her arts-informed ethnographic research focuses on the study of childhood and gender in early learning, family, and community contexts. She has published in *Review of Educational Research, Ethnography and Education, Boyhood Studies, Childhood,* and *Gender and Education,* among other journals. Her current work with transgender or gender-creative/expansive children has been supported by the Spencer Foundation. She is editor-in-chief of *Anthropology and Education Quarterly.* An award-winning cartoonist, Galman is author of the *Shane* series of qualitative methods texts.

DELIA C. GILLIS is professor of history and director of the Center for Africana Studies at the University of Central Missouri. For more than twenty-five years, she has taught a range of courses in US and world history including slavery, civil rights, African American women, gender and girlhood, the African diaspora, South Africa, and graduate colloquia on the social history of the American family and African Americans during World War I. She is a former project director for Created Equal: America's Civil Rights Struggle, National Endowment for the Humanities (NEH)/Gilder Lehrman Institute for American History, and currently directs university study tours to rural St. Elizabeth parish in Jamaica.

DEBORAH L. HUGHES is the president and CEO of the National Susan B. Anthony Museum and House. She began her tenure at the Anthony Museum in 2007, bringing more than twenty-five years of wide-ranging nonprofit experience to the national historic landmark. She holds a bachelor of science in religious studies from the University of Oregon at Eugene, a master's of divinity from Colgate Rochester Crozer Divinity School, and a certificate in fund-raising management from Indiana University.

CHRISTINE A. KRAY is associate professor of anthropology at Rochester Institute of Technology and the program director for the sociology and anthropology degree program. She received her PhD from the University of Pennsylvania, and she was the McKennan Postdoctoral Teaching Fellow at Dartmouth College. A political anthropologist who combines ethnographic and archival research, she has traced cultural dimensions of international projects such as colonialism, evangelization, and globalization and how they are experienced and creatively reworked at the local level, in individual subjectivities, reflections on the past, and ritual practice. Her prior research has focused on the Yucatec Maya of Mexico and Belize, she has published in several anthropological journals and book chapters, and she is coauthoring a book on *Negotiating Life in the Colonial Borderlands* with archaeological colleagues.

JIYOUNG LEE is a PhD student in the S. I. Newhouse School of Public Communications at Syracuse University. Prior to joining Syracuse, she graduated from Ewha Womans University in Seoul, South Korea, for both her master's (in communication) and bachelor's degrees (in journalism). Her research focuses on public opinion and interactive media along with social media usage under risky situations; analyzing emotional communication from social psychological perspectives. Her work has received various accolades, as her master's thesis was recognized as the top student paper at Ewha Womans University. As a research assistant, Lee was awarded prizes including faculty paper awards in the Association for Education in Journalism and Mass Communication and Broadcast Education Association, and top student paper award at an International Communication Association conference. Lee also has experience in journalism, having worked at YTN (South Korea), Thomson Reuters, and Associated Press.

CAROL M. LIEBLER (PhD, University of Wisconsin–Madison) is professor in the S. I. Newhouse School of Public Communications at Syracuse University. A media sociologist, her research centers on media and diversity issues, and particularly on gender as it intersects with race and ethnicity. Liebler has published in a wide variety of journals, including *Asian Journal of Communication; Communication, Culture and Critique; Howard Journal of Communications; Journal of Broadcasting & Electronic Media; Journal of Communication; and Journalism and Mass Communication Quarterly*. She is coeditor of *Media Scholarship in a Transitional Age: Research in Honor of Pamela J. Shoemaker*.

HINDA MANDELL is associate professor in the School of Communication at Rochester Institute of Technology and is author of *Sex Scandals, Gender and Power in Contemporary American Politics* and coeditor of *Scandal in a Digital Age*. She is under contract with Rowman & Littlefield to edit the essay collection *Crafting Dissent: Handicraft as Protest from the American Revolution to the Anti-Trump Pussyhats*. She researches news coverage of scandal, and her essays have appeared in the *Los Angeles*

Times, Chicago Tribune, USA Today, Boston Herald, Palm Beach Post, Politico, and in academic journals, including *Women's Studies in Communication, Visual Communication Quarterly,* and *Explorations in Media Ecology.* Her website is omghinda.com, and she's on Twitter: @hindamandell.

JOSHUA D. MARTIN is assistant professor of Spanish at the University of North Georgia. He obtained his PhD in Hispanic Studies from the University of Kentucky, where he specialized in the cultural and literary production from and about the US-Mexico border. He has worked extensively with the Latino/a communities of Tennessee and Kentucky, with the Migrant Education Program and as a medical interpreter, respectively.

RACHEL PARSONS is a Chicago-based educator, writer, and editor. Originally from Michigan, she spent eight years teaching high school math in the New York City Department of Education. She took a break from the classroom to pursue her MFA in creative nonfiction at Sarah Lawrence College, and served as editor-in-chief of *LUMINA,* vol. 16. She has taught writing at the Barnard College Summer in the City Program and Pace University, and serves as production editor of *Post Road Magazine.* Writing about gender, sexuality, race, work, family, teaching, and culture, her work has appeared in *Guernica, Bleu Magazine, Z Magazine, Schools: Studies in Education, The Culture Trip, Organizing Upgrade,* and other publications.

NEAL J. POWLESS, MS, NCC, and PhD fellow at Syracuse University's S.I. Newhouse School of Public Communications, is a traditional member of the Onondaga Nation, Eel Clan. He holds a master's in counseling from Syracuse University and a BS in psychology from Nazareth College. Powless has taught and presented nationally for nearly twenty years about indigenous culture and value systems. He is the cofounder and co-owner of Indigenous Concepts Consulting, a firm that bridges Native American ideals and culture with organizations and individuals all over the world.

EINAV RABINOVITCH-FOX is a visiting assistant professor in history at Case Western Reserve University. She holds a PhD in history from New York University (2014) and is currently working on a book manuscript, *Dressed for Freedom: American Feminism and the Politics of Women's Fashion,* which explores women's political uses of clothing and appearance as a means of negotiating new freedoms and modern gender identities. Her research has been supported by the CCWH, Hartman Center at Duke University, Smith College, the Schlesinger Library, Winterthur

Museum, and others. Einav has published on fashion, feminism, and advertising in *Journal of Women's History* and *American Journalism: A Journal of Media History*, and her public writings have appeared in *Dismantle Magazine* and *Public Seminar*.

DE ANNA J. REESE is an associate professor in the Department of History and the Africana studies program at California State University–Fresno. She is also the program coordinator of the Africana studies program. Her areas of emphasis include twentieth-century African American, women's, social, cultural, ethnic, and immigration history. Within these areas, Reese's work examines the intersection of race, gender, class, culture, and identity for Black women both historically and within popular culture.

O. NICHOLAS ROBERTSON is an assistant professor of criminal justice at Rochester Institute of Technology. He earned his PhD in sociology at the State University of New York at Buffalo in 2015, an MA in American history from the State University of New York at Brockport, and a BA in sociology at the State University of New York at Geneseo. He has research interests in crime, law, and deviance; race, ethnicity, and immigration; urban sociology; and the African diaspora. An article from his dissertation research on "West Indian Young Men's Perception and Experiences with the American Criminal Justice System" is forthcoming in *Race and Justice: An International Journal*.

ROY SCHWARTZMAN (PhD, University of Iowa) is a professor in communication studies and affiliate faculty in peace and conflict studies at the University of North Carolina–Greensboro. He also serves as a nonpartisan political communication analyst for Time Warner/Spectrum Cable News, has won more than sixty literary awards for poetry, and has won more than a dozen awards for research, including the National Communication Association Outstanding Dissertation Award. Schwartzman has published more than a hundred articles and book chapters as well as 350 poems and the poetry collection *Only This*. A Holocaust Educational Foundation fellow and Shoah Foundation Institute teaching fellow, he researches and teaches extensively about propaganda and Holocaust studies.

JENNI M. SIMON (PhD, University of Denver) is a lecturer at the University of North Carolina–Greensboro. Simon's research focuses on gender and cultural issues, as well as the critical and rhetorical intersections that exist between culture and social movements. Coeditor of *Michelle Obama: First Lady, American Rhetor* and author of *Consuming Agency and Desire in Romance: Stories of Love, Laughter, and Empowerment*, she has also published in *Communication Review, Southern States Communication Journal, Women's Studies in Communication*, and *Women & Language*. Her most recent work explores feminism and social change, resistance to women's movements, women in organizations and politics, and the changing role of motherhood in the postmodern area. Simon is a past chair of the Southern States Communication Association's Gender and Women's Studies Division.

ANA STEVENSON is a postdoctoral research fellow in the International Studies Group at the University of the Free State. In 2015 she was awarded her PhD from the University of Queensland. Between 2014 and 2015, she was a visiting scholar in the gender, sexuality, and women's studies program at the University of Pittsburgh. Her research examines transnational women's movements in the United States, Australia, and South Africa. It appears in journals such as *Cultural & Social History, Humanity: An International Journal of Human Rights, Humanitarianism, and Development*, and *Safundi: The Journal of South African and American Studies*. She cofounded the Suffrage Postcard Project, a digital humanities initiative dedicated to woman suffrage postcards from the United States and Britain, with Kristin Allukian.

LEORA TANENBAUM is the author of *I Am Not a Slut: Slut-Shaming in the Age of the Internet* and *Slut! Growing Up Female with a Bad Reputation*. In 1999 she coined the term "slut-bashing," the precursor to the term "slut-shaming." She is also the author of *Taking Back God: American Women Rising Up for Religious Equality, Catfight: Rivalries among Women*, and *Bad Shoes & the Women Who Love Them*. Tanenbaum has written for the *New York Times, Time, Seventeen, Ms.*, and the *Nation* and was one of the original bloggers for the *Huffington Post*. She has been a guest on *Oprah, The Today Show*, and *Nightline*. She is the editorial director of Barnard College.

KATIE TEREZAKIS is associate professor of philosophy at Rochester Institute of Technology. She is the author of *The Immanent Word: The Turn to Language in German Philosophy 1759–1801*; editor of *Engaging Agnes Heller: A Critical Companion*; coeditor of *Lukács' Soul and Form*; and author of scholarly articles in the areas of critical theory, eighteenth- and nineteenth-century philosophy, and American philosophy. She is currently completing a book on the Rochester-born American philosopher John William Miller.

ASMA T. UDDIN is a fellow with the Initiative on Security and Religious Freedom at the UCLA Burkle Center for International Relations. She is also a Berkley Center research fellow. Uddin previously served as counsel with Becket, a nonprofit law firm specializing in US and international religious freedom cases, and director of strategy for the Center for Islam and Religious Freedom. She is also an expert adviser on religious liberty to the Organization for Security and Cooperation in Europe and a term member of the Council on Foreign Relations. Uddin writes and speaks on gender and Islam, and she is the founding editor-in-chief of *Altmuslimah.com*. She graduated from the University of Chicago Law School, where she was a staff editor at the *University of Chicago Law Review*.

MARK WARD SR. (PhD, Clemson University) is associate professor of communication at the University of Houston–Victoria. His studies of evangelical culture, congregational life, and popular media have been published in numerous journals and edited volumes. His books include the multivolume series *The Electronic Church in the Digital Age: Cultural Impacts of Evangelical Mass Media*, for which he received the 2017 Clifford G. Christians Ethics Research Award, and *The Lord's Radio: Gospel Music Broadcasting and the Making of Evangelical Culture, 1920–1960*. He serves on the boards of the *Journal of Communication and Religion* and the Religious Communication Association, which named his ethnographic study of evangelical media its 2014 Article of the Year. His broadcast experience ranges from local radio to national syndication.

JOANNA WEISS is editor-in-chief of *Experience*, a new magazine sponsored by Northeastern University. Her writing has been featured in the *Boston Globe, Politico Magazine, Slate, Pacific Standard*, and the *Economist*, and she has appeared as a television and radio commentator on CNN, NPR's *On Point*, and Boston's WGBH, WBUR, and WBZ. Her first novel, *Milkshake*, a social satire about the politics of motherhood, is available on Kindle and in print.

KELSEY N. WHIPPLE is a doctoral student and the *Dallas Morning News* Graduate Fellow for Journalism Innovation at the University of Texas at Austin. Her research focuses on gender and class in the media and the influence of technology on mass communication. She previously worked as a writer, editor, and digital strategist for Voice Media Group's network of eleven alternative-weekly newspapers. Most recently, she served as the company's editorial digital director in Los Angeles.

JAMIA WILSON is the executive director and publisher of the Feminist Press at the City University of New York. Wilson has contributed to the *New York Times, The Today Show,* CNN, *Elle, Teen Vogue,* and more. She is the author of *Young, Gifted, and Black* and wrote the oral history in *Together We Rise: Behind the Scenes at the Protest Heard around the World.* She is the coauthor of the upcoming book *Roadmap for Revolutionaries: Resistance, Activism, and Advocacy for All.*

BARBARA WINSLOW, professor emerita, Brooklyn College, is the founder and director emerita of the Shirley Chisholm Project of Brooklyn Women's Activism, 1945 to the Present. A professor of women's and gender studies as well as secondary social studies at Brooklyn College CUNY, she authored *Shirley Chisholm: Catalyst for Change* (Westview Press, 2013) and *Sylvia Pankhurst: Sexual Politics and Political Activism* (St. Martin's, 1997) and coedited *Clio in the Classroom: A Guide to Teaching US History* (Oxford University Press, 2008) and the forthcoming *Dismantling Historical Boundaries: Essays Centering Women's Nontraditional Lives* (University of Illinois Press). She has written numerous articles and book chapters on feminism, women's activism, women's suffrage, race, class, gender, immigration, oral history, and sexuality in the K–12 social studies curriculum. She is currently writing a book about the women's liberation movement in Washington State, and working with the Williamstown (MA) Historical Society on an exhibition celebrating women's suffrage in Berkshire County.

Gender and Race in American History

Alison M. Parker, The College at Brockport, State University of New York
Carol Faulkner, Syracuse University
Amrita Chakrabarti Myers, Indiana University Bloomington

The Men and Women We Want
Jeanne D. Petit

Manhood Enslaved:
Bondmen in Eighteenth- and Early Nineteenth-Century New Jersey
Kenneth E. Marshall

Interconnections:
Gender and Race in American History
Edited by Carol Faulkner and Alison M. Parker

Susan B. Anthony and the Struggle for Equal Rights
Edited by Christine L. Ridarsky and Mary M. Huth

The Reverend Jennie Johnson
and African Canadian History, 1868–1967
Nina Reid-Maroney

Sex Ed, Segregated:
The Quest for Sexual Knowledge in Progressive-Era America
Courtney Q. Shah

An Architecture of Education:
African American Women Design the New South
Angel David Nieves

Nasty Women and Bad Hombres:
Gender and Race in the 2016 US Presidential Election
Edited by Christine A. Kray, Tamar W. Carroll, and Hinda Mandell

Gender and racial politics were at the center of the 2016 US presidential contest between Hillary Clinton and Donald Trump. The election was historic because Clinton was the first woman nominated by a major political party for the presidency. Yet it was also historic in its generation of sustained reflection on the past. Clinton's campaign linked her with suffragist struggles—represented perhaps most poignantly by the parade of visitors to Susan B. Anthony's grave on Election Day—while Trump harnessed nostalgia through his promise to Make America Great Again. This collection of essays looks at the often vitriolic rhetoric that characterized the election: "nasty women" vs. "deplorables"; "bad hombres" and "Crooked Hillary"; analyzing the struggle and its result through the lenses of gender, race, and their intersections, and with particular attention to the roles of memory, performance, narrative, and social media.

Contributors examine the ways that gender and racial hierarchies intersected and reinforced one another throughout the campaign season. Trump's association of Mexican immigrants with crime, and specifically with rape, for example, drew upon a long history of fearmongering that stereotypes Mexican men—and men of other immigrant and minority groups—as sexual aggressors against white women. At the same time, in response to both Trump's misogynistic rhetoric and the iconic power of Clinton's candidacy, feminist consciousness grew steadily across the nation. Analyzing these phenomena, the volume's authors—both journalists and academics—engage with prominent debates in their diverse fields, while an epilogue by the editors considers recent ongoing developments like the #metoo movement.

CONTRIBUTORS: Steve Almond, R. Brandon Anderson, Pamela Aronson, Beth L. Boser, Michael J. Brown, Jane Caputi, Tamar W. Carroll, Gina Masullo Chen, Sally Campbell Galman, Delia C. Gillis, Deborah L. Hughes, Christine A. Kray, Jiyoung Lee, Carol M. Liebler, Hinda Mandell, Joshua D. Martin, Rachel Parsons, Neal J. Powless, Einav Rabinovitch-Fox, De Anna J. Reese, O. Nicholas Robertson, Roy Schwartzman, Jenni M. Simon, Ana Stevenson, Leora Tanenbaum, Katie Terezakis, Asma T. Uddin, Mark Ward Sr., Joanna Weiss, Kelsey N. Whipple, Jamia Wilson, Barbara Winslow,

CHRISTINE A. KRAY is associate professor of anthropology, TAMAR W. CARROLL is associate professor of history, and HINDA MANDELL is associate professor in the School of Communication, all at Rochester Institute of Technology.

"*Nasty Women and Bad Hombres* does it right. In this volume, an inter-disciplinary group of scholars and writers comes together to think through how Donald Trump, a reality-TV star with no political experi-ence, could pull off an electoral upset against Hillary Clinton, an intel-ligent, highly qualified candidate with years of experience in public service. Among other things, contributors illuminate the function-ings of widespread internalized antifeminism among women, hashtag feminism, and slut-shaming; recognize African American women as torchbearers; and consider the use of misogynist and feminist popu-lar cultural artifacts then and now. Simultaneously broad-based and focused, *Nasty Women and Bad Hombres* does an excellent job of laying out how we got here and pondering what to do next."

—Micaela di Leonardo, Northwestern University

"Christine A. Kray, Tamar W. Carroll, and Hinda Mandell have assem-bled a superb, interdisciplinary group of authors to analyze a recent political history in which the politics of identity played a large, as yet barely analyzed role. A must read for organizers, scholars, politicians, and students of politics who are trying to reverse the effects of Trump-ism on our national political culture."

—Claire Potter, The New School